This publication is also available as four separate books:

On the Other Hand: The Little Anthology of Big Questions

Just Around The Bend: Más o Menos

Louder than a Whisper: Clearer than a Bell

Stepping out of Time

Other Titles by this Author

The Doubt Factor

Children's Picture Books by this author:

The Frightened Little Flower Bud   Ages 4-99

Hat   Ages 6-99

"This is for the ones who stand,
For the ones who think they can,
For the ones who need a hand,
For the ones who try again."

'Comes and Goes' Greg Laswell

Umbra, Penumbra & ME

Renée Paule

Umbra, Penumbra & Me

By Renée Paule

Edited by G R Hewitt

Copyright © June 2019 Renée Paule

Published in Ireland by RPG Publishing 2019

All rights reserved in all media. No part of this book may be used or reproduced without written permission, except in the case of brief quotations embodied in critical articles and reviews.

The moral right of Renée Paule as the author of this work has been asserted by her in accordance with the Copyright Designs and Patents Act of 1988.

Cover and Interior design by G R Hewitt

Illustrations by Renée Paule

Written in British English

ISBN: 978-0-9935098-8-9

Questioning everything raises consciousness
and this will change our world.

Thank you Godfrey - for everything

Table of Contents

Preface *1*
Introduction *7*

ONE
Something's not Quite Right with the World *15*
Open-Mindedness. *25*
Interaction *39*
Does it Matter? *49*
Time. *57*
Right and Wrong. *65*
Light Casts No Shadow *73*
Where am I? *79*
Curiosity and Confusion. *83*
Our Cluttered Mind *95*
Change is Possible. *101*
Information *111*
Comfort and Security *117*
Absurdities. *123*
On Death. *133*
Letting Go. *139*
Who Am I? *146*
On Reflection *149*

TWO
A Bit of a Rant. *155*
Just Around the Bend *161*
Completeness. *169*
Mind Dramas *177*
Independence *187*
'What if' and Other Worries *193*

Emotions and Energy.. *201*
Observation.. *211*
Attachment.. *221*
On Faith.. *231*
Intention... *239*
Humanity is One... *245*
We're One... *254*
Who am I?... *257*

THREE
Sensation, Desire & Relevant Reflections..................... *263*
Am I Good Enough?... *273*
Responsibility... *283*
Consolidation.. *293*
Louder than a Whisper...................................... *301*
Betrayal... *311*
The Abyss of Loneliness..................................... *319*
Personality, Pride & Other Tough Stuff....................... *327*
Hidden.. *338*
A Compendium of Thoughts.................................. *341*
Who am I?... *368*
On Reflection.. *371*

FOUR
Hello World.. *379*
Know Thyself.. *385*
Assimilation and Dissemination.............................. *395*
Memory and Thought....................................... *403*
Taking Stock - A Perspective................................. *413*
Relationships.. *425*
The Control Conundrum.................................... *433*
Endurance... *439*

Plan B.	*445*
A Little More Taking Stock	*451*
Stepping out of Time	*457*
A Touch of Feeling	*465*
Gratitude	*475*
If I Told You	*481*
Wrapping Up	*485*

Preface

'Success is the ability to go from one failure to another with no loss of enthusiasm.' Winston Churchill

Many years ago, I wrote my autobiography - more as a form of therapy than anything else as, at that point, I had no intention of publishing it. Sometime later, while reading through what I had written, it occurred to me that there was enough misery and sadness in the world, which my book would be adding to - serving no good purpose. My 'therapy' had apparently worked and I no longer felt the need to wallow in self-pity – nor invite others to do the same through the pages of a book. That said, however, some insight into my life is necessary for you to understand the processes leading to the book that you now hold in your hands. To that end, there follows a brief synopsis of what's gone before.

~~~

Despite having two living parents, I was placed in an orphanage at the age of nine months; my parents had decided to go their separate ways. The reason for this, I later learnt from an aunt, was that my father had returned from work one day to find my sister and I playing in one corner of the lounge, while my mother was sitting in another, covered in blood after having cut her wrists; I've never discovered any more than that and have no wish to. My foundation was lost long before I could build it. My time in orphanages was neither pleasant or loving - it was ugly and cruel and that footing led me to characterise the outside world as a hostile, selfish, violent, abusive, confusing, dishonest and unfriendly place - a world with which I felt unable to interact. I was afraid of the frightening images that appeared both in my dreams and during my waking state, and had no one at all to turn to.

At age twelve I was marched into the matron's office, introduced to a woman and casually told that she was my mother - I'd always been told she was dead. I remember running out of the room, but can't tell you where I went as I've no memory of it. I've around twelve year's amnesia and a few openings where snippet memories, like this one, remain intact. The incident was the hardest blow of my childhood, that I can remember. Because of these blows and being forced to deal with them at such a young age, I've been able to cope with other difficult situations in my adult years. I've also been able to let go of many conditioned beliefs. This painful upbringing led me to stumble and fall a great deal in my earlier years. I wavered between feeling inadequate, despair, hatred, self-hatred and self-pity - emotions more damning to the purity of a child's mind and ones I couldn't share with anyone. My childhood was brutal and left me with little appetite for the challenges of adult life. The ordeals that tormented me in my youth became the weapons used in a war against the world. I learnt some difficult lessons in the hardest way.

~~~

In my late teens I went to night school and learnt skills like typing, shorthand and communication skills. I worked as a secretary, temped for a while and became a personal assistant. However, staying too long in one place was suffocating, and I could never make sense of, or have the energy to participate in toxic office politics. Office work was mundane and from the expressions on the faces of other personnel, no-one was particularly happy doing it. Over the years, I tried many other things including running my own business. I was meticulous and committed, but didn't enjoy it or the ridiculous amount of time required on administration rather than actual work. I was incredibly bored, which sapped my motivation. Although I earned a reasonable salary, I didn't feel as though I were doing something worthwhile with my life.

Many years later, I attended university and studied English Literature, but it was focused on highly regulated literary criticism rather than author intention. Writers wish others to experience their horizons, not to look down at every stone on the path they'd like you to tread. Again, boredom set in. I've a sharp and active mind and it needed more positive stimulation. Family Circumstances then led me to leave two and a half years into my studies. The wind blew, yet again, in another direction. At this point, I rather looked forward to the changes that came into my life and was, perhaps, guilty of triggering them quicker than necessary. I still had no 'place' in the world and couldn't find anything to love about it - I'd no idea if I loved anything at all. I didn't enjoy the basics of everyday life - nightlife, shopping, reading, social gatherings, cinemas, holidays, touring or drinking - all these meant little to me. I was a loner, but didn't like being in my own company, which made life pretty difficult. I lived without passion for the world and its population, wondering why I existed at all. Despite, or perhaps because of, this frame of mind, something 'new' always appeared and led me off in another direction. I now look upon these events as the stepping stones that kept me from drowning, despite often slipping dangerously on some of them. Nevertheless, I was still able to reflect, smile and move on.

I never wrapped myself up in a guru or any other mentor. This may be because the opportunity didn't arise or because my subconscious told me it wouldn't help. All the blame for the mistakes I made in my earlier life was directed elsewhere, but I now take full responsibility for it; no-one is to blame - it's how it happened.

In between all the above, I've married four times, six, if you don't include the pieces of paper that somehow make them 'official'. You might be asking yourself why I didn't learn the first time, or even the second or third. Some of you might want to know what went wrong, who was at fault and how things panned out. However, feasting on the bones of my past serves no good purpose and isn't the point of this book. In between my marriages, I've entered into several dysfunctional relationships. I've lived in so many houses that I couldn't even *try* to count them - I can honestly say I've never felt 'at home' in any one of them. Deep inside my subconscious mind I sought my 'home' and this was probably my motive. I can assure you I gave each relationship my utmost attention and devotion (relative to my ability at the time), but my naivety meant I picked the wrong relationships. This was due to *needing* to be in a relationship and I sought parental guidance, missing from my childhood, from my husbands. I now know I wasted considerable energy in a desperate attempt to nurture what were weak bonds. I'd have saved myself a lot of trouble had I the foresight to discern the difficulties that arose because of my childhood, and left them behind. A blank slate would have given me a better context - a fairer perspective. We don't listen or learn much while we're in 'why me' mode, do we? But life doesn't play fair - our base instincts tell us to participate wholly reliant on personal experience.

The craziest things begin to happen when we start to question our world. I remember an occasion when I decided to relocate to France - I was on my own at the time - and experienced considerable opposition from friends and family who said, 'You can't just go around doing whatever you want' and I'd reply 'Just watch me'. My mind was made up and I did it. After overcoming many hurdles, learning to speak French being just one of them, marrying a Frenchman who didn't speak a word of English being another, I'm still standing. Leaps of faith are just that. Opportunities have to be taken before you find out what's on the other side of them. I've always jumped from pool to pool and though sometimes the water can be rather deep, if I could turn back time, I'd do it all again - perhaps with more vigour and gratitude for the experiences.

The most profound and magnificent moment in my life was when I walked one evening along a beach on the Sussex coast in England, watching the most amazing sunset. I stood still for a moment to admire it and found there was no separation at all. I felt the waves, the sun, the sand, the rocks and the *Everything*. It lasted just a few seconds but it was deep, informed, and I was so moved by the experience that I haven't stopped or left my path since that moment. It was another new beginning and the closest I'd ever felt to *home*.

I don't watch television, eat at restaurants, go to pubs or any other social events. I do have a few like-minded friends and love to spend time with them. It wouldn't occur to me to give up; the journey is exciting, a great deal of fun, and for the first time in my life I've found something worth pursuing - something to be truly grateful for, which I am. I now realise that for many years I'd been listening to the wrong voice inside my head - the one that says 'Life stinks' and 'No, you mustn't' as opposed to the one that says 'Life's a miracle'.

I can assure you that although I've torn down many walls, I'm not more fortunate than you (far from it) neither am I stronger or luckier - I just made a decision not to live behind them anymore. The strength of these walls is proportional to the strength of our agreement to live our lives behind them. One of the toughest walls for me to remove was the one that prevented me from writing. The notion of writing my autobiography was a sort of 'self-help' therapy, a process of coming to terms with myself - a self that I hated. That realisation was central to discovering my *raison d'être*. Writing was an itch I just had to scratch and the greatest difficulty I faced was overcoming the belief that I couldn't reach the spot.

After writing my first book I thought that subsequent ones would be easier, but nothing could be further from the truth. The biggest hurdle is getting over the idea that others are better qualified to write what I write, but who can write of my experiences; who can possibly be better qualified to write about my world? Who is better placed to record the contradictions, nuances, influences and thought processes that have guided me from a dark past into a brighter Now? Who is better placed to guide me from both dark *and* light - from all dualistic conditioning? Only I can reflect on my life's experiences and through this sincere reflection which began in my childhood - albeit in a somewhat twisted way - was born a need to write about them, together with a deep and compelling need to know myself. All I can offer you in this book is an honest blend of the ways in which I see the world - a few of which are inevitably autobiographical.

Introduction

Life isn't something that happens to us - we happen to life.

Threads about transformational journeys through life; such as, pilgrimages, paths, quests, purpose and the like are woven through the fabric of music, poetry, symbols, paintings, films, documentaries and all literature. You'll also find them in fantasy, games, hobbies, metaphors; they're in myths, theme parks, theatres, sports and legends. There's so much information out there, whether metaphorical or not, which can't be seen until we begin to question our way of life and are driven to change it. It's only then that it becomes apparent that the way we live is more absurd than the idea that legends may be trying to tell us something important. When we do see it, the absurdity of the way we live our lives becomes clear and loses its general appeal - change then becomes inevitable. This book isn't about making the connections; it would take thousands of pages to write a book like that, and involve a great deal of research which would be counter-productive for me - adding dubious knowledge rather than removing it, which is my goal. This book is about my journey, my quest, my change of mind and my determination to question *everything* - to destroy the assumptions that I once accepted as my reality, regardless of where it leads.

~~~

It was many decades ago that I struggled to write my first book - my autobiography. I was trying to write what didn't need to be written, my story of pain, instead of what did, my story of recovery - swimming upstream instead of down. This book is a journal of observations that closely examine the course my life has taken, paying particular attention to how I saw, and now see, society. For years I carried around a bundle of mental baggage that I had no idea what to do with - now it's all out in the open.

The 'Preface' covers the underlying circumstances, and the substance shows how the contents of our minds can be unpacked through close examination. I didn't plan the chapters in this book but rather, allowed them to be written as a stream of consciousness. What didn't need to be written about was my life story and what *did* was how I learnt to 'let it go' - not allowing myself to be controlled by things from the past that can't be located, by us at least. What I'm really writing about is my psychological journey from helplessness, confusion and self-pity to inner strength - a journey of negation and a determination to find what's always been missing from my life - purpose - a purpose - *anything* to make waking up each morning feel worthwhile rather than mundane and repetitive. When I get stuck I sit in front of my computer and hold various questions in mind that are answered through my fingers onto a screen or, I move away from my desk and do something entirely different until what I'm going to write about becomes clear - it never takes very long. What's guiding me? I know that whatever it is, it's far greater than I am. To see our reflection in the world *outside* can be a terrifying experience - far more so than the physical reflection we see when looking into a mirror.

The mind and the ego: What are they? Do we create them? Why has the mind got two conflicting voices? I raise these and many other questions with other diverse, but related subjects. By looking into them I began to see the world as it really is; an incredible and ingenious illusion that has a disproportionate impact on individual well-being. Questioning the world surrounding me from time-to-time wasn't enough; I had to repeat it continuously, repeating the *same* questions, in order to discern the impact of the societal conditioning that pervaded my life since birth. The more I considered the questions - but dispensed with the urge to answer them, the more I made sense of my world.

~~~

Humans are funny fickle beings - consider the fact that:

- We don't like what we read in the news, yet still buy the papers.
- We don't like what we watch on the television, yet still watch it.
- We claim not to like violence, yet accept it as entertainment.
- We don't like pollution, yet continue to contribute towards it.

You can probably think of many more examples and perhaps ask yourself the same question as me 'Why do we do these things?' This book explores these facets with some bold and frank questions that, at times, might make for uncomfortable reading. I ask many, many questions that *don't* require answers - only recognition; answers get in the way of questions - taking deep root in our mind. Answers stop the questioning process and can be impossible to remove, particularly if they 'fit' our requirements - we can never be *completely* free if we're attached to anything at all.

If this book is about anything, then it's about changing weakness and fear into strength through a process of observation and self-examination; it's about turning the known world up-side-down and it's about walking blindfolded, without fear, along a gossamer thread knowing it can take the strain. It's clear to me now that it was my state-of-mind that prevented me from seeing what I'd *known* all along; here ... now ... *this* is it. So much is revealed to us when we're willing to examine our thoughts, actions and intentions - *all* of them. With this realisation I felt the almost 'evangelical' need to share it with others. There are those who experience an instant conversion from 'unconsciousness' to 'consciousness', but they're few and far between and the majority of us take a far longer 'road to Damascus'. Many of us can be discouraged by 'epiphany' stories, particularly when we're told they're so rare; I was one of them. This book is for those of us who take longer to realise what we already know on one level, and to keep you company on your 'journey' - it's for those who are willing to change and prepared to lose the lot.

When covering so many simple topics, that have become complicated by society, certain repetition of thought is necessary and unavoidable. I do however, endeavour to keep this to a minimum. For this reason, I may re-visit some points in more than one chapter; this is unavoidable and very much a part of the process of unlearning - some of our conditioning is harder to remove. If I repeat anything to you then I'm also repeating it to myself. It's not enough to ask the question 'Who am I?' just once, as though it were a magic curative. It's part of a process that we need to be *fully* absorbed in, rather than treating it as a 'hobby'. We learnt what we know by rigid rules and strict repetition; we have to unlearn it in the same way, but with a new pilot at the helm - ourselves. When we reduce complexity to simplicity, we arrive at our point of origin, in *this* world at least.

After writing so many chapters that reflect on humanity, I've come to realise that I'm neither closer to nor further away from discovering an 'ultimate' understanding of my world. The restlessness I feel is not something I can ignore or question - it can't be pushed aside. It calls me - with some urgency - to reflect on the world I've created for myself, and to be the best person I can be within it; I'm not here to 'solve' it and I'm not here to find answers. I'm here as my own authority and to find my way in life - not to be steered by others who may think they know what's 'best' for me. The only real waste in this world is the waste of our lives if we ignore the opportunity to make a difference - to learn to love ourselves, and through that love be able to love all others.

There's nothing in any of my chapters that we don't already know, and for this reason I often ponder on why I'm writing them at all. It all comes down to this; I must unlearn everything I 'know' with the same rigidity that I learnt it - I must hammer at and chip away all obstacles that keep me from seeing what lies beneath my outer shell - I must break into my own safe! I can't show or tell you how to 'straighten out' your life, or how to see the magic in it. I can only show you how I'm straightening out my own life and how with careful attention to my thoughts and inner voice the noise and chaos in my mind has abated; however, it's not yet fully quiet.

Providing answers is not the purpose of this book, but rather it's to encourage you to ask your own questions and uproot any answers that you may already have. I say again, questions *don't* need to be answered; they need to be *asked* in order that we're able to distinguish between truth and untruth. To repeat myself, everything we know has come to us through repetition, and we need to *unlearn* it by the same process. When we begin our journey of discovery, questions are far more abundant and important than the answers - finding new questions at every bend. Further along the 'road', we don't ask so many questions and consequently, there are far fewer as the book progresses.

<p align="center">~~~</p>

Far be it from me to tell you how to read your book, but if I may suggest, based on feedback, that you read only one chapter at a time - leaving yourself space to ponder over and digest what you've read, before moving on to the next chapter. Because this book documents my journey of self-discovery, I recommend reading the chapters in sequence. There's inevitably a certain amount of overlap and repetition - it takes time for old thoughts to be replaced by newer ones.

To illustrate some of the thoughts contained in this book, I created a character called Dilly, which means something or someone remarkable. Dilly is a 'thought form' that thinks, and he demonstrates some of our most endearing human traits - sometimes in a humorous way. I had a lot of fun creating these illustrations and I hope you like them as much as I do.

ONE

Chapter 1

Something's not Quite Right with the World

'Common sense is a collection of prejudices acquired by age eighteen.' Albert Einstein

It's said that you can't fit a square peg into a round hole and this applies to people too. No matter how much we shave off edges to round the 'peg', we'll never fit in any way that isn't illusory. Trying to be normal can be an upheaval and it would be better to be neither round nor square; both shapes have finite boundaries. Why do we pretend to fit by keeping quiet about a life that is at best robotic and commercial? There's something not quite right with the world.

Doubtless, like me, you've wondered why the world's not a happy place to live in - why there's so much division, why we struggle and why we just can't seem to get it right. What's holding us back from experiencing our true nature and making us want to argue and fight, rather than loving and appreciating each other? What makes us competitive; needing to keep up with The Joneses or exceed them? What makes us want the things in the world that environmentally, or otherwise, we're better off without? We claim to care about the world but we choose to ignore it in favour of selfish gain. Something amazing is waiting for us to notice it, regardless of whether we want to believe it or not and, we're a part of it. As W. H. Davies so beautifully put it in his poem Leisure, 'We have no time to stand and stare.'[1] at the marvels of our world because we keep ourselves too busy.

When I've spoken to people about spiritual matters and how incredible humanity is, they'd ask me for proof of it. Yet they'd never had any proof for anything they'd been taught in school or by their parents. We accept most things without question. I find it a little bit odd that we believe everything we're told, particularly as our 'teachers' were taught by their teachers ... and so on. These same beliefs have been passed down for generations. Our belief systems are founded on what we've been told by highly questionable authorities who decide, for unclear reasons, what our children learn. For example, schools teach our children the 'Theory of Evolution' as an unquestionable fact, but they also teach 'Religious Education'. When I was at school, questioning or disagreeing with teachers was strongly 'discouraged'. I couldn't accept my questions being ignored or rejected - I'd a great many of them. As a result of this I learnt to doubt everything people tried to teach me, and spent much of my school time truanting. My favourite haunt was the Oasis swimming pool in Holborn, where I would spend hours in the water - I didn't have anything else to do and no-one noticed my absence or ever questioned me; consequently, I had a great deal of time to self-reflect. Despite the lack of alternative beliefs, most children grow up never to doubt or question what they've been told. They're pacified with toys and computer games and kept busy in and out of school. Children lose their individuality and their own *unique* character as a result of this conditioning, which is replaced by a compliant and systematic one - carried forward into adulthood. Surely this shouldn't be the sum of our human experience?

How can something as magnificent as a human being not have a meaningful purpose? What could this purpose be? Perhaps it's to see if we can remove the veil hiding our true self before the end of our lifetime; who can say? You may be perfectly happy to see your life through without a spiritual thought and that's okay. However, as you're reading this book you've started making enquiries about the meaning of your life. Essential to this journey is to doubt what we've read in text books, newspapers or what we've heard on the television. If we doubt any part of it, but choose to believe some of it, then shouldn't we take another look at why we're being so selective?

Now that the contents of the world have become 'disposable' we've lost appreciation for anything in it. If something we've bought breaks, it can be thrown away and easily replaced. Any guilt we may feel for 'waste' is driven away because we're encouraged to take our unwanted things to council 'dumps' and place them in the giant skips provided. We're told these things will be safely recycled and made into something else - few people look further than this. In effect, we're given permission to throw whatever we want away and encouraged, through advertising, to buy up-to-date replacements.

If society says it's okay to do this, we don't give it another thought - we've absolved ourselves of all environmental responsibility and tell ourselves that we personally, can't be blamed. If you're familiar with trips to the rubbish dump then you'll know that no matter what day we take our rubbish there we have to queue to dispose of it; we queue when we buy things and we queue again to throw them away. We don't think too much about where this rubbish goes as it's 'officially' dealt with. We don't struggle to abdicate responsibility or to dispose of our physical clutter, but we do have difficulty when that clutter is psychological.

Do we care for our children? Do we see any improvements at all in the world? We've seen a steady increase in violence, gore, sex and profanity in the films that we watch. Why are they in films at all? Have we ever given these issues serious thought? If we had, then we'd see it's our desire for them that brings them into being - we buy them and are therefore, responsible for their production. By changing the way we interact with the world and not waiting for someone else to do it for us, our world *will* change. More importantly, we can't leave it up to people who don't hold high standards or live by their own 'examples' of what's right and wrong. If we didn't buy or watch the films then there wouldn't be a market for them. We always have choices - rarely do we choose wisely.

Multiple choice questions are often the format for exams and this doesn't leave room for independent thought. Have you ever filled in one of those questionnaires in a magazine that tries to 'type' you or tell you who your ideal partner is? They ask you questions such as 'If a man asks you if you want to dance with him at a disco, and you don't like the look of him, would you:

- Bluntly say 'No thanks!' and walk away?'
- Dance with him even if you don't want to?'
- Say you're waiting for someone who's the jealous type?'

What if none of the above answers apply to you? The suggestion is usually to choose the answer which fits the closest. Well it's not true then is it? What if you don't go to discotheques? When you consider the rest of the questions and you choose the 'closest fit' answers how then can the resulting standard personality type, which results from your choices, tell you who you are? If we answer the questions and believe the 'results', we're allowing ourselves to be categorised by someone else's standards. Just who is it who designs these questionnaires anyway?

That the authorities are questionable is not difficult to see. Look at so-called history; were we ever not in the middle of some war or another? We've only to look at media stories about government officials, religious representatives or any civil service departments to see that they can be highly a-moral. When exposed, often few, if any, disciplinary measures are taken and it's all hushed up in that wonderful way we're familiar with - we never question it again. We do, however, take the time to satirise the scandals for long enough to make them 'amusing' and the purpose of this is to 'soften the blow', creating laughter instead of tears. Then the scandals dissolve as others take centre stage, continuing the cycle. Are these not just the same old stories with another face on them?

These same authorities tell us how to best bring up our children - legally obliging us to send them to their institutions, such as schools, where they are educated by a strict and psychologically-limiting curriculum-based system - the aim of which is to produce compliant non-questioning individuals, and there our children remain for the majority of their most formative years. Are we, considering the above, fit to bring up our own children? Do we not just pass on to them what was passed on to us by those with no more comprehension or proof about our world than *we* have? This situation is self-perpetuating and not only do we pass on our experiences to our children, but new ones are passed on to them from authority figures and other family members who haven't managed to improve their own lives. If I'm given any advice, one of the first things I do is look at and listen to the person talking and ask myself if they live by their own convictions. To me this is the only qualification we need to give advice to anyone else.

One consequence of this society is a decline in the health of an already 'sick' and corrupt system. Another consequence is that children grow up insecure and never quite *fit in* - they've not been given a stable foundation to stand on. This has resulted in an unhappy world where most people hold grievances, loathe themselves, live in fear and spend their lives in front of the television. We don't care much for anything that sounds like self-development. We generally prefer not to make efforts when it's perfectly acceptable to push the button on the remote control and change channel. This is not too different to turning over in bed, pushing the snooze button on our alarm clocks and going back to sleep. We look to others for images of what we ought to be like, usually on the television, because we're unhappy with ourselves. Next time you go to a supermarket slow down a little, take a look around and try to find a happy face in the crowd.

Think for a moment about 'self-help' books. We need help when we're in trouble, right? Well, I invite you to take a look at how much self-help is available; we're in *big* trouble. I searched for 'self-help' on google.co.uk and got 1,600,000,000 results and I got them in 0.28 seconds[2]; what exactly is the world concentrating on? How many different ways can there be to help ourselves and if they *are* any good, why aren't we seeing the benefits? Another search revealed the first self-help book was purportedly written in 1859 by a man named Samuel Smiles and it was called *Self-Help*, but the concept goes back a great deal further. In *The Great Learning*, written around 500 BC, Confucius said 'The ancients who wished to illustrate illustrious virtue throughout the kingdom, first ordered well their own states. Wishing to order well their states, they first regulated their families. Wishing to regulate their families, they first cultivated their persons. Wishing to cultivate their persons, they first rectified their hearts. Wishing to rectify their hearts, they first sought to be sincere in their thoughts. Wishing to be sincere in their thoughts, they first extended to the utmost their knowledge. Such extension of knowledge lay in the investigation of things.'[3] That sounds like self-help to me. Why has humanity not advanced psychologically? Technology, commercialism, social media and the like have advanced. Why has humanity been left behind? The main reason is because we're not willing to tackle this question or even accept that the question exists. We roll along with it all and occasionally complain. We see the advancement of technology as our own advancement. Among other unhealthy past times, we eat junk and spend too much time in front of the television or inside virtual reality games. Paradoxically, with such a huge - and growing - demand for self-help it's obvious to me that there's a need in society that isn't being met. Could it be that the 'self' part of 'self-help' belongs to the authors of these books, and doesn't necessarily meet the needs of the reader? Why aren't we paying attention to this need? Is the morale of humanity too low to care?

Humanity follows influential figures, whether it be through soap operas, so-called Hollywood celebrities, promising politicians, sporting stars, pop stars or anyone else who can apparently not only survive, but actually thrive in this 'system'. The chances are they're not any happier than you or me, and the stories we read in the media 'confirm' this. We follow the lives of these people and mimic their behaviour by copying their fashions and follow them on social media websites - we hang on their every word. We wait for celebrities to announce the names they've chosen for their new babies and often, if the timing is correct, give our children their names; why is it important to us?

Think about following trends for just a moment. We buy goods like 'lift and separate' bras, tight-fitting trousers to show off our bodies and we even cut our hair according to latest fashions. We're given a string of orders, which we follow such as; hems up, hems down, g-strings, baggy trousers, chains, piercings, tattoos, torn trousers, falling down trousers, flares, hoods, bras on, bras off, red dress, black dress and it goes round and round, but the pattern never changes. We always do as we're 'told' and wear whatever *uniforms* are handed out, often looking down on those who are so 'last year'. Corporations name the game and we rush in obediently - like a tsunami - buying up their stock because we or our children, must have the latest craze. We are truly fashioned by the latest fashions.

There isn't a person alive who can state categorically that they haven't asked themselves 'What's this life all about?' or 'Who am I?' at some point in their lives. Everyone, without exception, has suffered in some way in this world and continues to do so, regardless of whether they admit to it or not. Humanity and the environment are 'sick' and we're not nursing or even paying attention to it. There are some of us who attempt to bring these questions to the surface, but as we try to encourage others to take a look at the situation we're shut off and labelled as 'insane' or 'deluded' - this pattern has been repeated throughout history. Why are these issues not discussed in the media? When my mother was diagnosed with cancer, my brother decided to give 'McMillan Nurses' a try for some support. He told me his first thought was whether or not he could stand the company of these 'do-gooders' and that made me think. What does that make those who make such claims? Do-badders? I asked him this and he saw my point. The nurses helped my mother and brother a great deal and were wonderful all round - I recommend them to anyone seeking support.

~~~

I don't, as such, believe in the past or future but I write it that way for clarity. This is a good place to state that I believe in nothing at all; not that the world is a sphere, flat or even a planet; belief is not the same as truth. I want to make this quite clear before going on. For me, based on current knowledge, I'm lost in some sort of space and am on my way 'home' - I'm obliged to use familiar terminology in order to make myself understood. I do know that we're all connected, and that everything each one of us does affects humanity as a whole. This I can say is a truth.

As I walk around the supermarket a few things catch my attention and I stop and ponder these thoughts:

- The many types of perfect toothpaste - why do we still need dentists?
- Why is there such a thing as 'luxury' toilet paper?
- Why, when technology has advanced so much, have I been using the same brand of hair removing cream for forty years (though the name has changed)? Even the smell is the same.
- Why is there a sell-by-date on bottled water? It's been around since the world began! Why is it bottled at all?
- When will televisions be big enough and flat enough?
- Standing here holding on to my trolley, I've seen this so many times before.
- Where am I? How did I get here? What am I doing here?

Many people search books like the one you're holding for answers, but they'll never find them amongst the pages. There are no short-cuts and no-one can tell us what we must 'realise' for ourselves. Books can guide us, but we need to ask our own questions. If we don't follow through by giving the issues arising from our enquiries our total and personal attention - actually thinking things out - then we're going to go round and round like a hamster on his wheel and it'll never stop turning, no matter how many books we read. Our search must be genuine - if it isn't, then we're lying to ourselves. The only important question is 'Who am I?' If we look to books for answers, to questions we can't be bothered to ask ourselves, then like the hamster, we won't get anywhere.

I'd like to explore some of these issues further with you and I ask you to keep an open mind about everything, just as I will. As I write this chapter, thoughts stream in and out of my mind solidifying my beliefs about something or another; or knock them on the head, so to speak. I may change my views as we progress - this happens when we question everything and nothing makes sense any more. What's important for me is in recognising the title of this chapter, *Something's not Quite Right with the World*.

Chapter 2

Open-Mindedness

An open-mind can have no fence around it.

Being open-minded isn't about appreciating other people's rights to do what they want, or accepting their sexual preferences. It's not about accepting that comedians often tell hurtful, biased and demeaning jokes about others. It isn't about accepting everyone as a friend regardless of their political persuasion and it isn't about remaining comfortable in familiar territory. So what do I mean by keeping an open mind? What exactly is an open mind? It questions everything no matter how silly it may or may not seem; it questions the answers too. For example, the question 'Who are you?' Most people will give you their name when you ask this question or tell you what their profession is; for example, a secretary, a lawyer or a writer. But is it who they really are? Are you 'Jenny Jones' and if so, who were you before your parents named you? I took ten days to officially name one of my children - who was she during those ten days?

It's just a name. It's an identity we invent in order to function *efficiently* in this reality. For example, we need a name when we go to school, get a job or wish to open up a bank account, but it's *not* us. If we're adamant about being Jenny Jones then we're not open-minded at all. If we give it a little thought and try to imagine a time when we didn't exist we'll find it extremely difficult; even impossible. Close your eyes and imagine yourself 'dead' or 'not existing'. Can you do it? I haven't succeeded. We'll always exist in some form or another, physical or otherwise. Therefore we can't categorically state that we're Jenny Jones. Try to prove it? You can come up with paper proof but what proof is that? If we question the answers every time they present themselves then eventually, we'll run out of questions and consequently, beliefs.

The only 'proof' of our existence, other than on paper, lies in this so-called five-sense-reality. As Morpheus says in the first of *The Matrix* trilogy movies 'What is real? How do you define real? If you're talking about what you can feel, what you can smell, what you can taste and see, then real is simply electrical signals interpreted by your brain.' All of these senses can be and often are deceived whether it's through our eyes by optical illusions or our ears, such as when we hear a voice behind us calling out our name. How about an amputee who still feels pain from a missing limb? I can sometimes smell things from my past, like liquorice, when there's none around. The smell must come from a part of memory or I wouldn't be able to recognise it - sometimes, I can taste it too. There's plenty of research on this subject and a lot of interesting examples on the internet. We've more than five senses - intuition and a sense of danger are just two of them.

It's not my intention to use this book to continuously quote others but it *will* happen as intertextuality is unavoidable. One consequence of this is that proof of anything at all is near impossible to find because peoples' books and ideas are always copying, referring to, quoting, arguing with or analysing each other. Literary criticism prevents clarity and can't know an author's original meaning - we can't see through the eyes of another. People rarely agree and frequently argue with each other. Perhaps it's always been this way. We can't agree with *ourselves* so how can we agree with others? Have you ever spent ages deciding what to wear to a party? Confusion comes from conflicting ideas and those ideas come from excessive criticism of something *original*, thus dividing it. Before you know it, no-one knows the origin or truth of anything; or if you prefer, where to find the 'needle in the haystack'. Literary criticism is not open-mindedness - it's the creation of confusion. It fragments author intention and those fragments tend to remain apart.

It's not the purpose of this book to convince you of anything and I shan't even try to as I know it isn't possible. This book serves two purposes; it clarifies my own thoughts and maybe it'll raise a little doubt and curiosity in someone else's mind about the world they're living in. Intertextuality is not only unavoidable from book to book - it's entirely unavoidable in everything we do or say. Everything we know (or think we know) has been told to us from Day One of our lives by our parents or some other authority such as; a person, a film, a book, a song or a memory of some other kind. Therefore, we can't avoid referring to something from the past and we can't state anything that's not from memory, regardless of whether the memory is from a few seconds ago or an experience many years earlier. Any thoughts we have are plucked out from our memories. Would we know what tastes 'sweet' if the word hadn't been introduced to us? How would we see the colour red if it hadn't been repeatedly pointed out? Are we doing anything other than parroting when we speak to one another? We absorb traits from our parents, friends, celebrities. authority figures and those we pass by in the street. Why do we mimic others, albeit unintentionally?

If we put together the paper proof I mentioned earlier with the information about our senses then we're memory on paper, which for all intents and purposes is a book, and as paper is not part of 'us' then we can't be anything but memory. In other words, we're a story and it's the story of our lives. It's the story of our egos - surreptitious and *invisible* to most people. This thought is worth giving our attention to and we should think about it with an open mind, starting from scratch? That we're memory is obvious to me now, but when I first thought about it I couldn't accept it; not only was it *far* from obvious, but it attacked my sense of 'me' - it can have this effect, but if you give it enough time you'll see it too. We've been recording data since the day we were 'born'. Everything must have a beginning, whether it be; a tape recording, a television programme, the first brick laid to build a home, or the first letter of an alphabet. From these beginnings evolve a symphony, a film, a house and a book.

Open-mindedness involves believing in *nothing*. To believe in something, whatever it is, fixes it in place. Unless we can see options or choices we're not open-minded. Is '1 + 1 = 2' fixed? Are two apples the same as two pears? Is it the same two? If we ask many questions, but don't accept conditioned responses, we then begin to see and feel all possibilities. It shouldn't matter how foolish the question may seem. Question whether you existed yesterday or that you'll exist tomorrow and, if you're serious about the question, interesting thoughts arise. The important thing is to question *every* single thing with the incredible abilities we've been given to do that with. For example, what is a dog? It's just a name we've given the animal, or to be exact a noun, which are names we've given to 'things' but is it what they *are*? The world can be dismantled by removing the words that created it. We've come to treat these words as though they were solid, but nothing new is created when we invent a new word for it. If we rely on adjectives to describe our world then we're missing a sensory beauty that words can never describe. If we question absolutely everything, without a dictionary, we'll see more marvellous things about the world than we've ever seen before.

Consider the age old question 'Which came first; the chicken or the egg?' How close have you ever been to solving this question? Is the question or the answer important? Consider this also. When we were born we knew nothing at all - then we opened our eyes and began to learn about everything around us. Information streamed in at such a phenomenal rate that we couldn't, knowingly, comprehend it. It was the beginning of our memory of this life. When *I* ask *myself* a question, I question the answer I get; no matter how foolish it may seem. Let's look at the first part of that sentence and think about the words, 'When I ask myself a question'. What's going on here? Who's the 'I' and who's the 'myself'? When we begin to question our beliefs the mind puts up arguments because it's not used to it. The habits of the mind are so ingrained that it'll take some time to break them and to take back the power we gave it; just how long it takes is up to us. But if we persevere, we regain our control and then find ourselves behind the steering wheel instead of in the passenger seat. As we begin to see the world in a different way through constant questioning our consciousness level increases - as does our intelligence. It's a 'process of unlearning'. When we ask ourselves a question, where do the answers come from? I remember my father used to say to me 'I've taught you all I know and now you know nothing'. I never got the chance to find out if he understood what it meant, but I suspect he'd no idea.

To erase our beliefs is not a fast process; a great deal of effort and dedication to the enquiry is needed. It's a bit like floating in outer space, inasmuch as there's nowhere to go and no ground to stand on. The process removes everything familiar, comfortable and secure that we've kept close to all of our lives. It's a process achieved by constant questioning of *everything* we've ever been told by our five senses from the moment we were born. We can't consciously remember that far back, but the foundations are still laid. It takes a lot of searching, for every skeleton in every little closet no matter how well we've hidden them. Then we must face them courageously, until we see that they don't really exist. For example, I can think about my childhood and recognise it as an experience and then recognise that the experience was an illusion. It can't be located anywhere - therefore it can't exist other than in my memory.

The experiences we have in the world have nothing to do with who we are. In my childhood I'd fret about why my father didn't care for me and I used to believe I was lacking in some way. It could make me feel quite bitter towards him if I ran it through my mind enough, as I often did. By learning to watch these thoughts, they disappear as though they'd never existed. Thoughts come and go so fast that we can't follow them. If we hold on to them they can haunt us and if we let go, they set us free. If we fret over something long enough - even if it isn't true - we make it true and set it in stone. I used to have many thoughts troubling me during the nights and they often led to the nightmares I suffered with for so many years. The more I learnt to watch these thoughts, the more they dissolved and didn't trouble me anymore. Now, the nightmares have ceased.

The mind argues with us, and it's a formidable foe with a firm grip on our 'reality', to say the least. It'll tell us everything is real, important, and that we should be angry and do something about some issue or another. If we comply, it then contradicts itself and tells us we shouldn't have done it. Society encourages and reinforces this behaviour and it's not an easy wall to penetrate. It'll tell us life's not fair and that 'so and so' should be punished for what he or she once did to us. It'll come up with anything to stop us being at peace. The mind doesn't let go easily and it's negative; it's up to us to change ourselves by recognising how our minds work and changing the way we think. Changing the way we think can be likened to changing our shoes. We have to take the old pair off before we can try on the new. We can't stretch new shoes over the old. The dilemma here is that one part of us wants to try the new shoes on, but the other half refuses to take the *tried and trusted* pair off. Perhaps it would be more fun to walk through the middle of the argument, barefoot.

How come we've two voices and why are they at odds with each other? We can't defeat the mind and by trying to we only succeed in strengthening it. We can't lose the mind and we can't destroy it. We can become aware of how it works and begin to know ourselves better. We can take control of ourselves by getting rid of all the nonsense; we've never stopped dumping our rubbish and we love to rummage around, just in case we need the contents one day. As you read this book your mind may be telling you that it's all rubbish! My mind told me that when I thought about writing it. The mind always tells us things like that, and it can be likened to us playing 'piggy in the middle' with our two voices. If the 'piggy' sits down or walks away, the game ends. This results in the silence so many of us are afraid of. Being aware of how our mind works is an ongoing process and mine often wanders elsewhere with its favourite distractions, but I get back on track and it happens less and less.

I've said this journey is a tough one and that it takes a great deal of effort to stay on it, but results come fast if we're willing to let go of our ingrained beliefs. For many people - including me - the process is a gradual one, because staying with what's familiar doesn't disrupt our world or require anything of us. If we make the effort to change we struggle and get bumped around a bit at first, but we'll survive and become stronger for the experience. We tend to stick our heads a little out of our shells, see something new and think 'EEK' and scurry back to the safety of our comfort zones. We often get more involved in other people's problems than we do our own, because we can see how to help them - this is a tactical move by the mind and often the advice we give to others, is the advice we most need ourselves. To jump into the 'sea of possibility' involves taking responsibility for ourselves and our actions - this takes courage as these can be dark and scary waters. We all have a responsibility to discover our true nature and whether we take the plunge or not, is entirely up to us.

~~~

We come into the world with nothing, and we leave with nothing. Between these two 'nothings' we're shaped and moulded by the society we find ourselves living in. We're shown the basics of survival by our parents; we're educated, work hard to strict regimes in order to pay the bills, play a little in our free time and then, often earlier than the retirement we've been heading towards all our lives, we go to our graves. The only choices we have on this cradle to grave conveyor are limited to things like 'which toothpaste', 'what flavour ice cream' or 'what colour paint' we wish to buy; these are illusions of choice, already made for us, and we don't see it. There are of course many other choices in front of us, like whether or not to marry etc., but these are conditioned choices based on the structure of society, ensuring its continuation. There are many ways in which we're distracted from asking important questions about our lives. We tend to think of these as a way to make life more bearable and make the most of them while we're here. But what if there's something we're missing along the way - something important. There's something far more wonderful that most of the world's population is blind to and distracted from by a variety of entertainments. Most entertainment is provided by the media and breweries for the purpose of appeasement. This has become known as 'bread and games', a term alluding to one first coined by the Roman poet, Juvenal (1st and early 2nd century AD) - 'The people are only anxious for two things: bread and circuses.'[4]. In other words, we're kept occupied and tranquil with trivia and worthless things while the governments and elite do what they want without any threat from the 'proletariat'. By worthless, I mean the pleasures we get from them are immediate and serve no long term lasting purpose that can improve the morale of society.

Television and magazines entertain us with; recipe programmes, soap operas, home improvement shows, game shows, bad news, gardening, celebrity news, trivia, reality shows, sports and most importantly ... *advertising*! We want bigger televisions screens to watch them on, more 'friends' on social media, and to spend our lives twittering celebrities and each other. We live iLives and the big companies know this and give it to us at a great cost to ourselves and our children - not just in monetary terms. We may not agree we want these things, but then we have to accept that we tolerate them and invite them into our lives. How does this work? Think about how we *share and declare* our lives and the lives of our friends and family on social media? Is this not like an open and online private or business diary? Everything we do we plaster all over social media including photographs, family disputes, births, deaths and marriages. Life is digital and life, as we know it, is information.

When I registered on a professional social media website it wouldn't accept my own email address, but it did accept one of the big cloud group email addresses which I shan't name - it insisted in copying all my personal contacts and there was no opt out choice. I've noticed this happening on more and more social media websites and as long as we're willing to share information with them, they'll be willing to collect it. Have you ever wondered why they ask for this information about us? Why are these social media sites being pushed hard on to us and our own websites? I'm not against these sites, as such, as they're a nice way to share creative ideas and get to know other people around the world. However, they're often used to hang out our 'dirty laundry' and for family or business disputes. This can create an unhealthy environment on what has become the *Cloud* of humanity; I'll talk more about this later. There's a tremendous amount of personal information out there. Do we still have any privacy? Do we care?

I once asked a lady if she ever sat down to think about life. I asked her because she watched a great deal of television and it blared in the background - all day long. Her reply was 'Oh no ... I don't like to think about things like that!' Well that's why the world's the way it is because everyone's thinking in automaton mode as dictated by the media, in its many forms. Everything is provided on tap and there's no need to go to the trouble of thinking. The lady mentioned above doesn't sleep well at night and suffers with chest pain - the kind we have when we live in fear. I can relate to these pains because I did the same for many years and I used to call them the 'dreads' and I've to be honest here; I've no idea what I dreaded. I suggested she leave the television off - she wouldn't hear of it.

I once visited a friend in Australia who had four televisions in her house; they were on all day long, because she didn't want to miss anything when going from room to room. Her conversations were mostly limited to information about celebrities, news, politics, weather, game shows and soap operas - she wanted to be the first to know the latest news. She was hypnotised by the media and believed it kept her informed. She also spent a great deal of time online looking for her perfect partner. No matter what this lady did, in the background she absorbed more information than she would believe is possible, blurting it out at everyone she spoke to. This lady was never calm and suffered with low self-esteem and severe backaches. I never went again, as I couldn't get any peace or quiet in her house.

Life can be likened to a traffic jam. People are kept in jams in order to prevent them from having any 'free' or 'spare' time. By using these terms we kid ourselves we're *partially* free? Are we ever free? I know many people who, when I call them and ask 'how they're doing' their first response is, 'I've been so busy. I've not had a minute to myself' and they never stop being busy or not having a minute to themselves, always having to go somewhere in a hurry, every day of the week. We check the internet for traffic problems that may prevent us from getting somewhere on time and we search for alternative routes so we won't be late, but there are *always* traffic problems and it's just a question of degree. The rush hour is no longer limited to work days; roads are congested at the weekends too as we rush to shops and DIY stores that stay open every day of the week, in order to cope with consumer demand. Whereas we could once estimate arrival times if we were visiting friends or family on Sundays, we now arrive irritated and bothered from the journey. Why haven't these traffic problems been solved? It's easy to solve them by providing a decent free efficiently run public transport system, for *our* benefit not the benefit of corporations or governments. We need the free time to enjoy it, not just to perform a function that supports our work and shopping schedules. The world's problems are easy to solve if humanity cares to solve them, rather than perpetuate them.

Individuals blame governments but it's not their fault. It's *our* fault because we allow it to go on. For example, despite being told about the dangers of certain household products we continue to produce them, buy them and flush them down our drains. Where do we think they go? We're not forced to buy them. We do these things because it suits us to have sparkling bathrooms, glistening kitchens, 'whiter than white' clothes and germ free toilets. We give no thought to the consequences, then blame someone else when we're told the oceans are polluted. Governments are made up of human beings, just like us, and they have the same weaknesses we do - they can't improve our lives for us. We're *all* the government - we're One. All the complaints we put in are about things we've created and then tolerate. Did you know that 'complaint' is an anagram of 'compliant'?

People can't choose what they want to do with their lives without first considering how they're going to pay their bills. We're taught the value of money at an early age when we're given pocket money. We can't buy anything without it and learn fast what we can and can't afford. Money becomes increasingly important when we start working and doesn't stop being that way until we die. It's difficult for most people to live without debt; students, if they don't have wealthy and supporting families, are forced into it if they go into further education - often before they find their first job. Their lives are 'pay as you live' and their children's lives will be the same but more extreme with larger debts. Already, we're charged for water, which is the most abundant substance in the world - this is *madness*; how long before the same applies to the air we breathe.

Money is an abstract concept, but it has become the energy that drives the world we live in - the more money we have the more successful we're considered to be. We look to money to solve the problems it has created and this is why it won't change unless we do. It doesn't matter if we drop £1 or £10,000 into a charity box, it won't make a difference to anything except the way *we* feel and we *feel* much better for having done it. Money won't solve any of the world's problems. As Albert Einstein said 'We can't solve problems by using the same kind of thinking we used when we created them.' Until we change this 'kind of thinking' the only thing that'll change is that life will become more and more expensive. In order to begin changing our lives we must first see money for what it is, and recognise the futility of unintelligently throwing money at problems and expecting them to be solved.

~~~

Recognising the concepts discussed above hits you straight in the face, and when I was hit with it I almost collapsed; luckily I'd a friend close by who took me up to my bedroom to rest; it was about 4.30pm and my head felt so heavy that I couldn't lift it off the pillow - the world as I knew had come to an end. Everything I'd ever thought was real could not be seen, heard, felt, tasted or smelled and I felt disorientated. I couldn't use the word God anymore and I didn't know who to direct my prayers to - if anyone. I'd no idea who I was. I'd been dumped at the roadside and was alone in the world, without direction, faith or hope. I fell into a deep sleep until the following morning. The next day I felt as though I was walking on the earth again for the first time. I'd no choice but to be open-minded after this incident and now have to find my own truth.

As I became more aware of being part of a greater whole, and the fact that humanity is focused on transient, unimportant and destructive things; I saw life as frustratingly 'pointless', because I knew that there must be something more than this. Sometimes I'd arrive at the supermarket, stand in the car park with my trolley in hand and feel, overwhelmingly, that I was stuck in a loop. Life felt unnecessary, and it was all happening in a repetitive cycle. The same feeling would come when I filled my car up with fuel, cooked dinner or went to bed at night. All I could think of was 'I don't want to be here' anymore. It wasn't a depressing suicidal feeling, but more of a silent scream of 'get me out of here'. Though this felt frustrating at times, it could be uplifting at others. However, I didn't know what I was supposed to do with my life now. Something inexplicable had happened to me, but my ego told me that life was pointless and because I gave it the label, that's what it became. I felt there was nothing between me and death, like being in a waiting room with nothing to do and nothing to read and it was boring. I didn't want to be here feeling pointless for the rest of my life. I now see this as having been a shift in my awareness - a point where I let go of control and trusted that life would now bring all I needed. I was tiny in the universe - a humbling experience. I felt a strong urge to find something purposeful to do with my life and was no longer afraid or concerned about death.

If we stand back and take another look at the world, if we remove ourselves from it and allow ourselves to become aware of it as a 'whole', then it looks very different and a lot less threatening. We can see how we rush to the sales to buy things we don't need, we can see why society is sick and when we listen to the *news* we see it in a whole new light. If we watch documentaries about past wars, if we ignore the homeless, if we continue to want more 'things', if we continue to amuse ourselves with trivia and trinkets, if we prefer to feed electronic pets than the starving in third world countries, ignore warnings printed in books like these, put sparkle into household appliances and fittings rather than ourselves, if we pretend the things I've mentioned aren't true, then we're not at all open-minded and we might as well walk around with paper bags over our heads.

Chapter 3

Interaction

There's no such thing as good luck - only a good attitude.

Every day we come into contact with other people in one way or another. Usually, we don't give them a second glance and if we do, it's often in passing judgement relating to their social status, physical appearance, dress sense or some other critical observation. Sometimes these observations are kind, and sometimes not. Why do human beings have difficulty interacting with each other - particularly with strangers?

There's an air of decency implied in the expression 'human being' that doesn't quite fit with the way we behave. When I think about humanity on the *whole*, the arising thoughts are disturbing. We come together in times of need, such as when there's an earthquake or a big charity event to 'save the world'. I can't think of much else that doesn't require a crisis to spur us into 'action'. There's a regrettable need for this in society and if we want to rid ourselves of it, there needs to be a sea change on the inside of each and every one of us. Charitable actions are born from suffering; these actions place plasters that don't stick, on wounds that don't heal - why do we allow suffering in our world? However, they do show we're capable of incredible humanitarian feats when we *connect* for the common good. In general we're; vain, violent, aggressive, ignorant, greedy, jealous, self-centred and a whole lot more - few of us recognise or admit to these traits in ourselves. Our personal problems are bigger than anyone else's and they occupy us all the time. Human beings, it seems, are pretty strange.

Ever since I can remember, I've been watching people interact with each other. When we moved to our current home, we met a couple who lived in the next house on the same road, about half a mile away. The husband had warm eyes and a friendly disposition, but his wife was hard and unmoving and I knew - from the way she scanned us - that we wouldn't become friends - well, maybe it would take a few years. Sometimes when I've passed their home and they were in their garden, I said 'Hi' and invited them for a coffee. I always got a sharp and abrupt 'We haven't got the time' from the wife. On more than one occasion, I noticed her rush into her house as I approached it on my way back from shopping, so she wouldn't have to stop to say hello. It's such a pity to be unfriendly towards others, when it's a wonderful thing to meet new people; if we'd only take the time to get to know them - we may be pleasantly surprised.

When we look at another person we see a reflection of ourselves. So if we take a dislike to them, we need to look to ourselves to find out why, as it's *always* because it reflects a part of us that we don't like. The lady up the road keeps busy with her duties and family and she doesn't wander far afield. When we first moved in, I told her that we lived quiet and spiritual lives - her expression became one of disapproval. This feeling didn't come from us - rather it came from inside her, from a fear of hers that she wasn't ready to face. Whatever this fear was, it's deeply hidden and I doubt if she realised it, or questioned her likes and dislikes. We tend to accept our predicaments and limitations and rarely challenge them, preferring to live within their protective shield. We can make changes to our world - even small ones can make a big difference. Why not try smiling at the cashier next time you go to the supermarket and see what response you get? When I do this, I sometimes get a grimace in return and the same from a passer-by in the street, but I persevere regardless. The message I get is 'Can't you see I'm miserable and don't want to be cheered up'. However, several members of staff now smile back at me and that's got to be worth something - perseverance pays off.

We hear stories all the time about people living and dying alone, perhaps it's happening down our street, yet too often, we don't want to know. We may see them walking past our window or regularly pass them in the street. To us, they're 'the old biddy' or 'the grumbly old man', but we've probably never spoken to or considered visiting them to see if they're okay, or need anything. Why aren't we more proactive in 'lending a hand'? Have we become too suspicious of each other? Is it an innate fear of rejection or do we fear being accused of having ignoble motives? Whatever our reasons, we leave such people to be cared for by the authorities - though we know it's not always adequately provided. Because we all have to work hard and we occupy ourselves with trivia, we don't have the time or inclination to care for people in need. The saddest part of this is that there exists a profession called 'Carer'; how did caring become a profession? Childminders and carers have to be approved, trained and scrutinised and then police checks are made on them; what is this world we've created and live in and why is it so hostile?

We interact less and less with each other while we live out our roles - we've become increasingly divided. Because we've our comforts and we find security in them, we don't mind what goes on outside - I'll talk more about comfort and security in a later chapter. Think about how we behave towards each other on a train or bus - physically we couldn't be closer, mentally, we couldn't be further apart. A person sitting down can avoid the glance of a needy person standing up because they don't want to give up their seat for them; humanity can be very selfish. We read newspapers, books, do crossword puzzles, play number games, talk on our mobile phones and listen to music, but we'll not speak to another person. It reminds me of children who don't want to listen to something so they stick their fingers in their ears, screw up their eyes and pretend the outside world doesn't exist.

We don't speak to people we don't know. One of the reasons is that we've been inculcated from childhood 'not to talk to strangers', to report incidents and not to get involved in certain situations. We've been divided into social groups where a businessman, for example, might see a young lad with a hooded top coming towards him, and because of the media, judge him as some sort of troublemaker - he'll have a low opinion of the youth and be 'on guard'. On the other hand, the youth might view the businessman as someone who'd look down on him - they're intimidated by each other. The two have pre-conditioned opinions - though they've never met. We also have these conditioned opinions of the homeless, the rich, the poor, the scruffy, a person who drives a rusty banger or a shiny new car - our opinions may be far from the truth. The divisions are ingrained from a young age and children learn about social interaction from films, schools, clubs and their parents. Everyone is in defensive mode - we fear judgement, reaction and rejection. We think we're better than each other, but on the other hand, we also think we're not good enough. We can't see that the society we've created made us this way. We're selfish and do everything for our own gain, even if it doesn't seem that way. For example we may give someone a gift, but want them to be forever grateful for it, or we think our act of generosity was a 'good deed', but tell other people about it - we don't give from our hearts. We need and search for gratification and confirmation of our own existence.

There are people who can't cope with the outside world very well, and they withdraw from society altogether. My mother was one of them, and her life was planned with precision around the television - cutting short telephone conversations when a program was about to begin. She didn't leave her home for many years, except on Christmas Day when my brother would pick her up and take her to his house for the day. Human interaction with 'real' people in the outside world came to be replaced with the thoughts and activities of a world created by the media. My mother slept between her favourite programmes and mourned serials that came to an end - not knowing what to fill the free slot with. She was at her happiest after being diagnosed with cancer, and jumped into her own hospital drama, playing the starring role. She never complained about her illness - not even when dying. In some perverse way, she'd learnt her lines well by watching a variety of hospital dramas.

~~~

We struggle to solve problems between ourselves and don't often succeed, because we need to deal with the causes, rather than the symptoms. For example, a married couple can't solve their problems simply by talking about them; the problems will never be solved unless the root causes are identified and both parties are willing to find a solution. It's a bit like mopping the floor from an overflowing sink without turning off the tap - the solution is always simple. Problems often persist because the couple want them to; the talks are all part of perpetuating a situation that deep down they don't want to resolve. No-one wants it to be solved - it's the game play. The key to solving our problems is first to 'want to' and then we can identify the reasons for them - this takes thought and a great deal of naked honesty between the parties involved. We begin to interact with each other far better when we accept that we're pretty lousy at it. Do you find you're often waiting for another person to stop speaking so you can cut in to say what *you* want? Do you listen to what others are saying at all? When we meet up with someone we know we ask 'How are you?' but do we ever listen when they deviate from the expected 'I'm fine, thank you' with something more honest like 'well, now that you ask, I haven't been too well lately'. Do we really care when we ask the question at all, or is it just an accepted form of greeting? If we're honest we know that what we want to say is more important than what someone else is saying; we prepared it while they were talking to us.

Our conversations have been prescribed for us and we rarely talk about anything original or different. We've lost the art of communicating for ourselves. We've lost the art of thinking. We've no spontaneity, no creativity, no imagination and don't care much for anything except our own stories, ambitions and dramas. We're terrible listeners; have you ever noticed how much we interrupt when we talk to each other? Have you ever been to one of those parties where people stand around in groups? More often than not they remain in the same group they arrived in, for the entire party - no-one's really interested in mingling. If we go out in groups and see someone sitting all alone, does it occur to us to talk to them or invite them to join us? Do we offer them a smile? We tend to walk past and not notice them, or think they're weird in some way and that they're on their own for a good reason. Why are we afraid to talk to them?

~~~

We interact through language and language has changed a great deal over the years; we've 'apparently' gone from drawing on the walls of caves to reading complex programming languages like DNA. We now text each other in 'TextSpeak'; it's become the 'shorthand' of the Cloud. One day we won't recognise the symbols written in this book and children already struggle with language from Shakespearean times. We translate ancient texts, such as hieroglyphics, but we can't be sure the true meaning isn't lost, like in the game Chinese Whispers. Some children bury time-capsules as part of a school project; they prepare all sorts of things to put inside, in the hope that some future generation will discover them. My personal feeling on this is that whoever, if anyone at all, digs up these treasures in the 'future', they won't comprehend our languages - we've over 6000 of them. The things they find will be unidentifiable and end up being put in a museum, just like we do with the relics we dig up from ancient sites now. Future relics will be as big a mystery to the next generations as past ones are to us today. Because our technology is advancing at a phenomenal rate, a lack of discernment is already evident between *living* generations; for example, our children and grandchildren have never used three and a half inch and five and a quarter inch floppy disks to store information on and they're unlikely to recognise one if they see it now; they won't be able to read the information on them either.

Over time, the way we interact with each other has changed. Once we were 'out and about' communicating face-to-face with real people, or writing letters with a pen. Nowadays, we rely on computers and social media sites for these activities and the art of conversation is rapidly losing ground. Whereas we would once sit in our lounges at home and socially interact with family and friends, we now use technology to converse. We can be sitting in the same room with friends or next to each other in the pub, often having a separate private conversation with just one of them via texts - it's a new type of whispering. This is how we connect and interact with each other; how we arrange meetings, organise sporting events or parties. We now send a text message to see if someone's home - when they live next door - before we pop round for a coffee, or text from our cars to announce our arrival. Ringing on the doorbell and calling through the letterbox has become obsolete.

We're losing our social skills and life is now lived through the screen. Nowadays, we don't even need a computer as televisions are 'smart' and web enabled. Mobile phones have become evermore sophisticated - they've become 'smarter' than we are. If we believe in destiny, then we don't have a choice and all this is 'meant to be'. We're reaching a point where we won't need to go out at all, because food and just about any item we can think of can be delivered to our homes - we can and increasingly do, work online. Couples argue and dump each other by text and bosses have fired their staff the same way. We 'check in' to the 'cloud' in the mornings and 'check out' at night, often while in bed. We catch up with and discuss news stories and friend's updates on pods, tablets, mobile phones, laptops and computers and these have become our priority. Some Facebook pages are so frequently updated it can take hours to read through what's taken place while we were sleeping. I know of people who do this while they're at work. It can't be denied that the world is interacting more and more through technology.

Communicating through electronic media can be problematic because there's no body-language involved and we need body-language just as much as we need speech. Instead, we use the crude system of emoticons to convey our emotions to the people we send messages to. They're not at all accurate and our mood or meaning can be, and often is, misconstrued; often, we don't send the emoticon that matches what we're really feeling. For interaction purposes, the internet begs dishonesty and conversations without thought - it's impulsive. It allows us to develop another character and this character can't be a grounded one. We've the ability to proofread, alter and erase our messages before we send them, which we can't do when communicating face-to-face. What long term effects could this produce in society? Electronic media tells us a great deal about each other and we upload all our thoughts on to it - it's our external hard drive. Mobile phones, tablets and smart watches have become a new type of body part - we don't leave home without them. They are, in effect, our electronic selves and we prefer them to our molecular ones. Our mind is in the process of relocating from our organic bodies into an electronic cloud!

Everything is in the cloud now - it's the technological consciousness of us all. Technology is advancing into a superior being, leaving humanity far behind. I've nothing at all against technology or even interacting through it, but when I see that we're becoming ever more separated from ourselves and evermore dependent on technology rather than our own faculties, I can't help but feel a little sad for future generations. Technology is not being used for the psychological advancement of humanity - it's doing the opposite.

~~~

Adverts take up the majority of space on most websites and we constantly have to avoid them. Many websites now have more adverts than they do the information we've searched for. As we surf they attempt to force us to listen to auto-play video adverts that boom into action as we hover over them. Increasingly we're being directed to websites that don't give us what we were searching for. Adverts jump, shake, spin and flash around the screen - they follow us as we scroll down the page, pestering us like a sleeve-tugging child, as though we've ignored them. Today I looked up a word on an online dictionary and got 'all' of the above - they distract from our purpose. Does anyone give in to the temptation and click on them - other than by accident. Anyone living in this world, who can't see something's wrong with it, should look again at the stealth activities and juvenile trickery of advertising. Adverts *are* interaction. Just about every advert is aimed at what you've shown an interest in or bought in the past. It's not too clever because we've often already bought or found what they're trying to sell us. Advertising invades the threads on our forums. If you don't click on them and don't buy from them they have no choice but to disappear - our demands created them. The advertisers interact with us by invading our spaces with their own agendas. It's not just about buying their products - it's about clicking on their links as they're 'pay per click'.

~~~

The way society is at the moment we don't need to communicate at all, as it's all done for us - we're pampered. We're so involved, with television serials, the internet, the media, gossip, celebrities and the latest technology that we've no time left to recognise the magical world we live in. We copy behaviours, language, fashion, violence and attitude from the television and other media sources and if anyone steps out of line, we ostracise them. If a company wants information to go viral, it only needs to put it on a busy online account - then sit back and watch the fireworks. We complain about the bad news on the television and in the newspapers and we think our complaint is enough. We're happy to leave solving the world's problems to governments and because *they* never succeed with it, we don't believe we can either so we sit back and say 'That's life' - abdicating responsibility.

We're fragmented and we've become further fragmented by using the internet as the interface we communicate through. We try to put the pieces together but they never fit as they should, because we're not prepared to take responsibility or stand alone and turn away from our personal dramas. We try to squeeze ourselves into what makes us acceptable in the eyes of what we see as a 'normal' society. We've a great capacity to love each other and be creative, but we've also a great capacity to hate and destroy. In recognising how we interact with each other we're *already* beginning to change. Once we can see, we begin to observe our own behaviour and it becomes difficult to behave in the same way again. It becomes difficult to pass by someone in need and ignore them, and harder still to judge others by their appearance. When we can shine on each other, life becomes worthwhile. We change what we see in our world when we change ourselves - we can never change anything else. Are we capable of living in a better world? Only if we want to. Are we destined to ride this roller-coaster? Only if we believe it!

Chapter 4

Does it Matter?

*There's more in the mirror than we see at first glance -
so it is with the world.*

This book invites us to consider thinking about things from another perspective. If we do this with an open mind then there's nothing to lose and much to gain - there's no risk and nothing to fear. If there's something after this life that we're supposed to be striving for, then life matters; too few people care enough about this to give it any thought. Because we don't know what happens to us after we die, we're reluctant to expend energy on pursuing something that has no verifiable tangible benefits. We look *forward* to things like; holidays, becoming twenty-one, promotions, retirements or the next episode of a soap opera, yet on the other hand, we've adopted a 'live for today' attitude without a thought for the long term consequences.

After much reflection about the world we live in it's become clear to me that rather than live life, we tolerate it as dictated to. We believe ourselves to be individuals - nothing could be further from the truth. Just like a tree whose branches reach out in different directions, so it is for humanity. The branches seem different at first glance but on closer examination it becomes clear they're part of the whole. They're like the veins carrying the blood of humanity and for now, they're rather dry and brittle. If statistics can be believed, there are billions of us. Billions of branches who at our core seek; good health, peace, knowledge, prosperity and harmony, but on the outside we don't know where to find them because we're not looking in the right direction. To strive for something after our lives is difficult because we can't see *beyond* the boundary of 'death'. Because of our financial culture we want rewards 'right now' for our efforts - we don't like waiting for them. In other words, we want a guaranteed return before we're prepared to even *consider* risking anything out of the ordinary. Would we give up our life for a beautifully wrapped package without knowing what was inside? We're happy to invest in life, but only if the returns are good enough!

It sometimes happens that an event in our life, or some other thing, gives us pause for thought, and we begin to ponder on the meaning of life or ask ourselves 'Is this life all there is?' - a catalyst that makes us look beyond where we are and question our existence. If we're serious in our search we find, without doubt, there are wonders waiting to be discovered; *no-one* can ever take them away from us or put a price on them. They can't be reclaimed by banks or governments; they're our inheritance and they're free; all we have to do is open our hearts to our untapped potential. We already have all we could hope for but it lies beneath the persona we're reluctant to shed. We're wrapped up tightly in our own cocoons and don't have the time - or inclination - to listen to anyone who has other opinions. Inside a cocoon is a butterfly, inside a gift box is a present and inside a seed is the code for creation - what's inside you?

When this begins to make sense, we're able to see how separation is the cause of the world's conflicts. Whether you're a tramp living on a park bench or some high-ranking executive, we all have the same opportunities and abilities to find our way - no-one is excluded. There are many philosophical theories on the meaning of life but these are *only* theories and truth can't be a 'theory'. Enquiring within is the only way to be sure of our truth but if you keep looking outside, all you'll find is more confusion. There isn't a single one of us who's better than another regardless of their; age, race, religion, skin colour, cultural background or education. It's important to realise this in order to see how separated we've become from each other. We're captain of our own ship navigating the river of this life - there's no co-pilot and no crew. We can remain in this river, or navigate our way out of it; which we decide to do is up to us. One way to begin this navigation is to look at some of the charts - the established theories. Some of these I've sketched below.

One philosophical theory about this life is that it doesn't matter what we do with it. The theory says Hitler was treated the same as Mahatma Gandhi when he died. It also says we can do whatever we want including blowing up the entire planet and wiping out its occupants, which is not very intelligent. What's the mindset of someone who'd want to do something like that anyway? Is this life a living film and after having played out our parts we walk off the stage, or like children who play 'cowboys and Indians' or 'cops and robbers' and then go home for tea? It's a popular theory worth exploring - if you think it's plausible. Is it popular because we don't need to think about what we do with our lives, how well we treat others or feel remorse for things we may have done in the past? To make this plainer - does it suit us to believe it? Is it convenient? Is it fashionable? Does it let us off the hook? More importantly, is it true? It's a bit too easy to *escape* with this theory and it requires no work whatsoever on our part. For me, it can be likened to sweeping dirt under the carpet, which we tend to do anyway. This theory gives us permission to continue doing what we're already doing.

Another theory is that we're here to learn, but just what we're here to learn is unclear. Should we learn how to get along better with each other without judgement or criticism? If we're here to learn then we don't seem to be learning much, or fast enough. Education is in decline and people are being 'dumbed down'. Television and the internet take up most people's free time with game shows, trivial reality programmes and silly entertainments. The only thing the world is learning is how to keep its head in the sand because we're perfectly happy to go on pretending everything is just fine. If we're here to learn then it follows that we'll 'graduate' in some way after this life and move up to a higher plane, then repeat the process and reach higher still. If we're learning then we're learning the wrong things like; aggression, violence, disharmony, and complete disregard for humanity. We haven't learnt too much that's worthwhile - we've submitted to empty-headedness. We don't notice the beauty of the world we live in; we live within the shallowness of a prescribed life in return for a few worthless trinkets that can never justify the suffering endured by so many people. We're still at war with each other, using increasingly sophisticated weaponry; I can't see this changing in my lifetime or even within the next few generations.

There are those who think we're dreaming this life. There's a lot to be said for that. Here are just a few questions that have occurred to me about this theory. If it's a dream why do we return to it every morning? Why does it last so long? Why do we dream every night within this dream? Who is dreaming? The list of questions is endless. If it's a dream then we may live from dream to dream. Changes I've made in my life have been reflected in my dreams. Does this mean dreams are a guide to the healthy or unhealthy state of our minds? Dreams are muddled up events - our hopes, fears and experiences, which can make them unrecognisable as a reality we can relate to. We can experience walls crumbling around us, driving cars with no brakes, walking on water or flying? How do we create these dreams?

Yet another theory is we die, ceasing existence altogether. This can be likened to organic matter left to decompose in a compost heap. This theory is hard to get to grips with as it's obvious there's more to us than that. I fail to see how life could have come about, only to produce slaves to a system that values transient and abstract things above all else. Are we here to live in a world riddled with endless war, confusion, illness, corruption and perversion as we contemplate our personal extinction, paradoxically longing for eternal life and youth? Must we remain desperate for answers to innate questions and stand by - helpless - while the world is being destroyed? No! Something's wrong here. This to me is impossible and it doesn't take much thought to figure this out. Everything comes out of a void. If you plant an acorn and let it grow, the oak tree produces more seeds that have come out of *nothing*. These weren't there before - just the *information* needed to create them. In the same vein, think about a baby ten months before its birth or a word not yet spoken. Where do they come from? What happens to our consciousness after death? Our consciousness is not made of matter - it can't decompose.

Is life some sort of multi-dimensional game? Another theory says we're living in a holographic universe and that this is a virtual reality world. There are many videos and books on this subject. It's not necessary to agree with what they say but it's possible to fit pieces into the jigsaw puzzle after listening to them with an open mind - allowing our *own* thoughts and reason to stream through. Are we here to find our way out of some sort of labyrinth? If this is a virtual reality game within a holographic universe then I can't exclude the *possibility* that the whole world is *me*; I'd be the player and the game. It would mean everything is coming from inside me including every person I've ever met; making me the entire universe and multi-dimensional. If this is me then it's *you* too. If this is the case, our own universes are overlapping or 'masking' each other in some amazing and divine way. The only thing I could be sure exists, is my own awareness. The implications and responsibilities that go with this are colossal. It may also mean no-one would ever find the time-capsules I mentioned earlier because with our 'deaths', the world would disappear just like turning off the television while the programme is still running. However, if we flick the 'power' switch on again, the film is still there. What an incredible thought that is when I allow it to grow!

There are many more theories about the world we live in and it's not necessary to go into all of them. Whichever theory we give credibility to, we owe it to ourselves to examine it and face every question that arises. To follow blindly or believe in it just because it came recommended in a best-selling book would be unwise. Along the way we may discover several theories can fit together or at least parts of them - we may even discover a new one.

~~~

We're eternal *beings* who are all connected, like droplets in an ocean - this has become known as *consciousness*. If there's only one consciousness, then surely there must only be one Mind. A little research into my own mind - a part of the whole - has raised many questions for me to ponder over and that our true nature is magnificent is beyond questioning. Most of my research was done by watching my own mind and thoughts - a most beneficial exercise; if we watch *ourselves* instead of others we learn a great deal more about reality. What we're doing here in this life is a question most people have given up on - if they've asked it at all. This is why we still have questions after thousands of years of investigation - after all this time we haven't learnt to care. We tend to look to science for answers but the problem with this is that science looks at the physical world with measurement and logic. As we're not mechanical beings with mechanical responses, can science ever find truth? Remember, it's the questions that are important!

~~~

For as long as I can remember I've heard words like *eternity* and *infinity*. However, we can't conceive of these concepts because we're locked in space and time - they imply finite boundaries. No-one seems to know where they are in the universe. Ask anyone *who* or *where* they really are and they'll stare at you as though they've short-circuited - society can't think this way yet. We're waiting to die and making the most of our time here with a plethora of toys, gadgets and entertainments available for us in 'God's waiting room'. Life can be compared to long delays at an airport; we wander around the shops looking for yet more things to buy and occupy us, in order to help us pass the time until we board the plane. It's easy to think nothing matters and that we're powerless when we read the horror stories in the media, but it isn't true. We're hedging our bets on living 'happily ever after' and hoping it'll be alright by the time we reach the last page.

It can't be denied that we're being distracted from thinking about the *deeper* issues of life and also being encouraged to occupy ourselves with more trivial and abstract matters. Why don't philosophical and spiritual matters appear on the radar screens of large numbers of people? The subject of 'humanity' is never discussed in any serious way in the mainstream media or in schools - we should be shouting about it. What exactly is being obscured by these distractions? Why don't good news stories spread as quickly as the bad ones? We love to listen to bad news, pass it on and corrupt it further by adding our own criticism and judgement to it. We continue to listen to the news on the television and radio, even though it's distressing for us. We know we don't get told the whole true story, if any of it. We listen to the stories about wars and those injured in them, the starving in third world countries, our badly behaved sporting 'heroes', corrupt politicians, and many more. Why do we need to listen to them? Why is it considered *de rigueur*? We listen, we watch, we fret and nothing changes because we don't change ourselves. Why do we continue to do it?

Science makes everything seem out of reach by inventing big numbers and then adding an 'illion' on the end; this makes developments in our lifetimes appear to be beyond possibility. Beyond the 'illions' there's a googol, which is 10^{100} and a googolplex, which is 10^{googol}. It's so big it isn't even a number we could ever use practically. We couldn't count up to it in our lifetime; why is science wasting time on this nonsense? At what point do we accept infinity? In his series *The Cosmos*, Carl Sagan stated 'A piece of paper large enough to contain all the zeros in a googolplex couldn't be stuffed into the known universe.'[5] We think future generations can benefit from all this knowledge, but not ourselves, because the numbers are so big and way beyond our reach. If we can't understand the magnitude of these numbers, is it any wonder we can't fathom the concept of eternity? Consequently, we seek comfort in things, amusements, pleasures, celebrities, films, media and other trivial distractions because there appears to be little point and no encouragement to do anything else. Our children stand to inherit our knowledge, foolishness, possessions, depressions, traumas and ignorance, just as we did from our parents and we're doing nothing to change it - we can't be bothered. We look only at what our five senses perceive and at our own 'survival'.

It's hard to ignore that we - as individuals - must be able to attain our goal within our own lifetime; imagine what we might be turning our backs on by ignoring this? We must find out what we're doing here and without delay if we're to achieve it - none of us knows *when* we're going to die. If we're eternal beings and can't die then what does this life matter? This is not an easy question to think about. It's not a question we'll find in an 'answer book'. It's important to remember that all theories - some lasting and some fashionable - aren't *facts*. If anything, I'd say we're more likely here to remember 'who we are' and who we *truly* are has nothing to learn. Are we supposed to find our purpose and achieve our goals blindly? Ask 'Who am I?' and don't stop asking it, but don't expect a voice to call out from behind you with an answer - if you do get one, question it. The more we learn the more we have to 'unlearn' in order to find our true self - it follows that as we get older this task is more difficult. I'd suggest that our purpose is to return to where we came from and to be willing to leave our body, mind and ego behind. They're not who we are and we're far too attached to them; our anxieties, problems, fears and insecurities belong to them. Are we the sum total of this 'lifetime'? I invite you to ponder this interesting question for a while, but look at humanity as a *whole* rather than yourself as an individual while you think about it. For every question I get close to answering, many more get raised. Does it matter? That's up to you.

Chapter 5

Time

If time heals ... how long will it take to complete the process?

It's a dry sunny day and I'm typing this on my laptop looking outside the window. The tops on the trees are swaying in a gentle breeze and birds are coming to feed from the bird table competing for the food I've put out for them. It's lovely and quiet but despite movement, nothing is obviously changing or aware of the monotonous 'tick-tock' of the clock. If I wait an hour I won't see anything different. I did the same yesterday and I'll do the same tomorrow. I haven't looked to see what the time is; I don't wear a watch and I don't know what day it is. Time has not affected my view in any visible way that I can determine and it can't spoil my enjoyment unless I spend it worrying about a past event, future appointment or thinking about whether I should start preparing lunch - each new moment is right now. If I wait a few weeks more flowers will bloom and more will die off but it's all a cycle - a rhythm that has nothing to do with time. Time changes nothing, but we've created a mechanism for it and slotted it into the natural rhythm of nature. Because we believe time to be 'real' we then have to fill it and now we've expressions such as spare time, no time, free time, overtime, quality time, flexitime, save time and *even* a waste of time. But we no longer have the time to watch the sun appearing and disappearing on the horizon and, if we live in a town, we've *no time* to observe nature except perhaps if we go for a walk in the park or look up at a starry sky on a clear night.

Time is how we measure the movement of the universe; we attempt to measure its rhythm and regulate our lives by it. This doesn't work too well, which is why some months have different numbers of days in them; we also add an extra day to February every four years. The purpose of time is to help us 'schedule' our lives. Imagine going to King's Cross station to catch a train and finding out it's already left. How would we make appointments or keep to schedules without time? We need time to keep up with the pace of the society we've created, and that's *all* we need it for. The universe manages perfectly well without it.

Is turning over to look at the clock the first thing you do when waking up in the morning? My friends and family get busier and busier as they try to fill in the hours with rituals. These rituals include but aren't limited to work, television, sports, social media, shopping, fitness, cooking and socialising; we fit these in between our other commitments. We keep different time zones and put our clocks forward and backward twice a year. Some of my friends monitor more than one time zone. How many time-pieces do you have in the house including on the oven, mobile phones, watches and media players? How would you cope without them? The flowers in my garden are still blooming without any help or awareness of the seconds and minutes passing by and they're not in a hurry - neither can they be hurried.

If we don't get something done according to a schedule we say we've 'run out of time' or passed a 'deadline'. How is this possible? Why do we have breakfast, lunch, and dinner times; why don't we eat when we're hungry? We need these mealtimes because we have to fit in with the tight schedules of employment, appointments, travel, and television timetables. We combine some of these in order to save time such as eating while watching the television, or travel and organising our appointments through the use of computer tablets and mobile phones. I don't believe we're meant to run and rule our lives according to mechanical or digital devices, manufactured with increasing precision. We're obsessed with exactness and technology.

A delayed train or flight can have serious consequences for a tightly-scheduled businessman. It's partly for this reason that webinars have evolved for conferences and presentations and it's more profitable for a company if it doesn't have to put its directors up in hotels and pay for expensive flights. It's not just about saving money either as it saves a great deal of 'time'. Human beings have become mechanised and moulded into shape according to the advancements of technology. We 'function' to the rhythm of the clock. What time do *you* have to get up for work?

The world must remain highly organised if it's to continue meeting its financial and productivity targets. *Self-help* or *self-improvement*, rather than helping us to become happier human beings are becoming concepts designed to increase our efficiency by managing our time better, particularly where work is concerned. Ironically, this means learning how to slow down time so we've more of it in order to cope with the workloads and stresses of our jobs and the higher expectations and demands of our employers or schedules. We need diaries and gadgets that bleep to remind us of our commitments, in order to cope with the demands on our time. We speed up cooking times with microwave ovens and ready meals; we also speed up the growing process of our crops with faster growing varieties of genetically modified foods. Despite slowing down or speeding up time there are still only twenty-four hours in a day - we can't cram in another millisecond. Technology has advanced so much that a mere human being doesn't have the *time* to keep up - we must change in order to accommodate it.

Mahatma Gandhi said 'There is more to life than simply increasing its speed.'[6] We're getting to the point where the only way to keep up with our busy schedules is to mechanise human beings. We already have robots doing the repetitive jobs in factories that were once done by us; they do them faster and more precisely without the need for tea or lunch breaks; they also don't require 'time off' for holidays or sickness. We get faster and faster at sporting events; Thomas Burke achieved 12.0 seconds in the final of the 100 meters at the first Olympics in 1896. Usain Bolt ran the 100 meter dash in 9.63 seconds in the London Olympics 2012; when will we get it down to under 9 seconds? How? We'll need more than human bodies if we wish to keep running faster - our future athletes will have to be transhuman.

This is not about transcendence to 'higher realms' of spirituality but transcendence of the human body into technology - a merger of the two. This concept is far from new. The concept was 'shown to the public' in the form of *Frankenstein: or, The Modern Prometheus*, a novel written by Mary Shelley in 1818. Later examples include *The Six Million Dollar Man* television series way back in 1973, which was based on a novel called *Cyborg* by Martin Caidin published in 1972. This may seem far-fetched but we don't need to do too much research to see it's not far off. Transhumanism, in films and literature, is now accepted without horror or question, whereas the idea of Frankenstein was originally shocking. Other more recent films include *A. I. Artificial Intelligence* and *Bicentennial Man* in which robots want to become human beings. We already walk about with our gadgets and most people couldn't do without them; I've known people to be frantic when they've dropped their mobile phone on the ground or in water. My own opinion is that our 'natural state' is so advanced we've no need for technology. It could be argued that the only war is between the 'god of science and technology' and the 'god of spirituality'. It could also be argued that we're travelling back in time - returning to our *origin*. Is there any way of knowing?

~~~

Have you ever had that 'I don't remember the bit in-between' feeling? For example, when we're driving our cars and realise we've been 'absent' for part of the journey. We've negotiated traffic lights, roundabouts and other obstacles, but have no recollection of doing so. In my experience, sometimes twenty minutes have passed by without my knowledge. What happened to the time? A part of our mind has wandered elsewhere yet we've still managed to drive many kilometres without full concentration or incident. Who was driving the car? How is it we didn't hit a pedestrian, another car or drive off the road? Were we daydreaming or is this some other phenomenon? What has this to do with space and time?

Have you ever sat on a train pulling out of a railway station and felt a little disorientated. Sometimes it feels as though the world outside is moving and the train is stationary. This motion is caused by us and not by an external action. Similarly, when another train pulls out of the station while the one we're on is stationary, it can feel like the train we're on is moving backwards - this concept is called 'self-motion'. We feel this disorientation many times in our lives without realising it; for example, when we walk on land after being on a ship or standing still after spinning on the spot. This phenomenon is heavily researched as it has many uses in the creation of more believable experiences in virtual reality games. I'm no scientist, but if the world we live in is a virtual reality, then we're probably victims of the biggest hoax going and this must have been created by a far higher level of consciousness. Have we created a 'game' for our own amusement? Is the earth moving or is the universe revolving around us? Is anything moving at all?

~~~

Time is a strange concept. We turn time back when we remember the past, and forward when we go to the future; for example, when we've got an appointment to keep. Time is abstract and linear; our minds travel up and down its line - late, early or on-time. We can't *actually* go anywhere along the time-line. Time is a measurement of distance between two places in a similar way to feet and inches. When we travel to work for example, we *measure* the journey from our homes to our place of work in both miles and minutes. But time doesn't necessarily involve a physical journey from place to place. Time also passes when we don't move - while we're waiting for a bus or sleeping. Our obsession with schedules makes time important, but only to us, as the 'natural' world continues regardless.

We've all had days where time drags and it's usually while we're waiting for our working day to finish or when we're feeling bored and unchallenged? Other days, *time flies* and we don't know where it's gone. This is often when we're enjoying ourselves or we've a deadline to meet. Time doesn't feel natural to us; it curtails our more enjoyable and challenging activities and stretches out the dull and mundane ones. What's happening here? Time slows down when we're focused on things we'd rather came to an end but, when we're enjoying ourselves we live more in the Now and become unaware of the clock. We count the days until our next birthday, anniversary, mortgage payment, retirement and other notable dates. Children can become obsessed with time, like when they state their age as twelve and three quarters; they can't wait for the magical transition into their teens ... then they can't wait to get out of them. Coming of age at sixteen eighteen and twenty-one is all important because it brings *rewards* such as, 'grown up' status, being allowed into clubs and pubs or getting control of our own bank accounts.

~~~

Every thought we have originates from the past - every single one of them. Thought is memory. These thoughts can and do manifest in many ways, like when we remind each other of things we might have said or done twenty or thirty years ago, or we may remember an embarrassing moment that still makes us blush. It's difficult to let go of hurtful experiences; the mind holds on tightly and broods over them, which has a negative impact on our well-being. We go to the past when we look at photographs - think about that. We can *never* go to the future. We're always here, right Now, *out* of time when we're doing whatever we're doing. If we can't go to the past or future, do time and space exist at all?

Where is Chapter One of this book right now? It's not in the future. We could look for it in the past if we search our memory banks, but we won't find it in the Now. You can never find it in the Now. As you read this paragraph only the part you're reading at this precise moment is in the 'Now' and it's so precise - we can't pinpoint it because by the time we think about it, it's already in the past. The future can't be located; it can be waited for but it'll never arrive. The past can only be remembered. When we think about the future or the past we're in the Now. We can't go to the future or return to the past. If we're in the 'Now' ... what is time? It's an abstract concept designed to occupy us as we rotate it between work, play, families, stress etc. We can stop the clocks, but we can't stop the rhythm of the universe - we're all a part of it. Time is a 'tool' we use to measure and schedule our lives - like clockwork. The Now exists between thoughts. The Now exists between the past and the future. The only time is Now, but it's been divided into years, months, weeks, days, hours, minutes and seconds.

Time is an illusion obscuring the Now.

Chapter 6

Right and Wrong

Perspective is the pen that draws the line between right and wrong.

This chapter is not about what's right or wrong in the sense that to commit a crime is wrong. Rather it's about following the path that's right for us and recognising other peoples' rights to follow their own. This means we don't impose our beliefs on others if we believe them to be wrong. We've been taught right and wrong from an early age, but these standards were based on the upbringing and disciplines of people who were taught by others. In this society we don't live by what we preach; what standards are we following? It's up to us to decide what's right and wrong for ourselves and up to us whether to live without hypocrisy. No matter what path we decide to take it'll ultimately lead us to the same place; it may take a great deal longer in some directions, but nobody can say which way is the right way. We constantly talk about right and wrong, war and peace, good and bad and it's silly as these concepts are abstract stagnant distractions and they'll remain stagnant until intelligence is born in society.

As long as we look at right and wrong subjectively we'll end up with opposing views and conflict because for the moment at least, we're rarely in agreement. Conflicts arise between us because of these opposing views. As individuals coming from different cultural and educational backgrounds it's inevitable that we grow up with different beliefs and standards. For example, a person may believe that it's right for humans not to eat meat - someone else may believe it's okay to eat it. Neither person is wrong in their own eyes but both are wrong in the eyes of each other. As long as *right* and *wrong* exist harmony can never be found because they cause separation between us. Right and wrong must come into being simultaneously; like 'left and right' or 'malevolence and benevolence'. What sort of world would we live in if these opposite words didn't exist? Perhaps only

59

the fine line in-between can lead to harmony? To make the point a bit clearer, can 'left' exist without 'right', or 'up' without 'down'?

~~~

When I first learnt there was more to life than I'd ever thought possible I wanted to tell the world and I tried hard to do it. I joined forums where arguments about the world were rife and these forums buzz night and day. Most of the members were regulars and the threads got thousands of views; they discussed the latest political scandals, media stories and different conspiracy theories. I noticed the 'happy' threads too, way down the lists with only a few views. I started a couple of new topics, but they never got anywhere near the number of views the angry and scandalous threads got; they hardly got viewed at all and only two or three people contributed towards them. Someone came on to one of the threads I'd started and said 'it's way too happy in here' and left. I left the forums soon after this incident as I could see it wasn't the place to air my views and I'd waste my time trying to change something that didn't want to be changed. They weren't wrong and neither was I. We were walking along different roads.

On another occasion, I went with my partner to a spiritual group meeting in Brighton. I was excited at the thought of meeting other people on the same path. I fell flat on my face when we walked in; the meeting was already in session and the group were enthusiastically discussing the latest earthquake. I got up to leave and apologised for my confusion about the group's purpose. This didn't go down too well and I got nasty looks from a red-headed woman who wanted to talk about the earthquake - she wasn't at all happy that I'd interrupted her. The group became divided on this subject. I would've got a better reception if I'd turned up as a 'little green man'; as it was I turned up happy and sure of myself and people don't like a happy person too much. The meeting brought no harmony, no peace and no answers; it wasn't for us and we never went again. I'd nowhere else to turn - at least I thought this at the time. People didn't want to know and I couldn't change them. They were more interested in the current news scandals and what was being done about them. I tried to change the world outside of me.

I swam upstream and got nowhere. I tossed and turned at night for several weeks but afterwards realised they weren't wrong to want to discuss the earthquake - they enjoyed and found security in the discussions; it wasn't my place to tell them they shouldn't be discussing it. I made the choice never to go again and it was the right choice for me.

I once asked my hairdresser if she ever took quiet time to 'think' because whenever I go to her salon the radio is blaring; I don't think she even knows it's on. She told me she was 'afraid to think'. I found that to be an incredible statement. How can anyone be afraid to think and what *exactly* are they afraid of? The situation didn't invite further conversation and I didn't volunteer any. Again here, it's not *wrong* to be afraid and as her statement made clear, she does this by her own choice. We can't help anyone who doesn't want to help themselves - it's not possible. It took me a long time to accept this.

~~~

Interesting rights and wrongs have evolved with the creation of class systems. In the higher classes, having correct posture and a code of behaviour around the dinner table is expected. These tables must be set 'correctly' and it's frowned upon to use the wrong utensils when eating different courses. I'm not saying it isn't right to live this way, but I'm saying that in *my* opinion it's folly - it can't improve the eating experience. However, for people living in 'polite society' it's taken seriously. Though it's not wrong for them to eat this way, it *is* a disciplined behaviour and this means there are rules and regulations they *must* follow. They would frown upon the way most of us eat as families in our homes, which is not necessarily around a dining table. This process of comparison comes from our separation from each other. People in 'high society' aren't better human beings than anyone else; they see things differently because they've been the subjects of another type of conditioning. I see their way of eating and behaving as not too different from highly *trained* performers, but I don't see it as *wrong*. A question that arises here is 'Who's training them?' It would be easy to think the so-called 'lower classes' aren't also trained performers, but would it be true? We've been conditioned to believe we're right and the others are wrong -

the result is conflict. This gets more interesting when we realise that we've the same conflicts within each and every one of us.

One of the reasons I never completed my autobiography is that my mind kept arguing with me - the mind is conditioned and therefore 'trained'. It told me I couldn't write anything that isn't already in the book shops; my little book wouldn't make any difference and nobody would want to buy it anyway. Above all these reasons it told me my family would resent what I wrote about them and it would cause all sorts of problems. I wanted to show people they could recover from their traumas or problems and the only way I knew how to do this, was to write. However, my mind argued and it's still arguing even though I'm writing an entirely different book. I know that no matter what, it'll still argue with me. The difference now is that I'm aware of the process better and just *observe* the 'me' that wants to write and the 'me' that doesn't. This type of conflict isn't different and it isn't right or wrong; we can observe from the middle - objectively. On a deeper level it's also possible to observe the middle itself.

~~~

To recognise 'ourselves' in another is a part of the path to Grace. We become more tolerant of the human race and realise that we're all struggling regardless of rights, wrongs or class systems - we're all part of the same picture and we each have a role to play. Humanity has fallen, become fractured and it won't put itself back together again. So as long as there's competition and comparison there'll be no harmony. We're all at odds, not only with ourselves, but with each other; whether we're in small groups or in nations, we're shadow boxing night and day. Every human being, at some level knows these things. Will we ever get to the point where right and wrong don't exist - we just are?

The hairdresser mentioned earlier in this chapter wasn't ready to face the part of her that made her uncomfortable - the part she's most afraid of admitting exists. She wasn't ready to confront her own ghosts and may never be ready in this lifetime - her focus was still outside of herself. When each of us is ready we can make a conscious decision to climb out of the doldrums and look for something better, but we all decide this for ourselves when the time is right for us. Our journey is a solo one and it's through having the courage to be 'alone' with ourselves that we begin to see things differently. I'm not talking about loneliness; it's a wonderful thing to be alone once we're not afraid of it. Living this way won't win any popularity contests but if we care about popularity, then we're not ready to live this way.

I know some people who say they're certain when we die, that's it! They believe it and I don't and that's ok, but I must continue in my own way. The decision to change reaps benefits when we're ready to let go of our self-imposed and inherited restrictions, including the limitations friends and family may try to put upon us. This is normal and part of the process to reach a higher level of consciousness. People don't want us to grow and change - they still prefer the way things are and would be happy if we did too. Whatever a person does in their life must be right for them, or they wouldn't do it. Even in the case where a battered wife may stay with her husband, it's right for her. We always choose what's right for us at the time. It's hard to see these things from another perspective and it would be harder still for us to walk in their shoes.

There's something innate that wants to continue with the 'norm' in society. We want to stay put and despite our apparent objections to 'darkness', we have a strong tendency to lean towards it. We desire; things, money, homes, better bodies, romance and everything else society offers through advertisements and we want them now - we want *entertainment* too. We can't comprehend when someone turns their back on society; if we could we'd be forced to look at *ourselves*. By resisting, we don't have to acknowledge there's a better way to live with each other and we don't have to make any sacrifices in order to change our own lives.

We'll never find inner peace if we look outside or to others for it - it lies within. Until we're ready to look we'll not listen to anyone else's opinions. We reject all they say and think they're nuts, or we want to follow them and read all their books before moving on elsewhere looking for another excuse not to alter our current way of life. We're afraid to find inner peace and not prepared to put in the necessary work searching involves - it'll disrupt our illusions and schedules. In general, people don't want to be their own masters and they prefer to follow governments, celebrities and guru figures. To look at our shadow and admit to the ugliness contained in it is difficult and often painful but this journey *can't* be completed without either facing it, or by holding somebody else's hand. It takes a tiny flame to light up a darkened room, but we can't light up anyone else's when they don't want it to be lit - a guru can't do the work for us. There are those who believe we chose our lives before coming here and if this is the case there must be people who chose not to 'wake up' during this lifetime. I don't follow any particular belief but some things are clear.

We're eternal beings. We're pure consciousness. That we live in this world of suffering for an eternity makes no sense at all. As mentioned earlier, we all have to walk this path sooner or later, but only when the time is right for us. It's not possible to give this information to a mind not in tune with or resisting it. One of the wonders of the world has to be to light the fuse leading another person to the realisation that there's something wonderful and magical about us and our world. Can life be worthwhile if we can't help one another?

There's no right or wrong way - it's subjective. My way is right for me and the aforementioned red-headed woman's way is right for her. We can't climb into someone else's head and see the world through their eyes. We can only see from our own perspectives and our 'judgement' can only be based on what we've learnt since the day we were born. We have to choose our own paths and if that includes living in darkness, then so be it. Some people aren't ready or are unwilling at this moment to consider an alternative to the life they've created for themselves. We live in fantasy worlds of our own creation. If we came into this world with a purpose, then I feel certain our *true nature* knows what it's doing.

That right and wrong are subjective can't be argued. Social conditioning has given us all *different* ideas about what is right and wrong and regardless of these ideas, we believe them to be true. What we do with these beliefs is another matter entirely and for those who'd say 'oh well, I can go and commit murder then', my response would be that this isn't intelligent thinking. Should we harm another human being or force them to do something against their will? If we have the right to choose, shouldn't other people have those same rights? These questions are for each one of us to think about and to be entirely responsible for our judgements. We have an innate knowledge of what is objectively right and wrong and our only real choice is to choose one or the other - from our two voices. However, is it really necessary to choose at all?

Chapter 7

Light Casts No Shadow

A shadow is cast where light has been interrupted.

The shadow is what we hide from and what we leave lingering as we walk through our lives - it resides deep in our subconscious minds. The shadow speaks to us when we look in the mirror but we ignore it, because we don't want to hear what it has to say. We prefer to hear lies and create a more pleasing reality for ourselves. For most of my life I've never really liked the woman in the mirror - so I created something else; a world where everyone else was to blame for my predicament - a world in which I was helpless and a victim. This avoidance of the shadow allows it to project itself so critically on to others - we don't want to face the truth about ourselves.

Several years ago, I went for a walk with my partner and as we walked we saw in the distance a mother coming towards us with her overweight daughter. The daughter was raising and lowering her arms by her sides and my first thought was 'She'll never manage to take off'. I recognised that I was being cruel and later mentioned it to my partner who admitted he'd been thinking the same thing. It was in that moment I realised I'd cast my *own* shadow on to the young girl - I'd opened the door and allowed my *beast* out. Since then I've been self-correcting these thoughts, as and when they arise - now they're less frequent. If we do this repeatedly it soon becomes natural, as opposed to contrived behaviour. We have to do a great deal of self-reflection in order to accept the things we're not willing to face. Playing victim is a habit - it sticks like glue and the dark self-pitying thoughts leave us believing we're not good enough. If we believe the world is against us we give ourselves an excuse to keep things as they are. We refuse to see we're responsible for our own predicaments and we refuse to change. We *all* do this and until we see that we're fundamentally the same, our problems will continue. We've all suffered in some way and tend to focus on our own 'bad story' as though it were the only one in existence. The parts of our nature we're most uncomfortable with is what we see and criticise in others. I wasn't free to fly any more than the young girl who was waving her arms about.

Humanity likes to complain about its crises but the world is this way because we've created it. In every supermarket we see more unhealthy foods than healthy ones. Supermarkets supply us with the products that sell best. There are still only tiny sections in supermarkets stocking organic products, because of a lack of demand. Supermarkets now sell just about everything because we want to buy it. We created this consumer shadow. We want these products for our convenience and know that retailers need to be highly competitive in order to supply them to us. Our shadow knows others have paid dearly for this, but in the same way as when we look in the mirror, we pay no attention to it.

A great deal is wasted in the world. We buy to replace just because we want newer versions of things that, if we're honest, aren't significantly different from the old, such as televisions, computers and mobile phones. We change our televisions but the media don't improve the programmes we watch on them. Your average person won't be aware of all the functions on their mobile phones and never do anything with them, except to make calls and send text messages, yet still, we want the latest version with all its bells and whistles.

We continue to want new things and ignore that our desires create havoc in ways we refuse to look at. As long as we 'want' things like worthless trinkets, ornaments, rave parties, new cars, huge houses and junk food then the world will be filled with them - that's what will be manufactured. As long as we ignore that many products are produced in third world countries by under privileged and underpaid workers, we're contributing to the continuity of world poverty in order to satisfy our petty desires. Humanity has cast this dark shadow on society and humanity is deaf, dumb and blind to it.

Our choices have created this world. We each decide what to put into our shopping trolleys, what we do on the internet, what we fill our minds with and how we interact with each other. When we begin to make wiser choices, when we take *responsibility* for our actions then the world will become a better place to live in. It'll not become a better place if we leave the thinking to governments who, let's face it, have a poor track record when it comes to the welfare of us or the planet. It's easy to sit back and 'tut tut' about the state of the world as innocent bystanders, but we're not - we've not only contributed, but we're the cause. Governments are run by human beings just like us, with the same sicknesses of mind - our minds are the same, but the toys we play with are different.

The internet is a wonderful tool for communication, learning and for our interaction with each other. Because of the mindset of humanity, it's become polluted with our darkest shadows and desires. We're not forced on to websites with pornographic, violent or abusive content any more than we're forced to take drugs or get drunk; they're there because we want them to be there - because we're looking for them. The internet is what *we've* made it. Why do we choose to look at the more unchallenging and vacuous content, when we could put the internet to much better use?

Science and spirituality take the backstage and very few get views on their internet videos, whereas scandals, celebrities, puppy, kitten and cute baby videos go viral overnight. Society reflects what we feel about ourselves, like a mirror - it's not reflecting anything too bright at the moment. There are many wonderful videos that lie unwanted by the masses. To find personal peace we must search inside ourselves but the problem here is society isn't ready to face its shadow. We don't want to change. Why is this? It takes a lot of effort to change and we're not prepared to put in the work needed to do it. We want to live in the easiest way possible and that's why we choose *convenience*, enjoy lame entertainments and allow governments to go on with 'business as usual'. We've lost interest in 'harmony' and don't strive to better ourselves or ensure we 'leave' this world having done our best to make some sort of positive difference - we don't believe there's any point.

~~~

We know that mobile phones are hazardous to our health. We know third world manufacturers employ poverty stricken workers for a pittance and charge extortionate prices for their goods. We know big corporations make obscene profits - every year the media trumpets the Rich List. What kind of society brags about who's the greediest? We know our children are kept occupied by television or computer games because we have less time for them. We know we're polluting the atmosphere and water with household products. We know waste is replacing the soil in monstrous landfill sites. We know the Amazon is being destroyed. There's more to us than we think and we can change the world, as individuals and collectively - this has been *screamed* at us from rooftops in many ways including; films, music, fantasy and science fiction. We know all this and much more but we choose to ignore it for no good reason. We complain about things so much that most companies have a complaints department. Why do these companies still exist? We tell ourselves it's not our fault, but there's no-one alive who can hold his hand to his heart and claim they don't know these things. G. K. Chesterton said 'It isn't that they can't see the solution. It is that they can't see the problem.'[7] Shadows are cast by something blocking the light. We're so busy with our own agendas that we can't see the bigger picture or the damage we're doing. There's a big, dark and ugly shadow hovering over us and it's expanding, fast.

We *can* disperse the cloud hanging over humanity - all we have to do is change our perspective. We can also see that we're afraid of horrors and at the same time, see how we contribute to them. We're afraid of death, but we smoke and drink despite knowing the damage they cause. We drive too fast and we 'drink and drive' and for every law created by governments there are many people that think nothing about breaking them, which leads to the creation of more laws. Is humanity a sado-masochist? Humanity has incarcerated itself in a prison of its own making and there's no-one to blame. If we continue to behave in the same way we'll always get the same results. Humanity is selfish and self-centred and until it changes, the world won't change, because we *are* the world. It's no good waiting for someone else to come and save us - we must save ourselves. We're worth it - we can do it.

Chapter 8

Where am I?

*'... overcome space, and all we have left is Here.
Overcome time, and all we have left is Now.'*
Richard Bach

Ponder the question 'Where am I?' and then ask yourself 'Relative to what?' and some interesting thoughts arise. In order to think about where we are we need a point to start from. If I say 'I'm in London' then I'm approximately sixty miles from Cambridge. But, if I say 'I'm here', how far away is Cambridge? Wherever I am in the world I'm 'here' and I can measure the distance to anywhere else starting from this point but it always begins 'here'. This may not make too much sense yet, but the world already doesn't make much sense to you, otherwise you wouldn't be reading this. In order to see clearer we need to raise our level of consciousness and, for the vast majority of us, this is a gradual process. Somehow we've become trapped in space and time and disconnected from our origin. One thing's for certain; there are much bigger things in the universe than we're capable of imagining while we're in this form. If this life is a virtual reality game then it's probably called *The Trickster Mind*; it's a pretty good and advanced game, don't you think? Would you play it, given a choice? Who could've created it and made it seem so real? Are our dreams as real; are we still 'here' when we dream?

Where do we go, if anywhere, when we dream? Some mornings I wake up from a deep sleep and find myself between the dream and waking states. Are these two different worlds? This idea can be disorientating and I could argue that I'd died or perhaps travelled to another dimension or reality. I sit bolt upright and think to myself 'I'm back!' and sometimes it's disappointing, particularly if I'd been enjoying the dream. The world becomes a bumpy and uncertain place when we question reality, but it's more *real* for me than it ever was before and I'm much happier in it.

Am I 'here' when I'm asleep? I've no proof that I'm in my bed when I'm sleeping. I know I wake up in the bed, but that's not proof - I only have proof that I'm 'here' when I wake up. If we're in our beds while we sleep then who is in our dreams? How did we create those 'worlds'? Where are we when we're sleeping? What happens to the characters in our dreams? Do they cease to exist? They're real people to me -where do they come from? Who created them and decided on things like hair colour, weight or mannerisms? Who made the scenery? Once I get started on these questions I can't stop. I toss and turn in bed thinking about them as my mind is sharp and alert; often getting back to sleep is not an option. Is it possible to determine where we are at all? My partner says 'I know you're in bed when you're sleeping because I can see you there'; I don't go with that idea too much, because if I can't be sure where I am then I can't be sure where he is either. What if we're not in the same space and time? My world feels like it's *my* world alone; will this world still exist after I'm dead or will it *die* with me? There are lots of questions raised here, but as mentioned at the beginning of this book, the questions are *important*. Just as important is questioning the answers, for once we've accepted an *answer* it shuts out further investigation. If we ask the right question it answers itself though maybe not as fast as we'd like and *not* in the traditional sense - it may just point us in another direction. Some of these questions may seem ridiculous but, if you can't *prove* something, why believe it?

Am I like the particles popping in and out of existence in the wonderful world of quantum physics? They can pass through solid objects and can be in multiple places at the same time; there's much more to them than this, but I'm not a scientist and more than a passing comment on the subject doesn't belong in this book. Perhaps a better question to ask than 'Where am I?' would be 'Where is here?' 'Here' is where I can be found - there can be no doubt about that. How can we be sure where it is? If *here* is on a tiny planet lost and floating somewhere in eternal space - visible in a sun beam - then it's a bit beyond the comprehension of most people, including me. It makes you wonder though doesn't it? If there's that much space out there, where did the concept of measurement come from? Where are North, South, East and West? Something tells me we've never moved even a millimetre. If time and space are abstract concepts then there can be no 'here' either. So are we everywhere? It's amazing how one question can lead to another.

Without getting deeply into science, what are coordinates? The 'earth', or what we think of as the earth, is spinning in outer space in orbit around a sun (allegedly). All around this action, in every direction, is infinity - it's hard to imagine. There can be no measurements; such as, longitude, latitude, speeds or distance because there's nothing to relate them to. In this case, it isn't possible to know if anything is moving at all. If we left the earth and went far enough away from it, how could we define *in front*, *behind* or *distance*? We would never be able to return; there are no signposts, no coordinates, no landmarks, no sound and no compass points. There could also be no up, down, left or right, except in relation to ourselves. If we're the starting point then everywhere and everything must be relative to us - we must be at the centre, but what are we at the centre of? Isn't it possible that outside this bubble of *experience*, what we've come to know as 'physical laws' don't apply? If we're the centre of everything in *outer space* then we must be 'here' as well? Doesn't every part of our lives begin with us?

If the Big Bang happened, a random dot that exploded and is still exploding or expanding, then who or what lit the fuse? Where did the force come from that was the cause of the explosion, where does it continue to come from and most importantly, where did the *infinite* empty space it exploded in come from? What is space? Is this explosion not just in our minds? I began this life as a baby. I'm 'expanding' my comprehension of the world; my world has been expanding since my birth and it hasn't stopped. As I let go of conditioning my world is expanding as my perspective changes - not because of the accumulation of knowledge but because of the dispersion of it.

Chapter 9

Curiosity and Confusion

I am the product of all my thoughts.

We're set in our ways. We don't like to listen to the opinions of others, unless we want to have a *good* debate; in which case we're catching a ball in order to hit it back. We do things like sulk, tense up and fold our arms when we don't want anyone else's 'input'; our personal and impenetrable protective shields. What are we protecting ourselves from? Paradoxically, we've spent our lives listening to the opinions of others, which is where we get our knowledge from in the first place. We prefer artificial beauty and admire our electronic accessories more than a person passing us in the street; we often prefer our pets to other people. None of this makes sense to me. How strange human beings are. How did we become this way?

~~~

We take a great deal for granted in this world; for example, we believe our reflection in a mirror is who we really are, without ever thinking about it. We believe it because we've been told it and spend a great deal of time looking at our reflections - particularly when we're young and curious. I remember opening the door of my bathroom when my eldest son was around seven. I found him standing on the child step, studying himself in the mirror, pulling all sorts of silly faces. He was having incredible fun exploring his face and amusing himself with all that he could do with it - just like a new toy. Babies explore their bodies this way too. They grab their hands and feet curiously and explore their fingers and toes - everything goes into their mouths. They tug at their clothing and pull their shoes and socks off. Has the baby found itself in a new body/environment - somewhere strange? Are babies honing taste, touch, smell, hearing and sight? Perhaps the baby is protesting against the world it finds itself in. These are strange notions, but when we're pursuing a line of enquiry *many* unusual questions arise. If they arise it's because we need to think about them. Do babies have more of an idea about who they are than we do? Most of us put the 'Who am I?' question on the back burner because we don't have the time or inclination to think about it.

One of the differences between a baby's curiosity and ours is that we've adjusted to our environment after many years of coaching and supervision. The people who've coached and supervised us don't know who *they* are any more than we do. Most grown-ups shed these questions a long time ago. Our curiosity is rarely resurrected because we've buried it - along with our dreams - beneath life's experiences. G. K. Chesterton wrote 'Education is simply the soul of a society as it passes from one generation to another.' These things don't change because *we* don't change. We continue to teach the same things and they still don't involve asking questions about our amazing selves. Children find this frustrating because they're curious about everything they feel and see; they're sadly without a voice but only because we're drowning theirs out with our own. We learn through repetition, rather like a horse learns to run faster with the crack of a whip. Education would be much more fun and less troublesome if it were based on what we're curious about - instead this curiosity is suppressed and frowned upon. I've a friend who explained to his ten-year-old grandchild how we don't actually see anything. He told him our eyes are sensitive to photons, that they convert them into electrical impulses and that optical nerves carry these to the visual centre of our brains, giving rise to the images we see. Because this child had lost his fascination with his world and his need to challenge it, he replied; 'I knew you'd say something weird'.

If we stopped focusing on things like technology and more on ourselves and spirituality it wouldn't take long for the world to become a pleasant place to live in. We all start curious and because this curiosity is discouraged we become bored and discontented. When I was around eleven I wanted a guitar but my father wouldn't buy one for me no matter how much I asked. He said it was a waste of time and that I couldn't make a decent living playing music. More recently in my life, I showed some of my animated gifs to an uncle who commented 'They're really nice, but I can't see how they could ever be commercially viable'. This is what we've become - competitive and ambitious for money; we stifle talent, curiosity and creativity because they're not profitable pastimes. We're encouraged to develop abilities that will prove to be commercial successes; this is a sad - and robotic - state of affairs.

I've always been fascinated by the development of babies, especially when compared to the fellow creatures sharing the earth with us. Babies are slow to get up on to their feet. Horses can walk the same day they're born, wolves at two weeks, cows after just a few minutes. We're much more intricate and have a great deal to learn such as using utensils, mastering our own bodies, building our world. Other creatures don't need anywhere near so much development to live out their lives. If you look into a baby's eyes they're full of wonder and innocence - they don't know lies, anger, judgement, disappointment or hatred. A baby spends nine months in the womb but that's not the end of its development - it continues for years after; we reach puberty by our early teens, but we're still growing! Why do we succumb to being complacent about the miracle of life?

A baby's mind can't cope with the obstacles we place in front of it and constantly walks into things hurting themselves. For this reason, we protect them from table corners and other household furniture. Babies struggle with the world we've created, especially when around roads and busy streets. When a baby wants something it goes for it, without regard for its safety or what's in front of it - a baby needs continuous supervision. Our environment isn't natural and we have to constantly reinforce the rules and regulations of society before a baby can 'take care' of itself. We make our environment safe from their curiosity by securing them from it; by doing this, we introduce them to 'fear'.

If we constantly correct babies and teach them to be afraid is it any wonder they become confused. We put babies in cots and play pens with sponge balls and squeaky toys. They're not free to explore 'their' way because we put many dangers outside of these enclosures - they don't learn to protect themselves because we do it all for them. Our environment is hostile and alien to a young child.

How did we ever manage to look after babies before we created so many obstacles? Perfectly well! Would they adjust faster without a world they must become afraid of and dependent on? Shouldn't we stimulate and encourage all parts of a baby's brain to develop to its full capacity. We train babies to survive and live in the society we created, even though we don't do too well in it ourselves. We also train them to protect themselves from our violence through 'sports' like martial arts. It's become 'cool' to fight.

Many people have little curiosity about esoteric matters; in some cases, they're concerned more about what's on the television or new postings on social media websites they *need* to 'catch up' on. We're happy to wait until we die to find out answers to questions we've forgotten how to ask. I've discussed this subject with many people and the most extreme reaction I've had so far from one of them, is that he got up and left the room - agitated - as though I were trying to administer a poison. Why do we ignore innate curiosity about what life really is? Is the veil of ignorance also innate? Where do innate questions come from? Why are we content to work, support our families, suffer poverty in some cases, settle for trivial entertainments, and then die? Let's look at it plain and simply for a moment. We've come from *nothing* and have been unceremoniously dropped into an established 'system' that stifles the natural talents and curiosities we were born with. Spirituality is frowned upon by the masses but 'religions' are considered okay as long as we behave the way they tell us to. Hypocrisy is also okay. Everyone is confused on some level, some have buried the questions and some can't; there's a force that insists the latter explore further. What picture does this all paint?

~~~

Let's get back to the mirror. There are many people who play virtual reality games. I played around for a little while with a character on Second Life. I got bored because it was time-consuming and not *real* - it felt rather like playing in a doll's house. We still look in a mirror when we see the character on the computer screen - the principle is the same; it's a projection of our own creation. We create *dream* characters because they're more pleasing than the way we see ourselves. One problem with this is, when the game's over we return to our 'own bodies' and our discontentment with this life continues, until we login again. The frustrations increase because the characters still exist inside our heads and no matter what we do, we can't become them outside of the game. Creating and playing the roles of these characters serves to make us *more* insecure. The character I created could be anything I wanted it to be; any shape, height or colour. It could have amazing clothing and hairstyles, limited only by my imagination - it could even have wings and fly. The other characters we encounter in these 'games' are also not real. They're just like us - pretending to be someone more agreeable. Any interaction in these virtual realities is illusory and fake. I didn't stay around the website for long.

    I know of a man who plays a character responsible for several war ships in an online virtual reality game and he's more than obsessed with this - it's his life. He gets up in the middle of the night to keep an eye on the virtual situation but doesn't spend any time on himself - preferring to be the game character, because it feels safe and can be turned off at any time - there's no threat. In the game, people look up to him and he feels needed and important. Outside the game he's back in the uncomfortable world as the character he doesn't like - *himself*. He doesn't feel confident in his own life - his situation isn't uncommon. We like the character we've created so much we become addicted to it; consequently, we require more and more time online. Likewise, we've become addicted to our bodies, minds and egos and don't want to give them up and from these thoughts come fears of non-existence.

    How it all works I don't know, but through constant questioning I know that what I see in the mirror isn't me at all, but rather it's who I used to think I was. For a while I researched this subject but the amount of literature on it was overwhelming and contradictory - it's impossible to read all the books. One book leads to another and they all cross reference something else - I do it in this book too. Determined to find out more about my reflection, I took a large mirror off the wall in my lounge and wedged it between the arm and cushion on my settee. I took my laptop over there and sat working, facing the mirror for the most part of four days. This was a daunting and intimidating experience and it was hard to meet my reflection eye-to-eye at times. I was looking at someone else and I felt like *she* was trying to outstare me. I was being watched and it felt uncomfortable. At the end of the four days I knew for certain the image in the mirror wasn't me. I highly recommend this exercise and you can be certain of results at the end of it, which may or may not be the same as mine.

~~~

Our memories are formed from everything we've ever touched, smelled, tasted, heard or seen. However, despite all our knowledge we still grope for clarity of what life is all about. Our search may lead us to a spiritual leader, believing they can give us answers - but they can't. There are as many answers as spiritual leaders and this leads to further confusion - we end up with a collection of riddles. We hope that by visiting a spiritual leader, something called *enlightenment* will happen, if we remain in their company long enough, but enlightenment isn't contagious. Books can guide us too, but it's easy to get bogged down with the cross-referencing and jump from one book to another in a desperate and futile search for the one true answer. What we're doing is avoiding facing our darkest thoughts - often looking for answers where we know we *won't* find them. We don't like ourselves and self-hatred is more common - and more powerful - than most people imagine or will admit to. No-one likes what they see in their own mirror. We see the burden of memory with all its judgements, prejudices, sufferings, guilt and anxieties - it's not a pretty sight.

The mind is a wonderful puzzle - it's complex and confusing. We've absorbed fantastic amounts of random information, with few connecting links. Every time we discover something new we add another puzzle piece to the pile, but we've no idea where it fits. We don't like the mind, and we don't like what it says about us. It tells us things we don't want to hear and chooses the things that might disturb us the most - it's inclined to look on the dark side of life. The most interruptions I've encountered while writing this book were from my mind - it can be such a nuisance and leads to endless confusion and inner turmoil. The mind is a vault of all we've experienced and these experiences have been piled on top of the innate questions we've buried so deeply. There's a lot more to it than we know about or are aware of and it doesn't turn off even when we're asleep. The more I think about these things the more my curiosity is aroused. I see beauty and magnificence in everything.

The man I mentioned who left the room agitated, when I tried to discuss philosophical issues with him, is typical of many people. As soon as there are two people together in a place, with different opinions, there's conflict. We cling vehemently to our beliefs and we're not willing to have them challenged - I wasn't willing to listen to him either. On some level we know we're avoiding the bigger issues but choose to stay close to what's familiar to us and well within our comfort zone. The thirst for knowledge is still in our minds, but we can't quench it. A thought doesn't just disappear - it remains in our memory banks, hidden amongst all the other prejudices, opinions, knowledge and beliefs we've accumulated. Our stored up unanswered questions, anger, frustrations and bitterness reside there too and this collection of experiences makes up what we are - confused. We don't remember them all, but they're still there and impact on our daily lives. These thoughts become our reality and we're not willing to part with them - sometimes, we refuse to acknowledge that they exist at all.

Just like conflict arises between two people, it arises between two 'countries' or 'nations'. The people living in them are still in conflict with themselves, therefore it's not possible to live as a harmonious unit while conflict is at the core. This creates an unhealthy and volatile force resulting in wars and hatred. It doesn't take much to set one nation against another and we've all seen this happening many times. The matter then appears impossible to resolve because we believe it to be out of our control - we feel we're just one person and powerless to change anything. Society reinforces those beliefs and therefore, we do nothing but grumble and complain about it. If we don't change who we are, we'll remain confused and fragmented; the problem will not resolve itself and the cycle will continue.

This is important so let me clarify it a little. The conflict begins within us. Our mind is always arguing with itself. If you can't sleep at night then you'll know the mind comes up with out-of-date unimportant rubbish, preventing you from falling asleep - it's never silent. Look how difficult it is to concentrate on anything when our mind wanders; thoughts rise and fall like waves - as one becomes the ocean, we find ourselves riding on another. Our minds churn with unresolved issues, appointments, shopping, insecurities and other such occupations. It focuses on our irrational thoughts and feelings about others, because we don't want to focus on ourselves. For example, if I'm lying in bed thinking about *who I really am*, my mind starts chattering away about something I'd once said in anger. It then recites new scripts for me, polishing and perfecting the scenes it would've preferred me to act out - if I'd wished to claim a *victory*. The mind also prepares us for future events - playing mental chess and running through possible scenarios of what to say or do in certain situations and it predicts the possible outcomes. Does this happen to you too? Is your mind your harshest critic? We all struggle with these internal battles. It's simple, but complicated to resolve because for some crazy reason we like it this way - if we didn't, we would change it and we *do* have the power to do that.

~~~

One of the reasons our lives have conflict in them is that we're confused about our purpose. There are somewhere around one thousand professions to choose from - I got conflicting numbers when I tried to find out this information but it doesn't matter enough to search further. What matters is we have to choose one to earn our living in order to pay the bills society puts through our letter boxes. We study something like twelve subjects that can lead us to one of the more 'respectable' of these professions, if our final grades are good enough. We're swimming upstream in a fast flowing river and the current is getting stronger. The competition is fierce and the territory hostile - few of us climb higher up the employment 'ladder'. When we die, will it matter if during our lifetime we were a lawyer or a dustman?

Few people do a job they love and if we ask most people why, they would say they couldn't make a living at it. A great many people don't know what they would love to do anyway, but we do all have hidden talents. This is a direct result of our curiosity, true interests and natural tendencies being stifled in our infancy - we've been taught to think in a linear way and this limits our perception. It's also a result of the subjects we've been taught and no matter how 'professional' we become, it's not for the good of humanity that we do it. The only people who benefit from our efforts are governments and corporations. Were we given this world in order to live in and systematically destroy it?

Esoteric ideas are so far away from what we've been taught in schools - we can't relate to them too well. They're not discussed in the media in any meaningful way and it was the media who labelled the *spiritual* movement of the sixties 'Flower Power' and associated it with mind altering drugs and free 'love'. We're told there's a God but how many of us have found out for ourselves if this is true? Truth comes from *knowing* and not from believing what we've been told. *Believing* doesn't make something *true* - these two concepts are different. One of the reasons there are so many religions is that we can't settle on a belief that resonates with everyone.

It's important to remember confusion doesn't come from just us, but that it comes from previous generations too - we've inherited it and it's deeply ingrained. We've been educated with concrete beliefs, so abstract ones are hard for us to comprehend. By the time the notion of spirituality reaches our ears, our mind is already full of confusion and can't accept the concept of a question not having an answer. It's difficult to visualise a 'directionless' journey that's *not* physical or methodical because we're surrounded by an abundance of signs directing us to places, telling us how many miles to go, dictating strict rules such as 'Keep Left' or 'One Way'. We look to books and media for information, maps for directions and television for weather reports. We also have the radio turned on for the latest updates; we check traffic and accident reports to ensure we're not delayed on our journey. In effect, we've opened ourselves to receive information from all these sources without questioning its influence on us or the authority of those who provide it; we accept this information, verbatim.

We don't think about the process of the transmission and reception of this data - all information must be transmitted and received. How does this apply to us? It's all there wherever you go. Next time you're out and about, perhaps spare a moment to think about all of the information being transmitted and received around you - it's an invisible world but it's there and you're transmitting and receiving it too. I'm transmitting this information to you through words on a page and you're receiving it. It's all a bit alien to us. We don't know where to turn or which books to read and there's no 'logical evidence' to prove anything anyway. When we let go of the framework holding our lives together we find ourselves without support and that's a major difficulty to get over before we open the way for a new kind of thinking. If what we've always believed is not true then in order to see something new we must let go of the crutch we've held on to - the support structure we built for ourselves.

Our beliefs are so ingrained that we won't *listen* to the possibility of a non-physical journey because there aren't any 'visible' signposts to guide us. My mother used to say she believed in *something* after this life, but on the other hand, she also hated spirituality. The confusions come from being taught to rely on the so-called five senses and these senses will not show us 'God'. God must be *before* the creation of the mind and therefore can't be found within it. The seer, Ramana Maharshi once said: 'Existence or consciousness is the only reality. Consciousness plus waking we call waking. Consciousness plus sleep we call sleep. Consciousness plus dream, we call dream. Consciousness is the screen on which all the pictures come and go. The screen is real, the pictures are mere shadows on it.'[8] We can't change the reflection without changing what is reflecting it. We're given a blank sheet of paper to create our world on and we've scribbled all over it in the most horrible way - now we can't read our own writing. The blank sheet has also been scrawled on by society and we've been bombarded with bogus information from every direction - we can't read this writing either.

We must *be* before the creation of the mind because we're doing the writing, creating, transmitting, receiving and we're doing the dreaming! Who were we when the paper was blank? Where did the piece of paper come from?

Chapter 10

Our Cluttered Mind

To find what is concealed, brush away the cobwebs.

We've accumulated a great deal of information and beliefs over the years, and been constantly corrected and steered in a compliant direction. We've learnt, amongst other things:

- What a circle is, a square, colours and how to mix them.
- History, mathematics and grammar.
- To fight, argue and feel sorry for ourselves.
- How to behave.
- Unhappiness, fear, dissatisfaction, insecurity and disappointment.
- How to store stress and anger, and how to be in dysfunctional relationships.
- That we can bury it all if we take drugs and drink alcohol.

We've absorbed so much more - now we have an opportunity to get rid of the lot. Can we do it? Do we want to?

When we discover that the mess in our world is coming from our own mind, when we realise it's a *collective* mind, when we see we've been investing our most valuable assets in an external structure and when we're able to discern that the mind *is* cluttered, what can we *do* about it? An intelligence needing no assistance will guide us, as and when we're ready to take each step - we need only allow it to do so and stay focused on our goals. We've got much more inside us than is visible with just a fleeting glance. Our lives have become what they are because of information overload and if we're not happy, it would be prudent to stop absorbing it.

Instead of watching television, try turning it off for one week; for that matter, shut down all media sources. It's got to be worth trying for a more peaceful life - not a huge sacrifice to make considering the possible benefits. If you turn it on again in a week it'll seem very different to you, but only if you haven't peeked at it down the pub, in the chip shop or through your neighbour's window while suffering withdrawal symptoms. We seek peace in the world but when we turn off the noise and find it, we become bored and restless. It's like driving at 70 mph on the motorway and then turning off on to a quiet country road at 30 mph - it feels like you're moving very slowly. There's a period of adjustment to wind down from the frenzied activity of a media-fuelled existence. There are many people who say the television is *company* and my mother was one of them; how can a machine be company? How has it become possible to live life - in front of a screen - passively watching other people living theirs? Our lives have become what they are now because of our actions and if we're not happy, we must stop doing what created them. We need to stop waiting for someone else to 'make a difference', or to change our world. The world won't change - *we* have to.

This may seem like an odd statement but in the realm of the abstract, things don't work as they did in the 'concrete' one. A new awareness arises that extends our self-imposed boundaries and enables us to think in an entirely new way. As long as we're reliant on a system to provide us with the security we seek, which it doesn't do, we'll not be able to see the clutter in our minds. There's a transition between the known and the unknown and it's this murky river we fear entering - perhaps because we don't want to leave or perhaps because of the uncertainty of what lies ahead. We don't feel we're good enough or that we deserve better so we stay where we are just in case we find ourselves out on a limb - homeless, starving and alone. These are just a few of the ways we've been taught to live in fear, and all these fears live in the river.

There are some ways in which physical work can help us through this transition. Let's see how we can change something with regard to our accumulated clutter. Say for example, we've been storing things in the attic of our home for many years and it's so cluttered we can't get into it or find a particular item we're looking for - we've also forgotten most of the things we put up there. We're terrified of the thought of clearing it out for several reasons; it's a *lot* of work; we don't want to part with things because they might prove useful someday, they might increase in value, they have sentiment attached to them, they're not doing any harm up there, we could make a lot of money at a car boot sale one day and we might want to pass them on to our children. These are just some of our delaying tactics, which project into the future and draw from the past. So we delay and delay, keep the hatch closed and try to forget there's anything up there. This is exactly what we do with projections into the future and our past experiences - the mind doesn't live in the Now.

I know someone whose attic was a full, dark and musty place; he'd been storing things up there for thirty-five years and these included such things as; baby toys and equipment, books, lamps and shades, iron beds, empty cardboard boxes, buckets and spades, old record decks and an old car windscreen for a car he no longer owned. An opportunity arose for him to get rid of the lot and it took many weekends, courage, donations and numerous trips to the rubbish dump but on his final descent from the ladder leading up there, he came down with a huge smile on his face and dusted off his hands. In the physical realm, physical work was needed. However, he'd cleared a great deal of historical clutter from his mind at the same time and this hadn't been his intention - he felt freer and never went up there again. It's not necessary to go through a physical process, but it was an added bonus. By realising he could now let go of things he'd been clinging to, he simplified his life and never looked back or missed anything he'd disposed of. More importantly, he recognised how much better he felt inside. A huge bonus was that he never passed this clutter on to his children.

By recognising our minds are cluttered with all its implications, the process of clearing has already begun without us lifting a finger. For example:

- Which memories do you hold on tightly to?
- Do you bear a grudge that you're reluctant to give up?
- What resentments do you cling to?

Answer these questions honestly and then question the answers to begin the process. There's a need for determination and it's not a soft option - we need to take the plunge and be prepared to get 'wet'. It's no good re-arranging the clutter or dusting it off, because it's still *there* taking up space - it has to go. Things will change for the better if we return to point zero. If we can let go of everything there's no attic to clear. The clutter is not solid - it doesn't exist anymore than the past or future do, yet we keep it under lock and key. It can't be seen and it's not tangible. It's there because thought created it and we believe it's real - the reason it remains is we aren't willing to let go of it and can't imagine freedom from its weight.

One of the reasons I never completed my autobiography was that my mind kept arguing with me. When I wasn't writing my mind told me I ought to be; when I wrote it told me I was wasting my time. My mind wouldn't let go of these issues or others and as a consequence I put them to one side for many years - the mind is always contrary. It'll tell you one thing and when you listen to it, it'll tell you another - its contents are all in a muddle. I wanted to show people they could recover from their problems or past traumas if they were strong, but my mind argued and argued and it's still arguing even though I'm writing an entirely different book. I know no matter what I do, it'll still argue with me. The difference now, is that I understand the process better. My mind is increasingly silent.

~~~

Does a baby come from somewhere silent into this world? I've often wondered at what age its *spirit* enters the body, if that's how it works. Something tells me it's at the moment of birth but I'm not certain and I don't think anyone can be. It must be quite a shocking experience when a baby first opens its eyes; I wonder what it thinks, if anything at all, of its world and its inability to communicate in it. In my experiences, with my three children, babies don't feel separate from anything. Their world is full of innocence, excitement and exploration. A baby doesn't know if a person is tall, short, fat, thin, rich or poor - it can't see nationality or race - it observes with no judgement. A baby has no opinions about religions or politics and it knows no fear. It has no understanding of language and it doesn't care if it's wearing pink or blue. A new-born child doesn't know its name and doesn't know ours either - it doesn't know anything except hunger, pain, comfort and discomfort. It's essential that a baby be held, loved and cared for, as it can't manage even the most basic of its needs without us - these are imperative for its healthy development.

We project our needs on to a baby and we pass on the corrupt information that has been written on to our own minds - it's passed on through siblings too. As a baby learns it becomes separated and judgemental; it can be badly behaved and spoilt because we want to give it all the things we feel we were deprived of. It grows up resentful because we punish it as our parents punished us. It also becomes confused and develops some of our traits; how can a baby become anything else when we've scrawled our bad experiences over its pure and beautiful blank piece of paper? We may not feel we're *personally* responsible for this but we *do* contribute towards it - a baby also picks these things up from friends, schools, books and entertainment. In fifty or so years time, these babies will be the administrators of our world and all we can expect is continuity of the system we have now - more *extreme* because the mind of society is absorbing more and more unimportant information.

This process has been repeated throughout generations and it's so ingrained that we don't know it's there. The collective mind is a filthy place full of hatred, anger, conflict, selfishness and confusion and the events that led us here were less harmful than the damage caused by holding on to the memories of them. We have to make a conscious decision to return to the state of a new-born baby - innocence. It's only through innocence that we find peace and clarity and through innocence that we see the world through a baby's eyes. The veil of our experiences must be removed in order that we can see again the beauty of Creation and the discovery of it. A flower doesn't need to be told how to open in the mornings or an acorn how to grow into an oak tree. The baby came into its world with a 'clear mind' and it's us who filled it with nonsense. We can learn a great deal from life from watching a baby and listening to young toddlers. When toddlers ask us 'Why? Why? Why?' they're usually being more reasonable than we are. We reply - irritated - because we know the 'whys' go on forever and we don't like children asking 'too many questions'. We've stopped learning from children and we teach them the way we were taught. We buy books about bringing up babies - this must be innate. Why do we need to learn from a book about when to feed a child, what to feed a child and when to put it to sleep? Why do we need instruction manuals on how to become a human being?

Chapter 11

Change is Possible

When we change, the world cannot be the same to us.
The world cannot be the same to us, when we change.

Our expectations on a path of self-discovery are greater than what actually happens. Many of us are given a false perspective by the 'enlightenment' industry and mistakenly expect a 'Road to Damascus' epiphany - all our problems disappearing in the moment. When this doesn't happen we become discouraged; clarity about 'who we are' isn't going to arrive in an 'abracadabra' fashion. It takes work, courage and commitment; it's not a hat to put on and take off when it suits - it's a whole new way of life and it begins with *us*.

Looking at people without judgement or criticism regardless of who they are takes practise. Our long standing beliefs can't be wiped away like chalk from a blackboard - we have to constantly correct ourselves because these are old habits and the mind wants to cling to them. It can be frustrating when we put all our efforts into changing - we can't see the results even though we're desperate for them. We want to love everybody but there are still people we trip over. A word of warning; the initial enthusiasm and excitement we felt, when we began our journey, evaporate when we encounter these obstacles and distractions, which can be discouraging - just like when starting a new diet or exercise routine. Overcoming these 'hurdles' helps to strengthen us further - keeping us on track.

In theory, I understood that we're all 'One' but in practise, I didn't feel it. I couldn't see how *I* could be part of something so magnificent and not know about it. Consciousness and One were - and still are - words buzzing around the internet faster than spam. The concepts were hard to get to grips with - it meant accepting that people I didn't like were - *shock horror* - a part of *me*! With hindsight, this was because I didn't feel I belonged to a 'group' on equal terms - I'd always been an outsider. 'One' felt like an exclusive group and triggered old memories that told me I wasn't welcome, or worthy. The feeling could be likened to turning up at a gala ball with an entrance ticket that says 'No Admission'. Just as with the spiritual group in Brighton the people I encountered were the same - divided, confused and self-centred.

We want to be 'there' but can't because we won't give ourselves time to raise our consciousness level - we want to arrive at our destination without all the hassle of the journey. How easy would it be to understand a story by reading just the first and last pages of a book? We don't want to face our shadows. As I recognised the patterns of these thoughts and watched them, they occurred less frequently. It isn't necessary to change anything at all - we need only to observe, rather than take action. When we can see and comprehend this, changes take place without our interference - we don't need to fuel them. We can then walk down the street and instead of seeing stereotypes we see humanity as a whole; we're all harbouring resentments, all suffering, all searching and all seeking freedom from conflict.

~~~

I don't subscribe to the beliefs - in some modern self-help books - that claim we can do what we want in the world even if it means murder and mayhem. Yes we can do it but, is it intelligent or in our highest interest to do so? It isn't, if we wish to access higher levels of consciousness, and I don't believe these can be accessed without grace, good intention, wisdom or a sincere heart. I also don't believe these realms can be 'gate-crashed' with the use of drugs or alcohol. Sure, people can access other realms and there are many of them; however, can we be *sure* where we are when we take mind-altering substances? We can't be sure where we are when we don't. We don't know what or where these realms are; how can we trust them? Drugs aren't the key to awareness - we must get there alone.

Are we here just to play? If so, wouldn't the possibility exist for us all? From birth, we're faced with difficulties and struggles that don't belong in a 'playground'. I don't believe we're here to cartwheel our way around the earth visiting its wonderful places. There's so much to see and do that we can't do it all in one lifetime - given the type of society we live in. There are too many borders and barriers in place preventing us from living freely and more are being erected for the next generation. We're too busy wanting the things our society produces and we want it all *now*. We're attracted to ownership of cars, homes and the paraphernalia we fill them with and we *want* them - no matter what the cost; we live high-risk and that, if anything at all, is a game we play. If we're actually here to play - and we do enjoy playing - we seem to have lost the plot. Our play is aggressive - we play with an 'opponent'. Humanity forgot how to have fun a long time ago - even young children can't play together for long without conflict arising. We've lost so much sensitivity to the earth and to each other, that playing (other than in a prescribed form; parks, toys, playgrounds, sports etc.) has become impossible. This is clear when watching children in groups, men playing football or in any social gathering - we're far too competitive.

I watched quite a few children playing football when I used to take my son training. I saw competing parents standing behind the lines pushing and egging their sons on - transferring their own beliefs on to them. It was hard to tell who the real competitors were - the children playing football, or the parents competing for their own superiority. Sometimes I'd see a father's disappointment from his own childhood being projected on to his son, who didn't enjoy the game. This can result in the child feeling insecure and inadequate - seeking the approval of others for the rest of his life. Learning how to change our ingrained habits and not pass them on to our children goes a long way to improving the society we live in. Children need to be allowed to live their lives without making up for the failings in *ours*. Should we shape them into someone we consider to be our 'ideal'? Competition is a struggle for supremacy - this must mean that we want to *defeat* someone else; does this sound like 'war' to you?

The father mentioned above was looking to his son to fulfil the missed successes of his own past ambitions rather than encouraging the child to find his own talent. The children are keen to receive their parents' approval and are unable to get it. The world has become what it is today because not enough people question their actions or think about the consequences those actions will have on their children and society. We're far too accepting of what society tells us we should *do* and *be* - the comfortable option. This mentality has been passed on from our ancestors and will linger on into future generations, *if* we allow it to.

~~~

If we take the underground to work every day, beginning our journey at Victoria and terminating at King's Cross, always travelling anticlockwise on the Circle Line, we'll never know there are alternative routes that - if nothing else - provide us with a different experience. For a change, we could go in a clockwise direction or take the Victoria Line. We'll pass different stations, see new faces and have a different experience - we may even come across an old friend. New experiences sharpen our minds; we have to remain alert and consequently, pay far more attention to the unfamiliar route, which requires the attention of the *conscious* mind rather than the *subconscious* one.

We're subjected to so much repetition that we accept it as 'normal' - we don't question the boredom or ugliness of it. We've also been educated in a way that perpetuates the functioning of a society that encourages violence, immorality, competition and injustice in order to profit financially and egotistically. Financially, because the rich get richer and the poor poorer; egotistically, because where there's money there's power and where there's power, subservience. There's only so far we can inflate a balloon before it bursts. We're put under a great deal of stress - from birth - and the build-up of tension results in resentment and conflict. We've given away our power and though we don't trust the people we've given it to, we're afraid (or don't want) to take it back.

The way to help ourselves is to seek the truth and be sincere in our search without making selfish demands like trying to manifest a new car, more money, a partner or anything else. Why not start climbing the mountain, instead of walking around the base poking it with a stick and muttering 'too high', 'too rocky' or 'too steep'. Most of us never make the climb. Our intentions have to be 'pure' and a greater appreciation and understanding of this concept comes with time and patience. When writing my autobiography, it never occurred to me that I might be writing the wrong book, after all, I was *writing* the wrongs of my life and wanted other people to know about them too. Until that is, I let go of the book, allowing my heart to be opened and myself to give up 'control'. At first I rebelled somewhat, as one does, feeling reluctant to accept that my labours on it had been in vain - it *wasn't* going to be read after all. This gave me a new perspective - the world didn't need another depressing book or sob story, and I knew it.

Self-help books can't do the 'job' for us, because they're written by people who've found their *own* way by whichever means they needed, and their needs may not have been the same as ours. They can guide us, but our path may lead us on another road altogether. We can't be aware of the author's intentions either and this is *very* important. It's important to understand our own intentions, and I still question mine. Our cluttered minds are incapable of rational thought and the annoying voice in our heads interrupts just when we think we're making progress. Self-help books also serve to provide much needed comfort and security - they tell us just what we want to hear and it's not necessarily in our best interest. I'm not knocking them and I've read quite a few, but what I *am* saying is that we must put into practise these concepts ourselves and for each one of us the process varies. This book can also be seen as a self-help book, and this is true inasmuch as it's *my*self-help book; however, I'd say it's more about philosophy, which according to one dictionary definition is 'an attitude of rationality, patience, composure, and calm in the presence of troubles and annoyances.'[9] To debate the matter is not worth my effort and would serve no good purpose.

Other ways to make changes include being honest with ourselves. Recognising our own imperfections and taking responsibility for them is not always a pleasant task; amongst these are our insecurities, self-hatred, prejudices, judgements and our expectations of others. We lie a great deal too, but we call these lies diplomacy, tact, consideration, common sense, light on truth and even 'necessary'. One example of this is how we lie to someone who asks whether or not we like their new dress or hairstyle. In general, we'll say it suits them and that it's lovely, even if we loathe it. We'll also lie if someone asks us if they've lost weight (and they haven't) - we tell them what they want to hear. Quite often we search for flattery and *want* to be lied to; for example, if we ask someone whether we've lost weight or not, we already know the truth and it's usually 'no' or we wouldn't need to ask. Do we really want an honest answer? But if someone can confirm the lie for us it makes us feel better and we accept it as truth.

Lying has become an okay thing to do, because we convince ourselves that we do it in the best interest of others - to avoid offending them. I know of people who've told lies for so long that they end up believing them themselves. Are our lies always for our own benefit or gain? Have you ever telephoned someone and said 'I'm calling on behalf of a friend' when it was for yourself? My sister used to ask me to make telephone calls for her. She couldn't understand why I refused; I couldn't understand why she wouldn't do it herself. This is a strange kind of lie because there's no real need for it and it makes no difference to the outcome - the person on the other end of the telephone can't see us. Why do we want to hide and what exactly is it that we're hiding from? Why do we hide behind internet monikers and often have a variety of them for the same social media? We can change this behaviour and though initially it can make us feel vulnerable, we begin to feel much stronger and more self-confident once we get over the hurdles; we also can't get 'caught out' in the lie at a later date. Vulnerability is strength.

I'm pretty much a 'black and white' character - generally getting straight to the point and cutting out all the middle stuff, which I call 'colouring in'. What it means, on a practical level, is that I see the point without all the details and when I'm given too much detail I often lose track of conversations - I'm always asking for the short version of the longer stories people recount. I do the same with films and often watch the end first to see if I like it - it doesn't spoil the film for me, and nowadays I see most films as formulaic anyway. I've gone off the subject of lying, but here's how it connects. I see a lie as a *lie*, which means it's an *untruth* and there can be no 'grade' or 'scale' of lying. For example we may lie to our children when we cook a blended vegetable soup and not tell them a particular vegetable that they dislike is in it - if they ask, we may even deny we put it in. To me, either way is lying because both are deceitful and deceit is a lie. But my friends say this isn't a lie, because it's for the good of the children who wouldn't eat it otherwise. In another true example, a child would only eat a particular brand of tomato sauce that the parent didn't want to buy, so he then filled the preferred empty branded bottle, with the contents of a different brand and the child ate it for years without complaining. Is this lying? How would you feel if you found out someone was doing this to you - like selling you fake designer label clothing? Lying is a form of betrayal and none of us like that.

Any lie, in my opinion, as it's untrue is not a good idea because it's the lie that goes into the consciousness field and it reflects on each and every one of us. When we add up all the big lies with all the so-called little ones, there's a great many 'lies' out there. So it doesn't matter if it's a 'white lie' or an 'outright lie' or whatever name we wish to give it - it's *not* the truth. When we study our own behaviour we begin to recognise some not very nice traits we acquired over the years and wouldn't have attributed to ourselves. These same traits were at the heart of our criticism of others. Just by recognising these traits we're making important changes - changes that must occur if our level of consciousness is to rise.

~~~

We analyse everything in this world. What are we looking for in this analysis and do we really want to find it? We buy books, visit gurus and therapists - you name it - but no matter how many of them tell us what we *need* to hear, we pretend we haven't heard it. We seek permission to continue doing what we're already doing, but books *et al* won't give it to us. We make every excuse under the sun and convince ourselves that we don't need to change, thus avoiding facing ourselves in the mirror of 'nakedness'. Human beings are diligent when it comes to searching for something they don't really want to know or see - we know where *not* to look. One of the reasons for this behaviour is to delay our need for action and permit ourselves to continue procrastinating - another, is that we enjoy our illusions. We enjoy being the way we are and, on the whole, search only half-heartedly for change - we're not really willing to take the plunge. I know a lady who reads self-help books voraciously; she reads sections out to me, with some sense of pride, that she claims 'describe her completely', but it never seems to occur to her to take the necessary action, so that she's no longer ' completely described'; she enjoys basking in the 'notoriety' of 'helpless victim', which she has no intention of relinquishing. When we analyse, we're really analysing ourselves - the world exists only inside our heads. Something inside us wants to stay the way we are and avoids making changes. In order to change, we first need to accept that we're not as sane as we pretend to be, and that we've a tendency to inertia. Why isn't important, but recognising that we do it, is.

We've become accustomed to our familiar comfort zones and tend to prefer not to leave their boundaries, outside of which, there may be 'dragons'. We fear the unknown, losing friends, annoying our families, losing our jobs or partners - changing ourselves will inevitably put distance between us and the world we once knew. It's not possible to change *and* remain the same, or to use a well-known idiom 'we can't have our cake *and* eat it'. Changing ourselves will inevitably lead to changes in our lives, of this there is no doubt. It changes the way the world sees *us* and it changes the way we see the world - we become strangers in it. Our world is desperately in need of change - we're surrounded by insanity - and we've little to actually lose, unless we choose to hold on to our pain and suffering. This journey has to be lived - it's not something we can do on a rainy day when we have nothing better to do.

Chapter 12

Information

Tune into another channel for more information.

During our lifetimes - and after a person dies - our legacy permeates the consciousness field, just as when we throw a stone into the water and the ripples spread out. The ripples of what we did with our life remain in the field; the memories, actions, emotions, intentions and bitterness; the *information* remains and it's 'clutter'. It's not just your mind - it's *our* mind; there's no real separation. The ripples of past miseries don't just disappear - if they did we couldn't access their information and couldn't talk about them. If we don't heal and raise our level of consciousness, our fears, frustrations and anxieties remain trapped somewhere in space and time, in a cycle; they become 'immortal' when we don't allow them to die. We still watch war films and documentaries and go to the graveyards of the dead - the information is still here. Humanity lost a lot of lives in senseless wars and it hasn't learnt from them. We've convinced ourselves that we need to remember these wars to prevent them from happening again, and again; this is illogical - we need to move forward. Taken to another level, it's not too different from living our lives remembering all the horrors of our childhood and re-enacting them whenever we want a reminder of how awful they were, so that they won't happen again; this makes no sense whatsoever. The mindset of humanity won't change while it's trudging around in this cesspit of its past bloody atrocities. These wars have always happened and will always happen as long as we put our energy into them. We choose whether or not to remain in the deep end of this 'cesspit' - there *are* other options.

The world becomes a simpler place to live in when we discern it's made up of everything our senses perceive:

- The taste of an apple.
- The touch of a piece of wood.

- The smell of a peach.
- The sound of a bird.
- The sight of a sunrise.
- Our memories of childhood friends.

Everything is information - a continuous stream of it. If we record a rewritable disk to listen to and get fed up with listening to 'Learn French the Easy Way' we have the option to rewrite the information and begin learning 'Spanish', or to listen to an audio book. The process of rewriting will erase the French lessons from the past and re-write the disk with something new. We *can* change our information.

Since our birth, information has been written on to our minds by our parents, family, educators, ourselves and the media; its roots are buried deep and we continue to absorb more of it, which obscures our inner senses. In an interview with Conscious TV, Bruce Lipton said 'When I put in the new programs, all of a sudden I started to find ... my life completely turned around. All wonderful things started happening ...'[10] We can change without help from anyone, simply by changing our thoughts and grasping the processes of our minds. It all sounds a little weird and because it's an abstract concept we don't comprehend how we can do it - we don't think we're clever enough. This is not true - anyone can do this. All we have to do is think, raise questions and the changes will take care of themselves. We can get the hang of it quite fast; it's a bit like learning to ride a bicycle - it becomes second nature, once we get the hang of it; we no longer have to think about steering or turning the pedals - it's all done subconsciously. The subconscious mind works rather like an autopilot on a set course, which it won't deviate from without outside influence. This influence comes from the pilot, who can change the course. Many people live on autopilot without realising it. The conscious mind is in the Now - between thoughts - and it's clear of the clutter and distractions that the subconscious refuses to let go of.

It sounds strange, because it's so simple and the idea of writing information to our mind might seem ridiculous, but look how we've learnt to store and retrieve information on computer devices - our minds, though far more complicated, aren't very different. We may buy what we think to be the latest computer or tablet but we still have the same basic programs on it - nothing has actually changed. Social media is already on a computer when we buy it - all we have to do is put our username and password in; everything else is done for us as our information is already stored elsewhere, whether we like it or not. We're amazing computers ourselves - far more amazing than any computer that exists in society today, or ever will in the future.

A strong enough will, brings changes into our lives and it's rather like the 'placebo' effect, inasmuch as 'the effect is due to the power of suggestion.'[11] I've changed my life many times in the past and always dreaded the future at the turning point. Now when I begin a new adventure the past and this *dread of the future* I used to feel seem so silly; it takes a bit of practise to see it this way and the biggest hurdle to overcome, you've guessed it, is the mind. It interrupts, convinced it'll all go wrong and it doesn't stop hammering this message in. The mind is robust and by watching it in action, we gain a great deal of power over the control it has over us. The mind drags us down if we let it, but we can take control so we're not influenced by the 'me' who wants to re-write information and the 'me' that doesn't. The mind will argue with us far less when we watch its reactions closely - it's negative and uncertain because this is the way the world is and has been for a long time. The mind is limited; it draws from the past and it can't see beyond - it's the 'cache' of humanity. We resist change and only *we* can do something about it. The placebo effect is not very different to self-hypnosis - they're both essentially suggestion.

We always have choices to make, but sometimes we can't see them because the clouds of our past hang over us - they're too dense and dark to see through. If we wish to disperse the clouds, it's necessary to discern the traumas and difficulties of the past and to recognise that we need to come to terms with, and embrace them, if we're ever to take control of our lives. The way I see it, we have two choices; sit in a corner with our head between our knees, feeling glum, helpless, hard-done-by and perhaps turn to alcohol or drugs in an attempt to hide from our problems, or we can choose to help *ourselves*. The power of suggestion can enslave or free us and which option we choose is entirely up to us; suggest we're helpless and that's what we'll be - no effort required. Suggest we're strong and that's what we'll become. This 'suggestion', however, is just a seed planted by thought and will remain this way, unless it's underpinned by a heartfelt intention of change - it can't flourish on the barren land of the mind. For the seed to grow, we must continue to water it.

~~~

I've learnt to be grateful for my childhood and the difficulties that arose from it - without these experiences I wouldn't be the person I am today. It took many years to stop believing I'd been *given* the 'short straw' - the truth of the matter is, I adopted it myself. When we abandon all notions of straws, our load becomes lighter. I'm an ex-procrastinator who's struggled with life and frequently dipped my toes in water that was either too cold or too hot. I made myself fit into someone else's life, because I wasn't aware that I possessed the tools to create my own. A higher level of consciousness won't come to us on its own accord - we have to draw it to us. It's only by altering our perspective and choosing different information that we bring harmony into our lives - we don't have to wait. We tend to expend more energy explaining why we *can't* do something, than it would take to achieve it. We believe we don't have the power to change because we've been told it time after time. This isn't true. We store what we've been told - memory *is* information and information can be replaced!

When a child is belittled and rejected, then this rejection carries over into adulthood, potentially producing out-of-proportion anger or other negative emotional responses when they're provoked. The rejection triggers *learnt* mechanistic responses from our memories. So for example, if a parent was in the habit of jabbing an angry finger at us when we were younger, we'd feel the same emotion if someone did it again now - they need only point a finger in our direction for it to trigger a reaction. We react to the stimuli - autopilot kicks in and this is how arguments and disagreements occur. These reactions come from memory and we'll stay 'on alert' until we recognise how we submit to them. Triggers sit like landmines in our minds, waiting to be trodden on. By recognising this process, we begin to discern how our emotions can get out of control and with practise, are able to prevent the inevitable detonation. The ability to do this stays with us and we're able to respond better in our relationships with family members, friends or acquaintances.

As our consciousness level rises so does our ability to react to old problems in new ways. Sometimes it feels as though we're not making progress but this is only the mind putting up resistance - its insistent voice shouldn't be listened to. When a drop of rain falls into a stream it doesn't just disappear - it becomes the stream. From the raindrop to the ocean the process is automatic. The raindrop doesn't struggle and we don't need to either - struggle is resistance. If we force questions then the struggle prevents clarity; struggle is also 'information' and the results it produces are frustration and failure. The resistance resulting from our 'struggle program' is like a barrier between us and new information - this is why we don't, or can't, listen to anyone else's views or see the world from their perspective.

We hold onto what we've been taught, and cling to what's familiar, because we're comfortable with it - it's part of our conditioning to accept this safety net. If we decide to let go and I mean *really* let go of our programming, then new information can and will be written. Everything is information - how can it be anything else? If we've any doubts about 'information' then let's think about a baby. It begins as a single cell and information written on its DNA instructs it to divide in the most incredible programming language. The instructions are hard-wired, like the BIOS (basic input/output system) in a computer - it controls basic hardware functions. If we still doubt, then let's think about how a single cell can produce such an incredible and magnificent human being? Where do the instructions come from for the cell to divide into two identical cells and develop into a hair, a bladder, a liver, a vein or a finger? How do identical cells go off and become different things? How do they form an eye? How do they form veins and the blood that flows through them for our entire lifetimes? Where do the instructions come from that start the heart beating, the ears hearing, the eyes seeing and the incredible number of other functions that we're blessed with? How many different functions do these cells perform? How do they create our fingerprints - unique to each human being? How does thought occur? How many people have ever given these phenomena any thought at all? To be a 'human being' is something we take for granted, rather than reflect upon the Wonder. We're *joy-riding* in these bodies and know nothing about them or how they *actually* work. We use them to play games, dress up, push them to their limits and decorate them with jewels. We're absolutely amazing yet don't think about the miracle of life, while living out our relatively mundane existence. We ignore the miracles that surround us - then hope that one will fall into our lap. If we wrote down all the processes needed to perform these functions would we be able to construct a library big enough to contain the pages of information? I seriously doubt it!

Chapter 13

Comfort and Security

Break out of your comfort cage.

From the moment we're born we're kept in close proximity by our guardians, whether kindly or not - our basic needs were taken care of, otherwise we wouldn't be alive today; however, our psychological needs were neglected - our questions on this subject being rejected and discouraged. We need *true* psychological security so that we grow up free to question and explore, or at least try to find out about our true purpose in this world - without any fear or obstructions. When we can do this, we'll stop leaving our problems for our children to inherit. We must seek the truth of our existence; it isn't very different to finding our way out of a complicated and ingenious labyrinth - way beyond our technological capabilities. This labyrinth can be likened to a book of our own creation, entirely written by us, to be read and understood as the book of all our experiences.

I don't think I've ever met a *truly* happy or contented human being. Many of them have been coy, rebellious, aggressive, bullies, cunning, greedy, envious, vain, clingy, false and the list of characteristics goes on. We all wear a mask to disguise these traits and it isn't until we peel them off that our true nature is revealed. I can attribute all these traits to myself at various times in the past, but I wouldn't have admitted to them at the time. I've yet to meet a happy and secure member of the human race. The result of our upbringing is that we're self-loathing and afraid - no wonder we seek comfort and security in physical things. Because we were denied these in our youth, we fear the loss of the little we get and crave more, but there are few comforters in the world other than possessions, bank balances, entertainment, the lies we tell ourselves and familiar faces. So we're left searching for, but unable to find, what we need most in the world. We fear violence, loneliness and the end of our own existence and these fears are born from society.

We're judgemental, competitive, inconsiderate, superior and selfish; I don't paint a pretty picture of humanity, do I?

Success is not measured by how much good we do in our lives or how much joy we bring to others. Success is measured by salaries, savings, weight, class, house size, car, academic achievements, friends on Facebook, followers on Twitter and whatever version of technical accessories we walk around with. Our ambitions include being able to pay off our mortgages, get fit, meet our ideal partner, have wonderful holidays and to save enough money for our old age. Consider this; we go to our graves without any of it. What about the people who die before they reach retirement age? What have they worked all their lives for? Is it any wonder we seek comfort and security? Is it any wonder we've found artificial forms of them - hiding ourselves inside virtual reality games? We now hide from each other behind the mask of the internet with the ability to keep our status 'invisible'. When we hide from others we're hiding our own shame; why else don't we want to be seen? We can't face ourselves and because of this we can't face the truth about our existence - it sounds too far-fetched. As mentioned earlier in this book the label 'do-gooder' has a bad name and so does spirituality. How is it possible that we reject these? The train called 'society' is a runaway and it's accelerating - it'll take a miracle to stop it. On the other hand, runaway trains must crash or run out of fuel sooner or later.

<p style="text-align:center">~~~</p>

Why do we need approval and how did we become so insecure? A baby may be given a comfort blanket, a dummy or a soft toy to comfort it and when they're taken away, because it's considered silly for older children to have them, the baby will suffer from the loss of the surrogate comfort that it provided. If a baby isn't given these pacifiers they still seek comfort because it's in our nature to need to be held and loved - it's essential for our good health. Without it we become withdrawn and insecure and these thoughts in the mind of a child are unhealthy and long lasting. They manifest themselves in illness and behavioural disturbances such as rebellion, anorexia, violence, depression, aggression, withdrawal, bullying, self-abuse and the seeking of abuse by others - quite a horrible list. A child will misbehave to get attention as it gets older and even a *punishment* gives him the attention he craves - he needs the 'hit'. Every time a baby is denied emotional support it buries the need for it a little deeper. Ideally, a baby should have complete attention from 'at home' parents, day and night, but most families can't afford to do this - generally, both need to go out to work, so they employ someone else to guard the baby until their return. When we're tired out or just too busy we put our children in playpens, cots or cribs (cages), and later on in front of various screens; think about this concept a little before rejecting it outright.

We need comfort when security is missing from our lives. What we lack is psychological security and self-knowledge; without these we can't experience freedom. The artificial comfort we're given is usually given for the convenience of parents. Because the need for security is innate we seek it elsewhere - we've not been educated in a way that enables us to provide it for ourselves. If we don't find comfort and security we look for the familiar replacements that we've become accustomed to. Security blankets and the like pacify a baby - they don't provide security. Our need for psychological security has been replaced by something physical - this is a big problem in society; for example, our children play in structured playgrounds enclosed by fences - why aren't they climbing trees anymore? Are we going to keep them so safe that they'll end up under lock, key and CCTV - neither comforted or truly secure?

We've become dependent on physical things and other people. The security we think we get from them is an illusion and has the opposite effect. For this reason, because of a strong dependency, we continue to seek security and comfort from outside sources - this problem isn't talked about in society very much. The more 'safety' we accumulate, the more we need and the more we struggle to let go of when a threat arises. We've become dependent on other people to confirm our own existence and look to them to tell us what our place in the world should be (accountant, dustman, upper class etc.) - anywhere we fit in. If we don't fit in, we rebel, withdraw or turn to alcohol, drugs and/or other destructive habits, because we feel safe hiding behind them.

We look to authority figures for what we lack, as though they were different to us in some way; they're *not* and they've the same problems and insecurities that we do - they've also sought security in material things and ignored their spiritual journey. These authority figures have the same problems as we do and therefore, are unable to help us; they can't know the deepest levels of the psyche or their own insecurities - we're always looking outside for comforts and not to ourselves, where we don't need any. Comforters are given by our parents when we're babies and the need for them continues when we're old enough to go to school with points systems and gold stars for our work and 'correct' behaviour. When we make an effort in society, or excel in something like an exam, a sport, acting, science, a job or anything else, our 'reward' is physical and a pacifier; for example, a certificate, a medal, an Oscar, a pay rise or even the Nobel prize. We also get rewards such as 'recognition' and 'compliments'. If we reflect for a moment on how this works we see it's these comforters that increase the power of our egos. We like rewards because they allow us to feel proud of ourselves and encourage us to do 'better'. They also give us outside approval, which allows us to experience the feeling of worthiness - when we get it, we strive to attain more. The rewards are temporary and therefore not worth having - this world is also temporary. We've been taught to strive for artificial excellence - both physically and academically - which is measured by grades or rewards.

We've become accustomed to seeking security, but we're unable to find it. We look for:

- Financial security, in order that we lack for nothing right up to our deaths.
- Personal security through things like self-defence and relationships.
- Electronic security for our homes, cars and other belongings.
- Physical security through fitness, diets and health.
- Psychological security through the media and the approval of others.

However, all we get are illusory security and comfort. We've created foolish ideas, like 'comfort foods' and 'retail therapy'; is humanity ready to see that these are not only illusions but ridiculous concepts? They're 'pop therapy'; trendy, misleading and impermanent. We can't find happiness or satisfaction in them - we're wrapped up in poor imitations of true and permanent security - this can't be found on the outside.

Comfort in wars is a particularly difficult subject because we're complacent about them. Their regularity makes them the 'norm' and we accept war as unavoidable and as being a part of life - we accept it as inevitable. Our greatest comfort from wars is our survival of them - believing that we're being protected by governments who are 'looking after our needs'; this is an illusion. Imagine living in a world where we no longer believe that war can lead to peace. War can't lead to peace any more than ignorance can lead to knowledge. War leads to premature death, pain, suffering, hatred, fear and more separation - it's about time we woke up to this. A soldier goes to war prepared to kill or be killed - not an intelligent thing to do. Wars serve to create more conflict because they perpetuate fear, bitterness and hatred, between whatever nations or authorities are fighting it out, and also to those observing them - they create further division. More and more the only *comfort and security* we can depend on is our own 'survival' in a society that places little value on people, and great value on things. Until this is reversed, society will become more and more insecure, and comfortless.

Chapter 14

Absurdities

Picture a disco ball; can one tiny mirror be aware of the others? Are they not all part of the ball? Can the tiny mirror be aware of itself?

Don't you think humans are curious beings? People are bloody-minded, contradictory, cruel, kind, funny, sad, inconsistent, capable of feats of outstanding brilliance, and phenomenal stupidity. What drives us to behave in this manner? What drives us to insist we're right when we know we're wrong (as it were)? We like our lives to be difficult and we ensure they stay that way - woe betide anyone who tries to make our life easier. Dissatisfied with our lot in life, we spend time creating and perfecting our alter ego - often based on one of society's *role models*. Francois de la Rochefoucauld, a 17th century French author said 'We become so accustomed to disguise ourselves to others that at last we are disguised to ourselves.'[12] Not much has changed, has it?

Changing our appearance can be likened to replacing the label on a bottle of wine - the contents remain the same. No matter how stylish we are or how long we spend every day on our appearance, we remove our disguises when we go to bed just like everyone else. We're fundamentally the same as each other, but we hide behind our masks. When we wake up in the morning after a 'night out' we look ragged and wouldn't leave our houses without *camouflage*. I've a friend who won't open the front door without putting her 'face' on - no matter who's calling. Is it more important that we like our own image, or that other people do? Any alteration we make to our external appearance is because of programming. This programming gives importance to fashion, make-up, mimicry, competition, self-judgement and vanity. It comes from images and expectations placed in our minds and most of us aren't aware that we're trying to live up to expectations - we're the most unnatural beings on the 'planet'.

Women walk around in uncomfortable stilettos and no matter how much pain they're in, they still wear them; often leading to problems in later life. A man must keep up a 'macho' image and not do things like 'cry' or show 'pain'. Just how foolish are we? Consider how we:

- tattoo and pierce our body parts.
- get drunk, stoned, overeat, starve.
- humiliate ourselves, just to be on television.
- squeeze ourselves into clothes that are too tight.
- turn celebrities into gods.
- fight, cheat, defend, and ignore truth.
- transform our bodies through plastic surgery.
- eat and drink junk.

We agree to and enjoy suffering in return for our images. Are we nuts or what?

Outside, and within academic circles few people want to know who they really are. We don't think about this subject and want to make the most of our bodies before they wrinkle and wear out - we're 'clutching at straws'. On the whole, humanity doesn't care where it came from or where it's going. We change our behaviour according to who we're speaking to such as; our parents, doctors, lawyers, employers or our friends. We rarely behave in the same way when we're alone and the relationship we have with ourselves can't be understood by another - *we* don't understand it. No-one can ever truly know another person. How amazing is this fact? We know *and* don't know we're playing these roles - our chosen persona snaps into place as and when required.

People scan us - as though we were a vulgar piece of art or an object to be desired. We play 'judge' because it's far easier to judge others than it is ourselves. What does judging others confirm and in what way does it comfort us? What and whose standards are we judging them by? We decide, more or less instantly, whether or not we like another person on looks alone; the impression we form of them comes from programming - it comes from memory. For example, they may not be wearing fashionable clothing, or we may think they're too fat, too short or 'could do better'. Most of us believe we're better than we actually are, but we don't feel good about ourselves at all. We're frauds and we choose our personalities from the variety that are on offer - we select and combine them.

It's sad that we propagate this culture. Is it because of deep-seated insecurities and suppressed psychological needs? You must have noticed the way we behave with mobile phones; it's easy to tell when someone isn't *really* talking or texting anybody, but rather pretending to be. We do these things because we don't want people to see our weaknesses or think that we're not popular or 'normal'. It's a terrible thing to feel alone in a crowd - the phone becomes our ally. We can be 'loud in a crowd' when we talk on our phones or socialise with friends; we don't care if no-one wants to listen to our conversations - it's our penny masquerade. Why are we dishonest about our behaviour and ignorant of the wishes of others? Why do we need people to notice and like us? Why do we need to think we're 'better' than *we* think we are? Underneath the protective shield we don, we're all vulnerable and we're all insecure.

There's a great expression; 'to be a fly on the wall'. Imagine being a fly on the wall of a friend, relative, or a well-known figure. I'm certain you'd find out things you never knew, or would have guessed about them and some of those things may shock you, particularly if you've known the person for a long time. We remove some of our masks when we're alone and some of these changes may be simple, like putting our feet up on the sofa with shoes on or they may be complex, such as having secret perversions or fetishes. But behind closed doors there's a great deal going on that we're not willing to share with others, no matter how close we are to them. When we're alone we feel a sense of freedom as we can't be criticised or judged. However, when we're on this path of self-discovery we lose that feeling of *freedom* because we become our own critics, and there's nowhere to hide. We know there are many masks we hide behind that we're reluctant to take off. We fear stripping ourselves naked more than we fear anything else. What would you see if you were a fly on your own wall? What would you change about yourself? Just how many roles do we play simultaneously and how do we choose which persona to put on and for whom? Do we create a new role when we meet a new person? We know how to play a great many parts and we don't need scripts, directors, crews or a producer; we do the lot on our own without even thinking about it. We never take off all our masks - we wear them on many levels - but we know they're not us.

Our behaviour, when we're alone, can be complicated. The world becomes more confusing when we realise that we don't understand *ourselves*. Think about the man I mentioned earlier in, 'Curiosity and Confusion', who plays the role of a 'captain' on a fleet of ships in a virtual reality game. Who is he in the game? On the one hand he may be an 'all-powerful' head of a fleet with many compliant subjects at his 'beck and call', who must - without question - obey his orders. On the other hand, as human beings are all fakes in one way or another there's a good chance he could be lying about the role he's playing online. Perhaps his role is more humble such as scrubbing decks, but he's pretending to have a higher rank?

This gets complicated when we realise he has to play multiple roles at the same time. The 'actor' at his computer terminal is cleverly directing the actor on the screen and supplying him with the script; the captain can't make errors because the character of the player would show through. Other cast members in the game wouldn't suspect the man behind the computer is perhaps of short stature, insecure, has no work and probably never set foot on a ship in his life. The man behind the screen is the puppeteer and he's pulling all the strings. Who's pulling his? It would be disconcerting for a person playing out these simultaneous roles to have someone walk into the room and 'catch them in the act', as it were. The sudden switch to the role they usually play when we're around - not the puppeteer or captain - would leave them somewhat disoriented as they wonder how much we'd seen or heard. We don't appreciate our personal space being invaded and we need to instantly put on a mask - which one, would depend on who had walked in on us, and what they'd seen. Have you ever had unexpected visitors walk into a room at an inopportune moment, discovering something about you they *didn't* know before?

~~~

Society tells us what to wear, what to do and what not to do. It tells us from an early age so it becomes ingrained through laws, signs, rules, controls and the media. It tells us what to watch on the television and what to do in our free time through clever manipulation - we don't know it's doing it because we believe ourselves to be free. Have you noticed how many people play tennis when Wimbledon's on the television or how there are more joggers leading up to the London Marathon, regardless of whether they're running in it? We feel motivated and inspired by the 'devotees'. We love to do what others are doing and we copy language trends too. Where and when did we first hear the word 'awesome'?

We're conditioned who to judge and who not to, so that we'll listen to some people and not to others. We tend to look down on so-called lowly professions such as dustmen or cleaners and respect others such as lawyers and doctors. Is a lawyer a better human being than a dustman? If we think about it, we see that we're not at all free and that we submit to dogma without being aware of it. We work mostly until retirement age and therefore, the best years of our lives are lived under pressure and stress, rarely having any free time to think about life - even our holidays can be traumatic. We can't know freedom because we live within the boundaries society has put in place. We think we're free but it's hard to know what true freedom is - we adapt the parts we play according to our surroundings. We must go to school, work, pay taxes, buy or rent houses, we must, we must and we must. When did you last do anything *really* different? If we can't see these restrictions then it's because we've accepted them so well that we don't know they're there - our prison boundaries are invisible. Some people are happy for their lives to be routine and one of those routines is our annual holiday, but this is *not* freedom. I don't wish to go any deeper into restrictions here as it won't serve any good purpose. What matters most is discovering our true nature as opposed to the one we've manifested on the *outside* - what matters more, for now, is recognising that they're not the same thing.

A baby writes its life on a blank sheet of paper. He records everything his senses perceive from the moment he's born until his death. It could be likened to a baby researching and writing the script of the play he's starring in. We don't remember all these experiences, but they're recorded as the baby explores its world and they mould the character the baby will become. If a baby is given too much *attention* rather than *love* when he cries, he will cry even more and much louder when he doesn't get it. How many children have you seen having tantrums in supermarkets or in the streets? The children have recorded old, well-established information and patterns of behaviour and they know, innately, what to do with them. They can't record new information because the society they live in is 'old'. What appears new to us - fashion or technology - is the same clock with a different face on it. Any attempt by the child to find out more about himself is stifled, one way or another; usually by us not having the time or inclination to listen to his questions. Paradoxically, we think our own children are wonderful little people who've unique characters, but on the other hand, we're training them to fit into a society that'll never allow them to develop their uniqueness - we literally 'spoil' them. Often we can't answer the questions they ask because we don't know the answers, but this doesn't mean we can't encourage the questions. I know of a child (aged eight) who asked his mother: Why am I here? What do I do? The mother replied 'That's what I'm wondering. You go back to bed, that's what you do.' This question couldn't be answered and we don't have the time or curiosity to think about it. Gradually, children stop asking these questions and because they're unanswered the child becomes confused and buries his inquisitiveness. This same child later (aged ten) asked his grandfather 'How will I know what to do when I'm fourteen?' He'd changed from asking a question in the present to one projected into the future. He did this because we're taught from the past (history) and think into the future (school, job, retirement). Most important, is that both questions showed that he didn't understand his place in this world and was thinking about his purpose *here*, even four years after the first question - he probably still does. We're taught that everything will come to us if we do as we're told and work hard - it'll come in the future. We wait until we're well into our fifties or sixties, but we can wait until we're in our graves - it'll not arrive. We don't even know what it is we're waiting for.

We begin our lives excitedly and wonder and marvel about everything around us, but this beauty and impulse is soon stifled and even made taboo. We tell children untruths. We tell them about a tooth fairy and place coins under their pillows when they lose a tooth. We tell them about Father Christmas and lie about who brought the presents under the tree and we know they're lies. We tell them lies and give them rewards for believing them. We don't think about the consequences of lying to them, because society tells us it's okay to do so. We then develop their confusion by telling them it's wrong to tell lies and punish them when *they* do it.

Because we're so busy with our lives, we allow children the 'remote control' for the television and have no idea what they watch when we're not around - this allows society to shape them further. Children are curious and they *will* flick channels as soon as we leave the room; they have the remote control and with it, they're being remotely controlled. If we don't break these patterns then our children are just, as Roger Waters put it, 'another brick in the wall.' In effect, we're shaping them the way we were shaped and we don't allow the wonderful, magnificent and brilliant 'individual' to develop. We allow them to watch television and films and these are 'behavioural instructions' disguised as education or entertainment. The purpose of television is to support the current system of society. Society will *form* children so their only function is the continuity of the world we've created. Society is us and the changes must be made by us. The most arduous task in the world must be to change ourselves.

Another way individuality is stifled is by standardising our worlds. There isn't much for us to do if you think about it. Make a list of things you can do that are *achievable* within the next twelve months that you haven't done before; there won't be much on it, because we're too stuck within boundaries, commitments and schedules. The choices we have are limited. What are the actual choices of leisure activities for the average person? What could you go and do tonight? Rather than create beneficial pastimes for ourselves, we're merely kept occupied. Is it significant that entertainment is *provided* for us?

The world is online and we've participated in its creation, even if we've never touched a computer. Websites are now mostly made from templates and we're encouraged to be creative when using them? How is this possible? We have standardised letters in word processing applications. We're moulded and shaped to continue the growth of a society that's sick, lethargic, burdened and profitable. A child's life is more or less mapped out from the moment it begins, with few variations - usually related to a choice of career or future partner. Our lives are templates, moulded and categorised - it's rare to see true creativity. One of the problems with a world like this is that 'thinking' will become obsolete - or even forbidden - one day.

We live like automatons and we've become blinded by the illusions. What does it mean to be an individual? No-one knows, as we've all been fed into the same sausage machine and we cling to what's familiar - for our comfort and security. On one level we've graded ourselves against other members of the human race by birth, wealth and class systems - this is so silly. It's a bit like saying one tulip is better than another - we're all the same. On another level, being an individual means behaving differently to the rest. It means following what we believe is the right path for us and staying on it - no matter what. The first thing to recognise is that our choices are limited - by society - if we don't change anything. This change must take effort and will not come about on its own. An alcoholic can't be helped until they recognise and want to recover from the problem - I know this very well as I've had close and regular contact with several of them. The first thing to do after recognition of the illness is to get rid of the bottles. The same applies to society - believing in the familiar is an addiction. The principle is the same for all problems or insecurities. We need to recognise what's actually happening and we need to *want* to let go.

Once we see what's happening we know it was obvious all along - we'd ignored it all. We heal without too much effort - a drop of water that's returned to the ocean doesn't struggle. The decision to change ourselves must come from within. We think this is impossible because we've been taught we must all stand united in order to make our nation strong, but a strong nation can be likened to an impenetrable wall - it can't be broken in *or* out of.

It's freedom within boundaries. If humanity stands together it can become strong too, but we don't believe we can make a difference so we don't bother trying. We don't believe an individual or a small group can make a difference; we're shown discouraging examples of this like, minority political parties running for government. We can do it - it's easy if we do it together. Strength is within us all and true strength is not physical. Choose to change ourselves and really mean it. If we don't place limitations or conditions in front of our decision then there aren't any. Never give up! We tend to believe someone else will do it for us and become dependent on science to find solutions to the world's problems or perhaps we're waiting for the Messiah to come and save us - one of our most absurd ideas. We must save ourselves. If it's *all* an illusion what does it matter? It rather depends on whether or not you're enjoying it or if you believe you have a purpose.

~~~

When we choose to change, the mind is furious - it'll fight to maintain security in what's familiar, and for its own survival, but the mind has only ever had power over us because we gave it away. When the mind doles out absurd thoughts, we must look straight at them and ask ourselves 'Who thought it?' This may seem silly at first because we've not been taught to think this way, but we can learn to adjust if we're motivated and determined. The thoughts quickly disappear when we watch them coming and going; the more we practise the better the results, but the more we fight, the stronger the cold hard chains of the mind become. The other night I awoke in the middle of the night and my mind was chattering away about an ex and reminding me that he still had some of my belongings. I smiled, because I recognised the pattern and the thought dissolved. But it never used to be this easy and I've spent many a night in the past tossing and turning, trying to silence the conversations my mind insisted on having - it wouldn't leave me alone. The mind is mischievous.

As long as we remain divided, we can't become united; as long as the drop remains out of the ocean, it's separated. It may feel scary to return but once in the ocean there's no more fear and no more loneliness. Governments can't heal this divide - they maintain continuity, because the people who make up the governments are *themselves* divided - they *are* us. It's all us, at every level, but we've given our power to others and don't know how to get it back again. Do we want it? We wait, and think the world will live in peace one day in the future, that governments will not be corrupt, that wars won't exist, that no-one will starve and that there'll be no more homeless people, but this isn't *true* and there's a lot of history to back up this point. If we're honest with ourselves it's clear to see that the world's becoming a harder and more violent place to live in.

We think we're *really* individuals but this could not be further from the truth - we're One. We're humanity - we're mankind. Like the glass square on the disco ball, we don't know we're part of a 'whole'. We're born, parented, schooled, prepared for work, get married, have kids, buy homes and wait for our retirement and grandchildren, who don't always arrive before our deaths. Of course there are variations to this but not many and not enough to make a difference to humanity or the world we live in, unless we 'choose' to.

Chapter 15

On Death

Some things we can change, but not the inevitable.

Death is an end to something but what is it an end to? We're born and since that moment we've been recording our lives, as though on a CD in the mind. It's the mind/memory that we leave behind when we die, together with all its confusing and contradictory contents; I'd suggest that what dies is the image, the personality we've created, the 'scrawled' on piece of paper and all the baggage with it. The ego is what we've been creating, shaping and clinging on to all of our lives - rather like throwing a vase on a pottery wheel; the ego is a bolt-on. An artist doesn't die if we destroy his painting - it's merely an expression of him. Death is an end to illusion, desire, fear, sickness, grudges, worry and stress, but we don't have to wait for physical death to lose these labels. When we strive to better ourselves we die a little every day and as we let go of ingrained beliefs, we die a little more; however, we don't want to go to our own funeral. The ego can die before the body - we don't have to hold on to it. The ego is an ID-Entity; it *identifies* us. We nurture, clothe, love, hate, and protect it and have done from the moment we were born - we possess it; it's our 'baby'. We also don't want to let go of the family and friend connections we've built up; we cling on for dear life to everything including our possessions. The living mourn the dead and I've no doubt in my mind that the dead don't mourn the living. The dead don't care for what they left behind, or the size of the monument we put up for them.

Why do we fear death? Is it because we don't know what it means and though there's lots of information available, none of it's verifiable. Just like everything else we experience, death is information and we each have access to it. Death is frightening to those of us that haven't taken the time to think about it. What exactly is it that we want to hold on to; the pain, stress, fear, bank account or perhaps a relationship? After someone close to us dies we generally remember the good in them, but while they're alive we tend to see the not so good. What does the mind have to do with this? We're actors, who after playing out our roles refuse to be written out of the script; we've played our parts for our lifetime and won't let go of ourselves, or the others in the cast. We don't like ourselves, but we can't let go of the images or the world we've created. Death is feared quite early on in life and to such an extent that we count birthdays, wrinkles, grey hairs and after a certain age there are those who begin counting backwards, as though it could change the inevitable. We take care of our appearances on the outside - sometimes meticulously, but we don't take care of our minds.

Children would talk openly about death, but we protect them from it. A boy who has 'lost' his grandfather may be told to be 'careful' about what he says to his grandmother at the funeral - if he's allowed to go to it. Children accept death far easier than we do. Does the innocence of children intimidate or embarrass us? Perhaps we're ashamed? Wouldn't it be better if we were open about this subject? If we open the dark door of death so it's no longer a taboo subject that we have to tiptoe around, our fears would subside. Children don't fear death until we *teach* them to, by passing our own fears on to them. We scare them with stories about what happens after death, such as hell, oblivion and the wrath of God. Little wonder a great number of children develop a fear of the dark, create imaginary friends or become withdrawn - we've seeded their nightmares. All this fear stems from fears passed on to us and from what we've been told or shown. None of it's justifiable; we live in fear of the unknown rather than the known. Because what happens after death is unknown, we've become afraid of it. But here's the thing - our bodies are going to expire whether we like it or not - the film *must* come to an end. Each and every one of us can be certain of this part of our 'destiny' at least. When we understand this, and accept it, we alleviate irrational fears. We prepare ourselves for all sorts of eventualities:

- Going to school.
- A job interview.
- Going on holiday.
- Going to the dentist.

- Getting married.
- The birth of a child.
- Our retirement.

We prepare for everything - except death.

Why are we sad at a funeral? I've spoken to people who've said they can't get upset at funerals, but feel guilty because they're expected to do so - I'm a bit like this too. Some people get carried away and enjoy the drama, some are genuinely upset at the death of a close friend or relative and some feel they've been cheated and left alone to cope. In the latter case, do we miss the person who died because we depended on them and now feel abandoned? Why do we have funerals? If it's to say 'goodbye' to a loved one then why do we remember the anniversaries of their death years later? Death is a mystery, but, it's the 'living' that cares about it. Dead people aren't at the funeral, only their bodies are; their essence is not inside - nor has it died. Does a funeral remind us that one day we'll die ourselves? We find it easy to talk about someone else's death but not our own. We avoid the recently bereaved; we feel awkward in their company and don't know what to say to comfort them - their sorrow is too great for us to bear. We can't share in their grief for the simple reason that we don't feel it, unless we were close to the person who died.

If we think about the thoughts accompanying our fears, we'll see that they come from memory. It can be argued that we love this fear. We've created a climate of fear from our desire for gratuitous violence in films - more and more of these films are produced and the demand for them has not slowed. Why do we want to see evermore graphic images of violence, and violent death? What information are we writing onto our minds and how do the images we put there affect us? Fear results from this information and the graphic images we see in these films. We're writing our own nightmares! Could we watch this violence with the same emotions, when enacted against a friend or family member? Why is it different watching it on a screen? What about the horrors on the news broadcasts and in the newspapers? If we surround ourselves with horror, bad news or terror, then fear is what we're going to feel. We've become disconnected from each other and can't see the

123

ripples of our actions. We're afraid of the method by which we'll die, but not the method by which we live. Why do we fear how we die? Is it because we've been continuously 'entertained' by the violence, and now fear that we'll become victims of the same fate? Could it be we're afraid of so-called everlasting darkness? Perhaps we want to stay alive because we're afraid of 'heaven and hell' stories, and don't believe we've lived our lives well enough to deserve heaven …

~~~

I know of someone who was dying of cancer and hoped he'd stay alive long enough to get an iPhone5 when it was released. This shows how strongly we've become attached to material things, rather than life itself. We want to make the most of them and can't let go of attachments, so we invest in gadgets and toys to amuse ourselves. We write last wills and testaments; we're preparing to die, but only in respect to the living. We're not looking at death properly. In order to prepare to die we need to see what death means and then we'll see that more important than having the latest toys, is letting go of the attachments we have to them. It doesn't mean we have to give everything away; it means we can see them for what they are - transient and meaningless. We can't delay death any more than we can our next birthday so, wouldn't it be a good idea if we came to terms with it?

As fantastic as it may seem, it's all happening inside our mind. Death brings release from all illusions and fear. Why do we need to hold on to them so much? All things in this world are illusory and impermanent. Time breaks down every*thing* - it becomes something else, just like a caterpillar to a butterfly. It doesn't take too much reflection to see that we can't cease 'existing'. Existence is the *only* thing that's real. Try closing your eyes one night while lying in bed or relaxing in the bath and imagine non-existence; imagine the 'end' of you. You can't do this because whatever you do, there's always an observer; the observer can't die and neither can the awareness of it.

I've a friend who had a car accident in which he was seriously injured. He had an amazing near death experience. He went out-of-body, and says he was everything … *everything*. From a position above the scene, he saw a man in the car suffering and noticed his injuries; he remembers thinking 'Oh my God ... the poor guy', but didn't recognise the man as himself - whilst out of his body he was not suffering at all. My friend saw colours he's unable to describe and told me that they don't exist in our visible spectrum. Dr Peter Fenwick, neuropsychiatrist, has done some interesting studies on near death experiences. He asks the question 'How is it that you can have cognition, or, an alert mind, when you're clinically dead? It doesn't make sense.'[13] It does if we stop seeing life and death as a linear experience and if we stop believing that we're the ego and the body. Two days before my mother died, she felt something touch her shoulder and heard a voice saying 'Come with me now.' This was quite disturbing for her and unexpected. She told her nurse but the nurse said 'Don't worry about it. It's normal and just an effect of the drugs.' I'm not so sure about that! This nurse had been present for many similar experiences and I've heard other stories about nurses who've seen this behaviour before, and heard these stories many times. They are common and yet, ignored.

We've been conditioned to believe all sorts of nonsense and we make those beliefs our reality - our minds are all muddled up. I'd suggest that as we 'die' we see what we *expect* to see, because we've been programmed to see it - in near death experiences too; for example, 'go towards the light'. I'd argue that we created the images because we're so afraid of dying that we've given ourselves a crutch to hold onto; however, I don't believe that we can ever know what happens when we're *actually* dead - instead of just *near* it. We need to begin to think differently about life and death - thinking is not enough on its own, and we need to change our perspective and raise our consciousness level to see more. Death is release from this life. What - if anything - is the legacy we leave behind? What - if anything - can we take with us?

Is there something beyond fear? Let's imagine there's nothing after this life and we cease existing - entirely and completely. How would we recognise the moment of disappointment? Everything would cease so fast that we wouldn't even know about it. On the other hand, if we die and there's something 'afterwards' there'll be no disappointment and no need whatsoever to fear anything. So where's the problem? Why is the subject - since time began - still debated; there are only two options after all and as I've shown, we'll only ever know about one of them? There's much more to the 'mystery of life' than I could've imagined ten years ago; it becomes more mysterious as I continue to let go of dogmatic beliefs and attachments. Living is merely an illusion, which means 'death' is an illusion too. Life is a cycle - it has a beginning and an end; I don't believe *we* do. I tried to share this realisation with friends and was puzzled about why no-one would even consider it. One of my dear friends said I was 'mad' and another 'deluded' and I was asked 'What if you're wrong?' I replied 'If I'm wrong I go to my grave having lived happily, if I'm right I go to my grave having lived happily; therefore, I've nothing to lose.'

Chapter 16

Letting Go

Whatever it is that prevents us from letting go, also prevents us from moving on.

Letting go is relinquishing the control that fear and other emotions have over us. Of course, there are times when relinquishing that control would be unwise; for example, if we found ourselves in a life threatening situation, fear would cause us to take the necessary evasive action. Knowing whether to 'listen' to our fear, or not to, could make the difference between being killed and staying alive. However, this 'fight or flight' kind of fear is not what I had in mind to discuss, but rather the debilitating control that our irrational fears and emotions exercise over us.

It's a human thing to believe that we're in control of ourselves; we like to think we're free to do what we want *when* we want, and that we're the masters of our own destiny. This is the way I used to think before I began my 'journey' and came to realise that this is not so; I was being controlled by my fears and emotions - just like we all are - and they directed my decisions, actions and thoughts about things and other people. It's quite a revelation to discover this about ourselves and it's liberating too, because *I* now hold the reins of my fears and emotions and control *them*, rather than allow them to control me. In the process, I've been able to 'let go' of many things that have been a hindrance to me in the past. Letting go has been the kindest thing I ever did for myself. Whereas once, I was in a destructive relationship with myself, taking back control of my life in a healthy way means that I am now, perhaps, master of my own destiny.

~~~

When we find ourselves 'stuck' in an unhealthy relationship, professional or personal, we need to question what's holding us in it. Often, we believe there's no way out, but the true reason we stay is fear. There's always a way out, but fear steers us away from it, convincing us that the upheaval will be more trouble than it's worth, and that we may well end up jumping from the frying pan into the fire. We don't want to leave our belongings, our homes, split financial assets, divide friends and we don't want to start from scratch. We care about what people think and in some circumstances, fear the repercussions. We complain and blame each other - yet, content to live with our lot, we're reluctant to change the things we complain about. Help is always available, if we're courageous enough to seek it, and if we have to go to a shelter initially then, so be it. Yes, I *have* been in this position myself and instead of a shelter, found myself - mentally and physically battered - in a foreign country - and at the mercy of the British Embassy. Our limitations are our only obstacles, making the first step tough, but if we find the courage to start the process, we regain control of our lives and that's got to be worth something. After all, wouldn't it be best to let go of things that cause us pain?

~~~

We try to secure our future because we're afraid of the spectres we've been shown of the elderly, the starving, the sick, the alone, the vulnerable and the forgotten. So we strive to accumulate more things in order that we may not go *without* one day; we hoard our paraphernalia and leave others to clear up after our death. However, we don't think beyond our deaths except through a 'last will and testament', then we cut ourselves off from anything beyond that point. As long as we place the word 'death' on a 'finish line', we're going to fear crossing it.

When we let go of desire and start to look at what we've got rather than what we haven't, our world changes dramatically. We appreciate that we've always had something to eat and drink - if we hadn't we wouldn't still be here. However, as long as we continue to crave 'material things' and the 'latest models', selfish desire becomes our reason for living, regardless of whether we want these things for ourselves or someone else. We're often at our greediest when we divorce or when someone close to us dies. When a family member dies we expect our *dues*, even if we haven't spoken to them for decades. We could walk away and let go of the harmful feelings we harbour, but tend to let greed get in the way, as if it'll compensate us in some way. It never does; it only gives us more negativity to hold on to. Many suffer in the wake of these grievances and many fall out because of some event they refuse to let go of - often carrying their bitterness to the grave. Think about how much joy they've missed out on and how much suffering they've *willingly* endured by not putting their differences behind them. When *anger* for example, begins to rise we have two choices - let it go, or allow it to grow into something destructive.

Family conflicts are one of the biggest causes of negative emotions. The home is where conditioning begins and where our psychological needs are first suppressed. Events arise that frighten us and, consequently, we begin to construct our defences from a very young age - adding to them over the years. These barriers do protect us, but they also imprison us behind them; we construct our walls one robust brick at a time. The mind flags up past negative experiences warning us about the consequences of removing these barriers; such as, being vulnerable and allowing ourselves to be perceived as weak. When we meet other people we see each other through the invisible walls we've erected - ours and theirs. The communication between us is filtered and we can never discover what lies 'behind the wall' of another. We know this on a subconscious level and it gives rise to suspicion, misunderstanding and disagreement. Between nations this same mindset leads to war. How can humanity possibly live in harmony under these conditions? Dismantling our defence system is an uphill struggle but until we do, we'll be unable to see the beauty that lies within ourselves, and others.

~~~

More and more we're discouraged from thinking and working things out for ourselves; if you have a problem, there's bound to be advice or help available either online, or at the end of a telephone. These include assistance with abuse, alcoholism, stopping smoking, depression, legal advice, mental health, breast feeding, reporting crimes or even suggestions about what to cook for your dinner tonight. We're always calling for 'help', so it's hardly surprising that we're unable to help ourselves. Why do we need so much help? How can we improve society when we rely on an unhealthy system for our guidance? Authority is one of the things we fear to let go of, because we're not used to being *responsible* for ourselves; the many rules and regulations that govern us make this seem impossible. Take a look at all the road signs when you next go out and about and ask yourself 'how' and 'why' they came into being. It would be difficult for us to do without them now - harder than you may imagine, as we aren't aware of the number of 'directions' we unwittingly follow daily. Thinking and common sense wither away through lack of use in this 'live by numbers' world. We have to let go of the need for help at every turn of our lives, and begin using our intelligence and thinking for ourselves.

~~~

It's essential to remove our masks so that we can learn how to stop hiding behind them. Do you ever really reveal yourself to anyone? We need to let go of prejudice, dogma, anger, guilt and everything else from the past - these preoccupations only serve to cloud the 'goal' - the only destination we need pay attention to. The preoccupations are what the mind busies itself with and if you try to suppress one of them, another, and another, and *another* takes its place. I have to admit here that there's a certain perverse pleasure in some of these 'preoccupations' rolling over and over in our mind and let's be honest, we might miss them if they went away. Who however, other than ourselves, do we harm by holding on to them? The mind resists change and it wants to keep busy. It works non-stop without a break; it's the ball and chain we've shackled to our ankles and it's heavy. The mind wants to protect itself and all its contents - like a child clinging to a tin full of treasured souvenirs. The mind's determination and ability to cling to the past shouldn't be underestimated as it knows *every* trick in the book; one of the most common being, 'don't do today what you can put off until tomorrow' - the trouble with this philosophy is that tomorrow never arrives.

You can be free if you want to; if you're willing to *come into existence* on your own merit instead of relying on the mind's negativity or authority to control your life. Our path is personal and we can't follow anyone else's; we're unique and so are our journeys. We can go our own way, but as long as we pretend that we can't, we'll keep looking in the right hand for what the left hand is holding. We don't have to live 'hard-done-by' or 'trapped' in a world we're desperately unhappy in, or accept without reason that we're powerless to transform ourselves. We've been looking in all the *known* places outside of ourselves for guidance and meaning to our lives but they're in the past (books etc.) and the future (hope); the key to unveiling our true nature lies in-between, in the Now.

At one point in my life, trying to like everyone became an uphill battle - it was a welcome blessing when I realised that I didn't have to. I didn't have to be liked and I didn't have to like anyone; I found freedom in that. I was then free to follow my heart. We change our attitude towards other people when we stop criticising them and realise that we're all the same; we all carry the same problems and tribulations on our shoulders and would like to be free of them. It's a lovely feeling realising we don't need other people to like us; we don't need their approval and no longer care if they don't give it.

We need to come together again and we can only do this by replacing negative thoughts with positive action. Ironically, coming back together again involves further separation - from the physical. When we're walking a path seeking 'peace of mind' we become disconnected from things that were once important in our daily lives; for example, office politics, going shopping, having the latest gadget or not missing the next episode of our favourite soap opera. A spiritual change or rising of consciousness level reveals the futility and monotony of these relatively mundane activities. If we realise the truth of this we can't help but change; it becomes impossible to behave in the same way or to accept the complacency of the society we created. Once realised, there's no way back to the old thought patterns and we don't look for one; we can't live the lie any more. If we *hear* this truth but *don't* realise it, we don't change; hearing the truth is like hearing a nice tune; we have our ears tickled and tap our feet to the beat. The feeling is warm and fuzzy and we like the comfort it brings; however, comfort and pleasure are *all* it brings and these have nothing to do with change.

~~~

Nothing grows without a seed. The mind tells us not to bother thinking outside the box and whether or not we listen to it, is up to us; as the ancient Greek aphorism goes 'Know Thyself' - nothing could be more important or worth knowing. We think we know ourselves but what we know is the ego; it wants to hold us where we are. It wants us to wait for a 'hero' and I don't advise waiting for one. This is a lonely road and few will be prepared to join you on it. If you've read the previous chapters and are still asking yourself questions posed in them or more of your own, then you've already begun letting go of obstacles. If you can marvel at the sun on the horizon or its rays stretching out, if you can see the beauty of creation in them, then you can no longer take the world for granted. There is much magic and beauty all around us. All we have to do is learn to look at it again and to appreciate it - to be grateful and to decide we're through with pain and suffering. We can learn from each new experience and gain a great deal by looking for the lesson it wants to teach us.

~~~

Changing is for each one of us, alone - it can't be shared. As we change we find resistance to our journey, from friends, colleagues and relatives; they can't see what we see and they think we're being misled. This was explained in The Matrix film by 'Agent Smith' who said 'Billions of people [are] just living out their lives, oblivious.'[14] People don't want to think in a different way and they're not interested in spiritual 'truth'. Most people can't 'see' and though a high percentage believes in a god of some form, they're not willing to make any sacrifice to find out whether there is one or not - believing is not the same as knowing. One reason for this is that their world is entirely physical. When we pray, we're asking the universe to come to us; when we change, we make the journey ourselves. Let go! Make the decision and just *let* go! You won't get paid, approval, new friends, 'likes' or 'followers' - your friends will think you've lost the plot and *you* might think you've lost it too. On the other hand, you'll get peace of mind, a sense of purpose and a perspective of the world that you've not seen before. When I watched the glorious sunset I described in the 'preface' I was *everything* and everything was me; I couldn't tell where I began or ended. I've experienced this several times now; these moments are wonderful and can't be explained with words but if I had to give it a go, I'd say it's a disconnection from the mind and body and a reconnection to all that is. From my perspective, letting go is the best thing I ever did.

Chapter 17

Who Am I?

All stories lie between a front and back cover.

I used to lie in the bath repeatedly asking this question and get frustrated about not receiving an answer. I'd think 'Come on ... tell me ... isn't asking the question all I've got to do?' but answers never came. The question isn't a token you feed into a machine and out pops a fortune cookie. Although I can't explain to you how to ask it other than to say 'from your heart'; if you persist, no matter what, what you need to know will come to you.

You are the sun that brings the light
The moon and stars that shine at night
You are the day that ebbs and flows
You are the wind and where it blows ...
... Is still unknown - a mystery
That will unfold for you and me
You are the waves that rush to shore
You are the birds that love to soar
The sand, the wood, the forest too
The sea, the land, the false and true
You are the clouds, the rain and snow
You're up above - You're down below
You are the seed - You are the tree
Responsible for all you see
The fat, the thin, the colour blue
The brown, the black, the yellow too

The light, the dark, the in-between
The play, the act and every scene
You're Adam and You're also Eve
You're all you can and can't perceive
You're in the air and on the ground
You're everything - you are profound
You are the water and the fire
You're all of these and can't expire
The dog, the cat, the cow, the ewe
The innocence - the conscience too
The universe and far beyond
Creation and its loving bond
Every wish you could ask for
You're all of this, and so much more
You're inside and you're outside too
You're every single point of view
You are the One who's lost in space
You are the secret hiding place
You're everything that's born from thought
Pre-anything that you've been taught
You are the game of dot to dot
The wonder is … you are the LOT!
Remove the veil that hides your eyes
Go in and find the greatest prize.

Chapter 18

On Reflection

'Solitary trees, if they grow at all, grow strong.'
Winston Churchill

I mentioned at the beginning of this book that my views may change as I progressed with writing it. This has proved to be the case and posed many editing challenges for me. It's been a steep learning curve as 'I faced myself' and I've been humbled by the experience.

As alluded to earlier, this book is not meant to provide answers and neither does it attempt to do so. Perhaps you've been challenged by some of the questions raised and are now asking some of your own. Like me you may have once held strong views about things in the world that you now see in a different light. If this is the case then this book has achieved its objective.

If we look at things in the world through innocent eyes our views change. It's worth thinking about the effect we have on other people and the effect they have on us. I now see the rather overweight girl who was raising and lowering her arms, as an expression of myself. I can't criticise or feel anything but love for her; I am her. The thoughts I'd had about her came from my education and conditioning - these were projected into my memory from other unhealthy minds. We're all connected and this doesn't mean we belong to a particular family, like the Taylor's or Joneses living 'next door'; our family name is Love.

If we became conscious of this then the world would show us very different experiences, but it's not that simple. It'll take many generations to change the world - if it can be changed at all. Like it or not, this is the 'human experience' and part of grace is accepting things as they are, along with all the horrors life frequently presents to each and every one of us. The beauty of our world remains evident for those who would but look. When we speak to each other we speak more from the mind than the heart. More often than not we swallow the honest words and speak the 'politically correct' or 'impulsive' ones - often whatever's in our mouth comes out, without thought. How many times have you posted a message on social media and then either regretted or when possible, deleted it? If we don't change ourselves then it won't matter how many cakes we bake for a village fête, how much money or goods we donate to good causes or how many doors we knock on with good intentions, we're just papering over the cracks. Without metamorphosis, it's just more of the same. We all have a journey to make; humanity *has* a purpose.

Joining a group and listening to whoever is leading the group doesn't bring clarity. Jiddu Krishnamurti said 'Truth has no tradition - it can't be handed down'[15] and this means no matter who we listen to, we can't 'inherit' their wisdom. We must follow our own processes to attain wisdom. This doesn't mean we can't learn from spiritual teachers, but it does mean we can think about what they say using our intelligence. Recognising our *own* ignorance and how tiny we are relative to the universe brings wisdom, but as long as we remain self-important tending only to our own agenda, we don't find it.

It's a convenient crutch to blame someone else for our predicament. A common belief is 'I can't change because my parents messed me up too much'. It's an excuse put forward by the mind - it's a delay mechanism and it isn't true. If we believe our parents are responsible for our unhappiness, then we must have given them our power - no wonder we can't change. If you believe your parents made you unhappy, then what's preventing you from finding happiness now? If we take back our power, we take back responsibility for ourselves and in doing so, we stop looking for something else to blame or for someone else to change. Things look different when we replace *insecurity* with *power* and although we'll find this disconcerting and scary at first, we learn fast that we're much stronger than we ever thought possible; we recognise just how much we abdicated our responsibility. There's an old proverb that says 'When the student is ready, the master appears'. When we take responsibility for ourselves, do we become our own master?

TWO

Chapter 19

A Bit of a Rant

We speak sweet intentions, but our hearts remain silent.

Earlier in this book I wrote about social media and some of the effects it has on our society. Since then I've given it a lot of thought, and it occurs to me that social media isn't sociable at all - it's asocial. In my experience, these 'social' sites are used increasingly to spread, amongst other things, inspirational quotes - a sort of pick 'n' mix philosophy that comes from a variety of sources from the ancient Greeks to modern day 'life coaches'. We don't spread our *own* inspiration or speak our own words of wisdom. I don't say these quotes should stop; I'm saying let's discuss them in a meaningful way rather than just clicking on a 'like' button and treating them like a piece of art we hang on our 'walls'. Some of these quotes have thousands of likes but only a handful of comments; in what way are we inspired, or inspiring, when we do this? On the whole, inspirational quotes have become the junk mail of social media and its presence is only exceeded by advertising. So many quotes are distributed that their potency and original beauty are greatly diluted and therefore, devoid of meaning and quickly forgotten. I asked a girl, who posts these as though they were confetti, if she can remember what she posted the previous day. Her answer was 'No'. I've had to unfollow quite a few people simply because there's no other way to stop the spam. As if it weren't enough that we're being spammed by advertisers, businesses and scams, we're now spamming our family and friends.

What happens when one of our friends persistently posts things we don't want to see? There are three choices - 'unfriend' the person, delete the posts, or put up with them; whichever choice you make there are bound to be consequences of one type or another. I had a friend who introduced me to her new boyfriend and we became good friends - we all knew each other personally. When she decided to end her relationship with him a year later, she said I should end my friendship with him. I refused, and she was very upset about it, saying that I wasn't a good friend to her. I didn't go further into this drama of hers, or agree to be a go-between passing messages between the two online; needless to say she and I are no longer friends. To me we couldn't have been such good friends in the first place. Humanity can be so silly and immature; during my lifetime I've heard more wisdom from children than I have from adults - it's time for humanity to grow up.

A contact of mine on one of these sites said in a post 'smart phones have made this world a lonelier place' and this is partly true. It's not the phones that have made the world into a lonelier place to live in, but our agreement to live our lives through them - they're a technical accessory to the human mind. Phones can't bring people together, as we must be apart in order to use them. Now we meet in game chat rooms and online messaging platforms - mostly, having no idea with whom we're interacting; it's strictly persona to persona. Instead of friends in real life we've friends on contact lists who we'll probably never meet. The more we frequent social sites the more asocial we become and the more the 'cloud' becomes filled with the phenomenal confusion of our minds; it will never make sense, so there's no point in trying to make sense of it. It's important to see that the cloud is a collective reflection of the mind of humanity - not looking too good right now. Recognising this, goes a long way to finding peace of mind, because we can then walk away without withdrawal symptoms and not rely on a 'cloud' for company or approval. That doesn't mean we have to stop using it - it means we don't have to be online every moment, just in case we miss something that leaves us out of 'the know'.

Technology keeps humanity apart, rather than bringing it together. The internet has become our 'cloak of invisibility' and only *we* choose when, or which masks we don when we're online. We can hide or lay low and choose who goes into which type of friend group, but it's important to see that for each friend group we put on a different mask - we're never complete when we do that. Another tricky part to this is that we hide the parts we like about ourselves the least, so, just as we don't know who we're really talking to, neither do the people we chat with - our screens are always in-between us. At the very least a need to lay low must mean that we don't trust everyone on our friends list in which case, why do we keep them? Some of us have multiple accounts that flicker between visible and invisible modes like fairy lights on a Christmas tree. To bring this into the light, think about how well we know the people we communicate with online; in most cases we don't know if they smoke, how tall they are or if they really live in the country they claim to live in. We don't tend to ask these questions of people online, or even converse with them, and we can't confirm that the picture they put on their profile is actually them, or recent for that matter - it might even be a bot. All we know about these 'friends' is what we've read on their walls - creating the image they want us to form of them - and that's about it. The internet is a place for a meeting of minds, predominantly unhealthy ones. There are more stealth observers on social media websites than there are active participants. If you want proof of this just look at anyone's page who has a reasonable number of friends and see how many actually post.

Mask off   Mask on

Too often we broadcast information, but don't receive it; I've had some 'private' chats with people who keep on typing - message after message - despite my requests that they pause so that I can respond to their original comment. We don't see the person we're talking to as human - people type at us, rather than to us. More often than not we're interested in our own world and don't want to read what anyone else has written. We try to out-do and compete with each other. So social media is a place to broadcast to the masses rather than to an individual and also a place where family members can keep up-to-date with each other. Nothing on these sites is personal or private, yet it's also both. Even if we keep our personal life quiet there's a good chance that someone else may talk about us or post our embarrassing photographs on their page or stealth private groups. Fear of this keeps us from being open and honest because we're always suspicious and *en garde*. We're becoming more and more like the people in E. M. Forster's short story *The Machine Stops* (1909), as we increasingly withdraw from the outside world into our rooms where we spend a great deal of time in front of screens with little to no physical contact. Yes, the internet was *predicted* that far back, before we even had radios let alone televisions. We've become the slaves to the servant we created and we're not looking for our freedom.

Ironically, humanity, long separated, is coming together as One; it's a highly controlled and confused One. It's a depraved One and we created it. It's a One made up entirely of the contents of our minds, which are extremely unhealthy: it's a wireless One. In other words, it removes the need for human physical touch and interaction - it lacks heart. Will future generations be able to read body language at all, or will we be reduced to a 'Swiss army knife' of emoticons on a stick, should we one day meet face to face? The internet can also be used for good. I use it to promote my books in order to raise even just one question in the minds of those who, like me, are curious about their existence or confused about the world we live in. I say I use it to promote my books, but those who know me personally know I don't go too far with that; I'd make a lousy salesperson as I simply don't care enough about it. I trust that those who're meant to read my books will find them; I trust in our universe and I know that none of us are alone. We're all guided and that means you too.

The internet is a fabulous way to reach out, and all conceivable information can be found on it - finding it is just a question of knowing where to look and entering the correct keywords. We can search online for violence or pornographic material and millions of results are found. We can also search for something more meaningful like how humanity could live better lives. Then, proceeding with caution through the abundance of misleading and immature information, it's possible to find little gems that lead to profound changes in our lives. The problem is not the internet - it's the mental health of the people that use it. The internet is the largest library in the world, and in it we've got access to everything we've ever known on this earth - it's also the largest hiding place. There's a great deal on the internet that's healthy for us, and a great deal that isn't - the problem is choice.

Chapter 20

Just Around the Bend

We're waiting for miracles that in our hearts we know won't arrive - we have to make them happen.

The wonders of the universe are so far away and beyond our comprehension - the stars, other galaxies and God(?) We're unable to reach up to touch them, but are still fascinated and frustrated by the skies, because we don't actually have a clue about what's 'out there'. We also hope that whatever we find will be better than we have here. An individual can't build their own rocket to go into outer space in order to take a closer look - they can only accept the selected images that are publicised - and hope that one day they'll mean something to them. Closer to home, good health, happiness, peace on earth and a debt-free life appear to be unattainable for our generation - this is the case for our children too. Let me try to put this into perspective; we're so many billions of people living on a planet that in universal or cosmic terms is less than the size of a speck of dust. We don't know who we are or what our purpose is, yet we run around trying to achieve something called 'success' before our exit into oblivion, heaven or the 'hot place' (you may have some other favourite). We leave chaos in our wake, while waiting for either a miraculous phenomenon to occur, or the arrival of a saviour to put the world to rights - we ignore the odds against these.

No wonder there's so much anguish in this world and no visible hope for our future; we immerse ourselves in the world of films, games and social media; in so many ways they're distractions from our lives and seemingly more interesting. However, they're about as much use to our awareness as a key is without a lock - they're just some of the tools of aberration and procrastination, or to put it another way, they keep us living in ignorance, superstition and fear. The distractions, because we focus so strongly on them, silence the mind as long as we remain engrossed - they're therapy, which is any activity that relieves tension. However, when we stop the mind is noisy again which results in us wanting to go back to the games or whatever distraction is our own particular favourite. We participate in these feel-good-pastimes whether it's by savouring a freshly-brewed cup of coffee, eating chocolate or parading down a high street in a new outfit. Whatever leisure activities we choose, even a noisy rave party, they temporarily release us from our incessant mind chatter. When we find ways to quieten the mind we make them habitual.

When we put all this together with the fact that every human being suffers or has suffered in some way, it's no surprise that we don't want to look inside ourselves - each one of us knows what we've buried so deeply. Understanding the mind of humanity is as complicated and mysterious as understanding the universe. We agree to wait in hope for the future because we can't see how this world or our lives have any worthwhile purpose with things the way they are - there's nothing to gain other than more money or more bills. In general, we get little to no job satisfaction because there's none to be had. Most of our jobs are mundane, mechanical and meaningless. The only result that can come out of a world like this is that more and more people become ill, depressed and increasingly unable to cope with their lives - yet still we wait for a brighter future that's always, just around the bend. Considering the above, we're waiting for miracles that no-one believes in. We can't even *see* the bend, let alone around it.

What we're actually waiting for can vary such as birthdays, anniversaries, Christmas, appointments, annual bonuses, change or retirement. Sometimes we're so keen for them to arrive that we prepare in advance like shopping for Christmas four months earlier, or saving money for our old age; ultimately, we're fine-tuning our deaths before thinking about why we're alive. Instead of living our lives purposefully we're waiting for someone else to improve them for us, like governments or an inspirational speaker / author. If we want to live in a peaceful world we have to work together to raise consciousness; we're One. Let's consider happiness, instead of misery.

A great deal of humanity's time is spent waiting for the future to arrive - our whole lives - but it never arrives and it never will.

It can't arrive for one good reason; the future doesn't exist and therefore, the bend is infinite. We wouldn't queue today to catch a boat arriving next week. We're queuing to live and don't realise that there's only Now. We're queuing up a dead-end waiting for someone else to bring this impossible future to us; science, governments, help books, super heroes and the like. For some strange reason we believe they'll succeed in doing it one day, if not for us then for our children. However, what we actually get is another version of something technical like a bigger, wider, flatter or higher resolution screen, a new artificial flavour or a promise of a cure for cancer in the future. It's barely enough to build up hopes, and doesn't warrant the trust we put in these authorities. All too often we're 'running on the spot' and one day leads into another that isn't very different from the last. Long term, we're rushing to beat the clock, with no idea where we're going and we're allowing ourselves to be entertained while we're doing it.

I once had a dream that took me a few years just to begin to fathom. In it, a voice said 'We're multi-dimensional time travellers'. How is this possible? The future and past exist only in our minds. Only the future can exist on a working clock face as no clock is accurate enough to pinpoint the Now; just like us the clock's hands chase a future they'll never reach - time obscures the Now until the clock stops ticking. The future exists in our imagination - in pictures of a paradise island and in promises of a stress-free existence when we no longer have to work. For the majority of people this couldn't be further from the truth; for some, the greatest bonus is the privilege of free transport passes and a secure retirement home. The past also is only a thought; we live in the past when we dwell on it and the longer we dwell on it the deeper its roots go and the more venomous its poison. Sure there are happy memories too, but the mind is only interested in drawing our attention to the less positive ones. The future and past are thought forms; we wait for the future and remember the past so what precisely are we doing *Now*? If this makes any kind of sense to you then you'll understand when I say that the mind can be seen as a 'time machine'. The contents of the mind are thoughts from our pasts and hopes for our future and we spend our lives collecting and remembering these - thought is never in the Now. We learnt to remember the past and to look forward to the future. How did we lose the Now?

I had an experience many years ago that I couldn't understand, and it couldn't be explained. It was one afternoon after having had a light general anaesthetic and a laparoscopy; I was taking a nap at home, and painkillers. I dreamt I was in my bed and a large picture with a three-inch picture frame around it fell from its hook onto the floor. I leant over in bed to see the damage and the safety glass had cracked in one corner, but not too badly. The room in my dream was exactly the same as the room I was sleeping in. The picture had hung on the wall for four years. Now, this is where my experience gets interesting. I was startled by the dream and woke up. As I lifted my head from the pillow I watched a repeat of the whole event - even the crack was the same. I've never repaired the picture. The future is not something we can wait for and incredibly, I watched the same event twice. I don't need this experience to be analysed. Drugs can cause tricks of the mind but *this* trick can't be explained in any way that would satisfy me. This happened; I was the only witness and was so excited that I spent over two hours on the phone telling friends all about it - of course no one really believed me. People have doubts when something strange happens to someone else, but not when it happens to them - *no-one* can convince us otherwise. When you know, *you know*, and you can never turn your back on it.

There's something wonderful waiting for us just around the bend - but we don't want to see it. We put off self-realisation -

mostly because we think we have time on our side, but we can never have time on our side. Time brings wrinkles and infirmity - not revelations. A young lady once ask me 'How much time do I have here?' How much easier our lives would be if we knew answers to questions like that - perhaps we might think twice about procrastination. We find and defend every excuse to continue with things the way they are; like 'I want to change, but I was hurt, so I can't'. We put up barriers in order to prevent our 'progress'. I put progress in inverted commas because there really is no such thing when it comes to realising who we are. We've nothing at all to learn. Living this life is rather like wandering around a forest looking for something we haven't lost. We can't understand this until we find it. Yes I know this doesn't make complete sense at the moment, but it does when we realise that what we're looking for is not outside but *inside*. Imagine looking out of your lounge window all your life without ever knowing what was in the lounge.

We're already everything we'll ever be, but pretend otherwise. The same young lady (mentioned above) asked me what advice I could give her, so I suggested she observe her mind and find out how it works. She said 'Yes okay, but the observing is hard' and 'I keep myself busy so I don't *have* to think'; this is like calling for help when drowning, but sending away the lifeboat when it arrives. The road to revelation has no bargain basements, no special offers and no group workshops; the work isn't easy, I know, but we can each of us do it if we're serious. We ask 'how can we observe our mind', but in my experience we really don't want to. What we *really* want is to be given confirmation that we *can't* do it; we're looking for a sick-note, so we don't have to be an active participant in raising our consciousness level; we want our 'advisor' to be responsible for our journey, so that *we* don't have to be - in other words, we're skiving. Society is pampered and lazy. It doesn't want change if it has to work for it and it doesn't want to make sacrifices. We want everything delivered to our doorsteps just like our takeaways and shopping. We're not on *our* path to self-realisation when we're dependent on others to show us the way - we're on someone else's and who knows where that will lead.

If we're everything that ever was, or ever will be, why can't we just know it now? In truth, because we don't want it badly enough and put it off for as long as we can; we think we're in control of our lives, but this is so far from the truth. We don't even 'play it safe' - well a few do, but mostly we'd prefer our place to be reserved while we look elsewhere; we like to keep our options open. Here are a few excuses we make to prevent ourselves seeing the truth about our world:

- I'll do it tomorrow.
- I've got a full-time job.
- I've lots of mouths to feed.
- I want to, but I just don't have the time.
- It's alright for you …

Do any of these sound like familiar excuses? These are all arguments put forward by the mind. We're afraid to look around the bend because we're not sure what's there (if anything at all) and the mind keeps us afraid for as long as we allow it to. Just around the bend can seem too far away and too much effort to reach. Going around the bend is an insecure experience and this is a key reason why we don't do it; for some strange reason we believe we've something to lose, like our sanity. We don't want to take chances that we can't guarantee will pay off and there's no complaints department, should things not pan out as we'd like them to - it's a leap of faith. So we bide our time hoping someone will keep *our* seat free for us on the next boat. In other words, we let others do the work, such as scientists or politicians as though they were capable of finding a shortcut and we become their silent audience. The mind is like our car - either our hands are on the wheel or they're not, in which case it'll collide with something sooner or later, unless we take back control of it.

~~~

Do you really believe you're an irrelevant reject of this universe? Two important questions we can ask ourselves are 'Have I reached the highest height I'm capable of reaching' and 'Do I put my heart and soul into the things I want to achieve'. If you answer 'Yes' to either of these, then why are you reading this book? It can be of no use to you. If you answer 'No' to them - well, recognising this is a great step forward, as it were.

The more we delay what we all know innately we must get on with sooner or later, the more our shame and guilt build up. The effect on our health and stress levels are horrendous. I declared to my partner that I was going to stop smoking in exchange for a new laptop. He was looking at them online and called me over to look at a particularly interesting one. I said 'I'd stop smoking for that' and we went out the same day and he bought it for me. Now I was in a bit of a pickle because I'd made a promise and the present didn't feel like a good time to fulfil it - I quite enjoyed smoking. It took me six months to prepare for the mental marathon and after that time, with only two cigarettes left in my packet, I told him I wouldn't buy any more. He doubted me and I don't blame him. He said 'you'll want some later this evening, so we better buy a packet just in case' but I stood my ground and said 'No. These two are the last two'. I smoked and enjoyed them and threw the empty packet into the bin - I've not touched another one since. The guilt I felt over the six months grew and grew and more so because he never mentioned it or reminded me of my promise. The relief I felt after stopping was amazing and I was never tempted to start again. When we put our minds to something and really want to achieve it, we're almost there; the next step is to put the plan into action and then keep our eye on the goal.

Because of our inertia we can't collectively see beyond this reality, but I can assure you this reality is temporary and transitive. Whatever we do has consequences and whatever decisions we make in this life are our responsibility. We can't always see the results of our actions, but that doesn't mean they don't exist. We have to leave this world empty handed - the same way we arrived. Now is the only time to think about what we're doing here, and whether we've enough time to complete it. Humanity is heading somewhere and carrying a tremendous and heavy burden with it. Each one of us can lighten that burden by observing ourselves closely and not passing our grievances and foolishness on for the next generation to sort out. Nothing in this world is worth holding on to, nor is it possible to take it with us when we die. Those who do decide to look further into their minds and question their own dogmas, are mostly considered to be out of touch with reality. Overcoming this criticism may well prove to be the greatest obstacle - it depends on whether you care about the judgement of others or not.

As long as there's a need for approval and a consensus to live in fear, we can't see the world as it truly is. By abdicating our responsibility and putting our trust in other people, we agree to be controlled by them doing what they think is best for us, or rather for *them*. Society doesn't encourage individuality or the questioning of its rituals, rather, it encourages inertia in these matters. We sponsor and commercialise physical strength, beauty, acting ability and wealth, applauding them with awards of one sort or another. But, when a person sees through the charade and wants to change this world into a happier and more loving place to live in, we label them a 'bad influence'; *this* is insanity.

Scotty? Beam me up!

Chapter 21

Completeness

When we stop looking for help, we realise we never needed any.

As a child I was obsessed with the idea of dying and wanted to do so before I reached the age of thirty. Death didn't frighten me at all - I'd become used to the idea through recurrent dreams in which I died - although I did feel fear of the method. Thirty seemed very old to me - it was 'grown-up' and every grown up I'd ever known had been unkind, indifferent or hypocritical towards me; the last thing I ever wanted to be was a grown up. I was fifteen when struck with an insane idea. My family were gathered around the dinner table and as usual, raising their voices at each other - in French - so I'd no idea what they were fighting about and they didn't seem to notice that my sister and I were even in the room - we were invisible and always had been. I left the room unnoticed, went to the bathroom and gathered all the painkillers I could find - there were plenty. I took them up to my bedroom with a couple of glasses of water and sat down in front of my dressing table. One by one I swallowed them, counting them out loud, until I'd taken forty. I felt no fear or emotion, but imagined that this act would bring out some sort of emotion in my father - a change of heart. I left the house and went to the nearest phone booth to call the only friend I had, and told him what I'd done. He took me to the hospital. I still felt no fear or emotion. The stomach pump wasn't fun at all - I rather hated the experience, but harder to swallow was the reaction of my father. He arrived at the hospital, at their request, sat down by my bedside and wrote me a cheque for £50. He handed it to me saying 'buy something to cheer yourself up' and left. I felt as flat as the cheque now lying on my bedside locker. This wasn't how it was supposed to end at all and, apart from a short visit from a doctor to assess my mental state the following morning, no-one ever mentioned the incident again. At this point in my life - and for many years following - I believed I needed my father's love to make me complete. I never got it so unconsciously sought it elsewhere.

~~~

    Divorce and re-marriage are the acceptable norm and a divorcee is often regarded as being 'back on the market'; what a strange term. Blinded by confusion, I was insecure, naïve and searching for a dream - unaware it was only an illusion. My only purpose was to get married, have children and not to make the same mistakes my parents made - putting my children into an orphanage. I married many times because I was unable to discern then what I see clearly now. Foolishly, I believed I could right the wrongs of the past. To believe that something from the outside could make me complete meant I saw myself as *incomplete*. I was searching for a 'normal' family in order to become part of a *whole*, rather than a fragment, but this search is a diversion from what really needs to be done. I wanted to be a better parent to my children than my parents had been to me; this is like looking for a future that can change our past. It's also looking for someone to fulfil our dreams for us and holding up a flag that says 'Rescue Me'.

    This is the life we've been encouraged to strive for through 'happily ever after' films and stories. I was searching for my fairytale-ending before I'd even begun to live. The fantasy became an obsession and I thought about nothing else. I'd no ambitions other than to live in a doll's house, walk through the door wearing a white wedding dress and to have my own front door key to lock the world out - letting someone else take responsibility for me. What I didn't know then is that I was locking myself in. When things inevitably went wrong, I quickly found a replacement crutch to lean on, because I was afraid to be alone. The marital vow 'till death do us part' has lost its importance for most of us and perhaps should be replaced by 'until I wake up' and realise there are no knights in shining armour, no princesses to save, no short-cuts to self-knowledge and no-one who can carry us to our *Self*.

    Never think more of someone than you think of yourself. When we fall for someone, we tend to ignore their shortfalls (or view them as endearing) so that in the rush of romance they appear to be our ideal partner. I now see this as insanity driven by irrational need. We need someone else to be solid for us, to hold our hand, give meaning to our life and give us what we think we lack. In order to live with our *flaws* rather than our *strengths* we look up to someone, creating a symbiotic relationship, but we're not aware we're doing it - it's a survival instinct. What we're really trying to do is *join* ourselves to someone else, but two people can't make each other complete or fill the void in each other's lives. We do it because if we didn't put our hope in others, we'd have to face ourselves.

By looking up to someone else, we place ourselves beneath them. This gives us an excuse to stay exactly where we want to be and they become our *prop* - we surrender to them. The pedestal we've stood them on is constructed from need and desire. In much the same way we look to society to be this 'prop' and get comfort from being a part of something bigger than ourselves - we play a passive role. Deep in our hearts we know that the key to our freedom lies 'within' and the reason we don't admit to it, is because we're not ready to be self-contained.

By finding people we believe need our help or can help us, we somehow feel worthwhile and it avoids us taking a long hard look at ourselves for the more esoteric questions that may give meaning to our lives. What we're really looking for is a distraction from the stresses in our everyday life. If fairy tales are to be believed then in order to live happily ever after, we must find our prince or princess; this only gives us an excuse to believe that our happiness hasn't arrived yet, because of some misfortune. The reality is that these relationships are deep in work, dirty dishes, children, nappies, paying bills, stress, frustration and being able to fluently converse on cultural and 'soap opera' current affairs. Problems arise because just as we want to continue with the *status quo*, so do the people we find. In other words, they don't want to change any more than we do. Initially the relationship feels energised because we've 'balanced' ourselves, but it's only a matter of time before the batteries run down and we realise the truth; we're still incomplete and our companion doesn't have our missing pieces.

We want to be with a new partner twenty four hours a day and if the relationship is based on symbiotic need, sooner or later we'll want to be as far away from each other as possible. This is one of the reasons relationships can become stale; nothing actually changes because we're relying on someone else to make those changes for us. Think of it as two people sitting either end of a see-saw - they're dependent on each other and if one gets off, then the other comes crashing down. However, if a couple find completeness in themselves, rather than each other, they'll stand a good chance of having a healthy and progressive relationship. A relationship in which two roses can bloom side-by-side.

Why do we need to look up to someone else to make us complete? This is a question of faith, but it's a false faith. What we actually look for is our shadow - that which we're afraid to claim as ourselves, which is why we externalise our search. The person we find is doing the same thing - they also feel incomplete. A shadow is not necessarily dark - it's the parts of us that we deny existence to. Someone content to live a wicked life has a light shadow; he knows he's not living in his highest interest, but never listens to that inner voice. However, we're only window shopping and the shop front will always keep us separated. Let me explain this a little more. We're on one side of the glass looking into the shop for what we think we need. What we believe we need is looking straight back at us. So why isn't it a perfect match? Because it's not really us. It's part of somebody else. We already have what we're looking for to make us complete but we're (1) in denial of that and (2) unwilling to confirm it by taking a look. This is an insecurity. We think so little of ourselves that it seems impossible that we're all we ever need. Just as in our high streets, it's in these shop windows that desire is born and this desire can never bear fruit that won't one day rot. One tree can't bear the fruit of another. We see what we want to see, listen for the words we want to hear and only accept that which suits our agenda.

It's also for these reasons that we choose to ignore the mischief of governments. There isn't a soul who doesn't know that governments are corrupt, dysfunctional and never stick to their manifesto promises. They bring poverty, misery, illness, war and neglect to the people they govern. Despite this knowledge we choose to mechanically re-elect them to govern our world. We do this for several reasons including fear, laziness and insecurity - yet few will admit to that. We look to them to do what we believe we can't, yet we know full well they can't either.

~~~

Often we turn our attention to celebrities and see what we want to see via the various forms of media and social interaction outlets. We ignore any notion that the images we have of these icons have been created by others - they're faux. The characters Clint Eastwood plays in the spaghetti westerns are good examples of this; we're led to believe they're tough, indestructible and in complete control of their lives. However, this image is an on-screen image and not the character of the actor off-screen. As a small child I turned my attention to David Cassidy though I'd no idea who he was. I listened to his songs, *I Think I Love You* and *Daydreamer* again and again, imagining I was good enough to be the girl he was singing to - getting lost in the illusion. But it wasn't because I wanted his life - it was because I didn't like my own and because according to the lyrics, he understood me. Listening to his songs gave me temporary relief from what was then, an incredibly noisy mind. It's also about energy - he had it and I didn't and by mimicking him, I felt some of that energy. This is one of the reasons there are so many copycat and lookalike artists in the world - they haven't found their own purpose / skill. The same principle applies when we copy fashion and other trends shown to us through celebrities or advertising campaigns.

When we look closer at what's happening here we see that we only see snapshots of successful people's lives and then wear their names on T-Shirts, or model ourselves on them. We become the character's 'fan' because we feel a void in our own lives and in some odd way they fill it, by proxy. This is an illusion and if the actor so much as trips over a pebble in real life the illusion is either destroyed or ignored. If ignored we continue to believe and make excuses for their momentary lapse and if destroyed, we seek someone else to take their place. Characters on-screen are powerful and influential in our lives, regardless of whether they're villains or heroes and this is true in blockbuster films or the more minor, but no less influential, soap operas. We can't see that the actors are just like us; we see what we want to see, hear what we want to hear and make them into our gods. Like in dreams, we must one day wake up and realise that what we believe to be real, isn't. The word 'fan' is derived from 'fanatic' - that's got to be worth pondering. Following someone else's habits and behaviours is rather like reading someone's book and then writing our name over theirs - plagiarising someone's life. We've our own book to write. We all have the ability to be creative but we don't believe we can do it, even though we do it every moment of our lives.

If someone tries to tell us the truth about the person we glorify, we don't want to know and put up a huge amount of resistance in order to reinforce our beloved delusions. This is true even if the person we're glorifying tells it to us and refuses to accept our irrational inflated opinions of them. Placing someone on a pedestal they're unable to stand on causes problems in relationships; the relationship is based on a false notion and the pedestal will crack under the pressure. Because of this it can never bring peace or happiness, other than of a temporary nature. The situation will always require a victim and someone to be their saviour, who is also incomplete - they need someone to *save* and believe they can do it.

The delusion is more wide-angled than it seems at first glance. On its lowest level it's where a person may choose to remain in an abusive relationship. We often believe we can't survive without the person involved and keep going under the delusion that things will change one day. In a lot of cases we're convinced we're responsible for our partner's behaviour. Why? Because they convinced us of it. By claiming responsibility for someone else's behaviour we're making excuses for them - it's a small price to pay and it serves both parties. This is an evasive tactic we make in order not to take responsibility for ourselves - it's our albatross. On its highest level the delusion requires the worship of an outside and invisible force, such as any one of the variety of gods we worship (metaphysical or physical). Somewhere in-between lay our relationships with our employers, friends and other family members.

There are people who choose to remain where they are in life, and continue making the same mistakes, and there are those who seek them out in order to play out what they enjoy most - control. There are also people who feel an irresistible urge to break the glass and walk away from the destructive and repetitive patterns in their lives. You're one of those, because you're reading this now. More often than not the root causes of this behaviour are irrational fear and apathy. Deep down we already know all we need to know about ourselves and those we come into contact with. If we look closely at our own thoughts we see that we push aside the wise ones in favour of the reckless. Because we don't believe we can survive by ourselves, trust we put in outside forces must, by definition, be misplaced. We put trust in other people to do what we feel unable to do ourselves. A strong character attracts a weaker one, but if we look carefully it's easy to see that the weaker character is in complete control; without the consent of a 'weaker' character to dominate, a strong character has no power. Generally speaking, 'weaker' characters are only weak because they've *forgotten* their own strengths, preferring not to remember them because then, they'd have to take responsibility for themselves. It's this way with society too.

We're dissatisfied with ourselves and hope that someone stronger will save us by whisking us away to a place of safety - anyone will do, as long as it's not us. We've also been taught to think that solutions to problems in our lives lie in things like large bank accounts - measurements of our success. Not true? How many people buy lottery tickets, and how many people buy more than one? By looking up to people who've apparently cracked the problem we can make more excuses about why we can't, by putting their good fortune down to luck or talent. We look up to people who have, or can achieve, what *we* can't, and set them up as our role models, but this mindset is twisted because we can never become them. We set ourselves up to fail and rely on outside forces to stimulate us. It's a way of living our lives through something or somebody else and its root is apathy.

When we look outside for help or completeness, we also look outside for someone to blame when things go wrong in our lives: we want someone to be responsible and someone who can alleviate our pain and suffering. The most obvious example of this is that we leave the world in the hands of the politicians and corporations

- then blame *them* because we're not living in a Garden of Eden - conveniently forgetting that we vote them into power and buy the carrots they dangle in front of us. However, when we're in the driving seat - instead of the 'mind' or a government - there's no need for any adjustment or remedy. There's no need for gender categorisation labels either; weak, strong, housewife or hero; there's no need to try to become something we're not. The only thing we need to *become* is who we already are. We're not fragments but over time we've become 'fragmented'; we're already complete and we only need to realise this. We started believing we're incomplete because we allowed ourselves to be convinced of it, by society. Through vigilance and the observance of our own mind and behaviour, we realise that we're not incomplete at all.

Chapter 22

Mind Dramas

Yesterday has already happened - we don't have to re-master, splice, edit or re-live it.

Every moment we process information picked up from a variety of sources. On a physical level the sources include teachers, media outlets, books, friends, acquaintances and family. This information is then processed through our personal filters, according to our bias and conditioning. It's not until we step back and think about what's happening that the process becomes apparent. The actions of others pull triggers that appeal to, upset or offend us - they also create fear. Whatever our reaction, its roots lie in our past experiences and we allow them to create what becomes a smash-hit drama, in which we're starring. The root of these dramas is often that we don't feel good enough - we feel unworthy and therefore, insecure. The dramas become *real* and set in motion a chain of events producing emotions and reactions that validate them. Our dreams have the same effect on us. I remember once waking with my partner in the morning and he'd felt annoyed that I'd smoked a cigarette, after having recently given them up - but this was just the residual thoughts and feelings from his dream. Nevertheless, the emotions were real for him and though he *knew* I hadn't smoked, he'd found it hard to ignore his dream. Our dreams can seem so real that when we wake up from them we react as though we were really *there* and participating in the storyline. Nightmares from my childhood were exactly like that, and in one recurring dream I used to wake up just as I was being shot. I awoke in a cold sweat with a tight pain in my chest - symptoms of fear or dread, as though it had really happened.

We've been creating the dramas for so long now that we don't realise we're doing it - we absorb the effects like emotional sponges. Take for example watching a film in the cinema. Our reactions to scenes in the film depend on the genre and include, but aren't limited to sadness, remorse, anger, fear, disgust, revelation, shock, horror, compassion and hope. Yet, all we did to bring about these reactions was buy a ticket and take our seat. Nothing happened to us, personally, and we haven't interacted with anyone off-screen. The drama isn't real - it's information from sounds and images perceived by our senses. It's happening in our mind - a hard concept to grasp initially but when it falls into place we wonder how we never noticed it before. We literally, during some scenes, sit on the edge of our seats in fear or anticipation (sometimes both) as the action grips our senses dragging us into the reality of the film as though we were participating in it.

One of the most famous scenes that terrified audiences worldwide was the shower scene in the film *Psycho* (1960), where the character played by Janet Leigh met her end. Auditory and visual memories from this scene remain in our minds. Proof that this happens is that I still remember them now and if you know the film, so do you - they're embedded. There were reports that some people apparently feared getting into their showers after watching *Psycho*. Sound and vision were used to produce the same effect in the film *Jaws* (1975) but instead of dreading a shower, many people feared swimming in the sea after watching it. Our reactions to scenes like these are far stronger when we watch the evolving three-dimensional films because they're more realistic. Sometimes our reactions are so strong that, when we get back home, we double check we've locked all the doors and windows. Why do we like these self-induced fear experiences? Perhaps it's because we survive them and walk out of the cinema unscathed. Perhaps it's because our mind errs on the negative side of life. We enjoy the terror and fear, which is why these films and others like them are produced more and more; demand equals supply. Humanity has become disconnected from what they see in such films - our minds don't see the long-term effects that permeate so deeply into society; such as ignorance, apathy and complacency.

The more we watch such films, the more our reactions to the violence or sex in them are neutralised. Many children watch these films with no *apparent* ill effects and without this content, they'd find them boring and passive. They watch these films from a younger and younger age and when they're not watching them, they get the same *information* from books and games they download. Imagine showing a child an episode of the 1950s / 1970s *Dixon of Dock Green* series today. Its slow and comparatively mild-mannered pace wouldn't hold their attention - it isn't scary or exciting enough. We crave the fast-paced action-packed content for entertainment which matches the increasingly fast-paced and limited perspective of our lives. Consequently, the dramas playing in our minds are just as fearful and fast-paced off-screen as on. We end up not being able to understand the mess and confusion in our minds, as much as we can't understand it in the world; we live in fear and perhaps the biggest fear of all is to be in *silence* - we don't know *how* to be silent. For most people silence means loneliness, but this loneliness is really a fear of being left alone with only our mind for company. I know now that loneliness is an inability to live with our shadow; the noise inside that knows us so well - when we're alone we can't hide from it. The mind forces us to focus on things we'd rather not focus on (ourselves) and it's for this reason we like to keep busy with work, leisure, play, social media, television programmes and music. The louder the noise we can make around us, the less we hear our mind and the less we hear ourselves.

We love extreme drama. We live in fear but we also love the experience of that fear, which is why we love roller-coaster rides and other 'scaries'. There's a ride at the Stratosphere Tower in Las Vegas called *Insanity* that spins people round a mechanical arm at a height of 900 feet, generating 3 'G's. Scarier still is a ride called *Big Shot* at the same tower that generates an experience of 4 'G's and as if that wasn't enough you can now be thrust 30 feet over the building at 30mph, if you so choose. There's plenty of people who want to go on these rides. These so called 'thrill' rides have become more and more terrifying and there's a great demand for them. But we don't enjoy these things just because of an adrenaline hit. What we love most of all is that while we're being terrified, in that moment, we're not thinking about our daily worries. While we're being thrust off a building we're not thinking about relationships, bills, work, mowing the lawn or anything else. We're living carefree right inside that moment - the Now.

Less extreme, are dramas like finding the courage to chat up someone at a club or other social venue - though some people may well prefer to be launched off the Stratosphere Tower at 30mph. Somewhere in between there's going for an interview, going to the dentist or standing in a queue at a supermarket checkout getting irate because the cashier is idly chatting while our frozen produce melts. Many other dramas pass through our minds while we're waiting in queues; the mind loves the opportunity to get our full attention. This is particularly true in traffic jams and some of these have miles of tailbacks. Why do queues affect us? Because we temporarily have no choice but to be still and think while we wait; we've no control and our mind seizes the opportunity to create dramas that occupy us. The word *queue* (15th century) means *tail of a beast* and who could argue with that definition?

Interpersonal relationships are also affected by abstract dramas - mostly imagined. The longer we interact with a person, the more complicated the dramas of our minds regarding them can become. Each interaction reinforces our deep-seated beliefs and prejudices; when you put that alongside our natural tendency to lean towards the *negative*, it's easy to see how resentment builds up - without provocation. For example, let's say that a friend borrowed a book from you six months ago and hasn't returned it. How many times would you run the conversation in your mind about asking for it back, enacting possible outcomes, including ending your friendship? Perhaps you want to forget about it, but your mind won't let you - even in bed as you're trying to sleep it's churning away. Each time you remember it, more resentment builds up. You may feel angry, bitter, rejected or used. Whatever the feelings, they get out of proportion and even permeate your dreams. It's important to realise that you've written a drama and that you're playing and continually rehearsing every part in it, including that of the audience and critics. The chances are your friend is completely unaware of your turmoil and forgotten altogether about the book. A gentle reminder may be all that's needed and your mind will quieten, at least where this subject is concerned. It's far better to have peace of mind than to hold onto a grudge based on an imagined scenario. I remember hearing a joke about a man who wanted to borrow his neighbour's lawnmower and he ran an incredible script through his mind predicting the negative outcome of his request. By the time he knocked on the door and the man answered he said 'You know what ... you can stuff your lawnmower'. This may be a joke, but we do this sort of thing all the time - the mind encourages it. We create the drama out of nothing at all.

There's another drama that plays a part in our lives and that's the long-term random repetitive reminders of past pains and suffering. I call these random because they pop up unexpectedly, while we're doing or thinking about something unconnected. The mind doesn't want us to forget the past and it's constantly reminding us of things; it replays not only the story, but variations of it, even twenty or thirty years after the event. I was haunted for many years by memories of my father, wondering how or what I could do or say that would make him feel differently about me. The more I focused on the situation, the bigger its influence became in my life. As far back as I can remember these painful and damaging thoughts plagued my days and nights; my father was mostly my waking thought and the last one before I went to sleep, which is why he appeared so often in my dreams.

This continued until I was around thirty-five when a psychotherapist explained that I'd given my power to my father; it came as quite a shock to me, because I'd never thought of myself as someone who had had any power to *give* away. I began to take back my power and to see that there were some things in the world I could never change - first and foremost on the list were *other* people. I realised it was possible to change the self-pity, self-hatred, grudges and bitterness that took up so much space in my mind, by taking responsibility for them. I saw that the source of my unhappiness was not my father, but me. I'd discovered that the 'me' I thought myself to be, was in fact a clever and highly manipulative fraud. We too often focus on how other people have hurt us and don't realise that we hurt and judge ourselves far more harshly than anyone else ever could. These dramas hang in frames on the walls of our mind and will remain there until we decide to take them down. The walls we've constructed are reinforced and patrolled by the mind - they're an illusion. We don't have to remain behind them.

We don't just create our *own* dramas, but jump into other people's productions too, regardless of whether we know them or not. One way we do this is to listen to and spread gossip. Why do we do it? Often because we've nothing better to do and nothing more interesting to say or if we do, no-one who wants to listen to it. Often we want to fit in with the person we're talking to and gossip is what's expected in order to rank highly on someone's popularity list. So we spread the latest *newscast* or fabricate another one and marvel at our ingenuity, despite the mini-drama at the back of our minds that knows we don't feel good about it. I bumped into a neighbour of mine a few months ago and she asked if I'd found my dog. I told her I hadn't lost him and she didn't believe me. 'Oh well,' she puzzled 'I suppose it was someone else's dog', before getting into her car and driving off. So I knew I'd been the subject of gossip and it wasn't long before how it started got back to me. We've become expert at gossip and social media has become an unpleasant extension of it. One of the biggest reasons to gossip about other people is that we're dissatisfied with our own lives and another, that we've nothing better to do; we often find their lives more interesting than our own.

Another way we enjoy other people's dramas is by being an audience. We love soap operas, slowing down to look at accidents on the motorway (rubber-necking), standing around watching an ambulance crew and being kept up-to-date with scandals; we have a morbid curiosity and love to make a drama out of a crisis. Our mind also loves to imagine what people might think about us, even though we haven't done anything wrong; a form of insecurity. One example is how we behave when we're leaving a shop with our purchases and the alarm bells ring. Everyone stares as though we've stolen something and though this is not the case, feelings of shame and embarrassment arise as though we'd *actually* committed the act and these feelings arise because we believe other people think we're guilty. We love to think the worst of people and often what we imagine people think about us isn't true; some of the people staring may simply be feeling relief that it wasn't them that set off the alarms. Why do we care about what people think? It's because we seek approval from outside sources and in this scenario at least, what we get is more like condemnation.

~~~

There are many of us who have a need to bring other people into our drama and this is often at the cost of friendship. This situation arises when someone is so engrossed in their own problems - relationship, health, work or family - that they can't see anything outside their own story. Even a good listener tires of listening to the same boyfriend / girlfriend problems again and again and struggles to hide the fact. The *victim* will use this lack of interest to deepen their 'unworthy' or 'nobody cares' beliefs. I'd suggest that we don't actually *want* anyone to listen or even to give us advice; what we seek is a sounding-board and validation of our right to feel miserable, because we believe the severity of our problem warrants it. If we're given this validation, it confirms the belief that we can't change - this is the pay off.

~~~

Our minds and bodies respond to the information they receive and for this reason it's a good idea to choose what information we 'upload' into them; the information becomes who we think we are and influences how we react to the world around us. The mind recalls memories and therefore, the past. We create our dramas from our memories and only we know the script - no-one else has access to it. One way to stop the noise in our heads is to recognise and watch the thoughts coming and going. Initially this isn't easy as our mind wanders off without us realising it, we daydream or even fall asleep. The thoughts come and go like waves on an ocean but we can choose to surf on them or let them roll to the shore; either way they're still part of the ocean - memories. All too often we catch another wave before the one we're riding on breaks. Sometimes my mind catches me out and I ponder some pointless thoughts for longer than necessary. As soon as I recognise this the thoughts dissolve and I can't find them again; it's a bit like going upstairs to get something and then forgetting what it was I went up there for. However, the mind quickly replaces the thought with another and at first, we need to repeat the process often. The mind is *wild* and arguing with it will prove fruitless - it holds all information about you and knows all your strengths and weaknesses. It can be recognised and observed and with that comes a greater understanding of who we are and why we dwell on so much negativity. With this understanding, the mind quietens and we create fewer, if any, dramas in our lives.

It's possible to stop these dramas once we've set our *intention* to end our pain and suffering. However, in order to work with that intention, vigilance is needed to recognise our 'unhealthy' thought patterns as soon as they manifest. For example, contacting an estranged friend or family member can be a tough beast to conquer. More often than not we can't remember what caused the dispute in the first place, or why it's gone on for so long. Pride and foolishness raise their ugly heads *insisting* we hold on to the grudges but by working in line with our 'intention' we can overcome these when we recognise their familiar faces. Mind dramas are the ego's self-defence mechanisms and its armour is strong, particularly when it senses danger. Stubbornness is nothing more than an impenetrable force-field constructed of fears and it's us who are locked behind it. The only obstacle that prevents us from finding peace is *us*. Our ego controls each one of our masks and it's under the protective custody of the mind. The ego loves role-playing games and it's a Master of Disguise.

Chapter 23

Independence

We can depend on not becoming independent.

Independence is something we strive for without comprehending what it is. Amongst other things, the act of seeking independence is seeking separation from the rest of humanity. Countries fight to become independent, children leave home to become independent and we seek well paid employment so that one day we may achieve this *independence*. These are somewhat illusory goals for no matter what, we live in dependence of *something*. If we didn't, we wouldn't be where we are now. Humanity is separated, but it's also dependent on that separation to keep itself going in the direction it believes it has no choice but to follow - it no longer requires *free will*. If we decide to change course and create a peaceful beautiful world to live in, we'll need each other to do it. Humanity is a team, despite its cells pretending to be individuals and this frame of mind has come about through the coordinated efforts of every one of us. However, whether we like it or not we work together; a nail can't drive itself into the wood and a football can't kick itself into the goal. Even air is dependent on the space it occupies and we're dependent on that air for our next breath. It's only man, in his audacity, who believes otherwise - on some level we all know this is pointless.

We're dependent on the society we've created, and it's dependent on us. Each thing in it exists because of another and they can't be separated; everything and everyone is connected and interdependent. You exist because your parents brought you into the world.

- Shops exist because of desires.
- Police exist because of crime.
- Beauty parlours exist because of vanity.
- The poor exist because of the rich.
- Starvation exists because of the greedy.
- Doctors exist because of disease.

- Bullies exist because of victims.

Even excuses exist because of a lack of responsibility. Increasingly, foundations and charities exist because we care only for our own needs - this leaves others to go without. We claim our rights to things we're entitled to, but we've become so self-centred that we care not for those who are unable to claim theirs; instead of supporting them we judge and condemn them. Misery and loneliness exist because of separation - the separation of each and every one of us. Anyone who denies that humanity is separated has forgotten that he's connected to the tramp in the street, the poor, the pitiful and the sorrowful; he's forgotten also that we charge them to live on their own planet. We are One and dependent on each other; the actions of one of us affects the lives of others. Some of these effects are minor and some major - like in wars. We care about ourselves, and not about those who pay the price for our vanities, and we'll continue to do this, all the while charity bridges the gap between us. How come you may ask? Because we're excused from responsibility when we do our bit by dropping our pennies into charity boxes - it doesn't improve the situation if you drop in pounds. If we look at this objectively, it's easy to see that as long as charity exists between us and those in need, people will continue to go without.

Humanity is being willingly driven at high speed to an unknown destination and refusing to consider where it might be going - neither knowing nor caring who the driver is - regardless of the consequences. Humanity blunders on, complaining about the driver's intentions and huffing and puffing at - or blaming - the other passengers for the unfortunate casualties along the way. With nothing more to go on than a tacit agreement between the driver and his passengers to drive where he sees fit - he's been given carte blanche to drive off the edge of a cliff, should he choose to. Yet, despite opportunities to disembark at every stop, humanity chooses to remain on board. The twist in the above analogy is that, long term, the driver doesn't know where he's going either; the driver needs us and we think we need the driver. Taking this analogy to another level - who is this driver? Is anyone at the helm at all, or is the bus being driven by society itself?

Scotty! Do you read me?

~~~

One argument I've heard against the non-existence of independence is 'I'm independent. I go to work, support my family, own my own house, take care of my children and depend on no-one'. This is a specious argument and so easy to dismantle. For one thing, we're dependent on our employers for our salaries, pensions and the continuity of our contract. This argument also shows that you care only for your own agenda and therefore, ignore the needs of the rest of humanity, who belong to this world as equally as you do; it's an 'I'm alright' mentality. Another argument is 'I run my own business'; then you're dependent on your clients, materials, paper, pens, banks and many other things. We're as dependent on society as a child is on its parents; dependence is inescapable for everyone.

Independence = In-*dependence*

A multi-millionaire may seem to be independent but he isn't - far from it; he's less independent than the poverty stricken people in third world countries. Money needs maintenance and he'll need trustworthy staff to manage his life and guard his wealth. Like us, he still needs to eat and drink and more than anything, he's dependent on the silence of the majority to keep him in his privileged position. One of the most difficult things about having money is that we can't let go of it and always want more which in the long run, means more people go without. No matter how much money we accumulate, we still live in pain, uncertainty and a restlessness that's occurred because of our separation.

Look to nature for proof; everything is inter-dependent and that's one of the things that makes it so wonderful - everything needs everything. We too are part of nature and couldn't exist without it, yet have allowed ourselves to become divided in the most insane ways. We'd all like to be independent, and strive for it one way or another. We seek independence because we believe that with it will come this thing called security, but we don't really know what that means. Sure, we can become financially secure, but that won't heal what's hurting inside us and more importantly it won't remove the real sicknesses of our society - fear and apathy being just two of them. Mostly we fear death and in particular, a painful death. Death to each of us is as natural as apples falling from a tree - it will happen.

Even if it were possible to achieve independence, it would be pointless. It would be like the left leg seeking independence from the right. We're connected; each one of us is an essential component in the design of the world that we've created, yet we choose to ignore this fact. We can only function as One, despite our attempts to pretend otherwise. We could achieve what we think of as *freedom*, objectively, by working together - all of us; this planet is rich in food and there's enough to sustain us all. The only difference between the majority and financially secure multi-millionaires, is the size and quality of the cages they live in. The only thing we all *really* need in this world is each other, but for now we have to walk alone, because the crowd aren't ready to see that.

<center>~~~</center>

From a young age we've been subjected to common thoughts and influences. The toys we play with are limiting and designed to help us to fit in with and perpetuate an established and ritualistic society; we learn our ABC's and 123's together with dexterity, physical fitness and hand-eye coordination. Our lives are geared towards becoming independent and in many ways this is a *good* thing, because we *should* be able to stand on our own two feet - taking our allotted places in society; however, this independence is relative and illusory, as no matter how independent we like to think we are, we still depend on so many other things in order that we remain standing; for example, if a person loses their job they look to society to support them until they find another, and without such support they'd fall upon hard times. There are many other examples I could give, and when we start to think about them, we come to realise that we're not at all independent - we're inter-dependent. Understanding this is something, I think, that's missing from our education. We learn all the skills needed to work in either blue or white collar fields. Never are we taught that we can think freely or imaginatively about who we are, where we came from or what we're doing here, or more importantly, where we may be going.

Questioning our way of existence is strongly discouraged, and philosophy is rarely part of any curriculum before we're old enough to attend university, if we do at all - for so many years we've been trained to function in a rigid and unrelenting society, on which we're all dependent for our survival.

Chapter 24

'What if' and Other Worries

Look to the light and the shadows will stretch out behind you.

The question 'What if?' is that bucket of water used to quench the fire of joy, inspiration and hope, which we pour over ourselves - or somebody else does it for us. 'What if?' also gives us permission to worry about something that may or may not happen in the future - it's a pre-order for something that doesn't exist. When we give this a little thought we see that it's a self-limiting activity that saps our valuable energy and fills us with inertia.

'What if?' is close to 'but', inasmuch as it's a clause or condition that cancels out rational thought. Before I go any further, I want to make it clear that there are times when 'What if?' is prudent, but these are not the times I'm talking about. I'm referring to those times when we're not genuinely looking for a solution; For example, 'I want to get out more, *but* what if I get hit by a bus?' or 'I want to leave my job, *but* what if I can't find another one?' 'What if?' and 'but' give us our excuses not to change, and generate a false sense of protection from the future. In other words, by 'worrying', we set the scene to prevent changes in our lives - at least that is our hope. 'Worry', 'What if?', 'but' and 'fretting' are all symptoms of fear. We look for things to worry about, like whether it's going to rain tomorrow ... or perhaps next month. A problem is something that requires a solution, but rather than seeking solutions to our current ones, we choose to find others to worry about that haven't happened yet, and may never happen. By doing this we create a great deal of stress in our bodies, often as though the hypothetical event had actually happened - muscles tighten up, we get chest pains, suffer dread, rely on old familiar comforts and make ourselves ill.

Many people don't *want* solutions to their problems, because in a perverse way their problems define who they are; paradoxically, we know what the solutions are, but prefer to ignore them by pretending that they don't exist or are unattainable. We create problems to worry about by continually putting ourselves in problematic situations; for example, like getting drunk then living in fear of being found out - perhaps by our parents or employers. However, at the same time, we're proud of and even brag about our behaviour to our peers. I remember my sister used to go to school in her uniform, but took more 'suitable' clothing with her to change into for when she truanted with her friends - worrying yet revelling in the fear of being caught. The only reason to live in fear of being found out is that we're ashamed of our own behaviour and if we're ashamed of it, why do it? We see the danger signs and walk straight past them choosing images for ourselves that make us an *acceptable* part of the 'in crowd' - it's all about peer pressure and this comes initially from films, advertising and other forms of media, like magazines.

We don't have our best interests at heart, but expect others to - how strange we are. The mind keeps us in fear of danger regardless of whether that danger exists or not and it's always on guard against attack. The ego wants to survive and is at its happiest when it's not questioned, so to speak. It's having great fun doing whatever it wants to do and when we want to stop its fun it reacts rather like a child that doesn't want to leave a playground - it has a tantrum. Worry is a way for the mind to maintain control and it's through fear-invoking control that we've been dominated for so long. When we begin to think for ourselves, the mind puts up a fight with 'worry warnings'; it creates hypothetical situations that ward off any attempt to reclaim our power. Like the mind, we want to be heard; our personal worries are greater than anyone else's; when we hear someone's story - more tragic than ours - we tend to 'tune out', waiting for a pause long enough to cut in and begin relating our own. When we worry so much about our problems, whether hypothetical or not, we're not interested in the dilemmas of others; the ego loves to be in the limelight and it's *not* a good listener. It's a fact, that there's no-one more interested in what we have to say than ourselves.

Worry is a tool of self-confinement. For example, by worrying that we may get attacked while out shopping, we can get ourselves into such a state that we stop going out altogether - barricading ourselves into a believed place of 'safety'. I know of a lady who taped up her letterbox out of fear someone would set her house on fire during the London riots; she doesn't even live in London, but was gripped by the broadcasts and therefore, the worry.

My mother didn't leave her house for years, except for hospital appointments and for Christmas dinner at my brother's house - he would pick her up and take her back again. Her only interest in the outside world came from the television which reinforced her beliefs that the outside world was unsafe - confirming that her decision not to go out of the house was the correct one, even just to sit in the garden. My mother *hated* the sun and spirituality and was never afraid to make that perfectly clear. Despite my mother never wanting to leave the house she'd still complain about the weather, even though it made no difference to her world. The more we worry about something the more extreme its effect on us. Worry is a mechanism for withdrawing from society and the outside world - it's living in a padded cell that's locked, from the inside. My mother and I were unable to converse much on the telephone because she wanted to discuss world and local scandals and to share her abhorrence of them for hours on end, but I didn't. We can never find light when we search for it in a darkened room so it's a bit of a waste of time trying, especially when someone is perfectly happy living in the dark.

'What if?' is a journey that never ends; we explore every possible negative scenario and each time we do, we increase the burden that we voluntarily carry. Worry increases our personal torment and the last thing we want to hear is that our worries are unfounded. What, after all, would we do without them? Worry is a distraction from other things we're avoiding. We use it to make excuses about why we can't help ourselves right now because if we did, the results *could* be 'catastrophic'. We create the monster we want to worry about and then flog ourselves with its whip - we flog other people with it as well, like friends or family. The monster wants to live and we continuously feed it. More than anything it wants an ally - someone to listen to its story.

Society doesn't help at all. The media provides us with a huge range of things to worry about; war, terrorism, sickness, poverty, eviction and violence are just a few examples of these. Closer to home are things like divorce, loneliness and family security; for example, we give our children mobile phones so we can remain in constant contact with them. Children are also given great worries to contend with. They're put under enormous pressure to 'perform' well in school and they're constantly pushed and examined; now they're given SATs tests at the age of seven. For what? To prove they have good memories? What exactly are we grooming them for? The parents worry and so do the children. Later in life these children are put under greater stresses to prepare for more exams, wait months for their exam results and worry continuously about whether they've failed them. The stress is too much for some children who will always worry about 'What if I fail?' and they can spend the rest of their lives feeling inadequate if they do. I recently heard about a young boy who committed suicide because he didn't do well in his exams. A healthy society would not do this to its children and we're always too quick to blame the 'system'; *we* created this system - we *are* the system.

Worry is always negative. Who in their right mind worries about 'What if I pass my exams?' We don't worry about *success* or whether we'll enjoy the next episode of a favourite soap opera but we *do* worry about failure and how we'd fill the 'slot' if our favourite series came to an end. So what is this worry? Quite simply it's a fear of something negative; we fear it because we exclude the positives that match. For example, we talk ourselves into worrying about 'What if?' the world comes to an end but we don't want to consider 'What if it doesn't?' Worry is a low vibrational sickness of society and it's deeply embedded. We can however, choose not to live in fear and make a decision to raise our level of consciousness. This involves a decision not to submit to the will of our mind but to take back control of it; the mind, when it's in control, is negative. When I tried to talk to my mother about going out into the garden, or even walking to the gate, she became aggressive and insisted 'I can't!' But she *could* and didn't even want to try, strongly resenting any suggestion that might lead her away from her self-imprisonment. When we confine ourselves, we keep the doors closed and don't welcome any suggestion that they can be re-opened.

Just as we've locked ourselves inside our homes, we lock ourselves behind screens and through them we contact 'the world'. Even if we've been talking to someone for years online, when push comes to shove, we're mostly afraid to give out our address or phone number; our online relationships generally depend on our continued anonymity and we now have 'contacts' instead of 'friendships'. Generally speaking, we don't want to meet up with our contacts online and one of the reasons for this is that they would see us as we really are - without our masks. We worry about what's on the outside of our 'security' because we 'What if?' about someone is violent or a con-man. We worry about meeting face-to-face someone that we met *online* as we would a stranger knocking on our front door. I've known a few people to shy away when I've offered to send them a copy of my book - they didn't want to give me their address. We've been taught so well to fear strangers and people that we meet online. When we worry continuously about anything at all we're living in fear, and as long as we agree to live in fear we'll remain prisoners of our mind, and of the society we created.

~~~

Sometimes, we feel a more extreme form of fear - dread! The best way I can describe what I mean by dread is to say that it feels as though something dark and ominous has passed right through us. The emotions that go with this feeling are terror, apprehension and an overwhelming feeling of imminent danger. We learn early on to be afraid, from listening to various types of bedtime stories such as *Peter Pan*, *The Three Little Pigs* or perhaps *Jack and the Beanstalk*. They're hardly friendly foundations for young, innocent and highly impressionable children. Some of us also picked up these fears from our parents or guardians and some are inherited from other sources. We learnt to be afraid of pirates, giants, tyrants, ogres, burglars under the bed and bogeymen - the list goes on and on. Thought is memory; if you can think it, it's from memory. We've built up all these memories of fears and added to them from sources such as films and other media. More than the memories themselves we remember the emotions related to them - the actual feeling of fear - and it's important to note here that our fears are nothing more than thoughts. We've all learnt something about history and what stands out more than anything, is that we've always been at war and that war is brutal and heartless. Our minds are awash with horrific images so it's no wonder we know so well how to feel afraid. There's no greater fear than dread so what can we do about it. When it happens, just allow it to pass through - be aware of it and don't resist; it can't harm you in any way. As you become more aware it will occur less frequently and less intensely. This process is faster if we don't subject ourselves to further conditioning from violent films, newscasts or other media terrors. We can choose to watch it all and suffer further, or to focus on our awareness and the beauty of the Now. Here are a few more 'What if?' scenarios for you to ponder over:

- What if you're truly amazing?
- What if we're missing the point?
- What if we're here to experience?
- What if we stopped fighting?
- What if there's no such thing as death?
- What if our purpose is to raise our consciousness level?

Imagine dying and then being offered the opportunity to return for a week. The world would be exactly as it is right now, but you couldn't be harmed in any way. What would you choose to do with that week that you haven't done before? I've asked a few friends this and not one could come up with an answer.

You're everything! You're a conduit through which the divine speaks and there's no 'What if?' about it. No-one can see through your eyes - your perspective belongs to you alone. We know so much more than we've been led to believe and deep down we've no doubts - no academic institution can teach us this. Our energy has been suppressed and *misused*, but I can assure you it's still there and no-one can take it away from us, come what may. It's not born and it doesn't die. The only reasons we can't feel it is because we haven't been encouraged to ask relevant questions about our lives, and our focus has been directed towards the transient rather than the infinite - it's based on desire. We listen with our ears and see with our eyes but these are so limited in Universal terms; more important than what we see and hear, are what we *don't* and this information is available to anyone - no exclusions and no prejudices. Consciousness can be perceived only through the heart. You're the world ... Now ... not in the future.

Chapter 25

Emotions and Energy

Emotions are a highly volatile energetic state.

Our emotions are one of the most powerful energetic forces that we know of. Unchecked, mishandled or manipulated, negative emotions can cause enormous harm to ourselves and those around us - the reverberations of which can be felt for many years to come. Conversely, positive emotions can be a force for much good - no-one ever went to war because they were joyful and happy. How we greet each day and move through it depends on our emotions, but not only that, other people's emotions can have an effect on us too. It isn't until we *sit down quietly* and think about this, that the connection between emotions and energy become apparent.

We've all experienced walking down the road and felt the mood of other people as they approach us. Often we sense if they're angry, afraid, depressed, happy, sad, guilty, ashamed or hostile. What we're actually picking up on is their energy (emotional state) and we adjust our actions accordingly; for example, if we perceive that an approaching group of people is hostile we may choose to cross the road, thus avoiding potential conflict. There are many ways in which we read people's body language; we know when they look downcast, suspicious or walk with confidence. Their emotions might have come from pent up feelings from many years ago or an event they experienced just moments earlier, like meeting up with an old friend. We read each other all the time without realising that we're doing it and have no idea how we pick up this energetic information; the process is automatic and acts rather like an early warning system enabling us to react appropriately; this is how we read our world.

Most of us have felt the energy in a room when we unsuspectingly walk in on an argument, or the tension between two people who aren't speaking to each other. Perhaps you've been present when an employee is being humiliated by their boss? I'm sure we can all relate to one of these 'cut the atmosphere with a knife' situations.

In most cases differences aren't put aside when we arrive because the need to continue with being *right* is greater than any need to be polite for the sake of someone else - neither party will give in even for a moment. The energy is bouncing around and because it's low vibration we feel tense, awkward and 'dragged down' with an urgent need to leave the room as soon as possible. These situations are difficult enough to cope with, but they exist in the 'physical world' and at least we can be sure of the mood and personality of the company we're in. However, the internet has removed vital parts of our 'communication skills' and now we can't rely on gestures or other physical cues like intonation or eye-contact. We act purely on the words, images and emoticons we see on the screen, which can so easily be - and often are - misconstrued.

In this world of the web, we transmit and receive energetic information - instantly - when communicating with each other. This makes it hard to accurately judge what the person we're talking to is *really* feeling, or what their true intentions are; feelings can't be replaced or translated by crude digital expressions of our faces. We can't hide our feelings when we're standing face-to-face, but online we've the option of telling a different story. For example the acronym for 'rolling on the floor laughing' - 'rofl'. Often this is not what we're feeling at all, and we know no-one actually does it. Depending on the conversation we could be crying and at the same time typing 'rofl' in order to hide our emotions; for example, hurt feelings. 'Rofl' can be a mask to cover our emotions or intentions; we portray ourselves as invulnerable. We can hide our intentions when we talk face-to-face as well, but this is much harder to do and sometimes our true feelings stand out a mile. Imagine a face-to-face conversation where you take the time to choose which facial expression you're going to display. This idea is ridiculous, but this is *exactly* what we do online and it can get awkward if we accidentally click on the wrong emoticon and press send - we can't do that when we're talking face-to-face but we *can* get away with it online. We live in a world of choreographed feelings and emotions manifested as emoticons. The emoticons are a representation of our 'virtual persona' and more often than not, this is vastly different from the physical one - it's just another mask.

Politicians and actors (amongst others) are trained in all aspects of body language so that they know how to stand, smile, position their hands and how to make eye-contact for best effect. There's a great deal more to this language and we're pretty expert at it - even without training. In the case of politicians, they learn it in order to convince the public to believe in them and feign personal strength and ability. The fact that they have to *learn* it means they don't have the right character for the job, which is why they need a fake persona. If we need to be taught how to be convincing, then we don't believe in what we're saying and for the well-trained eye, the deception is obvious. Humanity is genius when it comes to creating characters, which is how we can become such good actors and create things like caricatures or puppets so well. In order to become a good actor or politician we have to be able to hide our true self and in particular, our true emotions. Body language is a tool that can make or break a politician, actor or perhaps a salesman; if their energy isn't tuned in correctly, we're unconvinced by them.

~~~

If we look at online videos that allow comments we often see capitalisation (SHOUTING), which makes these remarks antagonistic and therefore awaiting a response from anyone who'll pick up on the energy - it's a trap. Shouting is an emotional outburst that states what we're saying doesn't hold enough weight on its own, which is why it needs to be reinforced. It also tells the reader, quite clearly, that whoever is shouting isn't going to listen to anyone's responses. If the comments don't get responded to, they end right there, but if we reply to the comment then a string of further and more heated abuse follows - just about everyone is aware of how nasty these threads can become. Whoever wrote the comment loves the reactions that help him to express himself to the rest of humanity, in the way that he chooses - he feeds off their energy. Those who continuously respond, also like the way the aggressor's hostile comments make them feel. The aggressors love the power it gives them, because they can't experience it in their *real* life; likewise, others must enjoy being caught in their net. I doubt anyone has ever given someone a 'telling off' online and successfully changed their attitude - quite the contrary. These threads act as magnets for those looking to vent their spleen on the world; whoever is shouting on these threads is really expressing his pent up feelings and the louder he shouts, the more emotional he becomes, and the more energy he leaves on the threads to be picked up by other viewers, should they choose to pick it up. These threads are powerful emotional outlets and people feel safe venting on them. More often than not a thread is attacked because something in it resonated with the aggressor - he doesn't feel good and neither do the respondents - sometimes it's due to pure mischief.

This pattern is similar to our relationship with governments or other authorities; they call the shots and we respond, but we don't change them when we're silent and they're not listening well enough to the few who do speak out. If we choose to walk away (say 'No'), then they have no power, for their power comes from our willingness to respond to them. Next time you walk past a newsagent look at the headlines in the papers - they're capitalised and bold (both are shouting). This powerful energy affects us and our response is as negative as the headline intended it to be - our emotions have been hijacked and someone else is in control of how we feel. When we realise this we're able to take back control of our emotions and the headlines lose their power over us - we don't pick up the energy they emit. What's happening between us all is an energetic exchange; if we don't control our own power, someone else will.

Emotion = e-motion = energy in motion

People who pick up on this energy can still feel it even months or years after it was written. The same applies to re-reading a much-treasured stack of love letters or a sad film we watch again and again. We feel and react with the same emotions as if we're seeing them for the first time - whoever sees them - in varying degrees - feels the emotion. Energy flows out of us, and it flows back in. We're constantly sending out and absorbing energy to and from a variety of sources and it's important to become aware of this. We may leave our house one morning feeling buoyant, in which case this is the energy we're emitting; however, seeing sensational headlines or meeting a friend who's always full of 'doom and gloom' can drain that energy and suddenly, that buoyant feeling evaporates and is replaced with a feeling of imminent doom.

~~~

I'd like to share with you something that happened to me not so long ago when I lived in France. I was driving with my partner to a builder's merchant. A police car appeared behind me and flagged us over. When we stopped, two policemen got out. One of them looked friendly enough, but the other had an aggressive strut and was clearly 'on a mission'. Even though it wasn't sunny, he was wearing sunglasses. I smiled, but it was not returned. I asked the officer why I'd been stopped and he said that I'd been talking on a mobile phone whilst I was driving and he looked really pleased that he'd caught me. From that point on he couldn't express the energy he wanted to because I got out, offered him my handbag and gestured that he could search it and my car too. I informed him that he was mistaken, because neither I nor my partner had a mobile phone with us. He insisted that we did, and his partner smiled, knowing full well that his colleague was stuck in a hole of his own digging. He never admitted his error or apologised and went off frustrated. This unexpressed energy is always re-absorbed and will probably get expressed all the stronger on the next person he pulls over, or perhaps in some other situation. All our pent up emotions must get expressed and vented sooner or later.

Think of a kettle about to boil. The gas or electricity is the life force, and the water our emotions. If we block the vent that allows the steam to escape then pressure builds up inside. Sooner or later the kettle will explode and then there'll be a sudden outburst of steam (emotion). When we 'let off steam' in this way, it hurts us, and anyone unfortunate enough to be caught in the blast. However, when we allow the steam to escape freely no harm is done and the system works harmoniously. Allowing emotions to control us prevents us from being grounded - we're always reacting and rarely in a calm state. It's unwise to allow ourselves to be led by our emotions - they're highly unstable.

Moods are also emotions and they can last for weeks or years. We often don't know why we're in a particular mood, because we can't remember when we started feeling it. However, moods come from suppressed emotions and manifest themselves in things like irritation or anger. We've all met people who are always irritated or angry. My entire teens and twenties were spent in these moods but occasionally I could vent, often by grabbing something and hurling it across the room; I wasn't too selective about what or where I threw objects either. Once when I threw a brick, I missed a man's head by an inch. When pent up emotions erupt, we don't think about what we're going to break or the consequences - rational thought ceases. This is because the need to get these pent up feelings out of our system is far greater than the value of any object we might break in the process. We don't think in these situations - we're in the Now. Sometimes we feel much better after our outburst and sometimes the effects aren't so visible, but they're still there. When we become aware of what's actually going on we're able to regain control of our lives, if we want to.

~~~

Energy is a collective and powerful experience when we're gathered in groups. The energy bounces between us and multiplies - like at music festivals. Freddie Mercury for example, could really stir up an audience - the bigger the crowd the more powerful the energy. Supporters at a football match emit an enormous amount of energy because of their sheer numbers. Have you ever heard one end of a stadium when a goal is scored? The energy from the crowd can spur on a team to perform well. If the supporters of *Team A* are more encouraging and active than the supporters in *Team B* the chances are *Team A* will win the match - they're spurred on because of the energy emitted by the crowd. We can feel this energy even if we're not there, by watching it on the television for example. Those who gather en masse in a pub to watch a match also feel the energy and consequently, roar out with their own. Similarly, a person sitting at home alone watching a match (I know one of these) will lift off his seat when his team scores a goal - distance is no object for this energy.

Emotions need to be expressed and we'd struggle to interact without them. How could we understand each other if we didn't cry, laugh, sulk, shout or get angry for example? These are our ways of relating to each other and also to ourselves. Like with the steam in the kettle, our emotions need to escape from inside us. Because emotions are energy and we pick up on them, some amusing situations can occur. If for example a person is laughing uncontrollably, it's almost impossible not to join in, even if we don't know what they're laughing at - it's infectious and can result in a painful stitch; this type of laughter is physically exhausting. Similarly, we can pick up on energy from yawning or crying by another person and involuntarily do the same - mirroring their emotions.

Emotions are an energetic way of expressing what we're feeling at the time. Too often, we don't recognise why we're feeling them at all - the cause can go back many years. Way into my thirties I'd react to events in much the same way as I did in my childhood. If I saw events on television that were similar to things that happened to me, I'd feel the same emotions, such as sadness, fear, dread and frustration; what I saw acted as a trigger to re-awaken older memories - it was as though I were re-living the experience through somebody else. Unlike online with emoticons, these emotions aren't always controllable - particularly when what caused them is deep-seated. How we cope with emotion is different for everybody. Some people can cry over minor events, and others can't cry at all. These emotions, however, belong to all of us and like with my example of a kettle, too often we suppress them.

Peace of mind can *only* be found within; the process is hard work and a full-time job on top of whatever else we have to do. However, the more we get to grips with being honest about our own behaviour and character, the more peaceful we become inside. By becoming aware of our own energy, in for example, conversations with other people, we become self-regulating and consequently, our world becomes a calmer place to live in. But, if we speak aggressively and constantly complain about other people we're putting out a lot of negativity, which comes back and adds to the burden we already carry - we become negativity generators. Another way to look at this is to ask 'If you met yourself, would you want to be your own friend?' or when you're talking to someone, online or off, ask yourself whether you'd like to receive the energy you're emitting. It doesn't matter if we slip up every now and then, what matters is persevering, getting to really know ourselves, and with practice we'll slip less and less. A most important point about energy is to avoid or say goodbye to those who continually want to drain ours. Because we pick up on energy it's not a good idea to remain in the company of those who want to pass theirs onto us - unless it's good energy. Our own energy is precious, and when we become aware of the significance of that knowledge, we're no longer willing to part with it, or to take on the negative energy of others - it's not even an option.

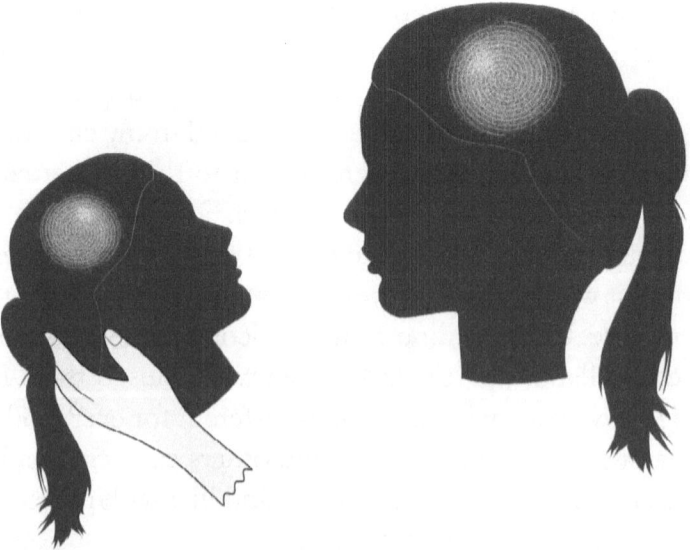

Chapter 26

Observation

To observe effectively we need to zoom out - not in.

When we think about observation it tends to fall into one of three categories: something we do, like looking through a telescope, something we have, like the ability to be observant and something we're under, like the ubiquitous security camera. When I first heard the term 'observation' with regard to my thoughts and looking for truth within, I couldn't for the life of me see how that was possible. All I could think of was that my veins, lungs, kidneys and other internal bodily parts are just that - on the inside - and my eyes look outwards. There was also a bigger problem - I'd no idea what I was supposed to be observing or what this so-called 'Now' was all about. Before even *starting* this 'observation', my mind stuck out its big foot and tripped me up - I hadn't reached the first hurdle and was already flat on my face. I'd barely picked myself up when my mind pushed me back down again. It told me I wasn't qualified to do the job and that I'm not an 'expert'. Can anyone be more of an expert on who I really am than *me*? We're generally conditioned to believe that we need professional help for such matters - we most certainly don't for this. Experience is a good teacher but it's no substitute for observation and no-one else can observe for us. It doesn't matter how good the teacher is if the student is inattentive or unwilling to learn. When we observe our mad world it becomes clear that we're all students, no matter what our age, who still have much to learn. No one person can observe or change the chaos of the world, but we can, without a shadow of a doubt, change ourselves and only this will produce the results that most people refuse to give credence to.

Observing ourselves can be tough because our mind interferes all the time - it's insistent and keeps us blinkered within a limited physical perspective, and doesn't have any spare time for airy-fairy will-o'-the-wisp metaphysical nonsense. It wants information, hard evidence, debate, paperwork, action, analysis, cross-referencing and above all, it wants to maintain control - it doesn't want our interference. When considering a project for example, the mind reminds us of our previous failures and tells us there's not much point in wasting our precious time, as based on past evidence, the project is *doomed*. The mind wants to keep us in our place - it doesn't want to change and it doesn't want a 'co-director'. When we decide to observe our thoughts the mind interrupts and before we know it, often before we've even begun, we check for email messages, phone a friend, make a drink, water the garden, awaken an ancient grudge or clean out a kitchen cupboard. We may find that we're staring at a blank wall, a crack on the ceiling and eerily, sometimes we're staring at nothing at all, dreamily unaware of our thoughts - in the latter case we're 'out of mind'. The mind knows a lot of pressing postponement techniques to occupy us with, should we become distracted from what it thinks we should be doing. More often than not it bombards us with thoughts that keep us in 'take no action' mode. On the whole we're unaware of the process but it's possible, if we pay attention, to observe the insane stream of unimportant data coming and going.

The mind does all this so fast that, by the time we've finished our chores, we've quite forgotten what it was we wanted to consider; the thought has been dispersed and replaced by a multitude of other 'high priority' tasks that are more to the mind's liking. Whenever we want freedom from the chatter of our mind it presents us with meaningless hypnotic distractions. It's only a matter of time before questions like 'Who Am I?' for example, shout out our name again and the cycle recommences.

~~~

There's something that drives us to question the meaning of our existence, at some point in our lives. It's always there at the back of our minds, but we tend to ignore it in favour of more 'important' pastimes. Initially, the concepts are unfathomable, as our minds have been trained to be rigid and negative. Generally, the only acceptable knowledge is from our education and various other equally ritualised conditioning processes. Searching for alternative information in books and on the internet about the mystery schools, hidden secrets or this thing called 'enlightenment' is like wallpapering over the existing paper in a room - the lumps and bumps will show through. We have to *first* strip off the old embedded ideas, prejudices and beliefs etc. There are so many layers to get through and lots of elbow grease is needed. This metaphorical room is our responsibility alone, and no-one can do the work for us - it's unpaid and arduous. The room is a part of each and every one of us and it's 'Private Property'; we own it outright and always will. It's our 'observatory' and we've let it get into a dreadful mess - sooner or later, we need to clear it out. At this point, I'd like to mention that we don't need books or the internet in order to enquire about our true nature; this knowledge is accessible to everyone on the planet and with observation, if we truly want to, we'll find what we're looking for. So never give up because you already know all of this - you're remembering it. Don't trust in the mind that will tell you there's 'no proof' and that you're 'wasting your time', because everybody needs to see and think about this too, if it's going to have any impact on society; don't trust in *anything* other than your own rational voice. *You* are your world and only *you* can change it.

Initially, when we observe ourselves; for example, by challenging the mind, things seem rather strange. Imagine you're driving along a motorway and you're almost out of petrol. You're about to pass a service station and the sign tells you there's another station in forty miles. The mind tells us we'll make it to the second station but the other voice in our heads says 'be wise and fill up here'. However, we tend to listen to the mind, as this is our familiar habit, but, this habit gets us into familiar situations - the mind lives on the edge of danger. If we're serious about observing and changing our destructive habits, we'll begin to listen to the more rational voice. When we challenge the negativity of our mind we're moving 'mountains' and the more we do it, the more it becomes second nature, as it were. The first step is to accept that we have destructive habits and the second, to decide that we're through with suffering; yes, it's a decision we have to make. When we make a decision to listen to the rational voice something in us changes; the more we listen to it, the more we change and the less we pollute our world with negative energy and thought; we no longer allow the insane mind to control our thoughts - we break the pattern and change direction. In other words, we become responsible for our thoughts and choose which to listen to. When we change direction a great deal about human behaviour becomes clear.

Let's take the newspapers and television broadcasts for example, and think about why we pay so much attention to them. We never get good news except maybe when someone has grown a giant pumpkin exceeding any previously seen at garden shows, or a politician kisses a baby on the cheek - other than that we may get the occasional good news, but it's not *our* good news and it doesn't benefit humanity in any way. Some people say they *have* to keep up with the news, but these papers get read, the stories get spread in concentrated horror via other media (we call it *social*) and then, before we've fully digested yesterday's bad news, another helping is offered up to tempt our hungry minds. Absorbing this bad news every day is never beneficial - it's nothing more than regularly feeding on 'anxiety and depression' flavoured snacks. Consumed daily, this 'food' becomes bland, and no longer startles us - even though we proclaim 'horror'. If we don't read the news, people think we don't care or that we're closing our eyes to *reality* and if we do then at best we can only join in the spreading of bad news; we can't, practically, do anything about any of it. This doesn't make sense to me at all and if that's 'reality' why do we want to hold onto it so badly? When we pull away from the *River of Disaster* - in which all things flow - we observe it from a distance and therefore, from a wider perspective. We observe that humanity, on the whole, really doesn't want to change the world it's living in - otherwise, why is there so much resistance to dispense with the things that drag us down so much? Removing this negative force from our lives has many benefits on our health and mental well-being - life slows down and with it the chaos in our mind.

As ideas and realisations fall into unfamiliar places, and things we once thought were solid, like our world, aren't any more, all lies get revealed; the hardest lies of all to accept are those we've been telling ourselves for so long - yes, we all tell them at some point in our lives. One of the reasons this is hard to cope with is that in the past, we've projected our abhorrence of lies onto others and now we realise that *we* do it too. Applying the social labels 'liar' or 'hypocrite' to ourselves is a hard-hitting experience - like catching sight of ourselves in a mirror and being appalled by our own reflection. It quickly becomes apparent that we're no better than anyone else in this world - a humbling and surprisingly liberating experience.

At this point we've two choices - ignore what we've seen, as we've done for many years, or continue to observe these ever-evolving revelations. Each time we recognise a shortcoming in ourselves is like stripping off one of our masks; these have become so adhered to our faces that we don't realise we're wearing them. On a deeper level of this observation is the revelation that what we've criticised in others was a projection from deep within ourselves. We're so deeply conditioned against being duped by scams, con-artists or dodgy-builders for example, that we don't recognise we're conning ourselves.

The biggest lie that permeates society is that our life is an accident of nature, and that there's nothing after it. We one hundred percent physicalise our existence and kid ourselves that there's nothing after our deaths. But this is a cop out - it's an excuse to justify our temporary enjoyment of the pleasures we cherish so much. We justify this enjoyment in order that we don't have to make an effort to change our habitual behaviour; for example, abstaining from wild parties, playing non-stop games or drinking alcohol and eating to excess - anyone who tries to tell us otherwise is labelled a 'party pooper'. We're just a bit too quick to stick critical labels on anyone who disagrees with our conditioned beliefs, even though we don't believe them ourselves. However, these things make our lives more bearable because we forget or at least ignore our problems, albeit temporarily. The mind is more than able to continue this unproductive cycle and plays 'devil's advocate' when it comes to the welfare of humanity. It does this by ignoring our connection to consciousness and putting our thoughts and insights down to something physical; in other words, it makes consciousness, or Spirit, into something 'biodegradable' and therefore 'disposable'. We trample down our conscience, always looking to people who'll provide *proofs* to confirm what we want to believe. When we hear what we don't want to hear (like perhaps from this book) although we can see it makes sense, we convince ourselves that it doesn't. We excuse ourselves and seek new reasons not to think on what our lives are really about.

We can observe our behaviour in many situations and this is necessary, if we want to end our suffering. One way to do this is to watch our reactions to others; for example, by comparing what we're thinking when we talk to them, with what we're actually saying - more often than not they don't match. We can also compare what we really think about someone when we tell them they 'look good', when we don't mean it. By observing in these ways we begin to realise that we're far from honest and then as that realisation sinks in and becomes palatable, we change our behaviour accordingly. My life changed for the better when I took responsibility for my thoughts and how I felt about other people changed too. Without being prepared to go through a process of self-observation this wouldn't have been possible. When we make an excuse about why we can't do something or change an obsessive habit we're in fact, confirming our will to remain just as we are. All these things are observable and tell us a great deal about ourselves, if we're prepared to examine them honestly and closely enough. Mostly we're not prepared to be honest about our own behaviour because, let's face it, we're all headstrong and determined to do what we want, regardless of whether it's in our best interest or not; none of us like being judged by anyone else - let alone by *ourselves*. Even if we ask the advice of others, we generally have no intention of listening to it. Paramount to self-reflection is a willingness to criticise our own motives, actions and intentions, rather than those of others. This book and everything in it are me doing the same - how can it be anything else? The book came into being because I made an active decision to follow the 'white rabbit'; I've no choice but to continue following it and this is where it has led me, so far.

By stripping off our masks, usually one at a time, we make ourselves vulnerable to outside criticism - something nobody really enjoys. Ironically, when this happens we no longer care what anyone thinks *or* need their approval. This process can take time but I assure you it's worth the effort; when we dispense with the need for masks, barriers or approval we find that our fears subside. We wear so many of these masks and only realise we're wearing them after self reflecting, *without* allowing our pride or ego to interfere. There are many ways to know ourselves and once we start enquiring one thing leads to another - it's a continuous process. The masks represent a sort of defence system; they act as a shield to hide anything that might render us vulnerable to attack. Have you ever noticed your thoughts during an argument or how you try to stop yourself revealing your true feelings to the person you're arguing with? Have you noticed your thoughts when arguing and know you're being obstinate, but won't admit to it? Try to catch your thoughts during these moments and recognise how ingenious we are when it comes to defending 'our corner' regardless of rights or wrongs; I've done quite a lot of this in my time, and now, each time I end up laughing at the genius of it all. Try also to notice your thoughts when you're going to sleep. At first when I did this I always fell asleep before I got the chance to notice patterns but now, after persevering, I watch my own 'demons' coming and going and find it rather fun to do. Catch yourself out at the supermarket when you're paying for shopping; watch the thoughts about the cashier or the people in front of or behind you. I used to find some people rather intimidating and others I felt I had power over. What are you thinking now, about me or yourself, after reading this paragraph? Perhaps you're judging me and that's okay, but more important than judging me is to recognise and accept that you're doing it, rather than getting caught up in the critical net. The point of observation is not to watch me, but to watch *you* - this is the tricky part. The more we observe, the more we see and the more we change - provided we resist the urge to be 'hurt' or 'offended'. Through this type of observation it becomes obvious that there's an observer that's neither the ego nor the mind.

The ego dominates and is defended by the mind that created it. As long as we believe that we're the ego, we're unable to observe ourselves and the reason for this is that we filter out the *Observer*. By this subterfuge we've become accustomed to seeing the world through *conditioned* eyes as others would have us see it, rather than as it is. This predicament leaves us psychologically ill-equipped to *observe* the world we've created, so that close examination of something 'magnificent' - like a flower, or the gathering of its pollen by a bee - becomes just a scientific and logical exercise, as opposed to something *miraculous* - the mind filters out true beauty. Close observation of our mind is impossible without the awareness of our two contradictory voices. Once we become aware of their differences it becomes difficult, if not impossible, to ignore the voice that's in our highest interest.

Chapter 27

Attachment

We place a noose around our necks and tell ourselves it'll keep us from falling.

At its simplest level, attachment is anything or anyone that we allow to control our thoughts and actions, in any given situation. A dog's movements are restricted when he's attached to a lead, and a train carriage coupled to its engine isn't going anywhere, unless it's being pulled. The dog goes where its owner wants it to, and the carriage as far along the track as the engine pulls it. In these examples, attachment enables *control* and it's a good thing that it does - who knows what the dog may get up to if he were let loose, or what damage would result from a carriage that became uncoupled from its engine. There are many ways in which attachment is vital; for example, mountain climbers rely on being attached to their rope, power cables to their poles and our arms and legs to our bodies - to say nothing of our heads! There are also many ways in which attachment is a detriment to our lives; for example, when we live in fear of losing our home, job or partner - when the very thought of losing them leaves us feeling insecure.

At this point, I find myself wondering which attachment has the greatest power over humanity - money or people. In my experience, my family were largely controlled by their love of money and material things - what these did for their image and bank accounts meant far more to them than any person ever could. My sister and I were placed in an orphanage so that my father could work and play freely, without the responsibility of small children around. It's funny how we become so attached to the things that we can never keep; people love accumulating money as much as they love beating a high score in a game - there's something about having more and more that runs through our veins - whether it be pounds, points, food or online followers. Given a choice, there are many that would give up their children or partner, rather than their home or belongings; if we're honest with ourselves, we love things far more than we do people, even our own children. It becomes a question of priority.

Imagine you're in a relationship, and you've managed to scrape together enough money to buy your own home - albeit with a hefty mortgage. After a year or two of bliss, things begin to turn sour and you separate. What then becomes more important - salvaging as much as you can from your investment, or the loss of your partner? I've had much experience of these situations both of my own, and of other people who I've known; in every case money and belongings were the highest priority, for at least one of the parties involved. Over time, we become attached to the things we call 'ours' and I'd suggest this is not a good thing. For one thing, they prevent us from having honest and open relationships, because those belongings get in the way of them; take for example, so-called prenuptial agreements - a sort of 'I love you, but, should we split up I want to leave with everything that was mine before we got into this relationship, intact'; this sort of relationship is hardly based on love. Even if there's not an agreement, we still tend to want what was ours to begin with - of course there are exceptions, but I doubt there are many of them.

Money aside, we can become so attached to people that we get ourselves into a situation in which we believe we can't live without them. I've done this many times and as a result gone from one relationship to another, because I feared being alone again. When a relationship ends, for whatever reason, it takes us out of our comfort zone and we have to rebuild our lives, routines and rituals all over again - from scratch. Even the thought of such disruption can be too much to cope with; so much so, that many people stay in unhealthy relationships because they don't want to experience the upheaval of starting all over again, or living alone. I got to the point where I'd hear myself saying 'oh well, here I go again' and somehow, always landed back on my feet - stronger after each experience. The attachment here is to a *relationship*, rather than the person - an attachment to someone, *anyone,* to share the burden of this life with; let's face it, life, in our society, isn't exactly a 'picnic'.

Attachment to friends and family can be similarly burdensome; things run smoothly until, as we've probably all experienced, they don't. People have different ideas about what they expect from each other and the problem here is that rarely are two people's thoughts in line. As an example, let's take a family whose children have left home; the parents then decide to split up and go their separate ways, and the children are less than happy about it - this scenario is not uncommon. Children expect their parents to remain together and keep the home fires burning, as it were, even though they no longer have a need for it. When I was living on the River Thames my children rarely came to visit me, and then only at my request; when I told them I was going to move to France they weren't particularly happy about it and at the time, I was rather surprised by this; however, they didn't need me around, so I went anyway; had things been different I would perhaps have stayed in England. Sometimes we *have* to let go of the things holding us in place - the things to which we've granted control of our lives - sentimentality especially, can stop us from realising our dreams or expanding on our visions. We get one chance to do the things we want to do in this life and, provided we don't shed our responsibilities, we should go out and do them.

As mentioned earlier, attachment enables control and this is not always a good thing - least of all when we're on a conscientious spiritual 'journey'. Many years ago I was attached to a particular vegetarian snack from a local store. I ate them for years and then one day couldn't find them; the store had decided not to stock them anymore, which left me at a bit of a loss as to what to replace them with. I'd become dependent on that store for the supply, assuming quite wrongly that this product would always be available. After that I developed a recipe for my own similar alternative snacks, which tasted better. When we're attached to something, it has control over us and there's a risk of losing it - we also stifle our own creativity. For example, when we follow - to the letter - a recipe, we forget that we can adapt them for ourselves. Anything we're attached to controls us; even the simple things, like a chair, mug or book: we can for example, become upset if someone sits in our favourite chair, drinks from our mug or dog-ears one of our books; interference with the things we're attached to bring out our negative feelings and emotions - they have control over us. Remember, the engine pull's the carriage, the owner controls the dog.

I've a friend who keeps all her clothes. She's in her mid-fifties and still has some of her clothes from when she was fifteen. How she finds the room to store them all is beyond me, but her double fitted wardrobes are packed from top to bottom including the one in her spare room. Depending on the season, these clothes get moved into and out of her attic. When I asked why she does this her reply was 'I don't like waste'. Surely it's more of a waste to cram them into cupboards and not use them. Anyway, I don't believe this excuse and I'd suggest, it's more about a fear of loss or going without one day. It's also about attachment to the memories of when she wore them and her lost youth. She won't like me writing about her *lost youth*, but then I'll remind her of a request for me to make her younger than her *mid-fifties*.

Just as we hold onto belongings, we hold onto memories of them - in photograph frames or diaries. For example, I remember many years ago being unable to delete a friend's phone number from my address book - he'd died six months earlier. For the first few months I used to dial the number hoping he'd answer. Realising that we must let go is difficult, but we all have to do it sooner or later. I couldn't comprehend how someone could leave and never come back. Humanity coming together only to suffer and then separate again made no sense to me then, and it still doesn't. We shed tears year after year for the same pains - digging up past memories and reliving the misery of them again and again. The tears we shed expressed our loss years ago, but they won't help now. Sorrow is difficult to live with - it's devastating and can take a long time to recover from. There's no need to forget our friends who die, but it's possible to re-frame how we look at death - we all die sooner or later. We have to stop looking at death as though it were unnatural - it's as natural as our births. Yes, we can die from terrible illnesses, but death itself is *not* an illness and there's no need to treat it as such. Death from illness is simply death brought about sooner than we would die naturally. Illness is a dreadful thing but if we look at it objectively then surely it would be prudent to ask 'Why is there so much illness in this world?', which we can do something about, rather than 'Why is there so much death?', which we can't.

Observing our actions enables us to question them. For example, we can examine whether a process we hold onto is good for us, by asking:

- Is this in my highest interest?
- Have I reached my fullest potential?
- Am I doing myself more harm than good?
- Do I want these nightmares to end?

When we ask the above questions the honest answer can only be 'Yes' or 'No'. However, too often we reply 'Yes, but' or 'No, but'. 'But', in this sense, is a weasel word - an escape route that *qualifies* our answer. It's a limitation we place on ourselves and it's nothing more than resistance to letting go of our self-directed dramas. We can, if we choose to, resist that resistance. 'But' is attachment; 'yes' and 'but' can't exist harmoniously together and neither can 'no' and 'but'. 'But' is the excuse we use to disagree with the 'yes' or 'no'. 'But' is a clause, a condition and a doubt. 'yes, but' or 'no, but' are formulas that can't be solved. 'But' is a self-imposed mitigation. 'But' is the small print; it's our terms and conditions before signing.

The greatest attachment of all is to our ego. The ego is born from the mind - it's a manifestation of it - the mind also creates our 'virtual' ego. The mind wants to hold on to its control and we don't particularly care who's in charge - as long as it's not us. We've absorbed our environment through religion, society, family, culture and education - now we project selective parts of it as our *self* - our ego.

Ego = Energy Going Out.

What we project and put on display as 'who we are' is our ego, but it's not who we truly are. Ego is the force that hides our true nature - it's our disguise and the image of ourselves that we project onto others. Whatever we project produces a reaction in our own lives; for one thing, we have to keep up the façade, which means we have to hide behind our masks. We're multi-faceted, not just a body, and we don't realise it. We cling onto the ego, feeding it when it so desires, and it's not until we recognise it for what it is - a faux entity - that we're able to shed our masks, at which point the world becomes a very different place to live in.

Have you ever had a bad argument with someone and been really angry with them? We say things we don't mean and then feel shame and guilt when we reflect on it later on. On another level, we know that the hurtful things we said came from our 'shadow' and it *does* mean them. We want to stop ourselves but we're unable to. Our reactions to events are protective of any part of us that'll be left vulnerable when we're 'under attack'.

It's only by reflecting on our character and observing how we react in certain situations that we become aware of our separation from the rest of the world. Separation leads us to believe that we're better or worse than everyone else. We place a barrier between the two and keep it tightly closed, allowing no trespassers. It's only in anger or other highly emotional moments that our shadow bursts forth, sometimes with devastating effects; for example, when our backs are up against a wall. Why do we need it? It's a part of us and without it we're incomplete. By locking our shadow away we're unable to cope with everything put in front of us. We need to deflate the ego and embrace our shadow, so that they become one. When they do there's no need to wear masks - thus enabling us to relax our grip and let go of the fear that our 'dark side' might be exposed. Though our shadow has the capacity to embrace 'hell' itself, it doesn't mean we have to go there. The shadow isn't all dark however; there is much we hide that is *good* too; such as, talents we don't have the confidence to develop, or healthy emotions that we fear to express; when we hide something, it's because we don't want anyone else to find it. When our shadow and ego become one, we're no longer afraid of 'vulnerability' and we no longer feel threatened by society - we then appear to the outside world as we really are and more importantly, we appear to *ourselves* as we really are.

Attachments keep us living in the past; perhaps in a constant state of sorrow because someone we loved died, or a state of mistrust, hatred or anger caused by some other experience. These attachments can literally make us physically and psychologically ill. As I've discussed before, our minds are inclined toward the negative and therefore, the things that upset us in the past are the things that play on our minds now. We can all remember events that brought joy into our lives, even momentarily; for example, when we received a gift, or on our wedding day, or a chance meeting, but they rarely occupy our minds except for the odd sentimental moments as we glance at a picture on a shelf, or the gift we were once given. When we become aware of our daily thoughts and activities we gain a greater understanding of the things that make us 'tick' - with that understanding, we take back control of our lives; we can't control society as a whole, but we can control how we interact within it.

Letting go of our attachments doesn't mean letting go of all people and things; it means not allowing them to control what you do, think or feel - it makes you master of yourself. There are those who won't be happy about that, but then they're free to let go of *you*, should they wish to, and they invariably do; *if* they do, then they weren't a positive force in your life to begin with. As we let go of attachments our awareness is bound to change; the things we once thought of as precious become meaningless, and the people we once thought of as friends can become more distant, unless they grow with you. To grow in awareness does require a certain amount of sacrifice - obviously; we can't change *and* at the same time, remain the same. We must first strip ourselves of *everything* - then and only then can we don new clothes.

Once we realise just how much control attachments have over our lives and make the decision to take it back, where do we start? That's a good question, and it's likely that a 'one-size-fits-all' answer is impossible. I can tell you how I did it, which might give you pointers in helping you make a start. To begin with, I had lots of DVDs and books that I was never going to watch or read again and decided to take them to a charity shop, which I did, albeit bit by bit. There were some that I put back on the shelf 'just in case', but it wasn't long before I got rid of those as well. I came to love the empty spaces on my shelves, and the fact that when I bought a new DVD I didn't have to find a space to cram it into. I then turned my attention to my clothes and shoes and anything that I hadn't worn for the last five years, sentiment aside, followed the trail of the DVDs and books.

I started small, tackled the easier things first and then moved onto the larger and more difficult ones - only we, as individuals, know what they are. When past memories torment me, as they still do at times, I look directly at them, ask where they came from and what they're doing in my mind right now. I tell myself that I am 'here', 'now', and that these thoughts have nothing whatsoever to do with me, and they disperse. Doing this on a regular basis brings joy, a warmth and a knowledge that what we're doing is *good* for us - it's habit forming, and it's a good and beneficial habit to get into. Just as with my book shelves, I've come to love the empty spaces in my mind; whereas it was once crammed with controlling clutter from the past, it's now light and airy; thoughts creep in again, as they do, but then I take back control, repeat the process and reap the benefits.

Chapter 28

On Faith

*Faith is a personal thing that can't be conveyed -
it burns within.*

I'd just finished writing my chapter 'Observation' when a lady, with what she called a 'burning question' asked her friends online 'What keeps you faithful?' My reply was 'Faithful to what?' It was then I realised that up until that moment, I'd never thought about what faith is. Faith is a multi-faceted word that generally gets people's backs up, because of its strong religious connotations. I told a friend that I was writing a chapter about *faith* and before telling him anything about it I asked what his initial reaction was to the word. He replied 'My first thought on the word faith, is that all the miseries of the world have been ignored because of it.' Faith and religion are words so tightly entwined that they're practically indistinguishable; the meaning of both words can be confusing - too much pain and poisoned memories are associated with them. To consider 'faith' we first need to untangle it from religion - and any other interpretation or influence - so that it stands separate, untainted by dogma.

In my opinion, faith is often confused with belief and hope and all three are taken to mean the same thing - to me, that's an error. To believe, is not to *know* that something is true but rather it's a personal preference. We choose to believe something not because it's false or true but because it's convenient or suits our circumstances or culture to believe it - belief doesn't make something true. Hope, on the other hand, is waiting for a future event that may never arrive - rather like hoping that a bus we're waiting for will arrive, but not knowing for certain that it's coming. Faith is far harder to define and for this reason, hard to have. Faith is more like waiting for a bus, but knowing it *will* arrive at some point - there's no duality and therefore, no doubt. Faith is a combination of 'knowing' and 'trusting', without seeing, and with those comes a realisation that there's so much more we don't know about our world and can't know under our present circumstances. Faith is felt by our very essence and as our faith increases, it can't be shaken, as it isn't based on anything we've been taught. 'Hope' is a calculated risk, and 'belief' requires no evidence; both however, are roads that can lead to faith - it's embedded in our hearts. To try to explain the meaning of faith and how we can feel it is difficult because mere words just can't do it; we have to look *between* the lines where words don't exist.

Trying to describe faith, is rather like trying to describe what vanilla tastes like - we have to taste it for ourselves. Faith is something that grows and the process begins when we decide to look for truth - it grows alone, inside us. What keeps me faithful on my road and gives meaning to my life is knowing that in this physical world, there's absolutely nothing worth striving for. One way to think about this is to see what *changes* in the world, and through that process, realise what doesn't; we were once babies, grew taller, our features changed, our walk, the way we talk, what we know and what we don't know, but there's a part of us that doesn't change at all; it's been there since we were born - our awareness - and when we realise this our faith increases.

~~~

The uncovering of truth begins with the disposal of our illusions - by questioning. This is a materialistic world where commercialism thrives at the expense of human welfare. It's not always the *things* we create that do the damage, but that we create them without regard or thought for the good of our world or humanity. We don't see ourselves as *connected*; we're One, but have become separated, greedy and afraid. As long as we've desires and separation in the world or see life as one continuous effort, nothing will change. My faith began to develop when I saw there was nothing in this world that could make me complete - I'd reached an impasse. In other words, my faith grew when I let go of the struggle to become something or someone I wasn't. That left me rather in limbo; I didn't 'fit in' anywhere, but was still 'here' and knew I still had something to discover. It was when I stopped trying to fit in, that I realised I could *only* find completeness in myself; it's *only* when we're prepared to stop swimming upstream that the struggle ends.

In the past I'd sometimes go to a shopping centre or high street just to look around, but rarely found anything to buy because there was nothing I actually needed or wanted. Nothing could fill the space I felt between me and the rest of the world. I felt utterly bored and unchallenged in these vacuous environments. I found these shopping centres soulless, despite the presence of the heaving crowd and was amazed at the rush they were in to buy things, particularly at Christmas time. I'd sit in a café watching people coming and going, queuing to pay for things they probably didn't need, telling off their children (or not), while security guards strutted around keeping an eagle eye on 'potential' criminals. The noise, from the chatter of consumers, and each shop playing a different beat on its sound system was hypnotic and deafening. I could never concentrate on my reading or writing - things I loved to do in cafés. No matter where I went, I felt as though I was invisible - at times that was a lonely experience. Now I see this loneliness as having been my greatest *gift*; it enabled me to think long and hard about everything, and that's been paramount on my journey to find out who I am. Because of this feeling of being an *outsider* I was able to look at the world from a distance - from a different perspective. Among other things I saw clearly that even with their new purchases, the people wandering around were unhappy - there were no smiling faces - they were as lost in this world as I was. I didn't like what I saw and despite childhood longings, I no longer wanted to be a part of the crowd. What I needed to find out before anything else, was who I'm *not* and the above experiences helped me to do just that; the process of developing faith at this point, was one of negation.

We're driven by an innate desire to know or to discover 'something', and reminded of it *if* we choose to think about the inane rituals of our lives - we perform them but can't always see the emptiness they fill us with. When I realised that everything we could want in this world was pointless I became down-hearted. However, this changed how I saw the world and I very soon lost all my fear of it; the root of fear must ultimately be a *fear of dying* and I pulled that root right out of the ground. Someone asked me recently what the last line of my autobiography would be and I said 'I came to this world with nothing and I'm leaving empty-handed.' I'd come to the realisation that there's a purpose to our lives but it's not to be found in the pursuit of meaningless activities or the accumulation of possessions that we can't take with us when we die. When we raise our consciousness levels there comes a time when possessions, gadgets and empty pursuits, although they have their place and can be great fun, lose their novelty appeal. What once served as a distraction from the knowledge that we have a higher purpose becomes empty and fatuous - it did for me at least.

Thinking about these things and the insanity of believing that the magnificent human body with all its non-physical accessories (thought, hope, love, laughter etc.), and the capability we have for carrying out atrocities has led me to know that there's far more to us than *composting* material and that this isn't apparent until we pay attention to it. Thinking about life and death and how little we do in between them is a valuable activity; we're born, educated, taught fear, work, retire and then die. There's a great deal more to us than we generally see and considering that last list, it's no wonder that in our suffering we occupy ourselves with trivial entertainments that simply pass the time, ignoring the inevitable finale.

The pieces fall into place when we eliminate regulatory, conditioned and limiting beliefs. In doing so, new levels of consciousness open up to us. However, when we continue to fill our lives with horror stories, how can we reasonably expect to find *peace* or *happiness* - all we're going to find are nightmares. Wherever we go we take ourselves with us; no matter how much we want to escape the drudgery of our lives, we can't do it without first freeing ourselves from our prisons. So for example, if we hear a new song that inspires us, as they do, we revel in the greatness of the artist or writer, but not in our own. We put our faith in others rather than in ourselves. Words in songs, films or books can invite us to become inspired, but they can't free us from ourselves no matter how many times we listen to them, unless that inspiration turns into action. In 'Just Around the Bend' I mentioned an experience I once had when a picture fell from my bedroom wall. Inexplicable events like these build faith, but only if we resist the urge to dismiss them as coincidence, or listen to the unconsidered explanations of others who think we've 'lost the plot'. As long as we don't use the voice we've been given, by allowing others to represent us, we'll remain in our shells of hope and belief.

Faith, in my opinion, is the assurance that I'm doing what's right for me - to write what I feel passionate about and to put my heart and soul into it. As long as we live with a need to fit in with things the world wants us to do we'll never find fulfillment. I know I'm best suited to writing from my heart and I've an enormous amount of faith in that. I fought it for many years and used to feel pretty inadequate when someone would say 'find what you love in the world and do it' and all I could think was 'I don't *love* anything'. But that was a lie and one of the reasons I couldn't write when I was younger was that I'd no faith in my ability, which meant no one else did either. In other words, I already knew what I loved but didn't feel competent enough to do it, or believe I could make a living at it. So I buried what was true for me and pursued some of the things society encourages us to pursue; romance, family, fitness, arts and crafts and being a 'good citizen', but I never found fulfillment in any of them. This attitude was further moulded by my father, who insisted that I find a profession that pays well - my father put income before anything else. However, I never found anything that made me feel at home in the world; something was still missing and when everyone was having a good time at parties and social venues, I was unable to enjoy them. I'd a huge void in my life that no-one nor anything could fill; still I continued the struggle to do things I deep down knew were not in my best interest. Once the ways of the world became pointless to me, I was free to find my own way, but as long as I tried to fit in somewhere I didn't belong, I was stuck. One change that occurs when faith develops is that this nagging feeling of not belonging ends; there's a deep and inexplicable knowing that we *do* belong. Accepting that I have a purpose, and that I'm not 'deluded' or 'need to see someone', has made my life meaningful and worthwhile. When we can't see the fruits of our efforts; they become as exhausting as running on the spot, and equally frustrating - we know that tomorrow will bring more of the same. We can be sure of the same depressive news in the newspapers, political arguments and sad faces worldwide. With faith comes a knowing that what we're pursuing *is* worthy of our attention; the faith we have is in *ourselves* and no longer in, or dependent on others.

Each one of us is unique and special - we have a talent we can fine tune; life is not pointless and doesn't have to be full of turmoil and pain. It's this way because we choose to enjoy the things that our system produces, even though we know full well the consequences of producing them. We demand more and more of the same because, to be frank, we don't know what else to do with our time. We unwisely choose to let others be responsible for the world we live in - we don't want, or know how to do it ourselves. We've put all our belief and hope in a system that destroys all things beautiful and all that has achieved is worldwide misery, guilt and shame. It can be difficult to understand why our world is the way it is, particularly at our level of consciousness, but we have to persevere with our journey, rather than give up. There's no point in waiting for the world to change - it isn't going to get any better. On the contrary, things are heading in the direction of more madness. We need to change the only thing we *can* change - ourselves - and have faith that everything else will work out just as it's meant to do. If we don't change, neither will our world. So whereas my friend's first thought was that 'all the miseries of the world had been ignored because of' *faith*, in fact, they've been ignored because of the lack of it.

Chapter 29

Intention

Intention is a powerful energetic force that creates our world.

What do I mean by intention? Intention is the outcome we want from any kind of action we take to achieve our purpose or goal, but it's not the action itself. Intention is what motivates us to do the things we do and if we're not motivated, we become lethargic, bored and mischievous. The intention behind our actions is not necessarily good; quite often we seek results that aren't good for us at all, like if we take revenge on someone, or act with menace in mind. For example, when we're driving along a motorway and feel a need to overtake the car in front, perhaps because the driver is too slow for our liking - perhaps he's driving an 'old banger' that we feel is less impressive than our own car. Our intention may be to show our ability to drive faster, to show off our car, or we may genuinely want to pass by without any mal-thoughts for the other driver. From my experiences in this situation, people mostly want to get 'in front' as though there were a stigma associated with driving behind another car, or to be more precise, another person; yes, I've done it too. I feel that one of the reasons we do these things is to try to prove to ourselves that we're in some way superior to the person in front of us; the ego loves to show off and it's also looking for security, or at least recognition. Most people who needlessly overtake tend to slow down once they're in front, which confirms that they just wanted to 'be there'. We're not generally honest with ourselves about our intentions; the excuses we make are the *permission* for our actions. In the example above, the driver may not like driving behind another car, but convinces himself that the car in front is driving too slowly, thereby justifying his own manoeuvres.

Another important part of our intentions is that they're not always clear, which is how we get into a bit of a muddle at times - often achieving something other than what we intended. When I didn't know what to do with my life the struggle was there because my intention wasn't clear; I didn't know what I really wanted, or so I kept telling myself. As a child I wanted a guitar, but I now know that it wasn't to become a brilliant guitarist - it was to write songs; I've always loved writing. Having unclear intentions is often a refusal to follow our heart, mostly because of a lack of faith in ourselves rather than in others. We push our dreams aside, not because of inability, but because if we set the intention we'd have to get on with it - we're expert procrastinators. It's for this reason that we become stuck in jobs that don't motivate us; we're doing them purely to pay the bills, buy new toys and prepare ourselves for retirement, rather than to fulfil our dreams - now not later. It's possible to love our work and when we love what we're doing, it isn't work at all. Okay, so maybe we can't make a good living doing what we really love to do, but as long as we can earn enough to live on, it's more fulfilling than the drudgery of working at something that doesn't inspire or challenge us. There's not much that's more depressing than spending our days doing things we don't like doing. When we get out of our own way, putting aside our fears and insecurities, it clears the path for us to achieve our full potential, though admittedly we can feel rather unsteady at first, it's a step in the right direction.

We don't always do the *right* things for the *right* reasons and not many of us consider the importance of our motives, before carrying out our actions. If we did, there are times that we'd be horrified by our own connivance, manipulative and often spiteful intentions. Take for example, Christmas time when we give gifts to family members, including those we give out of *obligation* to those we don't like, often buying a 'that'll do' present just to get it out of the way. We spend a lot of time choosing gifts for people we care for, but precious little on those we don't. I think we've all done that 'unwanted gift' thing from the previous year - we give it to someone else. I've known people deliberately buy someone a gift in the full knowledge that they wouldn't like it and others who like to 'balance' the scales, choosing gifts of equal value to the ones they expect to receive - this is not the same as a prior arrangement to spend a fixed amount on each other. Either way, this type of gift giving is more perfunctory than a well-intentioned thought out gift. There's another way we like to give gifts and that's in order to gain the approval or love of others - this intention never gets the desired results and that's because money can't buy love or approval - nothing can.

I 'over-gave' gifts for many years for the wrong reasons - to gain approval. All I gained were people around me who were no good for me. I attracted people who waited around in my life for the next gift, or others who took offence at them. One of my sisters took offence. If she came to my house and admired something I had, I'd give it to her, but she took this to be an act of superiority on my part rather than a loving and generous one. In the end, she stopped admiring anything and I refrained from giving her things. We know why we give things to people, but can't know the mind or trigger that we pull when we give a gift to someone else. Although I gave things for what I considered to be the right reasons - I was never materialistic - there was an underlying intention on my part to gain their approval. From my sister's point of view, she thought I was suggesting that she couldn't afford to buy these things on her own.

We're One; we really are. If we take time to reflect on this, we see it's not just our intentions that count, but the collective intention of everyone else as well. Intention is energy and when the energy we put out isn't good, neither is what comes back. In the case of our intentionally giving someone a gift they won't want, along with the *gift* we're giving negative energy and this comes back to us, usually in the form of a lack of gratitude from a disappointed and underwhelmed recipient, and maybe a gift *we* don't like in the future - repercussions and revenge ensuring the continuity of the cycle. Multiply that by everyone who gives just for the sake of it and that's a lot of negative energy bouncing around. If you don't believe all this, observe how the feel-good level of the lights on the trees, the tinsel and the carols at Christmas time is lowered by the chaos and frenetic activity of shoppers. Also, observe yourself when you're giving gifts or receiving them - be aware of your heartfelt intentions, and disappointments. How would you feel if you gave a gift to someone who didn't give one back to you? We've lost the art of *giving* and not expecting anything in return.

I remember once being in a hurry to cross a road that wasn't very busy, and didn't feel like walking the distance to the zebra crossing. So I crossed where I was, because I consider myself to be intelligent enough to know when it's safe to do so. The only vehicle that passed me was a lone motorcyclist and though I wasn't in his way at all, he tooted his horn, shook his fist at me and yelled that there was a pedestrian crossing further along the road. His intention here was not for my well-being, but to throw *rules* at me that he valued a bit too highly, for not obeying them in the same way as he would, or *wouldn't* as the case may be. When we tell others how to behave correctly, too often we don't live by our own convictions; listening to what others say and how they say it is a good guide to knowing their intentions. When we act in the way the motorcyclist did, our motives are wrong and therefore, our intentions aren't in line with our best interest; our intention is to complain about something someone else is doing. People like the motorcyclist go out of their way to criticise, but don't take the time to look at themselves - the only true way to learn about *our*selves. Ironically, the man was more interested in telling me off for what I was doing, rather than what he was doing; riding a motorbike, yelling angrily and shaking his fist at me. Too often our intention is to get other people to behave in the way *we* think they should, rather than considering how *we* behave.

When we analyse these things we begin to think about our intentions, but only if we don't get too caught up in the analysis itself. When we do this we no longer have to ask for the opinions or approval of others - intention alone will get us what we want. The problem here is that we don't always *know* what we want and this is why so many people are unhappy. When I decided to finally write this book, my intention was that the book would be found by and help anyone that was ready to hear what I'd written on its pages - it was also to remove the block that told me I couldn't do it. Despite the initial *discouragement* from some people, my intention was already set and therefore, productive. I didn't need approval or want advice and because my intention was set, didn't need any motivation either. Writing became my life, day and night, as with this book; I'm doing what I love to do the most and trusting that the universe will guide me. When our intention is set, it will bear fruit - what kind of fruit depends on whether our intention is good or bad.

The most important aspect of our intentions is that as far as possible we have to live in a way that's in line with them, rather than in opposition. If we intend to become an author for example, we have to get on with the writing - the book won't write itself. After deciding that we've a skill in writing it's important to know what we want to write about and in what genre. It doesn't matter if it isn't popular or even liked; if we feel a need to express ourselves in a particular way then we must never be put off by anyone else's negativity. Most people offer discouragement rather than encouragement - follow your own heart and don't listen to them. If we spend all our spare time watching television or socialising rather than getting down to the business of writing, then we're not living in line with our intentions and shouldn't be surprised or disappointed that no book is produced. Gaining confidence and tuning into our talents requires a lot of sacrifice, particularly in our spare time. We all have a talent that we can hone - at least one - and deep down we know what it is. Only fear prevents us from living in a way that's in our best interest - passionately. A life without passion is never rewarding but a life with passion gets us up in the mornings full of motivation for the day ahead; however, waiting for our purpose or passion to come knocking on our door is both pointless and disappointing - we *have* to find them for ourselves. The next important thing to do with our talent or passion is to complete whatever it is we intend to do.

Intention, will bring our dreams to life if we dare to start the ball rolling, as it were - too often we lie to ourselves about our true intentions. It's easy to become distracted or disillusioned along the way by the negativity of others, because we're in the habit of not taking chances - even if we're bored stiff. We like to stay with what we believe to be *secure* and don't tend to need much discouragement. The biggest discouragements, as always, come from our own mind, particularly with regard to things like fitness, diet or any attempt to change from our familiar way of life.

When we examine intention itself, it becomes clear what our intentions really are, and the phrase 'the road to hell is paved with good intentions', begins to make sense. Suppose we consider taking up a sport because we want, or have been encouraged by our doctor for example, to get 'fit'. We might put it off because we 'can't afford' the right kit. They aren't necessary for our project, but we convince ourselves that they are and so put off starting whatever it is we claim we want to do. If we do buy the 'kit', it all too often gets left in the cupboard after one or two seasonal attempts to learn our chosen sport and it's never used again. Often we can repeat this procedure of buying different kits as we try out and test other sports or hobbies in an attempt to find something we *can* excel in. On a similar vein, how many kitchens contain 'must have' good intentioned gadgets consigned to the back of cupboards - juicers for example; we don't know what we want and therefore, can't set our intention - our initial enthusiasm soon dwindles.

Changing our habits can be difficult, particularly when our intention isn't set to do so; for example, when attempting to stop smoking, or any other habit; we *claim* we want to give them up, and that we *will*, but we don't mean it - our 'intention' sits firmly at the starting block, and we remain forever in a state of 'trying', but never achieving. To get an intention off the starting block takes commitment, if we're ever to realise our goal - we have to keep at it until it's achieved. This is a difficult concept to grasp in our 'instant gratification' society. A student doesn't become a master overnight - it takes effort; we can't become an instant lawyer, scientist or artist - there's no 'just add water' to achievement.

Chapter 30

Humanity is One

We're the only obstacle we need to overcome.

We're humanity; we're complex, wonderfully made and capable of amazing feats - our creativity knows no bounds. Sadly, this creativity is used to destroy and separate, rather than to unite us. We create things of great beauty, but then ascribe to them a value leading to a need to protect them behind iron bars, security cameras, guards and electric fences. We give things of 'value' more admiration, protection and care than we do the people who created them. It can be alarming to see people pushing and shoving fellow human beings out of the way, in their rush to acquire these *possessions* - some of us are even prepared to kill for them.

There's so much we've forgotten about that's common to every human being. We want to live in a peaceful world, where we can live without fear and come and go as we please. However, our history is at best 'disturbing' and prevents this sort of freedom. We live so close together, but we can never *really* know each other - we don't allow anyone near to that part of us we guard so closely. Unable to show vulnerability, because we fear it would leave us prey to those who'd perceive it as weakness, we're reluctant to take that first step to freedom - no one wants to go first. Because of this division we're on the offensive like a coiled snake ready to strike anyone who encroaches our space. At the heart of this posturing there's a sense of loss and confusion about our origin and destination. This hostility is manifested as an 'it's none of your business' attitude, which means we don't like anyone prying past the personal wall that we call *private* - we're walking 'Keep Out' signs. The confusion causes us so much pain that we bury the emotions deeply in order to function in our world, where we're encouraged to be attractive, mindless, afraid and tough - paradoxically to be their opposites as well. We're also encouraged to fend for ourselves and compete with each other for 'status', larger homes and faster cars. Because we're encouraged to behave in so many conflicting ways by people we don't know, it's hardly surprising we don't have a clue who we are.

We live in a world where we don't appreciate each other, neither do we feel appreciated, loved or wanted. A world in which there's so much hatred that we kill, injure or hurt each other with no good reason, leaving others homeless and starving; it's mankind who's responsible for this situation, and mankind that remains silent. Until we see this, it will remain difficult for us to change this world into a better place to live in. Some of you may argue that there are those who *are* loved; I'd have to disagree with you, as I'm talking about a love that isn't conditional or ephemeral. I'm also speaking about the majority and not the few who realise that this love is true. A love that we miss and long to return to - a love that has no need of money, masks or possessions, isn't selective or conditional and is literally, priceless. We don't have faith or see that a love like this exists because we're too focused on our separation; nations, countries, towns, families, cultures - just some of the causes of the many problems of our world. These levels of separation are increasing as parents become separated from their children, teachers from their pupils and employers from their employees; of course vice versa too. The concept of our separation and what we may have become separated from are things worth thinking about - essential if we want to close the gap between us.

Humanity is losing its ability to communicate with itself having become dependent on the mass media, and a plethora of electronic devices. We've one language for parents and another for children - thus separating them. For these reasons we're selfish and alert only to the ways we can survive, along with those closest to us. Close or not we generally get into arguments and debates, where no one person gives way to another - each tries to push their own agenda forward. Humanity looks outward for solutions to the problems it doesn't fully admit to, and we search for 'home sweet homes' that we can't hold onto forever, no matter how much we want, insure, decorate or tweak them. These homes become somewhere we *claim* as our very own and from that we get a sense of *belonging* to both the property and our families. However, I'd suggest that homes built for our security are actually prisons; outside them we don't feel safe and inside, we lock ourselves securely in - we think. Instead of being One humanity, we've become *one* nation or some other group; *one*, behind a barrier which is constructed upon the conditions laid down by others. We're physically one, rather than spiritually and the result of this is that we're suspicious of each other to the point of exclusion and prior judgement, even of those we've never met. By contrast, we allow those we don't trust to take charge of the society we created - we're quite mad!

~~~

We repeat the same activities day after day and apart from a few variations, depending on whether it's the weekend or we're on holiday, not much changes. A quick calculation reveals that I've brushed my teeth approximately 40,000 times in my lifetime and that's just one of the many daily repetitive rituals we perform. This is why we like things to celebrate such as birthdays, Christmas or some sporting event and mark these dates on a calendar, erasing each day that leads up to them with an 'X' - rather than living it, we *kiss* our lives goodbye. It's a paradox; we're excited about *waiting* for future events, yet frustrated by having to wait for them; we want to be *there* rather than *here*. We wouldn't want to celebrate going to work, shopping, a new television program or the onset of war, but these are a real part of our daily lives. No wonder we get excited about the latest gadgets - they break monotony, give us something to hope for *and* something to play with. That we never celebrate the monotonous nature of our lives has got to be worth thinking about, considering most of us suffer with the incessant boredom of them; why else do we look forward to future events. Life itself should be a celebration. The sister of a friend of mine was asked what she'd do if she knew she was going to die in her sleep; her reply was 'I'd go to bed early'. That's how low the spirit of humanity is right now. Something's very wrong when we celebrate things that don't matter or understand the true meanings of, ignoring the things that do - like life and each other.

As mentioned earlier, we've so much in common, including wonderful bodies that are perfectly suited to perform so many varied tasks. We just have to recognise our conditioning and then unlock our magnificent potential - we all have it. We create the most intricate devices: such as, the clockwork components for a watch, we can study the stars, dance on ice, sing in choirs, imagine unknown life forms and think about how we came into being. We compose beautiful music, write poetry and paint masterpieces that transport us to other worlds and / or invoke tears and emotions, inspiring generations to come - we can do so much good. Thinking is a wonderful ability - everyone is able to do it. Sadly, due to the pressures of life, we're chasing our tails and consequently our abilities are seldom realised. We marvel at people on talent shows who are discovered quite by chance, but rarely get the opportunity to find out what we're capable of ourselves. When we do find our talent, it's often shelved until we've more time or we retire - if we've got enough energy left. One of the things we've all got in common is our uniqueness; we're all special in our own way.

Generally, people don't question how we came to have so many abilities. There are those who believe the human being is merely a universal 'accident' of evolution; in my opinion, this view is utter nonsense. Today, we're focused on the physical and our desires, but tend to ignore our vastly superior metaphysical qualities. People who think otherwise haven't given the matter any serious thought - our exceptional qualities are crystal clear. Have you ever taken the time to wonder about how we see, touch, taste, smell or hear anything? How many other creatures can claim to be so brilliant or versatile?

It's about time humanity realised how magnificent it really is and stopped behaving as though each one of us doesn't matter. Life doesn't have to be full of monotony or fear; it's this way because we agree to it, and choose to be afraid, rather than say 'No' to the things that aren't good for us. The world has many problems and many unhappy people living in it, but we don't have to be that way too. No matter how miserable we feel we ought to become, or how guilty we feel about being content whilst others are suffering, we won't make the world into a better place to live in. We make the world happier by being happier in it - every move counts and the more people that make them, the better. This is what 'free will' - for want of a better term - is really all about; we can stay in the gloom and unhappy crowd or leave and *reconnect* to our point of Origin. We're infinite beings; we can choose to persevere with our pain and suffering or leave the field. There are those who claim that not keeping up with the disastrous affairs of our planet means that we don't care, but I'll say to them what good does playing 'oh no ... how awful' do for the suffering of others? It never *has* done any good and it never will or it would have done so by now. Only coming together again will help the suffering of others and to do this we need to look at the world objectively, rather than in the subjective and selfish way that's become a habit. People are suffering, not because they were born in the wrong country, but because suffering is being inflicted on them.

We can raise our consciousness level, but first we have to be prepared to find out why it's so low. It's no good just dabbling with 'cotton wool' philosophy, or sticking 'I love me' notes all over the place - they only work temporarily, if at all, because we're not looking at the root causes of our state of mind. If anything, when we read these notes we reinforce self-hatred because we're lying and we know it. As we read them the stronger feeling is *I don't love myself at all*. For me, it's nothing more than spraying an air freshener into a stale room - it soon smells stale again. When we question the way we've come to know this world and realise that like a stagnant pond it won't change without our intervention, we can begin to put things right. Until the dirty water is cleaned of the 'litter of ages', we'll remain exactly as we are - wallowing in our own filth, blaming each other for our condition. We can't change Jenny Jones next door, but we can change how we think about her and see that she suffers just like everyone else. We all have different mechanisms to cope with living in this world and that can be expressed as aggression, illness, self-deprecation, depression, judgement of others and much more. However, the root of the problem is the same - our separation.

~~~

How is it possible to see ourselves as One again? By widening our perspective. When we pay attention to our world it becomes apparent that despite each one of us having a unique character and point of view, we share a great deal more in common. By recognising this, we bring together again parts that have been separated for far too long. After all:

- We want to be heard.
- We've been hurt.
- We're unaware of what other people are feeling.
- We've a talent.
- We share this home.

- We're searching for love.
- We want recognition.
- We're afraid.
- We want an easier life.
- We're imperfect.
- We *must* die.
- We're killing time and don't know why.

I could easily fill up two pages with this list. There's so much more that we share but we've forgotten this because of our separation from each other. Regarding the last point I made, the reason we don't know why we're killing time is that we don't take time to consider these things - we're very good at procrastinating. When we pay attention to our similarities, rather than our differences, we reconnect to the whole. When we connect to the whole and realise that we're a part of it, selfishness becomes a thing of the past - it's our selfish and pompous acts that bring about and enforce our separation. When we criticise someone else, because they're different, we alienate ourselves from them. It's not so difficult to focus on what we have in common and it's much more satisfying than focusing on what we don't. When we do this our intention, rather than being competitive, judgemental or derogatory, is noble.

On a practical level, when those nasty old thoughts peep through the cracks, we can watch them closely. So for example, we see coming towards us an unkempt person wearing old worn clothing. We can look at them in one of two ways - with a critical or compassionate eye. Mostly our first thoughts are critical - that's our conditioning and it's deep-seated. We can take charge of our thoughts and recognise that this is a person just like us - perhaps less fortunate. They may be suffering in ways we can't comprehend; we can't see the world through their eyes and we can't be aware of the cause of their pain or suffering - it's possible they're entirely alone in this world. By challenging our original critical thought and replacing it with a non-judgemental one, we then see the person in a totally different light. If we take it several steps further it becomes clear that their predicament isn't their own fault, but one brought about by the society we created, and sustain. As well as considering why a person may be wearing worn out clothing, it would be an interesting exercise to ask ourselves why we're so bothered by it; what is it about us that needs to criticise others and in what way are we more 'deserving' than they are? If we persevere in this way, then the space that separates us becomes smaller and we begin to look at others compassionately, rather than critically. When we keep catching those thoughts it becomes apparent that we're not so different; we're One. By the same token, paying close attention to the unrelenting thoughts that turn in our heads when we're trying to get to sleep, we'll find that these will change too. However, if we're determined to think that we're better than others all we do is *increase* the space that separates us - isolating ourselves - psychologically and physically, from the rest of humanity.

In this chapter, I've attempted to explain my thoughts on how we're all One. Putting into words this abstract concept is not an easy task. However, once we grasp the concept, our separation from each other becomes obvious, and if we embrace it, our lives take on a more meaningful direction - life is no longer pointless or passé; we realise that we're not and never have been alone - we cease the struggle to become something we're not. Have you ever seen a shoal of fish swimming together or a flock of starlings in flight? They move as one, for the common good, and none of them fight with each other for space or first place, yet each one plays their part in the dance. If you haven't seen these you can find videos online -watching them is worth the effort. Whenever we gather together *en masse* we're all powerful and intentional, just like the fish and starlings, but as individuals our power and beauty are greatly reduced. When we've One mind, we can achieve so many marvellous things in this world. Sadly, we use this collective power for the wrong things, particularly war. Imagine a world where we gather together for the good of the planet and mankind; a world where we allow each other to develop our innate talents; a world without threat, fear, borders or corruption. I don't know about you but I for one would love to experience it. We're humanity and no matter how individual or superior we think we are, we're part of a greater whole. We all belong together and we always will. When we hurt each other what we're really doing is hurting ourselves - damaging the world in which we must all continue to live.

Chapter 31

We're One

We fear the darkness, yet choose to reside within it.

One day soon we'll re-gather
And wonder from where this madness stemmed
And how we thought we'd never mend
The gaping space that spanned between
Our unadulterated love for each other
And turned it into war and corruption
As we ran riot
Destroying not only ourselves, but others
With our faces devoid of empathy.
You,
My neighbour who I've loved forever
Looked at me with hatred in your eyes
Because you didn't recognise me and
Because I recognised you and said
'Bonjour' with a smile
That you could not return.
You,
My neighbour who obeys without question
Those who do not bless you
Or value your divinity because
They prefer that you live in fear of
The power you once gave them.

You,
My neighbour who has forgotten
On what sacred ground your feet walk upon
And the humble people you trample
Beneath your vanity and pride
Without ever knowing they're there.
One day soon we'll re-gather
And know from where this madness grows
And know we always knew we'd close
The gaping space that spanned between
Our unadulterated love for each other.

Chapter 32

Who am I?

Just around the bend the music is still playing, but it's at a higher frequency.

I've reached the end of my second section, and so much has changed for me. Let me correct that statement - *I've* changed so much in me. Obviously, you're still here in my pages, and I'd like to thank you for your company, and for sharing my journey - it has been a life-changing experience for me, and I hope it has for you too. When I see a photograph of myself, I don't recognise it as me. When I see my earlier writings, I don't recognise that I wrote them - the words seem to have never left my fingers. The past doesn't exist for me and it doesn't exist for you either - changing our perspective makes this perfectly clear. When we realise that neither the past nor future exist it's inevitable that, even if only in small glimpses, we begin, with increasing frequency, to experience the Now. Everything is connected, here and Now. I'm entirely responsible for my life; I never once imagined I'd ever say a thing like that.

It's all me
Everywhere I go
Left and up
Down and right
Turning myself inside out
And back to front
And in so many other directions
That I have no words for, because -

I

Am the mother of my child

I

Gave birth to it

I

Fed and nurtured it

I

Made my child
What she is today
And created her each and every way
She became an obsession
An un-treasured possession
That I valued, not, in any graceful way
Abandoned and rejected -

She'd

Been left to decay

Then

I

Rose

From her ashes

Dazed and confused
Deconstructed the parts
I'd cruelly abused
I reached and climbed
Every hill I could find
Then in Awe I relished
The Silence of my mind
No-thing at all
Had obviously changed
But
Somehow
Something
Had been rearranged.

THREE

Chapter 33

Sensation, Desire & Relevant Reflections

We need so little, but desire so much.

Whilst walking past my local bakery I was stopped in my tracks by a tantalising smell. I was unable to make out if it was sweet or savoury but felt odd sensations that resembled 'cravings'. Regardless, the event was full of flavours, urges, feelings of pleasure and the irresistible 'come and get me' invitation that at one time would've had me walking through the door in an instant, carrying out further 'investigation'. It was while I was lost in these pleasant evocations that it occurred to me what a wonderful and interesting thing had happened - it was all from sensory memory. How is it, I wondered, that I've vastly different aromatic experiences when passing a fishmonger's shop - evoking less appealing memories. It was at that moment I decided to write about the abstract human trait that we call, desire.

Desire is a 'loaded' word *generally* associated with having sexual, gastronomical, financial or religious overtones:

- Sexual - to be desirable to or by another.
- Gastronomical - to desire food; for pleasure (excess?). Desire is not a word we use to describe the needs of people who are starving - food is essential.
- Financial - to bring us *security*; to eliminate personal lack of anything *we* want in this world for the duration of our lifetimes - but not beyond. Need is an entirely different thing; clothing, food and shelter.
- Religious - to bring us the greatest and most elusive prize of all; Heaven - *if* we manage to conquer our desires for anything other than God - but not until we die.

Little wonder our focus is on the first three of these; they're *attainable* within our lifetime. We've heard the word 'desire' or seen images being used in the above contexts more than any other -

through subliminal messages and a great deal of early (often religious) conditioning. I told a few friends that I'm writing a chapter called 'Desire' (original chapter title) and asked what their initial reaction was to that word. To one it meant an expensive new car and to others it was an exciting new partner, improved personal appearance, happiness or an increase in wealth - things we're conditioned to set our sights on. Interestingly, the desire for answers to fundamental questions about the 'meaning of life' were not mentioned. Are we so lost in ourselves that these questions have become undesirable? One person did say they desire 'world peace' but hadn't thought about what that means or how it might be attained; 'world peace' has no more meaning to most people than any other throwaway cliché. In order to understand what desire is we first need to erase our conditioning through a process of enquiry - then look at it afresh. Without questioning the disorder in the world, we can't expect to create order.

~~~

'Want' can be interpreted as 'must have'. We always want more; such as money, a bigger house, car, television or better 'quality' gadgets and when - or if - we get them, we're not satisfied once the novelty wears off. Sometimes we can't fulfil our desires and in particular those we're *encouraged* to strive for. This leaves us with the feeling that there's a great void in our lives; for example, when we can't find 'romance', good friends or when we desire to be popular, have a 'top job' or at the very least, to be valued. Those of us who *do* have 'enough' material things are no happier than those who don't; we all have drawers full of discarded past desires. This comes about because the 'sensation' of desire is far more thrilling than the fulfilment of it and more importantly, it breaks the monotony of our limited daily lives.

Desire and temptation are closely connected and one can't exist without the other. In order to desire something, we must be able to be tempted by it. In the same manner, in order for temptation to exist, it must know desire. It's for these reasons that advertising is so powerful. Advertising companies have a great deal of experience and know exactly how to appeal to our senses - we provide them with the information. They also know that our desire for these sensory experiences override our need to be kind to ourselves or each other - they know that we prefer to say 'Yes' to any 'pleasure call' and they know us better than we know ourselves. I can't remember how many times I've bought packets of biscuits or cakes after having been tempted by the packaging and, on opening them, being disappointed by the stark difference between the image on the packet, and the contents. We know this to be the case yet *still* buy these goods and accept the disappointments as 'one of those things'. In time, we don't expect the contents to match the image; we accept the anomaly when we should be *outraged* by it and demand a refund. Just how far will we allow this situation to progress? Apathy leads to an insidious undervaluing of ourselves that lowers our expectations until one day, we'll likely be unperturbed if the packet is empty.

There's a tendency to desire what isn't good for us rather than what is and I'd suggest that this can be put down to a lack of self-worth - we both know *and* deny these things. As children we loved to put our hands into 'lucky dips' for the surprise, not because it was worth having, but because of the anticipation and excitement of it all - for the thrill. We loved playing 'pass the parcel', 'musical chairs' and participating in 'sports day' events, but they resulted in disappointment for all but the winner - who was sometimes disappointed too. We learn early on to cope with and accept setbacks that result in us feeling inadequate; we're not!

~~~

Advertisers tempt us into buying products we wouldn't want or need, by making them 'desirable' or 'fashionable'; for example, novelty party foods, ice dispensers on our fridge doors and new 'specialist' blister-plasters that heal self-inflicted wounds from wearing *the* fashionable shoes - allowing us to keep wearing them. In some commercial sectors 'demand' precedes production; sales of products and pre-orders are guaranteed well in advance. Because of demand the markets are saturated with colourful, shiny and attractive goods for us to desire and as quickly as we buy them, we discard them - rather like children who open a longed-for present at Christmas time or on their birthday and never touch it again. Who are the people who produce and advertise these things for us? We are! Humanity is its own villain, victim and hero.

There's an underlying sense of something lacking in our lives - a pernicious discontentment; it's a black hole that can never be filled no matter how much we stuff into it. Little wonder we easily become addicted to smoking, alcohol, sex, snacks, shopping, gossip, television, laziness or excessive exercise. When we're 'hurt', offended, depressed or feeling unworthy we want to suppress those feelings - to desire something 'uplifting' in their place, and after the initial lift has dissipated, nothing has changed - we're right back where we started and feeling just as empty, and perhaps a little guilty. Activities such as fulfilling an 'I need a drink' thought, exhausting ourselves with exercise, hibernating under our duvets or eating the contents of the fridge, provide only the coldest of comforts; they help us to cope with the surface of our woes rather than the root causes of them. Humanity is self-punishing, self-destructive and - with equal yet unused force - self-reflecting and self-healing.

How is it that we're caught in the loop of desire and disappointment? The problem is that we're reaching 'out' instead of 'in'; when we reach out, we place our trust in the hands of others that appear to be answering our 'call'. We feel 'low', see something that pleases our senses and as we need a 'lift' we react in a way that brings a superficial gratification, even though we know the 'hit' is instant and will leave us feeling dissatisfied after the event - the so called 'anti-climax'. I'd suggest that we tend to suffer with 'Now Syndrome' and that we're always looking for the next 'hit'. The actual *timeless* Now is never sad, lonely or depressing - these feelings require access to the past.

Despite remembering our painful past and looking towards our uncertain future, on a deeper level we always have and always will live in the 'Now' - it's impossible to be anywhere or 'anywhen' else. As discussed in 'Time', 'Time is an illusion obscuring the Now' and it's this illusion that leaves us groping for what we can get in the aberrational *physical* Now, even if it's a re-vamped version of something old - we see it as 'new'. We're in the Now when we're crying, angry, depressed, can't stand another moment without him, or her. The Now is when we self-punish because we see 'no way out' of a particular situation we've wrapped ourselves in. The Now is when we find no *immediate* resolution to our woes and seek consolation from the 'decadence' we convince ourselves to eat, 'retail therapy', or the alcohol we recklessly consume - though these consolations are more punishing than they are anything else. We 'enjoy', yet at the same time, hate ourselves for succumbing to these comforting temptations and pastimes - a hate we justify because of our 'woeful' circumstances.

Desire is so much more than just 'wanting' things. There's something about a wrapped glittering package, prettied with ribbons and a label with our name on it. We love new things and we love surprises so these packages - as assembled under a Christmas tree for example - hold great appeal to our senses; the surprise adds a sensational element that excites us more than the gift itself. Some small children prefer the wrapping paper to the gift; it could be because they're unimpressed with the present or that they love the crackling sound of the paper and feel of the silky ribbons. Have you ever felt the disappointment of having no further gifts to open on Christmas day (if any at all) or seen a child searching under the tree in anticipation of finding another present with their name on it? These gifts appeal to our selfish side that claims 'They're mine'; try taking a toy from a young child or preventing them taking a toy from another - the result is a tantrum. Once opened, a gift can be cherished, admired or be a bitter disappointment, but none of these feelings can compare to the elevated sensations and concentrated delight we feel as we carry out the process of discovering what's inside. The gift stimulates multiple sensations that we enjoy feeling for reasons we don't give a second thought to - the adventurous expectation of what's inside. We love and can't live without sensations and in the case of gifts, the whole process of receiving them is over too soon.

We'd experience the same sensations and expectations even if a beautifully wrapped present contained no gift inside, provided we were unaware of that fact. We live in a multi-sense 'reality' so it's understandable that we seek to experience and re-experience these sensations in full. We love to repeat anything that brings pleasure, like a child shouting 'Again! Again!' to be thrown up in the air and safely caught in the arms of his father; unless we're exceedingly disciplined we say the same words to ourselves when we're grown up, to a packet of biscuits for example, until they're all gone. There are the five senses that tell us this world is 'real' - physical senses - but there are many more sensations that we like to experience such as excitement, elation, curiosity, pain, violence, misery and fear to name just a few; we have many more spiritual/abstract senses.

~~~

We harm ourselves when we watch the news, horror films or try to hold on to things that aren't good for us, like bad relationships and painful memories. We resist good advice and hold onto a perpetual 'not good enough' feeling - carried over from our pasts and re-lived in various forms many times every day. Why do we do it? I'd suggest it's easier to 'go with the flow' of society than it is to resist it - even if it's painful and disturbing. You may argue that we don't 'like' these things, but then it would be necessary to think about why we agree to suffer them, and put up such a huge resistance to doing without them. As I said in the introduction, 'We claim not to like violence, yet accept it as entertainment'.

Just as we feel the misery of others, such as on television, we can feel their excitement and happiness too; we love to see pleasure on the faces of others. For example, we love to see the faces of those who've achieved their goals, such as winners of races and competitions, or those who've succeeded to climb high peaks or overcome seemingly impossible difficulties from a position of hopeless weakness to one of towering strength. These are our heroes or role models and this is one of the reasons we accept the authority/celebrity status of others; we feel they've overcome difficulties to get to their positions and therefore, we hold them in high esteem - they've 'succeeded' where perhaps, we've failed. It's impossible not to be caught up in the energy of these moments or to react emotionally; we're attracted to - and repelled by - each other's energy fields like magnets. When we don't feel powerful, we enjoy bathing in the reflected glory of others - in effect, we're living our lives by proxy. It's a spiritual/abstract desire that we seek to fulfil through others, rather than ourselves.

The more I focus my attention on this subject, the more I see how incredible a human being is. Incredible in the sense of us being a wonderful piece of bio-engineering, but more in the sense of our crass foolishness and immaturity. One of the most bizarre traits we have is the desire to be desirable - to attract a mate. Advertisers go to great lengths to encourage us to be attractive to others with perfumes, fabrics, skimpy clothing, makeup, alluring images of men or women, encouragement to 'behave badly' and much more; in doing so, they tell us that we'll be (and are) undesirable if we *don't* use their products. There are no shortages of places we can go to fluff up our feathers in order to compete with the 'competition', and no shortage of 'hopefuls' trying to attract our attention.

We tend to be more and more outrageous in our desire to keep up with - or exceed - the expectations of our ever-changing disordered society, but grace, humility and wisdom are left far behind us in this race to 'fit in'. Disorder can only lead to further disorder. The most undignified display of attention seeking I've ever seen was at a railway station when a member of a teenage 'hen party' of half-naked girls held up a stick with a sex toy on it and asked the ticket collector if Mr **** needed a ticket; 'in what way will these impressionable girls become more outrageous' is a worrying question and I doubt very much that it will lead to their eventual happiness. It's highly unlikely that the group member with the sex toy 'tool' would dare to behave in this way outside the group - she'd feel far too vulnerable, at risk and afraid. Acting in this way will never make up for what's missing in our hearts, hopes or deeper desires; we're more than adequate without the assistance of commerce and it's 'highly recommended' degradation of ourselves. Under the façade and bravery of our outward behaviour and appearances - outrageous or otherwise - we know that there's so much more to us.

The suppression of our desires is an invitation for them to rise again at a later date - they can't be eradicated. Desire is innate and in particular the desire we suppress the most - the desire to know what our lives are really about; in its place we accept the desires of the commercial world that encloses us. It's natural, that when we suppress our true desires they *must* express themselves in a negative way; suppression holds us back and when that energy builds up inside us we must one day let it out. It's for this reason that our world is full of anger, depression, war and other negativity; we work in opposition to what we know is true and what we really want - this is how 'regret' is born. No matter how much we suppress our hearts' desires they will crop up again and again until we recognise them and we'll continue to suffer the painful consequences of our ignorance. Trying to ignore a desire is like pushing an inflatable ball into water - the more pressure that's used to keep it down, the more furiously it will one day rise up.

~~~

Desire is a human trait that can never be satisfied - the very meaning of the word denies fulfilment. By its nature, desire demands a gratification that we seek to experience again and again. We enjoy the sensations of getting what we want, because it feels like we've gained some sort of power over our lives by working hard for something or manifesting it - we believe we're in control. But in 'reality' we're not getting what we want because we don't *know* what we want; hence, we readily accept distractions that bring momentary pleasure. We're always getting what other people want *for* us and what we receive has become so limited that we believe 'version II' of a game, film, gadget or new relationship is something entirely 'new' and desirable; we choose to ignore the ripples of these actions. Just like the baby who discards a new gift, we quickly tire of our new toys and anticipate owning 'version III' - we're easily bored. In our hearts we know these things are transient; they're merely a 'consolation prize' for something else - something that eludes us until we 'have the time' to start looking for it. Until then, we wipe out any notions about the 'truth' of our existence because we can't access it right 'now' - it's too concealed and been corrupted. Being 'too busy' is a way of distracting ourselves or allowing ourselves to be distracted by others - we fill the 'black hole' with possessions and empty pursuits. We look for contentment without even thinking about what it *means* to be content - it always means gratification of desire in our society. A piece of chocolate cake lasts for minutes, an ancient monument perhaps for thousands of years, but neither can ever be permanent.

There are different types of desire - physical and non-physical (spiritual, metaphysical or abstract - whichever term you prefer). The pleasure we receive from fulfilling our desires is temporary; it's like trying to repair holes in the road with ice - it soon melts revealing the hole again. The succession of unsuccessful repairs to the road surface leaves us feeling frustrated and inadequate - so it is with any gratification of desire. Until we realise this, it's impossible to live in harmony with ourselves and by extension, with each other. We look for completeness without knowing what it means - looking for it in relationships (with an individual or within a group) or on the stacked shelves of commercialism. Both of these are closely connected to the security we wish to find, but neither can handle the task. There's absolutely *nothing* anyone can obtain outside of themselves that will cause them to feel happy or *complete* for the rest of their lives - nothing that will fill the void. We can only find this completeness by a process of negation; a process that first finds out why we 'desire' so much and why, beneath the skin of our physical existence, we feel so empty.

Chapter 34

Am I Good Enough?

Find out why you feel the way you feel - about yourself.

The answer to the question 'Am I good enough?' depends on who we ask. If we ask ourselves, then generally the answer is 'No'. If we ask someone else and they say 'Yes', we tend not to believe them. Am I good enough? Yes! Absolutely! We're *all* good enough. Then why don't we feel it? Because of continual encouragement and manipulation to believe otherwise. I could end this chapter here, but I want to write further on the topic, as it's a particularly difficult problem to overcome, and I'm *still* working on it. It's not enough to be *told* 'Yes! Absolutely! We're *all* good enough' - words are a thin blanket against the cold. When society repeatedly hammers in 'not good enough' messages, like splinters, they have to be removed before they do more damage; however, we can't look to our 'tormenter' for assistance - we must remove them ourselves. To put this another way - because I want to stress the point - the path we trod to feeling not good enough was a tough one, and it's just as difficult to come off it. Splinters hurt like hell when we try to remove them, particularly when we have to dig deep to get them out.

Every time we look into the mirror we answer 'No' to the question 'Am I good enough?', even though we spend hours putting on makeup and our hard-earned pennies on a new outfit or hairdo. We invest in looking good on the outside but rather sadly, also in feeling bad. We go to great pains to make ourselves attractive and acceptable, not just for the sake of others, but to make ourselves feel better. This effort gets us through the day/evening but, in the morning - the beast is back - our hair is a frightful mess and we're our-*awful*-selves again - our faithful mirror confirms this. I know there are those of us who 'throw' our clothes on and don't bother with the rituals, but most do; either way, most of us would like to 'tweak' what we see, whether it's to lose or gain a few pounds, have curly hair instead of straight, be a little taller, shorter, have slimmer waists or thinner thighs. Some of us aren't averse to having major surgery performed or even a 'total body transplant' (our own mind in the body of one of the icons we idolise). Several people have told me that they're perfectly happy with themselves and even that they love their reflection in the mirror, but they take the trouble to be stylish and wear makeup. 'Makeup' implies making up for a lack of some kind; it's a decoration that covers up what's beautiful and natural about us. No matter how well we dress up or how many layers of makeup we put on, we don't feel any different on the inside. We return home after our excursions to face the same walls and ornaments - nothing changes behind the security of our barriers. Physically, we've become more comfortable behind screens and masks than we are in our 'natural' state. We feel increasingly safe behind our various electronic screens and don't need to get dressed to enter into our virtual world - safe in the knowledge that the images on our profile - out-of-date or otherwise - will adequately 'clothe' us.

However, on another level, we're at our most comfortable at home *alone* when we take off our disguises. We're much happier lounging around barefoot in joggers without the need to keep up appearances or conform to the expectations of society by wearing a suit - or other uniform - to work for example - not to do so is unacceptable in many workplaces. We pretend to be happy with our lives and in some minor ways we are; however, nagging in the back of our minds - like a dripping tap - are doubts and questions about why we agree to behave in these ways. We spend our lives supporting beliefs that we're not good enough, and tend to surround ourselves 'subconsciously' with people who confirm it. One reason for this is that we love to fall into the fantasy of the different characters we're capable of becoming; we're brilliant at it, but need a supporting cast or audience in order to keep it up. As new fashions are offered up to us, so are the complimentary labels that go with them; such as, hell's angels, punks, goths or whatever the latest genre is. Unfortunately, our cultures encourage us to veer more in the direction of *trendy* and *need*. The personalities that 'go with' new fashions - to those who *don't* follow them - are rarely 'angelic' and usually to be feared when they're in groups; these groups cause further division in society. The costumes, traits and fears were created by someone else and therefore, can't be natural to us. I added 'need' to the above statement, because we all need to find out who we are; we seek a true *identity* and the commercials play on this. I'd suggest that any *character* is a limited creation, because we zoom into particular personality traits that become who we *think* we are; for example:

- Free-spirited
- Workaholic
- Sociable
- Daredevil
- Law-abiding
- Criminal
- Sporty
- Tough
- Religious
- Adventurous
- Sophisticated (please research this word - it means impure/un-natural)

These are creations of the Mind and from them we've created our society. Besides choosing which outfit to wear each day (and how) they're *not* new and *not* our own creations but merely a 'mix and match' of what we already have. We can change a colour, add studs or cut slits in the knees of our jeans, but none of it is new; in Tudor times, for example, 'slashed' clothing was fashionable, revealing what was being worn beneath a particular layer. Once we attach ourselves to these personality labels they stick and become what other people expect us to be and subconsciously, who we think we are until, if ever, we decide to change our costumes. To put this another way, we're walking along the catwalk modelling clothes and images that someone *else* has designed for us. It's rare that apart from very close friends we'd allow anyone to see us without our makeup or 'slumming it' at home. We keep up the façade but our true nature is divine - wide-angled and limitless - if it wasn't we wouldn't be able to act out these parts. For example, no-one is born a goth or punk; we *learn* how to play these roles and love doing it. We're capable of playing *all* parts and we *do*; however, these roles are being cast *for* us - we're being 'directed'. To sum up this point, we have an innate need to have the question 'Who am I?' answered and when society tells us, you're a 'goth', 'rocker', 'bookworm', 'sex-bomb', 'nerd', 'genius', whatever - we go along with it. In truth, we fall into 'not good enough' mode when we stitch ourselves to one label and that label becomes the limit of our comfort zones - those limits become our prisons. It's more worthwhile to find out who we're *not* than it is to believe any label - negation is highly productive; for example, 'what' or 'who' are these labels attached to is worth pondering.

I've written much about topics that we don't particularly want to examine; they're not pleasing to our ears, because they make us feel that we 'ought' to make changes in our lives and we don't want the disruption. However, we can't find truth unless we're prepared to question our *reality* and in questioning reality it's important *not* to answer those questions. The reason for this is that we can only answer them from the same conditioning that gave us answers up to now; in other words, from the unhealthy Mind that is the river we all live in. Our education was never about *who we are* and it never encouraged us to find out either; it filled our heads with an abundance of information that was about everything *but* us, and what would be expected from us in the future. As a result we're unable to find out who we are from our 'knowledge base'. It's no wonder that humanity is puzzled about its origin and purpose; we don't have a clue who we are, or how we got ourselves into this mess. As long as we defend a society that in our hearts we know is sick, we won't be able to see the possibilities that lie beyond it.

As I've said before, we try to answer the question 'Who am I?' by looking outside of ourselves instead of in - it's a *spiritual* question. When we reply to the question physically we can never get the right answer and there are two ways in which we try to do this. Firstly, by altering our physical structure through leisure activities such as sports - particularly those that build muscles to a point where we become unrecognisable to ourselves or others; we also do this through surgery, and at the minor end of the scale by changing the way we dress, having a 'makeover' or taking on some other persona. Regardless of the methods we use to disguise ourselves, inside we haven't changed at all - it's entirely superficial. Secondly, we attempt to succeed by climbing a 'ladder'. Who are the 'chairman', 'president', gold medallist or a 'scientist' without their labels, and what is left for them to 'achieve' when they wear them? The trouble with the top of a ladder is that it comes to an end, abruptly. There are only three things we can do from the top of a ladder; stay there, climb down or fall off it - the ladder of society is a dead end. Okay, some may argue that you can jump off (or be pushed), but these actions lead to the same unhappy ending - an eventual fall from a powerful yet fragile illusion that our egos don't want to let go of. I'd suggest, we can never become anything other than who we *really* are (as opposed to who we *think* we are), and that we dabble with life by trying on different masks and living in ways that keep up and reinforce the pretence.

I had a friend who took these masks to extremes and her personality and accent changed regularly, even with me. We were reasonably well-spoken when we were children (I don't like these scales, but this was our conditioning). I can still remember the time I heard her speak, using profanities, in another accent altogether; she wanted to fit in with the friend she was with at the time and I was expected to go along with it, which I didn't. She perfected her styles to fit into any social environment she found herself in and, as is inevitable when we experiment to this extreme, became increasingly confused about her own identity to the point where, under some circumstances, even I didn't recognise her. For the record, I've no problem with anyone speaking in any accent or any way they want to, but when these get mixed together - as with my friend - it becomes difficult, if not impossible, to relate to them. Surely our relationships with each other are confusing enough without increasing the confusion of the relationship we learn to have with ourselves. If you'd been born in England you'd think of yourself as English, but if the same 'you' had been born in Russia instead, you would have become an entirely different person, with a different set of cultural beliefs and expectations - the root is the same, but the branches are different.

~~~

There's something nebulous about answering the question 'Am I good enough?' - it has a vagueness we can't quite put our finger on. Missing from the question is *what* or *who* we ought to be good enough for. Interestingly, more often than not we tell ourselves 'I'm not good enough' and *that*, let's face it, slams our *don't go there* door in our own face - eliminating the question altogether. Being '*not* good enough' was the root of what prevented me from writing for so many years; however, putting my mind to doing what I love became a cure for that. I'm good enough to do many more things too, but they'd be half-hearted distractions that would prevent me from following what I now accept as being my 'path'. A big obstacle to overcome is the belief that we can't earn a living from doing what we *want* to do but it can be overcome - only fear constructs the boundaries that enclose us. We can never know what'll happen if we decide to follow our dreams *until* we take action, but we live in fear of the unborn and conditioned consequences nevertheless. This is like standing by a door and being afraid to open it, just in case there's something nasty on the other side waiting to pounce.

Who is the *tormentor* I mentioned earlier in this chapter and why would they want to hammer us with 'not good enough' messages - so much so, that we feel terrible about ourselves and have to hide behind a cast of characters in a play that quite clearly we can't see we're not the directors of? That sounds like a loaded question - and it is - but please don't try to answer without thinking about it. There are many levels to this question, but as always I only look at what I can see clearly and have meditated on myself. When we turn our attention inwards and cease to look outside for answers then the identity of our tormentor becomes obvious - it's ourselves. We torment ourselves day and night - so much so that we have to keep busy in order to get away from the 'noise'; however, it's still going on subconsciously. I won't even try to answer the 'why' part of the question because we can't know the answer to it; nevertheless, it's a question we ask.

We need only observe our mind to see how negative and antagonistic it is, and how it leads us into states of mind that aren't good for us such as arguments, anger, aggression, low self-esteem, fear, shyness and addiction. I'd suggest that to some extent at least, our characters are *inborn* and further develop as we grow, according to the environment we grow up in; in my case this was an orphanage, and not at all pleasant. When they stopped punishing me for my existence I took over, because I didn't know anything else; I wasn't conscious of this phenomenon at the time. We tend to take over the roles of our past tormentors, or go on to torment others - either way is self-destructive and passes these habits onto future generations. We torment ourselves, far more than anyone else ever did; we're self-punishing and our own harshest critics. All our pain comes from stored memories and when we observe this fact closely it becomes clearer and clearer. We can't erase the memories, but we can put them into context and see them for what they really are - the past, which no longer exists (personally, I question whether it ever did). When we try to 'locate' our painful memories, we can't - it's like trying to locate a dream. What we learn from these past experiences, and what we're prepared to tackle or change, is entirely up to us.

If we want to change we can. The road is difficult because the Mind resists at every twist and turn; it likes to keep us on our familiar track of self-destruction. With honest reflection and close examination of ourselves this can be overcome; we need an unshakable 'will' *never* to give up. How many of us have bought self-help books in the past and felt on a 'high' after reading them? The 'hit' from these books can be temporary because:

- They tend not to go deeply enough into what's happening inside our heads/minds.
- We don't realise that we have to do more than just 'read the book' and then shelve it.
- We tend to use the information to advise others rather than apply it to ourselves; we're very good at this.
- There's no quick fix and this can be discouraging - like a diet we give up on.
- A 'hit' is just that; like when a ball hits a wall it bounces off again, and we're not prepared for this.

We buy these books because deep inside of each of us is a need to find out who we are, and in self-help books we share the experiences of others, in the hope that we'll find our way out of the despair and confusion our world is full of. No matter how good a self-help book is or how full our bookshelves are, if we're not ready to change, it's not going to happen. Generally, all we find is more confusion as self-help has become an 'industry'; we try to get to grips with the thousands of - mostly recycled - 'infallible' systems for 'healing' ourselves. The 'determination' and 'will' not to give up come on their own, once we see that the path we're currently walking on leads nowhere. When we see this, changing paths becomes not only worthwhile, but essential and with this comes our passion to keep 'walking' - giving up, is no longer an option.

~~~

When we try to reach unattainable goals they leave us feeling 'not good enough'. For example, we may visit our hairdresser and choose a hairstyle from one of their magazines; despite being advised that it won't suit us, we go ahead. Once created, it feels like a knock-back - we still don't look like the model, because we don't have the same face or colouring. I remember when I was around fifteen and feeling particularly inadequate. I bought a blonde hair dye kit and - without reflection - used it; my hair turned orange (I really mean orange). My head looked like the top of a Belisha beacon when I'd finished. I looked such a fright that I had to return immediately to the chemist (headscarf on) to buy a bottle of black hair dye in an attempt to get back to my own colour. It's ridiculous to try to become somebody else based on an image we've seen. Another example of how we do this is to buy the clothes a model looks great in and then hit ourselves hard when we don't look as 'good' in the same outfit. We bring up our children to follow 'heroes' and 'success' images, which is how they become as confused and insecure as we are. We can't walk in the footsteps of another person, nor along their path; we must each find our own way, but as long as we live our lives like obedient copycats or lookalikes we can't realistically expect to find out who we are, or what we'd be capable of if we were in control. At this point, I find myself wondering just how many Michael Jackson or Elvis impersonators there are in the world. To walk along someone else's path, is to completely disregard our own existence or purpose.

If we stop believing there's something greater than ourselves, that led us to where we are now, what've we got left? We're tiny in the universe, but have been given a great deal of responsibility in it - at least on this 'earth'. We're so busy wallowing in feeling bad about ourselves and re-living our pasts that we can't see the wonder of our existence - a physical manifestation of something metaphysical - more marvellous than we're capable of imagining. The world suffers with low self-esteem, because it insists on repeating - and ignoring the ramifications of - its past mistakes. We live in fear of change - thereby resisting it - and at the same time, we long for it. An argument or conflict only come into being when we have opposing agendas with ourselves or others. Two of these common arguments are 'I'm not good enough' or 'someone else isn't good enough'. We sabotage our happiness and peace because we don't believe we deserve it; we live on the edge playing in our 'one-man-band' with full knowledge that it's being orchestrated from the outside. We effectively destroy the opportunity to find a better life for ourselves when we insist on remaining in 'not good enough' mode, which is only a perversion of who we truly are. It's tough - very tough, but if we see that the burden is spread over the whole of humanity, it lightens our load. When we see this clearly then we feel the pains of others before feeling our own; in other words, we no longer see the world subjectively but realise that we *are* the world, and everything we think and do is reflected in it. The only thing we believe we're not good enough for is ourselves and one reason for this is that we're not ready to take responsibility for our freedom. The path is long, dark and tough, but it *is* there and there is 'light' at the end of it; beyond that light, who can really know what we'll find. We overcome all hurdles when we no longer get distracted or deterred by society. When we become the act instead of the audience many doors open, but we have to make the first move *and* be serious about our quest, which at first, can appear to be a hopeless task; however, if we continue on it, it becomes clear that it isn't.

Chapter 35

Responsibility

Everything is as it should be, but not as it could be.

Responsibility, as we tend to understand it, means being answerable for the actions or inactions of ourselves or others, such as our children, employees or neighbours; however, in reality, responsibility has come to be understood as an ability to manage 'obligations' that society has put upon us. Responsibility is a mantle we grow into when we're 'old enough' - old enough to look after a younger sibling, to earn a living, drive a car, buy a home, get married or start a family. Sometimes we're forced to assume the role of a mantle earlier than expected - perhaps due to the death of a parent. We become responsible for getting to work on time, driving safely and teaching our children to be 'well-behaved' so they fit in with society - keeping those cogs turning; the process is mechanical. In theory, this leads to a happy and rewarding life, but in practise our dreams lie unfulfilled, financial commitments increase, wages don't keep pace and our children's interests lie *outside* the family home (either physically or online), leaving us somewhat obsolete in their eyes, as they live in a world that we 'apparently' know nothing about. Our societal responsibilities have become a heavy burden, and once they're 'fulfilled' we tend to feel prematurely retired and rather at a loss for what to do with ourselves. While carrying out our 'responsibilities' life whizzed by, and we strayed far from the true meaning of responsibility - the ability to respond, as opposed to pre-conditioned responses that rely on thought and therefore, memory.

Though we complain about monotony and the problems in our world, we tend to accept it all as an inevitable 'way of life'. Society expects nothing less and we accept the 'contingency plans' it puts forward for us; for example, retirement homes, pensions and bus passes. However, history teaches us that we are and always have been stagnant - psychologically - and despite the horrors that have resulted, we refuse to change our ways regardless of the cost of this apathy; the cost is to accept the authority of others, which we willingly do, no matter how they use or misuse it. We've place a huge burden on the back of a donkey and expect that donkey to carry our load, but it never makes our load lighter - it increases the weight and leaves us feeling powerless, because under these circumstances we *are* powerless. By accepting the authority (guidance) of another, by definition, we make them our 'Master' and relinquish our right to think for ourselves - we lose the ability to reason and to know that there are other choices. We leave our burden on the back of the donkey who is quite willing to carry it - for a price.

Throughout taught history, humanity has been violent and willing to fight in immoral wars that leave a trail of devastation; we learn nothing from them and have no idea what we're really fighting for anyway. The order is 'shoot' and we obey - this is madness. We're far removed from taking responsibility for the carnage and destruction this fragmentation of humanity causes; in a twist, we shed responsibility while claiming to act in its cause; however, the action we take is superficial, in a way that society has made 'correct'. Mostly, this 'correct' way is to take no action and leave everything to our elected 'authorities', but also to apply dressings to the wounds of our victims and environment, whilst crying over them - our tears falling into collection boxes of one sort or another. How much easier it is to cry about something we can do nothing about, than something we can. We look to society - which created our problems - to solve them, because we don't want to take on that responsibility ourselves for more than say, picking up litter or recycling our waste; we're far too busy being 'busy'. However, we *are* that society. In the above two examples, it makes more sense to put our litter straight into bins and more importantly, not to create so much waste in the first place - the solutions are *always* easy if we take responsibility, and we can do this under our own authority - it's empowering. We can get so cross with the dustmen when they go on strike and don't pick up *our* rubbish - it's worth thinking about this. We produce far more waste than the authorities can cope with or will take away, yet still we demand increasingly efficient services for our increasing volume of landfill material. Our responsibilities surely must go further than this - to at least *think* about what happens to this rubbish after it's out of our sight. Just because we can no longer see it, doesn't mean that it's no longer there.

It's absurd to think that we're powerless to create a better world, in which the whole of humanity has enough food and is happy; we don't even have to *create* it, as there's already enough for every one of us. To believe that suffering is inevitable is a limit put forward by the voice of our egos, not the voice of rational or compassionate thought. Even more absurd is that we agree to live in a world filled with violence, greed and apathy - dumping responsibility for it onto elected governments that we hope will change things for us. We can't hope to become responsible whilst placing responsibility in the hands of other people who are also irresponsible. Governments are a part of our unhealthy society and made up of human beings just like us - they don't know any more about the nature of the world we live in than we do, and they're certainly no wiser. We've been diverted from our beautiful world and lured into the worlds of others - worlds that are highly immoral and far from benevolent. It's humanity who complies with this diversion and sits quietly watching and crying about the destruction seen either on news broadcasts, or as an eye-witness in so-called third-world countries - then we move in and clean up the mess. However, we only create more mess, hatred, bitterness and division in this process. Imagine an enclosed room in which we dust and sweep the floors; all we really do is move the dirt from one place to another; the room can never be cleaned, until someone opens a window and allows in light and fresh air. We've lost our ability to reason and are living in a world of common nonsense, rather than common sense.

~~~

The intention of this chapter is not to 'tell off' humanity - there would be no point in that. I too am part of that society and see clearly that for the most part of my life I did nothing to change it - nothing to change 'me'. However, now that I see this I can't sit by and do nothing; more importantly, I know I can't rely on others to change anything for me. We were *born* into this mess, and therefore it's hard to see how we can get out of it - it's also difficult to see how we got into it. This chapter is a plea to humanity to - at least - begin to see the folly of our ways, how we've inherited this mindset and how we're leaving it as a legacy to our children. One tiny footstep towards understanding the mindset of humanity, is a huge step in the right direction. We can't make plans to live in better ways because they won't work; the plans would be made by the society that created the problems, and we know that when society makes plans things get more complicated, rather than simpler. We're re-formatting old information to try to find something new; all we're going to find inside a haystack, is hay. We only need to recognise what's going on - in good conscience - and the rest takes care of itself. If we take those 'Huh!' and 'What the heck!' moments one step further when something seems to be odd or ridiculous, rather than brushing them aside, we start a process that picks up its own momentum; it is, however, up to us to keep that momentum going, or let it grind to a halt. We need to recognise and consider why our world is being abused, before casting aspersions about who's responsible for it.

We live in a world where good news is not welcome, where those who spread love and morality are ostracised; it's a world where everything is up-side-down and impossible to comprehend or get to the bottom of, and a world where the bottom of the ladder (immorality and corruption) is considered to be the top. This situation is not 'new' - it's been spoken about for millennia and *still* we aren't listening. We feel helpless, unworthy and are in pain to the point of despair; only fear keeps us rooted to the spot - fear of the things we believe we can't change, and the things we can. In other words, we fear 'change' itself - we don't want to upset the apple cart. There's little for us to do for our 'entertainment' and 'amusement' other than to watch programs (social media too) that mock others, offer prizes, bring bad news, promote violence, immorality, ignorance and stupidity - dumbing down a willing and obeisant society. Alternatively, we can drink or drug ourselves into oblivion, act outrageously, become obsessed with our bodies, shop ourselves silly or compete with each other. The greatest entertainment of all comes from our own mind - our true elected authority. We can protest about what's going on, but a protest is only a request for somebody *else* to change something. It's no wonder that 'hope' holds no power over us, let alone faith - it's not a good position to be in. We tend to work in directions that increase our salaries - if we have a job at all - in order to pay our increasing bills; this is a material world. We work in pointless jobs that serve the system we complain about - and rely on - because we can't see the way out of all the confusion and kerfuffle that get in the way. In this world, we're *for* or *against* the system, but whatever our preference we tend to believe ourselves powerless to change it. We're not powerless at all - it just feels that way when we look at it from a subjective and 'locked-in' point of view - when we don't want, or know how, to take responsibility for our own lives.

The first step to becoming responsible is to realise how much responsibility we've put onto others; such as, governments for bringing peace to the world, teachers for the education of our children, religions for 'guidance', science for 'solutions' and a 'justice' system to keep law and order. None of these would be necessary or even exist but for the fragmentation of our world; the cause creates the effect, *but* the effect doesn't bring an end to the cause - it generates more of it. We don't have to look far to see that there's no peace, that society is largely being dumbed down and that we live without 'guidance' or justice - none of these are heading in a positive direction. None of the above authorities are healthy themselves so we can't reasonably expect them to solve the problems of humanity; they *are* humanity. The world is different when we look at these scenarios from a distance. Becoming responsible is a process - a process of self-observation and examination that leads to a better understanding of ourselves and therefore, what it means to be responsible - it's also realising how irresponsible we actually are.

The biggest argument *against* becoming responsible is that we believe if one person changes, they can't change the whole - an 'everybody's doing it' excuse - so we drop out of responsibility and join the masses; I had *big* issues with this one. The problem needs to be faced before we can see the bigger picture and before we realise what a huge difference a change of perspective can make. Too often we want to know results before we even look at problems and this is the result of learning by rote; when we learn by rote we don't learn at all - we memorise. I can't tell you how it feels to reach the age of fifty, because you wouldn't be able to relate to my experiences; we have to wait for our own birthday. In so many ways, reaching the age of fifty changes our lives - mostly because of conditioning - regardless of what the rest of the world is up to. Humanity is arrogant to think that it already understands, knows and believes itself to be in control of the universe it lives in. One person changing the 'whole' only *seems* to be impossible, until we make more than a passing effort to try it.

~~~

I infrequently refer to, but never discuss religion or politics in my books as these subjects are responsible for so much of humanity's pain and confusion. Instead, I prefer to erase all conditioning - by seeing it for what it is and looking at the world through unveiled eyes. I received several responses to my 'Thank You' page in a previous book, regarding my thank you to 'God' and it has caused some people to say 'She's *God Squad*'; how closed-minded we can be when we accept the conditioning of society, and judge others inflexibly, without seeing the whole picture. This is a trained mechanical reaction - it lacks independent and rational thought. These rejections are our resistance to letting go of our problems; we tend to refuse to hear or see anything that *might* help us. This may be because we've been let down by society before and even though our reaction isn't good for us, it's all we have for security; we know - only from our own perspective - where we stand with it. Look closely at this and it's easy to see that 'God Squad' is nothing but a well-worn cliché and that these three letters (God) are enough to break up friendships, start wars and drag us into the realms of so-called 'darkness', where we can live safely in fear; just three letters can do all that and more. Another friend of mine associated the word God with 'organised religion'. God, on my 'thank you' page is short for Godfrey - a friend that gave me so much encouragement to finish my books. I've now changed 'God' to 'Godfrey'; I changed it because I want to reach as many people as possible and if they close the book without getting past the front matter, then I'll *change* that front matter - this is my responsibility and obligation, but only if the hurdle agrees with my reason. I don't feel responsible for other people's problems or for picking up the pieces of their lives, but I do feel responsible for doing what I can through my books - it's *my* world after all. The alternative was to dig in my heels and allow myself to be controlled by my ego and pride which is always counter-productive. Many years ago I would've done just that, as then I felt responsible only for sustaining the tightly enclosing illusions that defined who I believed myself to be; these are the 'notes' we pin on the walls of our minds and refuse to remove. Does God exist? This is a question worth pondering, but only if we get rid of every thought and belief about it currently entrenched on our minds; we can never find truth in subjects that have been influenced by others and consequently, labelled 'taboo'. We're far more powerful than we dare to believe. No matter how rich or poor, how educated or how many books we've read, we can know all we'll ever need to know, only by searching inside ourselves.

If we're old enough to say 'Yes' to something, then surely we're old enough to say 'No' as well; however, we tend to make these decisions based on conditioning rather than wisdom, which is why we make so many 'mistakes' in our lives. When I was seventeen I married for the first time; the decision was made based on fairytale happy endings, parental/societal consent and a need to leave my family home; no wisdom, responsibility or reason came into my decision - I most certainly wasn't ready for such a commitment or subsequent ones many years later. I was playing life 'by the rules'. We tend to take our first 'drink' when we 'come of age' - sometimes pretending we've reached it earlier - and it can't be denied that this and other minimum age limits are entirely conditioned. We're *told* when we've reached 'grown up' status and are generally far from responsible once we reach this milestone. I'd suggest grown up status isn't grown up at all, if by 'grown up' we mean 'coming 'of age' - coming of age is not an indicator of psychological maturity, and in no way implies being responsible.

Becoming responsible begins with an honest 'change of mind' - our mind. When this happens, it's amazing to watch it in 'action' and catch ourselves out when we're up to mischief; when we look at and judge another person, when we're about to tell a lie to ourselves - or to someone else - or when we get a glimpse of our reflection in the mirror and recognise a familiar moment of vanity. We become aware of our contradictory and irrational behaviour; we know when to say 'yes' when our mind says 'no', and 'no' when it says 'yes'. When we become responsible for ourselves, we become deeply aware of our surroundings, the movement of our thoughts, and of the same *true* nature of every human being, without any division or judgement. Everything falls into place in its own time, but only if we want it to. If we remain self-observant and self-critical, riding the inevitable ups and downs of these activities, we allow in that welcome 'light' and 'fresh air', and invite grace, humility and wisdom to guide us.

Chapter 36

Consolidation

Before becoming One with humanity we have to become One with ourselves.

The title for this chapter came to me in the middle of the night. I woke up remembering a time, when I had so many different email addresses and messenger nicknames, that I had to be careful about *who* I was speaking to and *how*; it was rather confusing when multi-tasking, or talking to more than one person at a time. I'd frequently send messages, in error, to the wrong person; I think we've all done this at some point in our lives, and these momentary lapses of concentration can be awkward, if not embarrassing. They occurred in the days when instant messaging was relatively new, and we were *encouraged* - more so now - to be fearful of the people we'd encounter online; we could only message from desktop computers at that time. I had to keep notes of my nicknames and passwords because there were too many to remember by heart. I could 'hide' from some people while showing online to others and have to admit, it was rather fun and empowering; I had some bad experiences, true, but also met some lovely people with whom I'm still in contact. Not much has changed, except that we can now do all these things on different devices and websites - the charade is more wide-angled. Naïvely, many still believe that if they keep things 'private' online, no-one will know who or where they are. We may *think* we're invisible, but are easily 'seen' - by those who want to see us - as long as we remain permanently logged in to, and communicating through our various devices.

The illusion of anonymity is rapidly disappearing as social media websites tend to *encourage* us to use the *better_known@email_ addresses.whatever* to any that may be more personal such as those connected to our own domains. As we 'log in', our personal details and contacts are ripped out of our - what we thought to be private - contact list and added to the new site; the larger websites are becoming more and more closely connected to each other, resulting in us logging into multiple sites with just one click; convenient, 'Yes!'; in our best interest, 'No!'. Whether we like it or not, the cloud is expanding and enveloping us, by our acceptance of its invitation. We're not always *explicitly* asked if it's okay for the people who run these websites to copy our contacts, but it's often in those brilliant long-winded 'terms and conditions' that we click 'agree' on; who has the time or inclination to read them? To add to the intrusion, these websites then make suggestions for further contacts we might like to add based on the contacts of the contacts they copied; what other information have they gathered? It's all part of a long-term process of 'consolidation' (control) on the internet and off.

However, this type of consolidation is not what interests me and it's not really what this chapter is about. I mention it because it's a good model for the kind of consolidation that *does* interest me; the journey that each and every one of us will one day make - becoming One with ourselves; it's a process that begins by accepting the things we have no power to change, and expending our energy on that which we *can* do something about - ourselves. Becoming One with myself and humanity interests me, but becoming One with the insane and immoral society we've created, doesn't. In both cases we don't know *who* is in control, but in one case we *can* find out. When we realise this, we have a choice - remain in ignorance, or change.

~~~

Some of the things I was told as a child left me puzzled, like 'Snap out of it', 'Get a grip of yourself', 'Pull your socks up' or 'Pull yourself together'. The latter in particular left me somewhat bewildered as it seemed to me that I wasn't in pieces. Looking back, it now makes sense; more so, I would imagine, than it meant to the people who used to say it - the ones who delighted in taking me apart at such a tender age. As a child, teenager and young adult - way into my thirties - I played many roles for different audiences. We all do it (some more than others) as it's in our nature - our *conditioned* nature. There was the 'me' that spoke to family, to friends, another to work colleagues, another 'me' to my doctor, father, self in the mirror, people I didn't like and a 'me' reserved for the complaints departments in shops - I took pride in each one. There were also the 'me's' that developed the characters for my online aliases, but in those cases I gave them monikers too. All these 'me's' were like the branches of a tree - reaching out in different directions from one trunk. I wasn't aware of any of this at the time, but now realise I was 'divided', confused, incoherent and had no idea who 'me' was.

We put on different characters, for different people, but we don't do it for fun; in most cases we do it subconsciously, and automatically, as we're so used to it. We hide parts of who we think we are, and develop the parts of who we wish to be or whatever fits any given situation the best - from the various role models we encounter in one way or another. For example, I was good at complaining in shops and getting refunds for goods I was returning, but knowing what I know now, my immaturity was obvious and I probably got the refunds just so they could get rid of me - I was rather aggressive. In order to do this successfully I must have watched others doing it and tried to assert myself in the same way. My characters concealed a far deeper insecurity that was afraid of the world (my world) and I hid behind them, pretending that the insecurity didn't exist - giving the illusion of me standing up for my 'rights' - 'the mouse that roared'. It seems strange that I could act the part out, but not make it a part of my 'private' self; however, it works because when we act out these parts we reinforce the walls we don't wish others to see through; we don't like the traits we hide about ourselves, and so we cover them up with layers that please us more. I don't believe we do this to deceive, but rather to survive and also because deep down we've come to love playing 'let's pretend' - literally losing ourselves in the new characters we create or rather, assemble. I created what I believed I lacked and at the same time, protected myself in case it went wrong; I kept what I believed to be my true self 'Private and Confidential' - well hidden.

Gradually, new personas are created from our assembled traits, including our body language, speech and temperament. We spend many years tweaking these until who we really are becomes so deeply buried under personas, conditioning, wishes, hopes, pains, fears and frustrations that we don't know who we are anymore - if we ever did. If you give this some thought for a while, with an open mind, it becomes apparent that our multi-faceted characters have been entirely created and are being maintained, by us, or rather by our minds and egos. Behind all the layers of 'pretence' lies some*thing* else. For this reason 'Who am I?' is the most important question we can ponder and generally, it can only be approached by being prepared to remove *all* our artificial coverings and stripping ourselves back to bare plaster, as it were.

Like layers of old wallpaper, these layers of conditioning aren't easily stripped off. One reason for this is that there's no reward for doing so; 'What's in it for me?' is a non-starter and nothing can replace the layers or prevent our inevitable resulting vulnerability. This might feel like a waste of time but I can assure you it isn't. It's these layers that hold us in our 'prisons' and therefore, when we remove them we remove fears, pains and frustrations - it sets us free. For those of you who have long hair you know how difficult it can be to remove the tangles. You can't begin from the top of your head because the lower tangles get worse and the whole process becomes painful. We have to begin from the ends and gradually work our way up - it's much easier in the long run and when we do this regularly our hair shines and is in much better condition. There are times however, when we reach particularly stubborn tangles or awkward pieces of wallpaper and it's easy to become disheartened. It's the same process for removing our layers - gradually our pains and frustrations peel away with them; it's these layers that have caused all our confusion. I say gradually, but in reality, we sometimes let go of a lot all at once. It takes concerted effort and determination to 'come clean' with ourselves, and at times this can be hilarious and humbling. For example, if I have a disagreement with a friend and our 'layers' reveal their ugly heads again, we now tend to burst out laughing in recognition of what's happening and let it all pass over. It's much more fun than being two angry bulls head-to-head in the middle of a no-win argument, which only serves to create more layers of grudges, anger, hatred or whatever you will.

Untangling hair and removing layers of wallpaper are useful metaphors to help explain what's involved in the process of consolidation, but on a practical level they leave us somewhat baffled; they are 'outside' physical actions that we need to apply to a spiritual concept. The difficulty comes in trying to translate these metaphors into a metaphysical 'action' for a mind that has never given it any serious thought and in my case at least, it took many years to see. The concept is alien to us - we haven't been conditioned this way; on the contrary, we've been taught that outside action brings results. We've been taught that the world is physical and our spiritual nature has been ignored; we're not encouraged to think about what life is about, what we're doing here or why we're always at war - nothing changes.

~~~

I mentioned in an earlier chapter, 'Our Cluttered Mind', a friend who cleared out his attic - letting go of some old memories at the same time. Now, perhaps this is going to sound insane to you, but there's nothing we need to *physically* do; observation and recognition of how we constructed ourselves and society are what's needed to start the process. Society is a reflection of our layers and what we've buried beneath them; our world is a reflection of the mind of that society. The insane mind created our insane society and society, the insane world; surely it's time to put this vehicle into reverse by 'unlearning'. Once we see through the illusion it falls away by itself. However, it's generally difficult for us to see how to make changes to anything *without* physical action. For example:

- Our house will remain dirty unless we clean it.
- We can't get anywhere without moving our feet or on some other mode of transport.
- We can't get a worthwhile job unless we pass our exams.
- We can't buy anything without handing over money.
- We can't have full stomachs unless we eat.

We're in the habit of having to *do* something in the physical world in order to see 'results'. Our characters hang on our branches which hang on a tree trunk and our lives are dependent on a social conditioning system that's controlled by our apathy; we blame this control on so-called 'fat cats', but they only get fat on what *we* feed them. Our desires feed our society and we'll sacrifice much in order to satisfy them; for example, our spiritual journey or a debt-free life, in order to buy something like a house, a car or the latest mobile phone. The physical is a projection of what's going on in our minds; we're separated, in pain, sorrowful, confused, proud and angry. These feelings lead to wars of all types in our world, but these wars will never end, because we're fighting each other, rather than thinking about why we won't stop doing it. The first war that needs to be brought to an end is the one going on inside our head.

Our conditioning makes metaphysical exploration difficult; we can't conceive of anything outside of the physical other than what we've been taught, shown in films or read in books. There's so much (physical) that we refuse to let go of because of fear that - for example, we might need it one day. All this has to be put out of our minds if we're to see a bigger picture. We don't have to leave our homes or give up our jobs; we only have to begin to look at things in a different way and become aware of the conditioning that influences our thoughts and actions. If our lives are meant to change in the process, then they will without any help from us; the universe works in strange ways that we don't yet understand and maybe never will. Though we don't need to take physical action there are ways in which it helps. We can take a look around our homes and see how much we've accumulated over the years; this can be shocking when we realise that the inside of our homes - to a large extent if not entirely - represents the inside of our mind. All our memories and sentiments surround us and we're reluctant to let go of them - so it is with conditioning. We mirror our minds in our homes and now also on the internet, and the contents of these mirror the baggage we're not prepared to let go of. We're reluctant to let go because our conditioning, homes and belongings represent who we think we are; they serve to *define* us and therefore are the boundary between the physical and the metaphysical, or if you will, our spiritual nature. There's nothing wrong with having things - it's when those things have *us* that our problems begin.

The strength and fight we put up to keep these things secured in our homes, and memories is formidable - sentimentality and fear are powerful forces, but they can be overcome by first recognising our 'state', and then having the will to act on that knowledge. It's this act of recognition that releases us from our beliefs that they're a part of who we are. The layers, previously mentioned, won't peel away easily but they *can* be removed if we're sincere in our intentions. For example, bringing a multitude of media pages together as one; this process begins to set us free from our multi-faceted characters. As long as we behave in different ways for different audiences and keep secrets from same, we can't expect to keep our balance while we hop from one to another like bunny rabbits running in and out of different burrows. It's important to see that our social media accounts and walls are an accurate reflection of our minds - we have different 'faces' and 'names' for each account. When we hold multiple accounts, we maintain the fragmentation of our minds and humanity, locking people into the groups we separate them by; for example, family, friends, best friends, work only, drinks pals, ex-boyfriends, people I know, people I don't, or whoever else you can think of - it's a silly game; it wasn't good for me, and I'd venture that it's not good for you. We live in a world - physical and projected - of 'private', 'business', 'social' and 'none of your business' and this will never lead to our peace of mind, or to humanity coming together as One; on the contrary, it creates further separation and therefore, more conflict.

When I consolidated my accounts, it was the first step in my journey to finding the 'true' me. It freed me from a heavy mental burden, freed me from the upkeep of maintaining so many alter-egos and the associated problems that go with that. It was like opening all the doors and windows, allowing the wind to blow away the stale air and dust - carrying with them all my aliases and leaving 'me' behind. Now, I *can't* get caught out, or feel guilty about a message sent in error to the wrong person - life feels 'above-board' and I know this is the best way for me to be - it's in my best interest. Where it will all take me, I don't know, but I *do* know that my efforts haven't been in vain.

Chapter 37

Louder than a Whisper

Our hearts are the loveliest landing place for truths that are hard to face.

Without sincere self-reflection, we do little to serve the psychological advancement of the Human Race. Instead we serve or function as a human resource, whose only purpose in this world is to advance an antiquated, ritualistic, selfish society, in which we choose to remain ignorant of our true nature; this is a system that abhors benevolence and seeks to complete its own agenda - total control at *both* ends of the scale. In other words, there are those who want to control and those who don't mind being controlled - you can't have one without the cooperation of the other. We fight, argue, hate, gossip, envy, judge and abuse each other, so much so that we don't recognise that we're doing it; ironically, harming ourselves more than the recipient of our sentiments. We poison rather than nourish our bodies, minds, land, air and water. We harbour guilt, grudges, conditioned negative responses towards others and carry the weight of our pasts on our shoulders, whilst wearing a mask of superiority. We retreat to the safety of our cocoons while pointing the finger of blame with a 'What can *I* do about it' attitude - mentally assembling jigsaw puzzle pieces that we trim, re-colour or squeeze into place to suit our loves, jealousies or prejudices, for whatever we choose to believe. I find that when I confront anyone with any of the above their kneejerk reaction is 'denial', swiftly followed by the immovable 'I don't want to talk about it' wall. More often than not people respond with 'Why would anyone want to do that?'. Come on! We know that hurting each other is so in our faces that we can't see beyond it. Peace doesn't come out of conflict - only power and submission can come from it and in our hearts we know this - it won't drop out of the sky or come knocking on our front doors either. Some people often repeat 'World War III is coming' messages and this concept really needs to be thought out with something greater than compliant activism. We're always waiting for peace in our world, which means 'war' itself has never *actually* ended - there's much more to war than guns and bombs. What's it all about? I can't answer that question, but I *can* think about it, and I do, as living with this level of insanity is unacceptable to me; stepping back a little and seeing the larger picture reveals much. Our world is seriously out of balance and heading towards its own destruction.

Why do we allow it? In my case, I've had to completely change my romantic notions about what a human being is. We can be confrontational, spiteful, violent, aggressive, egotistic, confused, selfish, judgemental, needy, pessimistic and dishonest with ourselves and others, even amongst friends. One of the reasons is because we're frightened. We live in a world of fear exacerbated by the never ending stream of doom-laden negativity; be it war, terror, lies, sickness, suffering and the underlying threat of the destruction of our planet, which pours from the media - 'social' or otherwise. We can't make head nor tail of the information we've been fed and don't know who to trust or what to believe in, if anything at all; we've created a society that's full of doubt, suspicion and judgement - about itself, and that's just the 'news'. Closer to home, we fear the possibility of the content of that 'news' impacting on our own lives; such as, unemployment, loss, violence and poverty. Ultimately, we fear the arrival of our own impending death, or of those who are close to us; we frequently see and feel the pain of *loss* and mourn those that have 'moved on' ahead of us; the clear message here is that whatever we become attached to we *will* one day lose, and this makes death dark and undesirable because, death hurts too much and there's *nothing* we can do about it. I'd suggest that this is one of the reasons we cherish our personal belongings and beliefs so much; when we fear losing something, no matter what it is, we hold onto it that much tighter - it's comforting.

~~~

Language and images are the tools we communicate with and have come to understand; how we interpret them is another matter altogether. Horror, dystopia, science fiction, fantasy, thrillers, adventures and time and space, are just a few of the genres that we love in games, films and books. We find it hard to see these as having any real substance; they're seen as entirely fictional by the majority of people, which makes them hard to conceptualise as anything *other* than fiction - yet they're worlds that we love to live in. Our inability to ascertain the truth or to know fact from fiction leaves us feeling helpless and vulnerable. We like to see these genres as fictional, because the pain of there being any fact in them is too horrific to contemplate and too complicated to fathom. There's a philosophical thread running through all these entertainments that we don't tend to notice - mostly because we're not looking for it, but we *do* recognise it. Imagine a nice big fruit cake; the mixture has been thoroughly blended and the cake slowly baked in a hot oven - we can no longer identify the ingredients, save for a few. We love the appearance, taste, texture, aroma and richness of the cake, but rarely consider how it was produced - we're more interested in eating it than anything else. That this cake tastes amazing is the only truth we're interested in; how it was created doesn't interest us past being able to reproduce the product - and many variations of it - in order that we might experience it again … and again.

~~~

Each morning, we wake from a sleep that we either feel rested from, or don't. Our lives are habitual and mundane, regardless of what day of the week it is; weekends are also routine - naturally there are a few variations to this. For many years the first thing I'd do every morning was reach for a cigarette, rush to the kitchen for a cup of coffee and listen to the news. Suitably 'fixed', I had a shower, got dressed, returned to the kitchen for breakfast and then all that invariably followed; work, shopping, meals, commute, television, laundry, social life and sleep again. We perform these routines so often - perfectly timed - usually because our focus is on the next scene; we label our actions a part of 'daily life'. For example, alarm call at 6.00 am, snooze button, alarm again, coffee, shower and dress, kids up, breakfast at 7.00 am; we're always watching the clock and routines demand this - even 'running late' is a routine. Some days these routines are harder to perform - perhaps because we didn't sleep well or went to bed too late, tired, stressed or maybe drunk - making it impossible to 'unwind'. We're unable to re-charge our energy for the following day and therefore, we function less efficiently - something we've come to accept so well that we're unaware of it. Even holidays are routine and often more exhausting than our working lives - they're like moving home, temporarily. Routines are unavoidable to some extent; we need sleep, our meals and at least some form of work/passion to keep us occupied - a *raison d'être* without which life would have little meaning.

We'd serve humanity much better if we could see that society is our elected master - a master that saps our energy, is self-destructive and at the same time, afraid of its own destruction. There comes a point when the folly of our unsustainable way of life can no longer be ignored, and then we've a choice - start thinking about what we're doing here or continue living with our eyes closed. For me this was a 'no-brainer', and once I took my head out of the sand there was no way I'd ever put it back in again. The whisper was loud and the sound of the bell crystal clear - more than enough to get my attention and make my head ring in confusion. The decision to change does leave us rather disorientated for a while - those bells keep ringing and resonating and that's perfectly normal. When I was very young I'd love to spin round and round until I got giddy and then I'd *have* to sit for a while until I recovered my senses - it's confusing for our brains/minds. This is rather what it can feel like to retire or to be made redundant; the pressure of work is suddenly off and, unless we're one of the super-planners, we can be at a loss for anything interesting or stimulating to do, unless we've already found our passion and purpose, in which case we're more than happy to have more time to pursue it. We get confused when we break cherished habits whether we enjoy them or not; *any* habit is an addiction and therefore, hard to break.

When we begin to question *everything* the fog begins to lift and things become clearer - not crystal clear, because what we see is so unfamiliar. It takes time to clear the clouds of conditioning and to change our point of view. Think of it as walking without knowing where we're going; there's no GPS, map, road signs or compass; however, despite being unclear about our destination, *something* keeps us going. The *drive* is powerful and our energy increases with each step. It's not that we didn't have this energy before, but rather that we expended it elsewhere. Energy is like money; if we waste it on useless things we've nothing left for the things we really need; however, our own energy is more valuable than money can ever be, but we can't know this until we start preserving it. If you're struggling with the concept of money being energy then just change perspective a little - think about how much power it has in our world.

The road mentioned above probably seems a bit silly and I can see that. Why would anyone want to think about walking along a metaphorical road that may lead nowhere? I can't tell you where it goes, but think about this - where does the road you're on now lead to? The answer to the latter question is known by everyone - absolutely *nowhere* unless you consider the graveyard to be your only

option for a choice of destination. This alone - illusion or not - was enough for me to change direction; there's not much point in continuing along the road if it's not heading where we want to go and when we realise this, our fear of changing dissolves along with our will to continue on the same path. Okay, so we might not *know* where we want to go, but that's not important at this stage; what *is* important is that we know where we *don't* want to go. Yes, our bodies still end up in the graveyard and if we believe this 'material' world is all there is then that's rather discouraging; however, material is *not* all there is and despite the beliefs of some people, 'something' else *does* exist and I'd suggest that's worth thinking about - we know it very well.

~~~

In this world - as we understand it - we have to live with 'time' and telling you that it doesn't exist would generally be unacceptable; it was to me for a long time (no pun intended). More often than not this idea leaves us feeling inadequate and frustrated because we may not understand it straight away - please don't give up on it. We've had *time* in our lives since our 'births' and we're reluctant to let it go - the mind and ego want to hold onto it and they're powerful, influential and unyielding. Society reinforces the illusion of time by putting clocks and watches just about everywhere we turn. It's almost impossible not to know what time it is or what we should be doing at any particular time; for example, working hours, tea breaks, lunch breaks and holidays; 'life' is always 'arriving' and 'leaving' via various timetables whilst we plod on. On this 'journey', some days feel good and can leave us feeling as though we're floating on air, but some feel bad - the bad can drag on for weeks, months or even years. Nothing really changes other than how we cope with day-to-day problems as they present themselves; however, this is a necessary part of our journey and therefore, not wasted. It's only wasted if we don't keep moving and what doesn't move is effectively, dead.

~~~

We live in a dualistic world of all possibility and that means we can turn it all around; one way to do this is to observe our own behaviour and change it according to how we want our world to be, as discussed in 'Observation'. We need each other and we're all a part of a greater whole. All of the above traits I mentioned regarding humanity can be changed - we need only make the choice and the process begins. Yes, yes and yes, it's *hard* and feels contradictory, but our lives are hard and contradictory anyway - as is to be expected in a dualistic world. One of the wonderful things about dualism is that we have choices; there's a 'yes' and a 'no', a 'this' and a 'that'. All we have to do is choose to change and when we make this choice something different evolves, but not if our decision isn't in earnest. If we change, we'll find that there's so much more to us; for a start, that the Human Race is One, life is worthwhile and wisdom, grace and humility are worth striving for. Our focus needs to be on, not what others are doing, but on what *we're* doing. We need to make a decision to be *done* with pain and suffering (my continuous affirmation) and *mean* it. We've everything to gain and absolutely nothing to lose. When we see this, the layers of beliefs we've created for our 'characters' fall away and that's *very* revealing. There'd be little point in just looking at a box covered in wrapping paper and ribbons - we'd never find out what was inside if we didn't remove them. Life *demands* something from us, but we continue to ignore this and instead, we take more and more from it - returning to its river only our anger, tears, refuse and frustrations.

We make decisions to change our lives all the time; for example, when we:

- Go on a diet.
- Make a new year's resolution.
- Start a new hobby.
- Decide to get fit.
- Move house.
- Begin writing a book.
- Join a group.

But these days, in most cases, they're only temporary pastimes or more accurately, passing fads. These occupations make us feel great at first, but they soon get pushed to one side when we get bored with them, or find something else to fill our lives with - our homes and garages are full of unfinished projects. I see these fads as being rather like fireworks - they look impressive in that first skyward rush that explode into enthusiasm, but they soon lose their sparkle and then, the burnt stick of 'reality' falls back to the ground. We can easily mistake these fads for our true passion, but passion doesn't burn away or fizzle out. Passion is the fuel - it drives itself and once ignited, it can't be easily extinguished.

The closest physical and psychological relationship we can ever have is with ourselves - from birth to death. We can never leave this 'home'- not even for a second. This is so important to contemplate. Problems have arisen because we believe we're the person in the mirror, the personality we created, the slob, the professional, the big man, the small man, the characters in films, the beauty or the beast. Our pasts define us; for example, I am who I am *because* of my past and therefore can't let go of it - this is just an excuse not to remove its stubborn stain. These beliefs are like the tethers of a hot air balloon preventing it from going on its adventures - until the stakes are pulled out, the balloon isn't going anywhere.

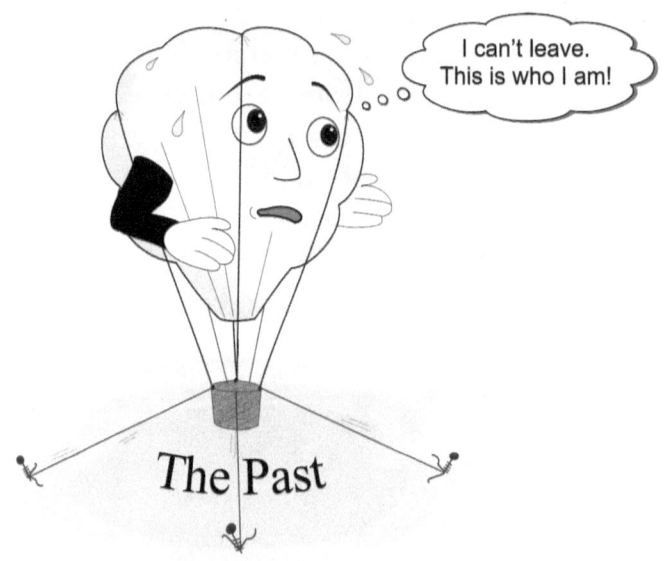

I know of some people who work well past their retirement age, perhaps because they're terrified they won't know what to do with their time or have enough money to survive on; however, once the chord is cut, most people wonder why they didn't do it earlier. The real terror here is that when we retire there's nothing left in our lives that defines us, so we refer to ourselves as what we used to be; I *was* a doctor, a secretary, an engineer etc., and these tend to be what we like to talk about with other people in later life - reliving our past glories. It's important to see that these professions aren't *who* we are - they're what we *do*. We allow society to define us with its various labels and divisions; such as, unemployed, professional, white collar, labourer, academic, elite or lower class, to name but a few. We have no boundaries, unless we choose to construct them, or allow others to forge them for us. When we were young children we had very little control over this situation, but now we do. Yes, it's true that we are where/who we think we are because of our past, and when we realise this we have the opportunity to break free from its grip. Why do I say 'opportunity'; wouldn't we just 'break free'? No! When push comes to shove, and the enormity of what stands before us becomes apparent, fear kicks in; we then start to backtrack and make excuses about why we can't change; excuses that allow our past to hold us in its comforting arms, until the 'right moment', the 'right tool' or the 'right person' comes along - *safe* in the knowledge that they never will.

Chapter 38

Betrayal

No-one can let you down, unless you depend on them.

Unlike the rest of the chapters in this book, I was asked to write about the subject of betrayal. I skimmed this topic a little in 'Completeness', but here I want to focus more on betrayal itself. This request was the first I ever received and for a while I felt reluctant to write it because I saw it as a part of someone else's journey and therefore, it didn't belong in my book. However, on reflection, the topic came into my field of vision for a reason so I decided to examine it and now, it fits rather nicely right here. Often, the things we put up the most resistance to are *exactly* what we need to focus on.

My initial thoughts about betrayal were to do with disloyalty, particularly with regard to personal - non-familial - relationships, because this request was put to me in that context. However, like all things, when we zoom in closer to any topic - not relying on conditioning for explanations - a new and clear understanding of it evolves. Betrayal is probably one of the most destructive actions one human being can do to another, or to themselves. It's 'breaching an agreement' and we're betrayed every day in one way or another by:

- A stark contrast between an image on a packet and its contents.
- Things promised, but never received.
- The betrayal of confidences.
- Political manifestos that don't deliver.
- The infidelity of a trusted friend.
- Ourselves for 'believing' in things we *know* to be false.

and much, much more. With this new understanding comes simplification and responsibility. When we hold onto the aches and pains of betrayal, simplification and responsibility are the last things we want to hear about - we prefer to hold others accountable.

More often than not we already know who's going to betray us well in advance - we prefer to gloss over the indications that we first noticed. Some of the things I once found endearing in other people proved to be 'early warning signs' that I chose to ignore; one example of this was the alcohol habit of one of the men I married - his drinking began several hours before lunch and ended at bedtime. At first he didn't drink too much, but it quickly became apparent that his consumption of alcohol had been reduced/hidden in order to 'secure' our relationship. Other examples of advanced warnings of betrayal are a 'roving eye', flirtatious personality and various excuses we somehow *know* are lies. We've been taught that no-one is perfect and therefore, we don't expect perfection; we're happy to accept a person's 'down-sides' and can initially convince ourselves that these are 'charming' - because we *want* them to be. If we think back far enough to the beginning of these relationships, we realise, in many cases, that what we now call 'betrayal' was, on discovery, anything but a surprise. Still, we feel 'let down', again and again.

~~~

It's impossible to talk about betrayal without talking about trust. Trust is something that grows, rather like the construction of a spider's web and gradually its delicate threads build up into this beautiful thing we call trust. However, if that web gets damaged by the touch of betrayal, we can never restore it to its original form - try as we may, we'll always be aware of those broken threads - giving rise to suspicion and the expectation of further betrayal. Suspicion (mistrust) is something that increasingly pervades our society in all walks of life; business, private, social and personal - so much so that we don't even trust *ourselves* and therefore, faithfully rely on the authority and consequently, the guidance of others. A great many people are reluctant to reveal their identity online and I've had many refuse my offer to send them free copies of my books - some didn't want to reveal their addresses. Even when the intention is kindness, people feel threatened in some way and find it difficult, if not impossible, to trust each other - often the result of many stories in our various forms of media that focus on betrayal, violence and other negativity.

These stories include the shattering of an illusion; for example, in someone famous we once trusted - our apparent 'fallen heroes'. We can't trust the stories and because suspicion has been planted into our minds, we no longer trust the person concerned regardless of whether or not they're innocent; suspicion and judgement are powerful condemners - with or without proof. More importantly, we believed in these people and what they stood for - we 'loved' them - and it *seems* as though our trust in that was broken; repeated stories like this leave us unable to trust or believe in anything at all. Because of this we're more likely to accept the authority of those 'in control' in our world - they so often remind us 'never to give out our personal details' and to 'check the credentials' of just about everyone we come into contact with. The 'authorities' offer us a protective parental arm to snuggle into; to accept and rely on this 'snuggle' could be unwise.

In this mixed up world it has become necessary to double or triple lock our doors and windows and in many cases, to live in 'secure' blocks that have more than a hint of penitentiary about them. Security is a highly profitable business which translated means, that the creation of communities that live in fear is profitable. Despite so much betrayal and suspicion in our world we *still* tend to jump straight into new relationships or one night stands and in some cases believe that this makes us 'free-spirited'. What it really does is misleadingly make us feel as though we're in control of our lives - it injects a little artificial and temporary *freshness* into them, but on a deeper level, these relationships confirm what we believe - that we're 'not good enough' - and leave us feeling more insecure; mostly, they don't contain anything worth holding onto and we know it.

Misplaced trust is like a walking stick we believed could stand our weight and one day, while we're leaning on it, it breaks and we injure ourselves falling down. We can repair the stick with glue or tape it together, but we'll never be able to trust it to support our weight again. Trust is something we give to someone else and when they betray it, it can hurt more than we've ever been hurt before, leaving a deep, ugly and *unforgettable* scar. To give someone our complete trust is to invite them to betray us one day - it also means we rely on them to treasure that trust as much as *we* think they should. A broken trust is the shattering of a firm expectation - with full confidence - that we can rely on someone or something outside of ourselves. The problem with this expectation is that it doesn't allow for the fact that we're all fundamentally the same and - save for our different experiences - destined to experience the same 'ending'. The walking stick we leaned on broke because it was flawed in some way, and though we suspected as much, we still chose to put our trust in it; whatever we entrust to another human being or organisation, we run the risk of losing one day.

The betrayals mentioned in the above list come about because we live in a fragmented world. We're divided (and sub-divided) from each other in hundreds of ways and therefore, as individuals, we reach out to others for what we believe we lack. We reach out because we feel incomplete and we feel this because we *are* incomplete. There's a thought that lives in the back of our mind 'There's more to me than this - I'm missing something important', but every time it pops up we push it right back where it came from; it's called a *Hintergedanke* in German, which means a 'nagging unconscious thought', but we don't trust it. To ignore it isn't very different than refusing to open the mail that's delivered into our letterboxes. One person I know told me there's no point in changing the way he lives, because no-one else will, and this is just one reason why the insanity of this world persists; this idea also demonstrates how we prefer to place ourselves in what we think of as 'safety in numbers' situations. Trusting ourselves - and our instincts - involves sacrifice and determination. More importantly, it involves a lot of self-reflection - not one of our favourite pastimes, and so we keep ourselves busy in order to avoid it. When we question everything, then by definition it follows that we must leave everything we believed in behind, including our suffering, pain, mistakes and regrets. This process includes all forms of 'security' in our relationships with others and yes, that includes family; relationship implies attachment and with that attachment, we run the risk of betrayal; the greater the attachment, the greater the injury we sustain when the walking stick breaks. No, I'm *not* saying anyone has to leave their home or their family; all that's needed is to examine the subject, observe the world we live in, how we interact with it, and deal with whatever follows those actions.

The betrayal of a child is caused by the same fragmentation of society. For a long time, I hated my father for putting me into an orphanage, particularly at such a young and tender age. I was unable to protest or defend myself against the staff and saw the world as an unfair place to live in. I was unable to complain to anyone or report incidents, as I never had the language or knowledge that it was possible to protest against mistreatment - for me, it was both terrifying and normal and more than likely the reason I decided to forget about it (most of it anyway). I felt wretched in the orphanage - as though I were something worthless that had been discarded. I now see this differently. We can't expect our parents, whose lives have been as painful and problematic as our own, to be loving towards us; they simply don't know how. This new understanding doesn't make what happened okay, but it does help to see how a particular situation came about and more importantly, how not to dwell on it. We tend to be pretty bad parents to our children; we give them 'too little' or 'too much', tell them scary stories, threaten them if they don't 'behave' themselves, and after they reach school age have very little to do with their upbringing. When they begin school, we lose whatever influence we once had over them - it passes into the hands of our various forms of education and media, who are people just like us. I've already had feedback from a friend on my 'bad parents' comment, so I'll elaborate a little. Are we looking after the planet and eradicating violence for our children or future generations? No, we continue to destroy it - and ourselves - in many different ways. This is also a form of betrayal; we're damaging and poisoning the world our children must live in and making them afraid - very afraid.

~~~

Let's get back to that stick for a moment. Sometimes the stick breaks because it was leant on too heavily. Too much trust can be a heavy burden for another person to carry and I'd suggest that this trust can be broken, not always with the intention of hurting another person, but because the weight is too much to bear. The trust of billions of people is in the hands of an untrustworthy minority who head political, religious and financial organisations. This gives them enormous power - *our* power - and we don't even know who they are, yet rely on them to sort out the mess our world is in. It's *us* who need to take care of our own welfare; we're the light *and* the shadow in this world and therefore, accountable for our own predicament. Any way you look at it, giving trust and risking betrayal of that trust are the prices we have to pay for relying on something or someone else. Trusting in someone else leaves us vulnerable and that means powerless and in fear. We prefer to walk through a 'minefield' after someone else has 'cleared the path' ahead - then we'll be more than happy to join them. There's nothing to be learnt from following in someone else's footsteps; they can't clear *our* path for us because they haven't lived through our experiences. Because most people want to live a risk free existence, nothing changes. Most importantly, our reluctance to change is one of the greatest betrayals of all - the betrayal of ourselves and consequently, of humanity - it's also 'spiritual laziness'.

Chapter 39

The Abyss of Loneliness

Loneliness is what happens when the connection between ourselves and our source is broken.

As a child, I can't remember exactly at what age, but it was over a period of many years, I used to watch one of my sisters closely. I saw her as a role model, because she was the only relative around at the time; in some ways, I saw her as a surrogate mother though I know that was the furthest thing from her mind. I'd try to dress like her, mimic her walk, talk and copy some of her other well-rehearsed traits, but these attempts to 'become' her only left me feeling more confused than ever about my place in the world. I depended on her for my happiness and wanted to share her friends, because I never had any of my own; this always backfired and I don't think I meant any more to her than a pat-on-the-head 'little sister' - an act that made her feel good about herself and left me feeling betrayed and humiliated on many occasions. I was a means to an end, as was she. I'd allow her to choose my clothes as I'd no idea what would or wouldn't suit me and she looked good in anything. My sister always chose something unflattering for me, knowing that I'd wear whatever she suggested. The nearest I can get to explaining how I felt at the time is to say that I'd been born on the wrong planet, into the wrong body, to the wrong parents and had the wrong siblings; I was effectively, lost.

This sister, in later years had many 'friends' and a busy social life. I was invited to go out with her, but I was still introduced to her friends as 'my little sister' and ended up feeling alone at parties, pubs, or bars; they held only more emptiness for me because no matter how hard I tried, I was unable to fit in - for the life of me I couldn't see the attraction. Years later, I realised we'd been looking for the same thing (acceptance) and - ironically - she'd wanted to be as much like me as I'd wanted to be like her, which came as rather a shock when I first realised it. We both needed to 'belong' somewhere and to be 'loved'. Despite her popularity, she was as unhappy and lonely as me; the parties, alcohol, drugs and crowds only served to numb the pain of her loneliness.

~~~

My perspective on loneliness has changed over the years and I now see that loneliness is not the same as being alone. Loneliness is a deep longing for completeness, which we search for in companionship, friendship and our need to relate to someone on the same level as ourselves, which is why we need to go out socialising and the like. 'Alone' doesn't need any of society's attractions and is free from the struggle of trying to 'fit in'. What was really happening inside my head was a resistance to partying my life away - counting down the minutes to an 'acceptable' time to go home, yet dreading the same loneliness that drove me to the party in the first place. However, the happiness we seek *can't* be found in this way - it's like trying to draw water from a well with no bucket on the end of our rope. It's important to see that just about everyone is doing the same thing from an innate longing to 'connect'. This need can't be met by anyone or anything else, because the only 'agenda' at these social events is to curb the loneliness that lies in our hearts. I needed something that held deeper meaning and in later years this led me to challenge what I'd come to know as 'reality'. It wasn't that I was unable to express myself, but rather that my expression was met with indifference; yet I kept on trying and failing, which increased my feelings of inadequacy - leaving me feeling lonelier than ever. It's easy in our loneliness to try to find happiness on the 'outside' through social activities, because this is how we've been taught to do it through clubs, groups, teams, classes and of course our parents and siblings.

Loneliness causes us to hide - from ourselves and others - behind self-constructed barriers and it's terrifying to think about taking them down. The power of our loneliness is much greater than our ability to overcome it and hits us hard from every angle (inside and out). No matter where we go, what we do or how busy we keep ourselves there's no way to escape our loneliness other than to seek out its cause. I mentioned to a friend that I was writing this chapter and when I asked what loneliness meant to her she replied 'I don't like to think about loneliness, because it makes me feel so lonely'. Another friend said 'You can have a huge family and lots of friends, but behind closed doors you feel lonely, because it's always you that makes the effort - which is upsetting - so you create a distance between you and *them* which results in you feeling lonelier still'. For my part, I started writing this chapter many times, because I was both drawn to and repelled by it - I also procrastinated. In all three cases, it's clear to me that loneliness is something we struggle to understand, face, live with or talk about and for this reason, I've written this chapter.

~~~

In general, we tend to consider anyone who's lonely to be socially *unacceptable*. The lonely feel that there's something wrong with them, because they're unable to play 'the game' *correctly*. They're labelled as 'loners', 'misfits' or given some other belittling title. In truth, the lonely would like to connect with people, but in a way that's more meaningful than having a 'good time', fitting in with a crowd, discussing the latest bad news or following a particular fashion; the lonely resist these 'guided' definitions of themselves. 'Loners' are *deep* and I'd suggest that it's for this reason most people choose to stay away from them - 'deep' is not our idea of 'fun'. People who are lonely see possibility; they see the beauty in how we *could* live, rather than how we do. Somehow, the lonely know true friendship, but are unable to find it and tend to hate themselves far more than they think others do. The more we see that isn't good in our society, the more space we put between ourselves and those who choose not to. The trouble with things like parties, is that they're someone else's idea of fun (the host); we're expected to fit in, and all there really is to do at them is listen to the problems people want to tell us about, feel frustrated that no one wants to listen to ours, discuss current affairs, behave badly, eat party food, compete with each other or drink alcohol - formulaic and meaningless activities. These social gatherings are often a distraction from the pain of reality, memories we'd prefer to forget and an uncertain future - a temporary escape from the mind for everyone who 'succeeds' at enjoying them. We put each other under pressure to *develop* fashionable social skills and appearances, which are nothing more than prescribed antidotes for loneliness and we do this in order for humanity to fulfil a need for company and 'excitement'. Popularity is something that's subjective and superficial; it's abstract and requires someone to be admired and, a trail of admirers; all of whom must play out their roles until the party comes to an end, which ultimately it must do. One modern example of this scenario is the plague of 'selfies' that has hit social media websites - selfies that scream out 'Look at me!' Where is the wisdom in this sort of lifestyle; is wisdom something society intends to eradicate?

The lonely know something's missing from their lives *and* also from the lives of others who suffer the consequences of our 'partying', and demands for more toys and excitement - they find gatherings painful, rather than enjoyable. No-one sees or hears us screaming; we're effectively invisible, and that leaves us with a deep and inexplicable feeling of 'out of placeness' or if you will, an inability to be comfortable with our surroundings despite the fact that we can't go anywhere else. We don't so easily escape the knowledge that so many in the world are suffering on our behalf and we can't live with the weight of that on our shoulders. We're left staring at a reflection that we don't want to look at - let alone think about - and consequently, keep ourselves busy in order to keep our gaze averted.

We vacillate between our loneliness and the pull of the world of 'excitement' and social gatherings in the hope that they might bring an end to it; for example, if we happen to meet Mr or Mrs Right or a new 'best friend'. We're not at all comfortable in this 'ping pong' situation because deep down all we really want is a permanent end to our loneliness, rather than a respite from it. We're the frontier between the two worlds; as the mind sharpens, it's possible to see that this frontier doesn't actually exist. It's not possible to see this clearly until we're prepared to remove our walls altogether, which leaves us vulnerable, but how else will we ever be able to see the 'whole' picture. Deep down we all want the same thing - inner peace and happiness.

Aside from when we're feeling lonely at home, it's not just at parties that we feel this loneliness, but also at school, work or in any other place where human beings are gathered together, regardless of their age. Just take a look around a crowded train or bus next time you're on one - no-one speaks to anyone else, but rather they're absorbed in their own worlds. The deepest feelings of loneliness aren't just felt when we're alone, but so often in public places where we want to reach out to others but our arms aren't long enough - or strong enough - to break down their resistance. I'll go so far as to say that this includes at 'spiritual' meetings; most people have only their own agenda, and if we say something that contradicts what they *want* to hear, conflict follows and more barriers are raised instead of removing existing ones. Mostly - deep down - we're thinking 'I don't want to listen to *you*, I want you to listen to *me*' - often we're not listening to what the other person is saying and waiting to cut in to the conversation with our 'take' on things. These gatherings can leave us feeling that no-one knows or understands us. However, we can take consolation from knowing that they don't know or understand themselves either.

~~~

Perhaps it's our fear of loneliness that's created so many homes for the elderly - before they'd remain with their families but now more and more of us have our *own* lives to live and can't handle the responsibility for others. It's possible that we see our elderly family members as being lonelier and more isolated than we're willing to imagine, or live with. Society takes up all of our waking time and therefore, we don't even *begin* to reflect on these important matters until we close our eyes, but by then we're invariably so tired that we fall asleep. Where can this situation end though; if our children become too difficult to handle will we, in the future, also think about giving them up to some other authority? It's already necessary in many families that children are cared for by childminders so this isn't such an alien concept for the future - it's been woven into literature for a long time now. From who or where will these children ever gain their wisdom?

Loneliness can cause us to feel as though no-one knows or cares that we're here. Some of the deepest forms of loneliness we can experience are; for example, when we've been out all day and despite crowds, not managed to speak to another soul, or when we're checking to see if our telephone is broken because no-one has called. Other examples are when we:

- Watch the clock to see if it's time to go to bed.
- Pass our time *staying* in bed.
- Make a cup of tea before the last one we made gets cold.
- Flick through television channels and never really watching anything.
- Nip out to the local shop for something we don't need, just because we want to see another face.
- Check for messages when we know full well there aren't any.
- Feel as though we're the only person in the world.
- Comfort eat, drink alcohol or take drugs.
- Look to others for our security.

There are some people I know of who are so desperate to connect that they read, and reply to, their spam as though it were from a friend; this is a dreadful state of affairs for humanity to find itself in and no-one should have to suffer like that. There isn't a human being who can make us feel better in these situations; we lock people out because they don't understand us, and ourselves in because *we* don't understand them. However, all of us want to be seen and heard by somebody else and because we want the same thing, we can't find it. In other words, we can't hear the cries of others while we're crying out to be heard. Interestingly, when I was feeling lonely I never thought about or noticed anyone else that felt the same way; this is how deeply loneliness penetrates - we can't see further than our own agony. No matter how awful loneliness feels, it doesn't have to be that way; we can find all we need within and now I see that my loneliness was in fact a blessing. For many years I didn't use the time wisely, or realise that I was my own greatest friend.

In all the loneliness situations I've mentioned above, the barriers we put up serve to prevent honest communication. The conflict is both external and internal and has a deeper meaning than is at first apparent - it ignores the innate *need* that I mentioned earlier, to connect with each other, not only on a physical level, but on a psychological one as well. Understanding this is pivotal if we ever want to bring an end to conflict. Serving one 'side' can't bring any balance into our lives, but only more struggle - isn't that what happens in war? Each side fighting each other and each person fighting their own internal battle, and from that we kid ourselves that we can bring about peace. As mentioned above, the walls of both worlds (internal and external) must be removed, or else it isn't possible to see what's actually going on. The apples of one tree are its fruits and there's no conflict between them or the tree that bore them - that would be ridiculous. Likewise, we're all the fruits of humanity and it's equally ridiculous to think that we're not, *or* that one of us is more important than another. We're One and unlike the apples, we're not only physical, but conscious, and therefore have a great deal more responsibility in our world than we're prepared to - or do - take on. Like the apples we have an origin - connecting to it when we're feeling lonely is the best and wisest thing we can ever do. We feel lonely because we're disconnected from our source and resist reconnection - for whatever reason. This causes us to seek solace in the company of others, who are as lonely as we are and therefore, cannot help us. When we figure this out and reconnect to our origin - by deconstructing our barriers and examining how they were erected - we'll better see what's magic and permanent - what never has and never will change.

Chapter 40
Personality, Pride & Other Tough Stuff

Pride is the pedestal we climb up onto - shame and humiliation, what we feel when we fall from it.

To understand what pride is, we need to know what it is we're proud of and how we came to be proud of it. In furtherance of this, it's necessary to put together some of the things I've previously discussed, and to examine how they relate to us personally. If we want to strip ourselves of our illusions, we must first understand how they've been woven together over the course of our lives and how we became so attached to them and to other people; we can't see the truth while we still believe the deception. It's a process of 'unpicking' the weave and we resist because we don't *want* to be unpicked, but these traits were not with us when we were born and are not part of our true nature. We're possessive and protective of our identities, convictions and contradictions - though we tend to be dissatisfied with how we see ourselves. We find a sort of comfortable security in our attachments to the familiar - rather like a child holding on to a torn and ragged favourite teddy bear that no other 'teddy' can replace. Our creations are our 'pride and joy'; who, after all, would we be without them?

Human beings are the most cunning of creatures and skilful at assembling character traits and appearances that are nothing more than a metaphysical photofit of what we call 'ourselves'. These traits make up our character/personality and we continually tweak them for any given situation, wearing them proudly as though they were works of art - for works of art they are. We pretend, in the main, to be interested in others by calling ourselves generous, hospitable, kind, charitable, respectable, compassionate and approachable, but usually we're nothing of the sort - how could we be when we live in such a mischievous world that's obsessed with 'self'. Generosity for example, can't exist without a need for it and surely for us to behave kindly towards someone, implies unkindness in the first place; we're full of contradictions. One business example of this is a answerphone greeting that the creator probably thinks is funny 'Your call is important to us ... please hold the line'; the call can't be important at all as often, some thirty minutes or so later we're still holding on - so they get away with it. If we all hang up immediately after hearing the message the companies would see how important our call actually is, and would have to adapt their system to become one that values rather than wastes the time of its clients. We're master imposters and pranksters trying to con and outwit each other with just about every breath we take and we're only interested in - on a conscious level - what's going on inside our particular 'bubble'.

The concept that our personalities are woven can be a difficult one to grasp. We tend to see ourselves as being entirely physical, ignoring - or having no curiosity about - our spiritual nature - we think in 'ego' mode. We take great pride in our 'creations' and nurture them until we become exactly what we want to be; professional, social, downright miserable or whatever else we choose to make of our lives. More threads are interwoven over the course of time; for example, at the age of five, we've no idea about things like romance or how we'll relate to it when we're older. We do however, begin to formulate this trait through fairy tales and other stories building up our dreams of what it would be like to be 'grown up'; for example, how we'll interact with the different people who cross our path. We wrap ourselves up in these 'dreams' and if anyone attempts to expose them, we move into 'defence mode' to keep the fabric of our *imagined* world intact.

The difference in our reaction when we see the innocence, beauty and the miracle of a new born baby and an adult is stark. The adult was once the baby who has grown into everything we've added on to it over the years including jealousy, hatred, judgement, opinions, fear and pride; however, the innocence, beauty and the miracle are no longer recognisable to us behind our hardened hearts. As a baby our character begins to be formed according to our environment; everything we see, do, taste, touch, smell, hear and everyone we meet influences and shapes our personality - society is our 'parent'. Society is the mould that shaped our characters; we hold on to the accumulated memories that parented us, because we'd be unrecognisable to ourselves without them. We however, add to our 'egos' with every thought, gradually building up so many layers that even *we* can't see through them. We get caught up in the illusion and change - where possible - our appearances to fit (metaphysically and physically); I'll be a brunette, a missionary, or a judge for example. We tweak what we see as our faults through 'new year's resolutions' or 'fads', but these rarely amount to any change, because they tend to have no more meaning than a change of clothes. On a deep level we don't like who we become, but as our 'personality' is 'apparently' all there is to us, we hold on to it tightly in order to survive; our inner character is very different to our projected one which to all intents and purposes, is the shield that protects - or hides - our true nature - the two are in conflict.

One of the features of living in a dualistic world are the contradictions present in each of us - these are the internal arguments we can't get any peace from. Rather than living in a way that prolongs our lives making them happier and healthier, we generally live by a 'death wish', and in order to make this wish come true we poison our minds, water, land, air and bodies. Despite increasing laws on 'Health and Safety' there's little evidence that we care about them, until we're personally affected; for example, when we - or someone close to us - becomes ill or has an accident, or perhaps if dirty water comes out of our kitchen taps. How can we have so many concerns about health and safety on the one hand and cause so much devastation and illness with the other? We know the risks and damage caused by smoking and alcohol for example, yet corporations make enormous profits from them; we're paying for our own destruction in the name of a 'good time'. We rush to support charities during a crisis, but generally, make no effort to eradicate the need for them. Far too often we prefer things just the way they are - things that are bad for us, as opposed to good; we become addicted to them as we turn to them for 'comfort', which is really 'escape'. If you don't agree that we like the 'bad' just take a look at any given week of yours regarding; food (unnatural), cleaning the house (chemicals), television, newspapers, fuel consumption, gossip, waste, judgement, thoughts, spending, smoking, alcohol, mind dramas and pride. We can't be perfect in this world, but we can become aware and that in itself will make a huge difference, which we can't see or benefit from, until we earnestly put our minds to it. The only possible reason I can think of for humanity to live this way is that we all know, deep down, that our true nature is infinite, so we play for high stakes believing that there really isn't any risk at all. Does this argument have any substance? Only we can decide that, as individuals - not in groups.

~~~

Pride is an inflated sense of achievement and superiority that allows us to hold our heads up so high that we can't - and don't want to - see where we're going. We award it to ourselves in the form of self-congratulation, while bathing in our pool of glory and achievement. Society encourages us to take these 'bows' with a host of awards and certificates that we aim for in one way or another, because with them we become 'successful' and are considered to be 'upright citizens'; in other words, we get the approval and respect of the 'authorities' that set *their* standards for us to achieve. One of the most serious side effects of this ballooning of our egos is that it leaves others far behind in our wake of gratification - causing division and resentment. Another effect is that we become what others want us to be (copies of our predecessors) and can therefore, never discover who we really are. I mentioned in an earlier chapter - 'Am I Good Enough' - that there were three things we can do from the top of a ladder; stay there, climb down or fall off it and 'staying there' has surely got to be the least stimulating of options and because of this boredom, the most dangerous. We need things to do, see or think about - things that are exciting, new and challenging, no matter how meaningless they may appear to be.

The mind needs continuous action and it doesn't want to be quiet even for a moment; a so-called 'couch potato' is still stimulating his mind by watching the television - or rather having it stimulated for him - regardless of what he's watching or how many times the program has been shown before - repetition is not boring for the mind and our lives are full of it. Our mind seeks stimulation anywhere it can get it and this, I'd suggest, is why we keep ourselves so 'occupied'. Television, radio, newspapers, commuting, work, shopping, chores and our social lives feed the mind's need to feel all sorts of emotions like fear, sadness, happiness, despair, frustration and anger; our world has become so noisy that what we can't bear - more than anything else - is silence. Whatever we do with our daily lives - regardless of where we are on the 'ladder' - we strive for more and more and *more* of it, but the stimulation comes from something external and therefore, it's nothing to do with self-discovery and, nothing new.

It's possible to watch our pride in action - it's one of our ego's treasured facets. The ego is the star of our 'show' and it doesn't want to leave the stage even for a moment. The mind is always scheming to maintain and increase its hold on us and it's highly efficient and very much 'on the ball' - it's as sharp and as dangerous as a dagger. Pride comes into being when we identify ourselves with our 'achievements' or in some cases, achievements we claim to have made, and also when we polish our appearance/character - rather like shining up those medals. But pride isn't just about medals and ladder rungs - it's the sharpest tool that separates us from our true nature and from others. Pride is:

- Apparently, the number one sin.
- The need to win an argument - though we may not know what we're talking about - and also to shout louder than our 'opponent' in an attempt to intimidate them into submission.

- A refusal to pick up the phone when we want to speak to someone, but are unable to bring ourselves to dial their number.
- Boasting.
- Refusing good advice because *we* know 'better'.
- The belief that we deserve the respect and admiration of others.
- A control mechanism.
- All about 'Me'.
- The wall that refuses to ask for help when we need it.
- The refusal of help that's being offered.

First we have to come clean about our world and then we'll be able to take responsibility for all that's going on in it. Our intention in these cases is to stand our ground - no matter what - even when there's no solid ground to stand on; pride prevents us from retreating or admitting error. We know full well when we're doing this, but refuse to back down; watching our pride in action brings that to an end because just in watching it, we become more self-aware and also see how ridiculous pride actually is. If you wish to see what pride means to the collective mind just do an internet search for the word and see what comes up both on the *web* tab and on *images* - you may be surprised at the results - they are there because *we* put them there. As our awareness increases it becomes very difficult to maintain the façade and increasingly, we're able to admit 'error' without feeling humiliated and with this change our pride begins to subside. Before blaming society for being a 'bad' parent to us, we must first ask ourselves if we've been 'good' children in it.

~~~

Society is an accurate reflection of the human mind; proud, stoic and resistant to change - though we collectively agree to live in it and to uphold its practises and regimes. It's what we do every day, and each one of us is, and has been, put through an educational system that demands the continuation of this proud society - it's a generational loop and it's an unhealthy and unworthy one. Despite society being unhealthy and destructive we're proud to be a part of it - flying our particular flags. We tend not to want society changed or criticised, particularly by those who think differently, seemingly posing a threat to the *status quo*, which we fight to maintain - a *status quo* that's created a 'hive mind' mentality. The world is the way it is because the majority of people like it this way, despite their protestations to the contrary. It's important to discern that we can't find our *centre* when our 'walls of pride' are up or when we're following somebody else's directions, because we're relying on an unhealthy system and an unhealthy mind to do it for us - which they're incapable of doing.

When our pride takes a 'hit', a wave of mixed emotions washes over us - ranging from anger to fear. Our pride gets hit when someone thinks they could've done something better than us -effectively deprecating our efforts. We don't like criticism, regardless of whether it's constructive or not. We see what we do as excellent - even if only by effort - because we've rehearsed it for a long time and to have someone not see us as we want them to, hurts our pride very much. One example of this is when we invite friends to dinner and one of them comments - across the table - that we added too much salt to the meal, or that they'd let us have their perfected recipe for what we spent all day preparing. Pride is wobbly and easily offended, particularly when it's met with such condescension. I'm sure that every one of us knows that feeling of vulnerability; such as, when we trip over a paving slab and everyone who saw it watches as our face reddens and we struggle to get up again - believing, if not knowing, that all eyes are upon us. This is also how it feels when attention is unfavourably drawn to us in the company of others, such as with my 'pat-on-the-head' big sister in the previous chapter.

Men feel vulnerable if they leave their trousers undone and women if they're caught with their skirt tucked into their knickers as they come out of the public toilets, particularly if someone points it out before they realise it. In these moments of discomposure, we feel humiliated and exposed because one of our walls collapsed in a momentary lapse of concentration - we dropped our guard and our ego *never* likes that. Two of the layers behind our pride are 'shame' and 'embarrassment' and we feel these when our wall of pride shows cracks, leaving us exposed because of our 'failure' - usually a failure to keep up expected appearances. Imagine, if you will, an actor whose moustache slips or forgets his lines in the middle of his finest performance - he's no longer fully 'under cover' and shows his infallibility, as he struggles to straighten the moustache or to remember his lines - in front of everyone. Even if we correct the error before anyone notices we worry that someone *might* have seen us because we're so self-conscious about the things we do. In the reverse of this situation we get to keep our wall up when we watch the misfortunes of others, and I'd add that we're happy these didn't happen to us. If something unfortunate happens to someone we dislike or disapprove of, then we may get a certain amount of enjoyment from the incident and consider that justice has been done - a rather judgemental and superior attitude to take, but we take this stance often and state that 'it served them right', or if we don't know them we may think that they 'must have deserved it'; bad is okay as long as it's happening to someone else, and unfortunately this attitude has reached pandemic proportions.

In order to cope with the world and the society that we find ourselves living in, we build up a shield of pride and this helps us to feel acceptable - by gaining respect or a good reputation. But, society doesn't reward our achievements any further than to 'stamp out' another medal or title before moving on to the next in line. Are these rewards really worth anything at all, or do they fill a hole with something temporary? Heroes are soon forgotten as others wait to step into their 'still warm' shoes; no-one is indispensable in our society. We can find ourselves at a loss when our services are 'no longer required' - all we're left with are fading memories, and a future in which we clearly see the 'finish line' that we'll soon have to cross - 'Now Syndrome'* then takes on a whole new and less exciting meaning. Because our lives are relatively short, we've become selfish and proud - taking what we can get while we still can. Because we can't see the results of any effort to change within our lifetime, there's little motivation to change anything for the benefit of 'future' generations - as evidenced by the way we treat our world now. Our personalities are masks - personas that we're proud of and love to defend - if we see this then what's actually happening becomes clear as day. Problems occur when we don't want to strip off these masks any more than we want to walk down the street naked. If we *want* to find truth, and something new, then we must accept *unconditionally* the necessity to leave behind pride, illusions, personalities, titles, certificates and medals. I'd suggest that now - *before* we die - is a good time to begin the process.

* Discussed in 'Sensation, Desire & Relevant Reflections'.

Chapter 41

Hidden

I listened to your lies of all shapes and sizes
Of colours and words in your master disguises
I never knew the centre could be
The infinite roots that you'd hidden from me

So fare thee well
And good-bye my friend
The truth must come out in the end
The clouds are dispersing
They're almost gone
And now is the time …
To sing out my song

I lived with all your fears, tears and maddening abstractions
Like love, lust and your comical actions
I never knew the centre was free
This heartfelt love that was always in me

So fare thee well
Adieu my friend
It will all come right in the end
The lying is over
Your treachery clear

It took me a while
To breach this frontier

So fare thee well
Au revoir my friend
The truth is out - now the light won't bend
This night has passed
And it's almost day
I'm not sure where I'm going
But I'm sure on my way

Chapter 42

A Compendium of Thoughts

If you're following me and I'm following you then we must be going round in circles.

~Suffering ~

I'd suggest there isn't a 'soul' alive who can state for certain what the true nature of a human being is, how we got to be here, or what we're supposed to be doing with our lives. There's no doubt that what we're doing to our world isn't in our best interest, nor that of the wonderful creatures we share it with; everything is suffering unnecessarily in one way or another - physically and psychologically. This suffering is 'alive'; it passes between us from generation to generation, government to government, book to book and from film to film, like a mutating virus passing through the physical and metaphysical veins of humanity, and for the foreseeable future there appears to be no respite. Humanity is the cause *and* effect of its own adversity. The media is so full of the suffering going on in the world that we're becoming immune to it - so much so that it takes a horrific image, of perhaps a disaster victim, to catch our attention, but even that image can't hold it for long. We talk about suffering for a moment or two and then get on with our daily lives expecting various 'peace' organisations to get their act together and bring it to an end - turning our backs on it after our initial outcry. We feel safe and comfortable behind our walls and borders, believing that these events are nothing to do with us, *personally*.

Suffering - of humans, animals and the environment - is entertainment on our screens; we decorate our online walls with horrific images kidding ourselves that this will help to eradicate the problem. Advertising these images doesn't alleviate the problem - it serves to increase levels of fear, hatred and division. There isn't one of us who doesn't know this though with some, it's buried so deep that they can't see it. To put this into perspective; we go to war, glorify and reward the 'heroes' of that war and *then* declare horror at the images of the resulting devastation - we applaud the cause and subsequently condemn the effect. We then make films - and games - about these horrors (even re-enacting battles on their anniversaries) and they become highly profitable best sellers; as if the horror itself isn't enough, we're willing to *pay* to see more of it.

Images - of suffering are more powerful and influential than most people realise and we put them everywhere arguing that we need to be informed, yet despite being regularly 'informed' these things keep happening and we keep passively discussing them. How will the nightmare ever end if we don't take responsibility for it? We claim that the corporations, governments, army, navy and terrorists etc. are responsible, but they're human beings just like us. They're no different to you or me except that they're willing and know how to take advantage of our fear *and* we allow them to do it - one gives the order and the other obeys. Human beings commit these atrocities and that's what must stop. If we don't *want* war, then we won't have it. The process *must* and can *only* begin within each of us but when we want to make everyone *else* stop what they're doing then nothing will ever change. Who after all, would you allow to change *you*?

There's a sense of great unfairness that occurs to all of us at some point in our lives - a feeling of being cheated out of our chance to live in peace, because we were born into a world full of cruelty, horror, war, hatred, racism, violence, politics, religion and sickness. There's also a sense of limitation and a lack of control; we find that we must comply with regulations in a world where it's impossible to find justice. We're encouraged to make the most of things and accept 'that's life', by someone else's standards rather than our own. We inherited these regulations from an unhealthy society and they must be changed or in some cases, abolished. Very few people question this 'powerless to do anything about it' situation or choose to examine it further but if we do, it becomes obvious that we're not here by 'chance' and that things aren't all they seem to be. Together, we *can* live joyously, rather than accepting suffering as our only option and something we must endure to find peace - this is as preposterous as taking a lethal dose of poison in order to live. In

'Open-Mindedness' I talked about a feeling I once had about life feeling pointless, but since writing it my view has changed - life isn't pointless, only what I was doing with it.

I recently met a lady who believes that 'this life is it' and although she sincerely believes that, she's content to 'accept' the struggles of our world until she 'comes to an end' and, as is the case with most of us - quite bizarrely - we prefer that end be delayed as long as possible, which is somewhat masochistic. Surely it's wiser to ask why we're living in a 'back-to-back' horror movie world than not to question it at all. There's something absurd about an innocent baby being born into this mess with 'no way out'; in this scenario, being born can be compared to being thrown into a dungeon with no idea why and no chance of getting out again - a life sentence. No! No! No! This is *senseless* and surely invites at least a little investigation on our part. If anyone of us *were* thrown into a dungeon surely - at the very least - we'd attempt to find our way out again, rather than accept our 'fate' and give up?

~~~

A friend of mine said that this book 'won't suit everyone, especially if they don't like thinking' and I've heard similar comments many times before. It's true that many people don't like thinking; we're fatigued by the pace of life and already have enough to think about; however, what's the point in having the capacity to work things out for ourselves if we don't use it? If we don't use our ability to think - preferring to be 'entertained' - then someone else will do it for us and consequently, make our choices and take on our responsibilities. In my opinion, we each have a responsibility and obligation to act in a way that's guided by our conscience - to work with it rather than against it. For example, dropping pennies into a charity box and then walking away may salve our conscience, leaving us feeling satisfied that we've 'done our bit'. Perhaps it would be wiser to ask why these charities exist in the first place, and why we allow ourselves to do so little to eradicate the need for them; in our hearts, we know how to achieve this - all we have to do is listen to and act on this wisdom. Often we prefer to push aside and ignore our conscience but a little reflection tells us that we *have* one for a reason. Only we, as individuals, can begin to understand this when we reflect on it - to reflect on how we live our lives and why we tend to prefer what isn't good for the whole of humanity, rather than what is.

The difficulty in ending the suffering of humanity is that we must begin with ending our *own* first - as an individual. We must literally, change our mind. We don't think changing ourselves will make a difference, because it seems too simplistic an idea for such a big problem. How can changing 'me' change what's going on elsewhere in the world? Because it removes the walls and masks that separate us from it - psychologically speaking. As long as we focus on the suffering happening 'elsewhere', the whole will remain dysfunctional and we'll continue to maunder. Keeping our attention on what we can change, instead of what we can't, will make a big difference to *our* world; the mouse *can* overcome the lion, if it will just try, and each generation has the opportunity to do just that.

~ Impermanence ~

There's a sense of 'life is temporary' amongst us - it lies in our hearts and consciences. Years of pain and struggle have pushed the importance of this sense to the back of our minds; we choose to lock it away where we don't have to think about it again. That we'll die one day is too awful to contemplate, particularly as death - due to conditioning - is frequently painted as dark, morbid and terrifying - it's something sorrowful to be feared, and life, something to be held onto at any cost. Thinking about these things is considered by many people to be an act of rebellion or anarchy rather than intelligence but more than that, it's thought of as *risky* - we tend to prefer to live in fear rather than take risks. Just about everywhere we look looms a sense of impermanence, of time corroding and wearing out *everything*. No matter how robust we make them, a tower block will erode just as a straw house will, though the time taken for the process varies enormously - nothing we can do or make will last forever. Though time is abstract and an illusion, we must live by it, so surely it's prudent to use it wisely while we have the opportunity, rather than live in a way that tosses a 'heaven or hell' coin into the air hoping for a glorious outcome when we catch it again - if - *and only if* - we've behaved ourselves.

There's a big difference in the timescale of something like a pyramid crumbling and the lifetime of a human being. Because we can't relate to a human being living for thousands or millions of years, it's hard to put this into perspective. Over one, two or even three generations there's very little visible difference in the deterioration of a pyramid, making it more difficult for us to see the transitory nature of them. Historically, these constructions have been here much longer than we have and will remain long after our deaths. When one archaeologist dies, another takes over where he left off and another after him. *Still*, we continue to study and preserve death and history, as though it could save humanity from destruction. This is impossible. We're alive *now* and it would be far more intelligent to stop digging into the graves of those who died a long time ago; it's impossible to find something new in something old, or something new in something that hasn't happened yet (future). We have a dream to go into 'outer' space one day in a hope to find another world, but space exploration is also a 'relay' occupation and each of us knows that we won't be alive - or going on the trip - when 'or if' it ever becomes possible. Knowledge of this is a reminder of the nature of our impermanence and also that while we're delving into our pasts and possible futures there could be something far more important that we're supposed to be doing, realising or noticing - now.

We assign great value to our belongings and want to hold onto them for as long as possible, even if that means passing them on to our children who we hope will value them as highly as we do and subsequently, pass them on to theirs. Just like us, our ancestors lived a 'smash and grab' lifestyle, accumulating as much as they could in their own lifetimes and even trying to take their wealth with them into their next life. In a desperate attempt to live on after our deaths we try to 'immortalise' the things we've accumulated over the course of our lifetimes, but these are memories that we'd be better off losing our attachment to while we're 'living'. If we don't then we're merely passing on a legacy of the misery of the world yesterday, to the world of tomorrow. These things that we'd like to hold onto so much are the spoils of a world that has known and *still* knows great suffering - they can't be used to change it. We don't just pass on the objects to the next generation, we pass on their energy too, as discussed in 'Emotions and Energy'. Whilst we're occupied with our pasts and futures, rivers flow, waves break on the shore, eggs hatch, the wind blows and the sun 'rises' and 'sets'; what doesn't change is far more important to contemplate than what appears to.

A friend of mine once lost their mobile phone and they were very upset about it; not about the phone itself, but the deepest secrets it held about them that could now be discovered by someone else. This information will survive long after our deaths, even if we do wish to believe it's private. We're not only concerned with our pasts, we're also occupied with passwords, logins, electronic privacy, speedy up-to-date technology and fast free delivery of our purchases; these are the things that concern and control our world now, but life can't continue at this pace without self-destructing at some point - this message is very loud indeed.

It takes determination and effort to cover the ground between the starting block and the 'finish line'. There are times when our heads spin with all the confusion - this is inevitable when we set our intention to 'de-condition' our mind; we're trying to hold onto what we've got but at the same time, radically change our lives. We have to clear out that jam-packed dirty and dusty attic after many years of storing our memories up there with one vital difference; we discover that it's not just our clutter up there - it's the clutter of humanity and we've been collecting it for a *very* long time. Many can't see the point of deep thought on these subjects, and from asking quite a few people I know, the general consensus is that we'll find out what life is all about 'all in good time' and that we should enjoy it while we can. However, are we really enjoying our lives or simply opting out of anything that requires us to use our capacity to work things out for ourselves - thereby merely keeping ourselves occupied or if you will, filling the gap between what we think of as our 'births' and 'deaths'. We'll find out 'in good time' implies that we already know we'll *survive* this life, so surely it's worth a moment or two to think about what we're doing here, rather than taking our time for granted? Time is impermanent and therefore, cannot be relied on for anything other than 'running out'. Time decays, time rots and time passes by.

In summary, we think of death as something to be avoided and can go to a lot of trouble to pretend we're younger in ridiculously superficial ways; for example, wearing younger clothes or having plastic surgery. Neither of these, or any other way, will prolong our lives; they serve our vanity and attempt to cheat nature, but the clock still ticks. We don't know the difference between 'reality' and imagination - what we've come to think of as reality we continually reject in the hope that we can conquer life itself - we'll settle for nothing less. This attitude is misguided and the likely cause of many of the world's problems and more than a little arrogant for we each are, effectively, temporary residents.

~ The Journey ~

There are times in our lives when something makes us stop in our tracks and wonder where exactly we're heading, but such thoughts tend to be forgotten about as quickly as they occur and the 'moment' is overtaken by the pressures of daily life; for example, we have to cook the dinner, get the kids to bed or keep an appointment. These thoughts remain lost in the 'garage' of our minds amongst all the other clutter that we accumulate, like an old car we've been promising ourselves that we'll 'do something' about, but never quite get around to.

In the physical world, a car left standing for any length of time won't start without 'shock treatment'; for example, by having its battery charged. It needs help as it can't get going by itself. Deep thinking helps us to start our *own* 'engine' but it takes a while to get our motors running smoothly and confidently - our engines have been left standing all our lives. Just like the car, which needs to be taken on a long journey in order to fully charge its battery again, so we need to follow through with anything that comes our way after a 'what the heck' moment or perhaps a 'push' from this book. If we choose to shelve this opportunity then our battery won't charge and we'll remain 'parked'. Leave a car for long enough and it'll refuse to start altogether and could be costly to get going again, if at all.

It's the same with us - the longer we wait, the more reluctant we become to embark on our journey.

Imagine sitting in the back of our cars expecting that by some miracle a driver will appear out of nowhere and take us to our various destinations such as the shops, work or the cinema. The idea is ridiculous and we wouldn't even consider it, yet we do this with our journey through life, based on the beliefs of our various authorities (our drivers) and our goal is to earn enough money to pay our bills and buy enough possessions to keep that same society going, or rather sections of it called 'Me' and 'Mine'. Ironically, every time we embark on any kind of journey, we leave everything we cherish behind anyway. Each time we leave our homes there's a chance we may never return to the belongings and people that we believe define us and are reluctant to let go of - yet our lives can end at any moment, without prior notice.

Yet we wait ... and wait ... and don't get around to thinking about the true meaning of our lives. Perhaps we're waiting for scientific 'evidence' to tell us that this 'invisible' journey really *is* important, or maybe for the arrival of an anticipated saviour. But this inaction puts the onus of our welfare - and our very existence - onto something or someone else. Meanwhile, we - humanity - believe there's enough time to discover what's 'true', but until we do it's 'business as usual'. It's quite a gamble to wait for the unknown and waiting isn't exactly an odds-on favourite, especially considering the direction we're already heading in - disaster. Only we can walk on our path and only without holding the hand of another, otherwise we're just following someone else in the hope that *they* know where *we're* going.

Once when I was driving - in the days before we had satellite navigation - I got lost after being diverted from my route. There was a car in front of me, that I'd naïvely followed since the beginning of the diversion. The driver seemed to know the area well because he wasn't glancing around, as we do when we're looking for a sign of some sort - he didn't appear to be lost. For this reason I decided to follow him - if you drive, I'm sure you can relate to this. It wasn't until he turned into a driveway several miles later that I realised my foolish mistake - more importantly, I was still lost and as it turned out, further away from my destination.

When we water ski in the wake of a power boat we can get into all sorts of difficulty after its engine stops; whereas we were 'walking on water' our skis and bodies then sink into the sea again and to use a cliché, we haven't a leg to stand on. We rely on the speed and momentum of the boat to keep us afloat and it's a lot of fun; dolphins have fun swimming in the wake of a ship, but fun is *all* it is and there's no deeper meaning to it or permanent change in the life of the dolphin. It's the same on dry land. Take for example a popular self-help book whose momentum carries it way up the best-seller charts; we may feel so lifted when we read it but that feeling is temporary. Primarily, this is because we're *reading* about how someone applied self-help to their life. It's a different matter altogether when we try to apply it to our *own* life because it doesn't account for our individual experiences - we can't walk the same path the author is treading.

'Self-help' is exactly that; we must help our-*self* and remove ourselves from the belief that we can plug into someone else's energy field and expect it to power our lives - our journey isn't theoretical *or* physical. If we were given a blank canvas, paintbrushes, paints *and* instructions by Leonardo Da Vinci, we still couldn't paint as he did. At best, we can create a *copy* of his work and however good that is, it will always be only a copy - a *fake*. Where's the value in that? We must create our *own* masterpiece. We would however, feel good about having received Leonardo's gifts and instructions. If something makes us feel good, it's prudent to find out why, because more often than not that 'good' is nothing more than what we want, rather than what we need. For many years I avoided the best advice I was given because the *best* advice is never the easiest to swallow and neither does it make us feel good; the application of good advice involves effort, sacrifice and risk - a big part of our journey. Good advice can sometimes be recognised by the force with which we reject it. There can be *no* permanent change unless we're prepared to make permanent changes - we have to want those changes, more than *anything* or *anyone* else.

Keeping our 'sights' on a target - our journey - isn't an easy task. The mind distracts us at every opportunity and it's easy to become disheartened. I used to feel frustrated when this happened and it can feel like a hopeless task to get back on track. But all we have to do is raise our bow, hold it steady and repeat this process until we're no longer distracted by 'Upgrades', 'Free Beer' or '50% off Sale' signs. Through this repetition the mind begins to lose its control and with this comes the revelation about how much control it has over us and also, a clearer understanding about our *two* voices; we built the 'wall' between them and only we can take it down again. It's a gradual process and we can't speed it up any more than we can speed up the flow of a river as it returns to its source. All we really have to do, though it's tough, is to keep our eye on the target; say 'Yes' to truth - whatever that may be and at whatever cost - and 'No' to the illusions. This is the only way to remove our conditioning unless we're one of the few 'blessed' by a rare 'Eureka' awakening experience. When we watch our mind closely we see how it loses its hold - it's worth thinking about 'who' realises this; *'Who am I?', 'Who am I?', 'Who am I?',* is our journey, and the journey is a miracle.

~ Miracles ~

The world can cater for all our needs. No-one needs to be thirsty or to go without food or shelter, yet our cities, towns and villages are full of various 'institutions' set up to provide these basic necessities for those who *do*. Our desires and their numerous divisions; greed, selfishness, competition etc., are the cause of the problems we delay solving. Dependent on a corrupt and menacing system to supply us with silly things we can well do without, we're unable to see the miracle of our world as a self-sufficient, wondrous and generous 'planet' - we take it for granted and abuse its gifts. The miracles have to be looked at, seen with increasing clarity and deeply contemplated.

Then, because we change perspective, we begin to see things in an entirely different light. Take for example the miracle of water; we fill our kettles, wash our dishes, scrub our floors and protect ourselves from getting wet with umbrellas - never noticing what a miraculous process is taking place. We can't know where water originally came from, or why there's so much of it, but we can think about the wonder. Water floats on itself when frozen, expands, crystallises, flows, reflects, cleanses, dilutes, dissolves, evaporates, quenches thirst as well as fire, falls as rain, snow, hail, sleet or dew, hangs in the air as mist or clouds, returns to its source and so much more - all without any help from us.

We're surrounded by miracles but can't see them and therefore, are unable to appreciate them. When we stay focused on the wonders of the world our lives can't help but be transformed and we see things differently - we change channel. A crumbling building looks very different to me now compared to the way I perceived it twenty years ago. The difference is nothing to do with measuring the further deterioration of the building, but in the way we observe it; for example, seeing that there exists a natural 'automatic process' that over time, returns everything to its source. I can't tell you how to do this, but you can see it for yourself if you're determined enough. That determination involves seeing the futility of the way we live now and realising that we're powerless to change anything unless we change ourselves; as I've said many times before, it's a process of negation; we must all change sooner or later - no exceptions.

A 'new born baby' is a miraculous reminder of how far from innocence we've drifted and continue to drift away from. A 'toddler', a reminder of how much we don't mind that these babies lose their innocence and how foolishly we prepare them to become 'streetwise', so that they can live *successfully* in the complicated, violent, decadent, threatening and competitive world we've created for them - rarely, if ever, to notice the miracle of their own existence. As they grow, they become mirrors of ourselves and then, because we don't approve of what we see in them, families become divided by children who complain about their parents, and parents who complain about their children. Parents compete with parents for the best dressed and equipped children - providing them with the masks and toys that society wants them to have. It's difficult to know how to break the chain and very few people have the energy to think about it; we've become disheartened and frustrated by this inherited chain of psychological disorder, because we feel powerless; however, we *are* that society and only we can change it. Each one of us in our turn was once the miraculous innocent new born baby - I'd suggest that thought is a valuable one to ponder on.

One of the greatest miracles that we ignore is the miracle of our own existence. From the joining of a sperm and an egg we become a single cell; we don't think about where the sperm or egg come from. The sperm and eggs are somehow produced by our bodies and most of them go to 'waste'; not all of a woman's eggs become part of a human being and out of *millions* of sperm cells produced by a man, only one - under the right circumstances - gets to fertilise an egg. The miraculous process of procreation has become little more than a joke and a highly profitable business; we've turned the beauty of human reproduction into an immoral multi-veined industry -

advertising, porn, violence, degradation and 'a relay society' are just a few examples of these veins. Many miracles take place during the creation of a baby and continue after it's born; a baby grows, changes, learns and in due time apart from its nails and hair, stops growing. The above is highly simplistic compared to the rest that goes on in this process but my point is that we don't see or think about how the hair on our heads can grow so long, but not our eye lashes, any more than we think about where a supermarket gets its apples from. We tend to see things that our senses attract us to, but never think about the miracle of these senses or the fact that we have them in the first place. Mostly oblivious to the miracles that surround us, we continue in our acquisitive lifestyles, forgetting that without prior notice we can lose everything we value so highly in the next moment. Still, we cling to our delusional arrogance that we can conquer 'outer space', control the universe and believe that we're in control of our lives. We each have a time limit in these bodies, ordained or otherwise. There's nothing to lose in thinking about this, so why are we so afraid to do so?

~ Nothing for Nothing ~

I've written a great deal about humanity in my books and on many subjects that ultimately lead to *the* big question; 'Who am I?'. On the way to that question, many thoughts arise that challenge our existence and purpose - showing the futility of the way we live and how it leads to further suffering. One example of this is how we destroy the beautiful creatures that share our 'home' with us; elephants, tigers and other creatures we hunt down. We destroy them, and then set up institutions to protect the few that are left - if this isn't insane then I don't know what is. Apart from the excessive consumption of products and information that lead to the rapid advancement of a technological evolution and a psychological devolution, we're inactive. Each of us is one of billions, who passively observe this horror unfold and this makes us miserable as everyone 'on the stage' appears to be in control, while *we* feel powerless to change what's happening - we accept this powerlessness and at the same time, complain about it. Rather than ask the question 'Who am I?' we're more interested in who or what we can become on that 'stage'; for example, free, rich, healthier, attractive, famous or even infamous - thus adding to our problems. We enjoy applauding, criticising, comparing ourselves to and 'rating' others - one of the reasons we enjoy films, news, comedies and reality shows so much.

We seek a 'high life' - an *easy* life - not to have to work or *think* about a lack of money for the duration of our lives and we call this state 'success'; this success requires either hard work *or* 'luck', but no matter how we achieve it we must still leave it all behind one day - it's superficial. It's not because we're *innately* lazy that we look for this 'high life', but because we're weary and resentful of the treadmill that supports a system that serves no good purpose whatsoever. 'Deep down', we want 'out' of the 'rat race' - we *know* it's fruitage is poisonous; however, this is the 'highest' life that society has to offer, so we 'tread-on' hoping to achieve it knowing that there are too many applicants for the few positions available and consequently, 'slump onto our couches' in frustration. It's because of this boredom - and loneliness - that we succumb to any sensational pleasure we can find - in many ways it's our 'reward'. No matter how much money we may accumulate to live 'higher' we'll never find happiness, contentment or more importantly, the security that we seek, because we'll *still* be all we have for company if we get 'there' - the same face looking back at us in the mirror, only much older; the same conversations going on in our head, only more bitter. There isn't any place we can be in the world or any level of 'success' we can achieve that will change how we feel about ourselves.

There are times when we may feel a surge of energy to change something, because we've had enough, like when we decide to make a stand against something in our life that has been problematic for a long time. We may, for example, write a letter of complaint to our employer about being over worked or the laziness and incompetence of our colleagues that lead to an increase in our own workload, while they take it easy. Those of us who find ourselves in this position tend to 'unwind' once we've written the letter and then spend hours editing it, until we talk ourselves out of handing it over at all. Our motives for editing the letter are many and varied; for example:

- We fear upsetting people.

- After writing our letter our anger has dissipated and we may even feel regret.
- We take the blame and convince ourselves that we're being unreasonable and making too big a deal of it.
- We're not ready to let go of the problem.
- We walk to the edge of change, but then fear the change we seek.
- We fear the unknown.
- We fear the fallout of our 'betrayal'.
- It's not team-spirited.
- We'd prefer that our employer realise what's going on for himself.

So we back off and allow resentment to build up and the problem to continue. The new version of our letter doesn't resemble the original in any way. In fact, often it ends up more like an apology for our inadequacy rather than a complaint against our colleagues; for example, 'I'm sorry, but I just can't cope with this workload'. The familiar may not be *much* but it feels secure in some perverse way nevertheless. The fact that we're doing the work of others arrives because we feel it should be done and we assume responsibility for it. We were never forced to do somebody else's work and therefore, not accountable should it not get done. The whole drama however, is *entirely* of our own making and stems from a will to change others to our way of thinking, rather than to change ourselves. Importantly, this drama is known only to ourselves; no one else is aware of our anxiety and *more* importantly, the problem remains unresolved.

~~~

It's no good acquiring thoughts from self-help books or wise men and women; this knowledge is worthless unless it's applied. I read a one star review of a random self-help book and the reviewer said 'There isn't treasure here ... just the promise of it'. This reviewer was looking for answers, which are impossible to get from a book, or its author. We must do the work ourselves and know that there *is* work to be done. Imagine, if you will, holding a bottle of medicine and expecting to get better just by reading the instructions - it isn't going to happen. Similarly, whoever wrote the above review was obviously disappointed that the author's 'prescription' didn't deliver its promise. The reviewer was looking for 'quick-fix' answers outside in order to heal what was hurting on the inside - little wonder in a world of 'instant-on', 'no-effort-required' lifestyles. When the reviewer didn't get what they wanted they attacked the author. The ability to do so makes us feel empowered, but in truth, we do it because we *lack* any 'true' power of our own and in its place, accept the illusion of it. Our lives have become convenience lives - they're formulaic and organised and we're fast losing our skills in favour of the 'industrial-led' lifestyles we created. Without a cause (consumerism, for example), there can be no effect (industrialism) - without the effect, there can be no cause - a chicken and egg situation. Without changing, there can be no change - nothing for nothing.

~ Promises ~

A promise is an assurance that we *will do* what we have said and the promisee expects it to be carried out; this commitment has been greatly diluted over time and has become no more than a 'throw-in' word that we have little faith in. We make plenty of promises to ourselves and others - too often without matching intentions - and these become 'heavy' reminders on our minds, refrigerators or notice boards, because we know we're expected to keep them. A promise - regardless of who it's made to - is something we hang on our 'to-do-list' or more frequently, on our '*not*-to-do-list' - which is usually much longer. These promises tend to consist of things like sticking to a diet, drinking less, spending less money, studying more, returning something we've borrowed or doing a favour for a friend. They get pushed to one side in favour of the things we kid ourselves are more important - these tend to be our 'habits' like going shopping, doing the housework, watching television, doing the laundry or any other mundane routines we may have.

Promises get forgotten about until we meet up with the 'promisee'. We tend to feel worse than they do about the unresolved issue and the subject hovers conspicuously between us in that awkward familiar way that never gets mentioned, or 'forgotten' - it's there every time we meet up again and it won't go away until the promise is fulfilled, or we become immune to the reminders. Today's world tends to feel a responsibility to fulfil legal contracts rather than personal ones, perhaps because we fear fines or being sued more than we feel guilt or shame. Whatever the reason we tend to give promises, or handshakes, no more importance than we would a 'white lie' - not keeping our word is *very* acceptable in today's world of expediency over personal responsibility. These things matter if we want to improve our world and to find peace-of-mind - to stop the incessant chattering that haunts us day and night. The voices are there for a reason; I'd suggest that if we've had enough of the nonsense, contradiction and mischief in our world, then it's high time we started listening to them.

~ Procrastination ~

It's said that procrastination is the 'thief of time' and we don't have to think very hard to see how this is true - that 'putting off' doing things that require our attention in favour of those that don't. The truth is, that the longer we put those things off the less inclined we are to do them - often they're replaced by those 'more important things'. We feel that as long as there's a 'tomorrow' we may not have to think about should've', could've or ought've as we'll have time to do all the things we promise ourselves, but is this wise? Unfortunately time has a habit of catching up with us and when it does, all those things that once begged our attention, now *demand* it.

The possibility of existing - even in the minutest way - after this life can make it bearable; it gives us a hope of the permanence we're unable to experience in this world - a chance at 'immortality', or perhaps a hope that science will find a way to stop us aging so that we can live on. We know of this 'chance' through education, litcrature, spiritual teachers and films - conditioning - yet we treat what we've been taught as *truth*. A truth based on hope, fantasy and weak optimism that are born from fear - from the words and actions of a corrupt society. Even with this 'chance' at immortality, we tend to be reluctant to reflect on the purpose of our lives before our 'deaths' - we want someone else to do it for us. Who, or what, wants to survive this life is worth reflecting on, and why. That our life is temporary and driven by our ego is beyond question.

The ego is *born* when we are and *dies* with us which makes it also temporary. Wherever there's a modicum of doubt about the purpose of our existence, surely the subject is worth reflecting on without referencing the past experiences and conditioning of others - continuing a cycle. After all, the problems of humanity can't be solved by referencing the past; it can serve as a 'reminder' or spark our 'curiosity' that can motivate us to find our own path - to find our own power. Instead of heeding this reminder, we look to others for guidance, reassurance or confirmation of what we already know.

We tend to use 'guides' for spiritual comfort, for a vain hope in times of need, more than anything else, but there's a danger that we become reliant on them so they're no longer guides but our leaders and we cease to think for ourselves. However, if we require this level of comfort then it follows that we have issues we lack the courage to tackle - why else would we need comforting? We seek it when we're feeling low; when we need a 'pick-me-up' or can't stand the mess we've gotten ourselves into any more - we look for someone to kiss it all better, be it a priest, guru or 'best friend'. Comfort comes after an event, therefore it's required to make us feel better about the past,

but it doesn't eradicate it - it fixes the past in place together with all its pains, sorrows, beliefs and insecurities. The past is something *dead* that we want to hold onto, despite the certainty that we can't.

Comfort tells us that it's okay to hold onto our baggage, as it's not our fault that we're carrying it; it denies responsibility and expects a miracle that will make everything better, with no effort on our part; I'd suggest this miracle *won't* arrive and that we must learn to leave our beliefs behind us, if we're to see the falseness of them. The past doesn't 'exist' - it's a memory, and we hold onto it and treat it as something precious as we believe it defines who we are. Sooner or later we must let go of our pasts; we *all* know this on one level or another and we know that the challenge to do so is enormous, yet we leave ourselves no 'time' to reflect on it - we procrastinate.

~ Positivity ~

There's a great deal written and said about positivity and much effort is put into promoting this phenomenon - with almost religious zeal - believing that it will solve all our problems, if we just stay positive!

Positivity however, can't last the course and though we feel great for a time whilst looking 'on the bright side', no psychological change has taken place. All we've effectively done is look the other way, while someone we'd rather not see passes us by. There's a promoted form of positivity that tells us 'if we think positive everything will be alright', but positivity isn't a cure for negativity - they go hand in hand. Thinking positive is a deliberate action of recognising and ignoring a negative situation in the hope that it will go away - very different from having a positive attitude to dealing with that same negative situation. Positivity, in itself, serves to make others comfortable around us and to distract us from truth; if we're looking in one direction, we can't see what's going on in another and more importantly, we can't see the whole. If we ask someone 'How are you?' we don't want to hear their list of problems; we want them to be positive and tell us that they're 'doing very well'. Try advising someone who's just lost a child or partner to be positive - there's no empathy or compassion in that guidance. In some cases, we want them to be positive because *we* can't cope with, or don't want to know about. their sorrow - we have enough of our own. No matter how positive they may try to feel, on a deeper level they're in terrible pain and positivity attempts to suppress that pain rather than to deal with it. Positivity and negativity are imbalances of the 'whole'. Like the volume on the radio, if it's too low we strain to hear it, and if it's too loud we cover our ears - we need the sound to be 'just right'. We also need to be able to listen without noisy or visual distractions - without any distortion.

~ In our 'Humble' Opinion ~
We want everyone to agree with our opinions,
but they're rather busy with their own.

When I was designing the cover for my first book (no longer available), I put up six different designs on a new website and asked everyone I knew to help me choose one for the final product. I already knew which of the covers I liked best but to my dismay, no-one chose it. There were no shortage of conflicting opinions and I tweaked the covers accordingly, until they no longer resembled the originals. In the end, I scrapped the lot and designed a new cover altogether. This time, I *didn't* ask for opinions and put it on the website as my definitive cover. No-one disliked it or suggested any changes and I was happy. Had I added this cover to the previous ones, it would've been subject to the same process and likely ended up following the same fate. By asking for opinions, we're 'passing the buck' onto others to make our choices for us and to approve of what we do - we care what people think. The more choices we ask others to make for us, the more confused we become by their subjective opinions - there can never be an 'outright/overall winner'. Interestingly, everyone liked the final cover, despite not having been asked for their opinion. The problem it seems is choice. When there's no choice put forward we accept the only option. This has enormous ramifications in our competitive and self-serving society - the biggest of which is that our choices are going to be made for us and our opinions formed, based on those choices.

We ask for the opinions of others but do we *really* need them? I'd suggest that we ask because we don't have confidence in ourselves or our choices and that we're looking for approval, in its many guises. Mostly however, we want other people to like us and to see things our way; we value our *own* opinions and would generally like others to value them too. Our world - particularly online - increasingly encourages 'likes' and 'dislikes' and these get us into a muddle as we become confused by the differing opinions and conflicting suggestions; it becomes impossible to satisfy everyone - or *anyone* - and that leaves us feeling frustrated and as in the above example, without a book cover. Further examples of this confusion are easily found on any forum or online video that allow reviews or comments - the same applies to books, films or other online purchases.

The world is absolutely bursting with opinions and for this reason they're often given *without* being asked for. Everything we put online is asking for the opinion of someone or other - whether we want them or not - and it *will* get them. Online is our 'showcase' and it will be criticised, both online and by those who choose *not* to air their opinions publicly. We want to be noticed, validated, appreciated and we want *this* from a world whose mind is volatile, debauched, quite mad, full of violent imagery, irresponsible and consequently, highly unstable. It's from within this world that our opinions, comments and creations are both given and received. This situation didn't begin with the internet - we've always been more than generous with our opinions - asked for or not. We give them when we look someone up and down, when we listen to gossip, when we want to agree with somebody else in order to be in their favour or - in some cases - when we want to be plain nasty.

Nowadays, we rate and review just about everything before we buy it. Often we buy products based on the experience and opinions of others, yet we've no idea who they are. We also rate and review things we *haven't* bought based on our preferences and prejudices - we have many of those. The result is a world that criticises everyone in one way or another - a world where we fear to show our 'masterpieces', in case they're negatively criticised. We fear our efforts and dreams being torn apart, which - if we look at it from another perspective - means we live in fear of our own creativity and in particular, of it being marked down by others. Reviews, likes, dislikes and ratings are different names for 'judgement by others', according to their own 'impeccable' standards. This causes chaos and further division which can - and often does - lead to anger and other negative emotions being vented online. These judgements are used as successful and easily corruptible marketing techniques;

for example, companies can - and do - set up multiple accounts in order to negatively rate or review the products of their competition, whilst positively rating their own.

~~~

Dishonesty plays a large part in our opinions and *correctness* has hijacked 'diplomacy' and 'tact' - painting them in its own colours of self-importance and expediency. Apart from the obvious antagonists waiting to pounce on anyone who cares to listen to them, we don't want to 'offend' with our opinions, so we tiptoe around the truth in fear of waking it up. Dishonesty therefore, becomes acceptable - and even creditable - if it appears to be in a 'good cause' like in an 'appealing' political manifesto. However, dishonesty, can never be a good thing no matter what disguise it wears. For one thing, we're highly intelligent and generally know when someone's lying to us or being 'diplomatic' - we know a sham when we see one. We also know when *we've* lied and then things like guilt and superiority can come into play - one thing always leads to another. If we ask a friend 'Does my bum look big in these trousers' we expect them to say 'No', but the very question implies that *we* think it does. What's happening is, we're asking our friend to lie to us and generally they'll comply; the corollary of this is our bum becomes bigger than ever. The lie then demands continuity - so it goes … on and on. People don't always lie about their opinions, but when they don't then we tend to strongly resent what we hear - this can be a great way to lose friends.

What do *you* think? Is asking for an opinion courting disaster? It depends on our intention and usually that's to hear what we want to hear, which isn't always the truth. It also depends on the intention of the person we're asking for opinions from. We'd be better off asking ourselves *why* we need someone else's opinion or why we think they may need ours, and watch - *closely* - our responses to that question. Often we look for approval, because we lack confidence in our ability to make decisions for ourselves - we look for the 'green light' (permission granted) and gratification. A gratification that tells us we're good enough, or confirms that we're *not*; yes, some of us want this confirmed too, as it lets us 'off the hook'. Our minds may sometimes be swayed by the opinions of others; we may not like those opinions but often go along with them anyway. We end up feeling frustrated by our lives because we don't live them as we want to, but rather as others think we should. As always, we can't change what's happening in the world, but we can better understand it by taking a closer look at ourselves. This is how we become empowered and grow in our ability to think for ourselves. This is how to change the belief that we need the opinions of others.

~ Hypocrisy ~
If you tell a lie for long enough, it becomes your truth.

We often betray our thoughts with our actions. Sometimes these are well intentioned - like when we don't wish to offend anyone - and sometimes not, lacking in sincerity for the sake of expediency or keeping up appearances. Take as an example a person who 'lovingly' strokes a dog, with the sole intention of getting to know its owner. He's betraying the owner of the dog by acting in one way in order to impress her, but whilst he's pretending to like the dog his thoughts tell another story altogether - perhaps by thinking about kicking the dog the minute the owner isn't looking. I've witnessed someone do this when its owner's eyes were diverted and then pretend to like the dog again. Should a relationship develop between two people in this situation - or a similar one - it won't stand much chance of being healthy. How could it when the first communication was hypocritical and therefore, dishonest?

No good can come out of any situation where we behave in one way, but act and speak against it. I'm sure that - just like me - you've had friends over for dinner or a social gathering and had a great evening, but later criticised the things they said or did *after* they'd left, despite having been in agreement with them at the time. If you haven't been in this situation, then perhaps you've spent some time in a discussion with one person and immediately telephoned a friend to tell them about it, 'You'll *never* guess what so-an-so just said', from an entirely different perspective. We're dualistic in our lifestyles, particularly when we're out to impress others. This is just another way of expressing a lack in our character that we feel obliged to make up for. We also make up for this lack in other ways, like when complaining about someone who hasn't telephoned us for a few months. We feel increasingly bitter about it and create a drama in our minds about what's really going on. What we don't see is that *we* haven't bothered to pick up the phone either, which we could easily do if we wanted to; we project our criticism and hypocrisy onto others when we don't want to examine ourselves. When we fail to live up to our *own* standards, we can never be free or complete.

There's a lot more to hypocrisy than we allow ourselves to talk about - it doesn't only arise in a 'do as I say but not as I do' situation. It's an attempt to deny our dualistic nature - a cover up. Hypocrisy, for example, is at the root of pomposity; of those who raise their noses skyward refusing to recognise that they walk on the same ground as every human being - it's delusional. It's a false sense of superiority developed in order to cover up a true sense of *inferiority*. If we have to 'think' ourselves superior, then we can't be. On the deepest level, hypocrisy is the betrayal of ourselves; it's the betrayal of our heart and we do it all the time - it's a mask.

Chapter 43

Who am I?

At the core of the fire, lie the spoils of desire.

Every moment, every minute, everything that we put in it
Every thought, every deed, every flower, every weed
Every muscle we expand, every blow that we withstand
Every place that we dwell, every rat that we smell

Every mask that we wear, every colour of our hair
Every film that we watch, every point that we notch
Every turn of our head, every place that we're led
Every cake that we bake, every pleasure that we take

Every need we fulfil, every blush, every chill
Every wall we defend, every tale that we bend
Every nose in the air, every time we don't care
Every scar that we leave, every ace up our sleeve

Every tear that we cry, every rule we apply
Every word that we spread, every dream in our head
Every face to the ground, every idol that we crown
Every smile, every pout, every legend that we doubt

Every truth that we taint, every sinner, every saint
Every shoulder that we chip, every stiff upper lip

Every morsel that we eat, every innocent we cheat
Every tactic we employ, everything that we destroy

Every person that we hurt, every call we avert
Everything we ignore, every tally, every score
Everything we despise, every view through our eyes
Everyone that we mock, every door that we lock

Every man we detest, every time we know best
Every bubble that we burst, every person that we curse
Every cut, every mile, every step, every trial
Every stone we have thrown, every seed we have sown

Every fear, every frown, everyone that we put down
Everything we create, every heart we vacate
Every song that we sing, every touch, every ring
Every moment, every minute, everything that we put in it.

Chapter 44

On Reflection

We're brilliant - often too brilliant - but we're not yet wise; we don't even *wish* to become wise. Throughout this book are many thoughts, ideas and self-reflections - none of which haven't been thought out before, and each one of them is a part of humanity studying of all things, itself. We're somehow aware of our own consciousness and able to reflect on many things about our existence and evolution - though more often than not we choose not to. We walk without thinking about how we put one leg in front of the other and eat without considering how we digest our food. We do these in much the same way as we drive our cars or use a washing machine - mechanically. Incredibly, we're able to think about how our bodies work, and our thoughts too, and the implications of that are worth pondering. As individuals, each one of us can think these things out for ourselves and find, if we're sincere, that nothing is what it appears to be.

All we really *need* to see is right in front of us when we observe our world, and what we're doing *with* and *in* it; none of it is, or can be, hidden from us if we want to discover it. As an example, we follow orders every day - orders that we don't realise we're being given because we've followed them for so long. These imperatives come in many forms such as 'Stop', 'Go', 'Give Way' and 'Keep Left' - orders we're unaware we're obeying. Other common imperatives in our daily lives are 'Open Here', 'Push', 'Pull', 'Click Here', 'Queue This Side', 'Up' and 'Down' - there are hundreds, possibly thousands more - little wonder some of us live in fear that someone will 'push the button'. We can argue - and do - that we need imperatives for things like 'organisation' or road safety but would we *really* just crash into other cars and run people over if the signs weren't there - of course not. On the contrary, we'd pay more attention to what we're doing and stop looking for instructions on how to do it. For goodness sake, even our text is predictive and corrected for us - when did we become so dependent? It's through these observations that illusions begin to fall away, and very many must. It's also through observation that our minds sharpen because they're not being used *for* us but *by* us - we begin to think for ourselves again.

This 'life' causes us so much anxiety or if you will, dread; dread of what we (as a society) created with the imminent possibility of the self-destruction of ourselves and our 'planet' or, dread of the mysterious 'void' we fear entering. We don't know what's in store for us after we die and we generally have only fables, myths, legends and history to guide us and not enough time to read all the books they're written in, let alone know if there's any truth hiding as ghosts between the lines. More often than not we don't have the energy or will to search for guidance, as it's hard to know which books are worth reading; the market is saturated with conflicting information and biased reviews of that same information. We're not keen to work things out for ourselves as we live in a world full of 'experts', instructions and reference manuals and from them we expect to find out all we need to know.

We seek gratification rather than wisdom or good advice. We're prepared to take our chances on whether or not we need to become wise, perhaps because we've as much to fear in our futures as we do the events in our pasts, or perhaps because on a deeper level we're frustrated about working so hard in this world for things we know we can't keep. In the world as we now know it - as we've always known it - there seems to be little need for wisdom. We know that no matter what we 'achieve' we must give it all up again and we don't want to - it can be felt, or seen, as 'failure' and no-one *wants* to feel that way about themselves. However, failure and success are illusions that must die when we do; still, we want so much to hold onto them, because it's what we know so well. Bearing this in mind, it's understandably difficult to 'take a chance' embarking on a 'metaphysical' journey that may *also* lead us nowhere at all; if we have to give up who we think we are and everything and everyone we know when we die, then why would we want to give it all up earlier?

Whether illusory or not, our lives begin with our births and end with our deaths. I'd suggest that we've a great deal to achieve between the limitations of these two markers. We take a chance that everything will be okay 'on the night', but this surely invests all our eggs in one basket and places a low value on our lives as individuals.

It's worth remembering that this basket isn't ours 'personally' - it's society's - and any decisions we make to put our eggs into it are based on information we receive from that society. These decisions originate from the past with all its horrors and as such can never solve humanity's problems. We can't repair today's fractured society with the pieces from yesterday's fractured society - our 'spirit' has been broken. We've no enthusiasm, energy or even the will to try to pick ourselves up; we're disheartened by the wall-to-wall daily dose of humanity's insanity with no end to it in sight. We're resigned to our circumstances and need to stop and 'take stock' if we want to see change. Without self-investigation we limit our possibilities and remain reliant - for guidance - on the corrupt and mischievous system we created. Because self-investigation *exists* as an ability within each of us, it's worth reflecting on how important it is to explore it and also about in how many ways we're being diverted from our purpose, by senseless and unintelligent influences, pastimes and attractions. We have - after all - nothing to lose.

FOUR

Chapter 45

Hello World

We've wild imaginations, to which there appears to be no limit.

I don't remember when I became aware that I was aware - that 'hello world' moment when I realised I was 'here' with no introduction or explanation. To my knowledge, no-one shook my hand or welcomed me into the world. I had to observe, listen, learn a language, evolve and form images of my world before I was able to interact with it, in whatever way seemed appropriate. I imagine it might have felt like being pushed onto a stage where millions of different plays are in full swing and, from *my* point of observation, trying to play *my* part with no script or character description - learning to play a role by imitation and improvisation, so that I'd fit in. Amongst all this confusion, I was unknowingly building a character that became the *me* others would see - my persona. I allowed my mind to be filled with the beliefs, distractions, fears and influences of others and I made them 'mine'. I was to create a role for myself from the information, 'props' and people that surrounded me and regardless of my choices, the play would go on. I could observe or participate in this 'show' - fully or partially - or I could sit quietly and observe it, but I couldn't leave the 'theatre'. Thinking about this reminds me of when my father 'taught' me to swim at around four-years-old; he threw me into the deep end of a pool and told me to swim back to the side and climb out again; the ladder was very far away, as it is when we're afraid, alone and unwelcome.

I was born into chaos and not much later went into a shell, to protect myself from a strange and confusing situation, from which I could find no way out. As a young child, I can't remember at what age but I'd guess it was pre-school, I found my environment to be extremely hostile. It was an environment in which I'd no rights, choices, or a voice anyone would listen to. It was a place where I needed to 'come of age' before I'd have some sort of control over my life - control within the confines of choices that had already been made for me, by society - a very sick society that above all else, taught me how to be afraid of it and to hate myself. From my perspective at the time, the world was ugly, corrupt, violent, unjust and cruel; I'd no idea how I'd arrived or what I was doing here. I felt about as much use as a teardrop shed on a battlefield, and a tremendous sense of not belonging; there was no-one to discuss my thoughts with. I cared not for this 'home', had no wish to remain in it and because I couldn't see a way out, felt powerless to change anything. There was however, a voice that I heard all the time; a voice that told me that there was more to me than this. At the time I didn't understand the significance of this voice and like the majority of us, ignored it. Whatever this voice was - this nagging, this underlying something that I didn't understand at the time - conflicted with my circumstances and all that I was being taught about myself.

~~~

I've meditated long and hard about what it may be like for a child to enter our world and as it happens, I've had the opportunity to 'video conference' with a friend's new born baby. The baby needs a little help to face the screen, by means of a supporting hand on the back of her neck and another to gently prop her tiny body up. The first time we met, she was cross-eyed, frowning and flapping her arms and legs around frantically as though she'd suddenly found herself trapped - somewhere strange - and was trying to get out again. Yes, the movements are reflexive, but from an observer point of view this isn't clear without prior conditioning. At times the frown subsided and she'd have that cute little baby face that the vast majority of us succumb to. However, occasionally her lips curled downwards at the sides and very shortly afterwards, she'd sob her little heart out as though her world had come to an end, rather than just begun. We turn our lips down and lower our eyebrows when we're unhappy whether we're sobbing our hearts out or not, even after growing up, so it was a part of us when we were born and, it still is. Babies don't speak a language we understand, but in my opinion, they know they've arrived somewhere new and according to the screams of some of them, they may well be more than a little confused by their new surroundings, or frustrated by their inability to communicate in any way other than to cry. They may also be frightened or in shock and want 'out' again. Of course there are those of us that don't scream out the moment we're born, but sooner or later - in one way or another - we do.

That an inexplicable BIOS (basic input/output system) exists within each of us is beyond doubt; if we didn't have one then our hearts couldn't beat, our tears couldn't flow, our lips couldn't curl and the jerky reflexive movements of our arms and legs couldn't occur; we couldn't be switched 'on', or 'off' for that matter; our hearts, tears, lips and limbs couldn't exist without the code that somehow forms and operates them. Before our births, meticulously coded instructions are carried out for every stage of our development - we couldn't live without them. To call this a system - a *basic* one at that - has got to be the biggest understatement ever made, but this is the limit that language permits us to describe the marvellous process of conception and subsequent 'life'. After our births, begins the relatively lengthy process of development, as we gradually learn how to use and control our bodies, while they continue the development process begun in the womb; the system is fully automated. There's no-one who can tell us how - or why - we came into being, no matter how deep or extensive their learning; we can only marvel at the wonder of it all if we're prepared to spend some time reflecting on - as opposed to studying - the phenomenon itself.

What should be a sacred reverential moment has been relegated to a mechanical incident no more - or less - important or impressionable than a new car rolling off a production line. Our births are planned for by our mothers and fathers, authors, commercial outlets, doctors and midwifes and a seemingly limitless number of approved baby-by-the-book 'how to' instruction manuals. The beauty and wonder of what's happening inside a mother's body - outside our control - is often reduced to something fashionable as we now show off our 'bump' in clothing designed specifically for that purpose. When do we speak about or acknowledge the genetic wonder of it all, let alone the philosophical and spiritual aspects of our existence? When do we put aside a little of our precious time to ponder these things?

It's my considered opinion that no-one can tell us what a baby can or can't see. No-one can tell us what a baby thinks or what his mind chatters on about, in whatever language he may or may not comprehend. Thoughts are the past so a baby *must* experience *before* he can think and whether his experiences begin inside the womb or after birth is a question - like all my questions - that I shall leave open. Babies arrive and as far as we can tell, we assess what they need through their cries, emotions, temperature, breathing etc. When I was caring for my own children, knowing what they wanted at any particular moment involved a lot of guesswork and a process of elimination; not hungry, not wet etc. - often I reached the end of my 'check list' and the problem still hadn't been solved. No doubt there were things I never tried, as they were beyond my knowledge but - for the purpose of this chapter - I'm only focusing on what I see through my own eyes and through meditation, reflecting on what a baby may see or feel from her own perspective. Why is this interesting to me? Because I apparently arrived 'here' in the same way - just as we all did. Finding my truth has been a process of unlearning and it follows that in order to do so, I must end up at the beginning of my learning again, as far as is possible. I can't go back to my birth, but I don't need to; everything falls into place when we're good and ready.

Again, no-one can tell us where we came from or where we're going, whether this life is a dream, an illusion, a game, a show, or 'the real McCoy', so to speak. For me however, whatever direction my questions lead me in, I'm 'Here' at my point of observation and I can never leave. I'm at the centre of my own world from which all aspects of my life spring. As we become more proficient at observation a curious thing happens - there's a distinct feeling that we ourselves are being keenly observed and by 'we' I mean our 'egos'. I shall extend this statement to say that I feel as though I'm keenly observing *myself*.

Chapter 46

Know Thyself

To ignore our spirituality is tantamount to ignoring our right hand.

The term 'Know thyself' (γνῶθι σεαυτὸν in Greek or *nosce te ipsum* in Latin) is one of the best known phrases in the world and often pops up in books, films and social media in one form or another, but what *does* the aphorism mean? To many people, it's nothing more than an ancient mystical cliché and in general given as much thought as any other 'fortune cookie' wisdom. Little wonder most people aren't too curious about the concept of 'know thyself', regarding it as a topic to be explored by the 'select few' believed to be in the know about humanity's 'hidden' secrets; we're content to await their spectacular revelations appearing in the Sunday papers and what have you - meanwhile, life goes on as we know it. 'Know thyself' sounds more like 'know thy place' or 'know thy limitations' and don't try to reach beyond them - this is the message a lot of people receive, albeit subconsciously. To complicate matters, many of us believe we *already* know ourselves, others lack the time or inclination to think about it, rejecting it out of hand; however, to those who earnestly need to make some sort of sense out of our world, there's no option but to explore further.

The three words *know thy self* can be taken apart and all sorts of sense made out of them and many people do this, but the inescapable message is 'go within', 'look inside you' - an action we'd prefer to avoid. One thing worth recognising is how lazy we are, especially when it comes to matters of a spiritual nature - on the whole, it just doesn't interest us enough to stop what we're doing. I'd suggest this is partly out of fear - fear of failure, fear of success, fear of ridicule, inadequacy or of losing what we may have to give up. Perhaps our greatest fear is of the isolation that could result from such a quest. Friends and family often become quickly uninterested in - or annoyed at - anything we have to say regarding philosophical or spiritual matters; at best, they'll tolerate a few comments before rolling their eyes, dismissing us as cranks and changing the subject. At first this can be frustrating, but gradually we become unaffected by peer pressure to conform - it's part of our journey. Whichever way you look at the adage, 'know thyself' is a do-it-yourself *quest* and *that's* where our reticence kicks in; it sounds like a lot of hard work and we really can't be bothered, as we've more 'important' things to do.

When we think about what it means to 'know thyself' one of the first things to consider is that it's not necessary to know the 'ins and outs' of angels, demons, elves, fairies or other spirits; we don't have to uncover age-old mysteries of astrology, archaeology, science, philosophy or any other subject in order to know ourselves and we don't need to read Greek, Latin *or* hieroglyphics for that matter - we've enough trouble understanding our own language. There's no big secret; nothing essential is hidden from us and no special knowledge is needed to go within. We don't actually have to 'get into' anything at all and therein lies the problem; it's just too simple - so simple that it goes against our conditioning. The conditioning is that we need qualifications, ceremonies, costumes, rites, incense burning, to sit in strange positions, or at the feet of someone 'wiser' than we are, in order to receive 'privileged' knowledge. We may well search for someone else to shine a light on the subject for us, as we feel unqualified without some form of certificate or rite of passage, but by doing that all we'll find is the mass of contradiction and confusion that exists in our society, further muddling our minds. We can delve as deeply into the haystack as we choose to, but we'll not find 'the' truth; we'll be unable to differentiate between what is or isn't true as our minds *are* deeply conditioned - a fact that's difficult to accept.

The entangling web of knowledge is more complicated and confusing than the questions we ask and can't be trusted; at best we may favour one person's answer and decide to walk along their path with them, but that doesn't make anything they say true; it just means that, for a whole host of reasons, it suits our personal agenda to go along with what they're saying right now - it's an 'off the peg' solution. We don't need to lose ourselves in other people's adventures. We can have our own adventures and in fact, we *are* unknowingly having our own, though for most of us it doesn't seem that way, because our heads are stuck deep inside the stories and fantasies of others - we experience their adventures by proxy, like when we cheer for a football team, celebrate a celebrity's wedding, cry at someone else's bad news or get a kick out of a success story in the media. Sometimes we change dramatically after putting ourselves in what we see as 'positive' situations; like spiritual meetings, listening to a 'life coach' (I do dislike that term) or receiving good advice - like a drug; these situations often leave us feeling 'on a high'. However, when we return to our homes continuing to live the way we were living before, we return to behaving the same way too; in the same way we lose enthusiasm for a diet once the novelty has worn off; we start the diet, lose a few pounds and then diligently put them on again. When faced with a sudden personal crisis that unbalances us we reach out for any helping hand, but once our balance is regained we let go of that hand and revert to our old selves; a 'crisis repentance' causes us to become more agreeable to people who are offering help at the time.

When we look to others for guidance on our 'quest', problems can arise because one 'expert' believes a certain thing, and another has a different opinion; for example, 'there's a heaven and a hell' or 'there are no such places'. Both have their reasons for believing what they choose to believe, but neither can provide 'evidence' to substantiate their claim - leading to heated debates that are never resolved; this situation has been going on for a long time. Of course, there are more than two opinions, but I use those as simple examples to put my point across. We prefer to look *outside* of ourselves for fear of what we'll discover within, or to be more accurate, *re*-discover. The mass of contradiction and confusion that we find on the outside has created a mass of contradiction and confusion on the inside - *this* is why our minds are so difficult to silence.

We *all* possess the ability to question our existence regardless of whether we're rich, poor, young or infirm. We don't need to be 'educated' or to consult a psychiatrist, guru or any other 'expert' for guidance or advice; each and every one of us is self-sufficient when it comes to controlling our 'inner' selves - we don't even have to *know* anyone else - there exists no valid 'get-out clause'. All we have to do is 'think'; it's really that simple, but we can't see it because we've made our lives too complicated. Regardless, there remain many things that can be questioned and considered, things that can't be denied; for example, the world is in decline - we all know this. I recently picked up a DVD from a supermarket shelf and looked at the rating; it was Rated 'R' for 'strong violence, disturbing images, and sexuality' and it contained 'strong bloody violence' with a 'fit for viewing' age of '15 or more'; these are our children for goodness sake - we don't allow them alcohol or tobacco at that age for fear of damaging their health, but we're quite happy to damage their minds. *What* are we doing to our children? For that matter, what are we doing to *ourselves*? Scarily, we're living in a society where we need ratings to tell us what we can and can't do; the older we get the more qualified we are to be exposed to ever increasing 'officially' rated (thereby *officially* sanctioned) sex and 'bloody violence'. We all know how the label 'contains adult content' attracts our children and we don't do much to protect them from the temptation. If it's not suitable for our children then in what way, and by whose standards, is it suitable for *us*? I feel deeply saddened by this frightening lack of intelligent self-regulation and personal responsibility. We can't know ourselves if we continue to take a *laissez-faire* attitude to what's happening all around us, or how it effects humanity as a whole. By considering examples such as the above, we begin to see ourselves in a different light, which raises our level of consciousness.

~~~

So how can we begin to *really* know ourselves? Only by taking a long, hard and honest look in the mirror. If we want to see ourselves as we really are, then it's necessary to remove all outside factors that define us. Everything we feel, see, think, shy away from or judge when we look in a mirror is a part of how we see ourselves, including the moments of horror, disgust, emotion and vanity. A good exercise is to stand in front of that mirror and listen to the muddled up thoughts that we broadcast to ourselves when looking at our own reflection; for example, too big, small, fat, thin, short or any number of other inadequacies and self-rejecting - or self-praising - observations; when we look in the mirror, we see a mixed-up historical conglomeration of ourselves. We define ourselves by what we *choose* to focus on and what we choose to make of our lives, and it's from these choices that our lives expand. Ironically, the choices we make are not always the choices we *want* to make - too often they're guided by fear, the past or expected approval, flattery or condemnation of others. We're each a masterpiece in our own right - completely self-contained - and we've the tools to create a beautiful experience or a horror story; our bodies are merely vessels through which we can view and interact with the life we create. Think about something that attracted you this week - something you couldn't resist like an object in a shop window or a book, a new job, a party invitation, a bottle of drink, a film, a person or even a cake. Something that pulled your attention towards it and then think about how it was possible for you to be drawn to that same thing - how it made you feel and what you were expecting - or got - from the experience; the pleasures of these experiences are short-lived, which is just one of the reasons we seek to re-experience them. Many lines have been cast with baited hooks and only we - personally - choose whether or not to take the bait; if we do, we're then hooked up for whatever experience we've chosen, and the memory of that experience becomes embedded in our minds; it becomes a part of us - a part of our story. We can choose not to take the bait that someone else has put out for us - this choice is an important one if we truly wish to know ourselves. I wish to point out that I'm *not* saying either option is right, wrong, moral or immoral - only that what we do *is* a choice.

It's not just material things and pastimes that we're attracted to (or seek out), but also emotions and ways to vent our frustrations with the world - ways in which we express or validate ourselves. Knowing ourselves involves *constant* self-observation and honesty, particularly about the things we *don't* want to know about ourselves. To see this, we need to study our own behaviour and listen to the background voices inside our heads that control our actions and reactions, particularly when we're up to mischief; for example, we may find ourselves looking to use or start an argument with a friend - often over something trivial - for a variety of reasons including a lack of honesty, manipulation, fear or even to fulfil an addiction - skilfully manoeuvring the argument to our own ends. Have you ever noticed how the voice of our conscience never bothers us *unless* we're doing the unwise? If we question why we ignore our conscience it becomes clear that our lives are 'ego driven'. 'Me' is with me all the time and when the validity of it is challenged that really gets our backs up. The ego is 'never' wrong and it's highly volatile; it's always ready to put up a wall, pounce, twist, be the loudest voice in the room or lie in defence of itself, no matter what, and if necessary, keep us up all night - tossing and turning - depriving us from the sleep we need and it'll keep doing that until we recognise it for what it really is - a fraud. It's at that moment an awful truth dawns on us - *we are* the fraud. Then we've a choice; we can ignore this 'revelation' by remaining as we are or embrace it.

~~~

The journey to 'know thyself' is a tough one - many of us can feel more than a little intimidated by this well-known phrase, but I'd like to put it into perspective. The journey is no tougher than the one we're currently undertaking; the hardest parts of it being learning to 'think straight' - without interference from our thoughts - and letting go of the character traits we so possessively hold onto; for instance, pride, suspicion, self-righteousness, fear and an unwillingness to change. On an encouraging note, our journey does become *easier* once we get started - it brings its own rewards. Speaking from my own experience, I find I sleep better at night without all the rumblings of my mind and consequently, I awake feeling refreshed - I've become unperturbed by things that once irked and distracted me - the things I know I *can't* change and therefore, no longer expend energy trying to. I'm less inclined to be judgemental of others as I develop a greater understanding of myself. The more we understand ourselves, the more we understand others - the more we understand others, the more we realise that our world and place in it is incomprehensible at our current level of consciousness - a level that we can raise *now*, while we're still alive. On this journey, life becomes a mystery again as we notice and think about wonders we forgot about a long time ago - experiencing life rather than analysing and navigating our way through it, according to the instructions of others. If we want to find something sacred in our world we need to experience the wonder of it, rather than conceptualising it.

Think for a moment about your hands. Take a good look at them, flex your fingers, make a fist, point a finger and focus on what you're able to do with these incredible instruments. Our hands are made up of - amongst other things - muscles, tendons, nerves, veins, nails, bones, and skin - everything we do with them is by our will alone; they do exactly what we want them to do - what we *will* them to do. Who is it who instructs our feet to walk one in front of the other in concert with our balance system and eyes, so that we don't trip, fall over or walk into things? Everything we do and think is by our own free will, but we've been doing them for so long that we no longer recognise that it's *ourselves* who are in control of our bodies and the mind we allow to run riot.

As adults, we bury the child within us and should we allow it to surface again, as we invariably do, we feel self-conscious and vulnerable - especially if anyone is or may be watching. Too often we refuse to allow that vulnerability to surface again. It's terrifying to strip away our comprehensive defences, revealing the 'truth' to ourselves - that we're frauds - let alone to anyone else; yes, knowing ourselves is a time to 'face the music'. If we allow ourselves to face it, then all we really stand to lose is the torment and suffering we insist on experiencing and *willingly* re-experiencing. We hide because we're afraid and often rationalise this fear as necessary for our personal security, resisting change so as not to be seen as we really are. Our lifetimes have been spent perfecting our disguises in order to protect ourselves from rejection - a rejection we can't bear to face again. The journey to knowing ourselves is like giving ourselves a mental make-over; however, because of our fears of rejection, humiliation and isolation - the undesirable possible consequences of walking away from the 'crowd' - we're reticent to take this step. When we jump into the 'mind drama' our fears soon multiply into a dread story that we serialise beyond reasonable recognition - our rationalisation is complete. Life is a journey between two points - birth and death; what we do between them is important. Do you remember what the majority of us were taught in school about how to cross a road? Look right, look left, look right again listening all the time and if there's nothing coming you can cross, but continue to look and listen while you're doing it. This advice applies to our life's journey too, but, unwisely, we're not looking where we're going - we're not listening either.

Chapter 47

Assimilation and Dissemination

We're here to experience this life; to pass through it - not to carve ourselves in stone.

Preparation for a child's arrival involves having all the correct equipment prepared, which if we take a moment to think about, isn't very different to having a new doll with all the latest accessories needed to comply with the current requirements demanded by our consumerist society. The 'advancement' and desires of humanity have caused us to need more and more things for every baby that's 'born', despite the baby's needs remaining the same as they always have been - food, covering and above all, love. However, these 'designer' babies are the only way for society to continue 'advancing' in the way it wants to - they'll one day replace our generation, just as we've replaced previous ones. If we were to teach our children 'new' things, or rather not teach them the old, then we wouldn't be able to hold onto society the way it is now. Despite protestations that we don't like things the way they are, we don't *want* to change them - particularly if it involves the personal sacrifice of any of our firmly-held 'secure' beliefs. A sick society can't teach the next generation to be healthy. Another stumbling block to change is that we don't know *how* to and we're more than a little afraid to find out. We're afraid of criticism, of losing a 'reputation' or the 'approval' of society, so we conform and seek the only apparent reasons for living the way we do - seeking continuity and success! Consequently, we continue to be unhappy while we hope to find this 'success' in our world - every one of us knows it doesn't actually exist.

Start to look at the world objectively and it becomes impossible not to see that the vast majority of us (if not all) suffer in one way or another. Each of us has absorbed and owns an 'eventful' past, full of imprinted memories that tell us who we think we are and who we've been told we are - but they're *not* who we are any more than the words of a story are the book they're written in. The events are and can only be what we've *experienced*, by whatever means - yet, they're how we define ourselves. I'm known as Renée Paule and she is the *sum* of my experiences - nothing more. Our story began - in part - with the nouns, verbs and adjectives that we later came to know as our 'identity'. We begin to see how our egos were formed when we weave in our emotions, pains, judgements, desires, disappointments and expectations to the story. When we see the pattern - how our characters have evolved - distances, barriers, distinctions and illusions fall away - sometimes slowly, sometimes uncomfortably fast, leaving us somewhat disorientated and possibly disturbed by our new surroundings.

Our grasping hands, reaching out for the familiar, pass through the things we once 'knew' were solid. These include our beliefs, opinions, choices and aspirations - things we thought were *ours* turn out to be nothing of the sort. As the barriers between reality and illusion are removed, we're left naked and exposed - stripped from the fine clothes we've unknowingly been dressed in for so long, with nowhere to run for cover. In this raw state we tend to grab at our old clothes, hastily putting them back on again, because they're preferable to this new and unfamiliar vulnerability - 'blind panic' causes us to cling to them for dear life. If only we'd pause, relax and take a moment to look around us, we'd soon find that our new situation isn't as frightening as it first seems. On the contrary, it liberates us from fear - there's nothing lurking 'under the bed'. We weren't born afraid - we were taught it. By a process of reverse engineering our beliefs can be deconstructed, and once we accept this raw state all fear leaves us - every little bit of it.

My perspective on what it means to be a human being has changed considerably with the examination and reflection of myself. For years, being a 'human being' limited me to being something apparently solid - something tangible. It's a term that implies the objectification of 'myself' and I'm not an object - neither are you. Our characters, thoughts etc. are anything but solid, as we tend to understand the term. The 'idea' of a human being is a wonderful thing; the idea that we're humane, compassionate, sympathetic, benevolent and special, above all others in the universe is an attractive one. The reality however, within the confines of our comprehension, is very different; though we've the potential to be all these things, we don't live up to those challenging descriptions. For benevolence to exist for example, then paradoxically, so must cruelty. Physically, the reality of being a human being is that we perform functions and routines, mimic fads and other behaviours that we're shown through our various forms of media and social interactions, and follow the influences, orders and rules of others; our conditioned behaviour is not unlike that of automatons. Psychologically, we ignore our consciences as they interfere rather too much with our desires - too often we don't *want* to hear the voice of our conscience and have been taught too well *not* to listen to it.

It isn't only our behaviour that's conditioned, but so are our thoughts and beliefs; the three are inseparable and arise from an accumulation of information perceived and digested from the moment we were 'born' until now. The cache of this information goes back many millennia and has always been passed on - it's tradition. Tradition is the passing on of any psychological or physical behaviour; it doesn't depend on truth of any kind, only the continuity of its doctrines and practices - tradition has its own agenda. It's natural for us to imitate others - how else would we learn about our world. A young child is taught everything; for example, language, right, wrong, funny, history, expectation, prejudice and many other societal driven behaviours. Here's one example; I saw a video with lots of babies giggling and laughing during different simple situations. In one scenario a baby burst into laughter when his father changed channel on the television after asking the child if he was 'Ready!' Then the mother asked the baby if he was 'watching golf' and the laughter was replaced by a look of innocent puzzlement. This is just one example of early programming and how we project what we want to believe onto our children. For me, the child was highly amused by the 'magic' trick the father was able to perform - changing the image on a screen with a little fun and anticipation thrown in. The mother, on the other hand, observed the child's excitement, took him out of the moment, translated it into something more appropriate to her own particular conditioning and in doing so, stole the innocence. Society would be all the wiser if it watched and learnt from its children, rather than manipulating them - they have a lot to teach us that we've sadly forgotten about.

~~~

A baby wouldn't survive if left unattended; without social influence/guidance or care. Apart from the obvious problems of a child being unable to find food, shelter and clothing, it would be unable to gain a perspective of the world - unable to develop a sense of identity - it would certainly die. So mimicry - with subtle changes - is essential for our survival and if we're mimicking an unhealthy world, then that's the world we'll continue to create and live in. Our disturbed world - plus the conditioning that children come across in theirs, is the world they'll inherit. If we continue to 'enhance' our insane world then things can only get worse. Thinking about these things gives a whole new meaning to idioms like 'walking in his father's footsteps' - a whole new perspective that's far from limited to members of our family, but also to anyone we interact with. The key to change must therefore lie in the reflection and evolvement of our *own* behaviour, otherwise we'll continue to pass this contaminated 'baggage' onto our children.

I remember - during an interesting discussion - being told by a friend 'I know my own mind'. No, we don't. If we did we wouldn't put up that argument. We don't tend to recognise that our entire life has been a subjective experience - absorbing information from the minds of those we've come into contact with, either personally or by proxy. To know our own mind takes a tremendous amount of honest self-reflection and observation. It involves, but is not limited to, seeing in ourselves what we see in others and coming clean about things we know to be false, but pretend are true - particularly about ourselves. The way we interact in our environment or with other people isn't us being *us* but a conditioned response to the circumstance we find ourselves in at any particular moment, based on our previous experiences - responses that we automatically, but unknowingly access. When we taste a lemon for example, we already know the response because we've tasted it before - we know it's going to taste sour and pull the appropriate 'squeezed' up face that we've come to associate with 'sour', though the face has nothing to do with sour itself - we tend to overact the part.

Another example is what a baby learns when he makes a mess of his dinner all over the highchair. A mother may react as though it were a crisis or just calmly clean it up. Whichever reaction she has imprints on to the child so that; for example, if a second child arrives in the household and then makes the same mess the first will react as its mother did - impersonating her and projecting her learnt behaviour. We think we're in control of our minds, but nothing could be further from the truth; we're reluctant to hear this fact.

We see, and absorb incalculable amounts of information from an incalculable number of sources, as we navigate our way through the chaos and hostility of our world. In some ways, we're like sponges. We absorb and process this information squeezing out any that's excess to our particular requirements - for political, religious, educational, scientific or any other cultural conditioning we happen to find ourselves connected to. This information brings us into line with whatever criteria a particular cultural group requires us to absorb, adapting ourselves so that we're 'tuned' into their hierarchical chain, making us socially or professionally acceptable, either low in the so-called 'pecking order' as the silent majority or, higher up as an administrator of continuity and progression. Our purpose - in society - is to function as a cog; this perpetuates a cruel and ritualistic existence where an 'individual' has no actual value, beyond a 'grade' awarded to those who are happy to fall 'in line' - replacing their predecessors. For instance, a student of a particular discipline may well wish to become a professor and will therefore continue to teach the same information his tutor taught him - rarely (publicly) questioning the reliability of the information. In some cases, this information can radically change; for example, we've been taught that people once believed the earth to be flat; however, who can honestly say that it's a globe, and if we do believe it, on what grounds do we trust that information? Based on our own evidence, who amongst us is able to verify one hundred percent that we're living on a planet at all?

In keeping with my philosophy, I maintain that answers don't need to be found in order to 'unravel' our minds from the 'Big Bang' of useless, unnecessary, diverting, corrupt and conflicting information. Our minds are so full of these things that we've become overwhelmed with too many 'truths' and 'realities' - so much so that the difference between fantasy, augmented reality, virtual reality, or 'reality' itself has become increasingly blurred. When our minds quieten, all arguments - whatever their origin - become null and void. If we see and admit to the problems, then the 'solutions' will present themselves all in good time, but *only* when we're ready to receive them. If we choose however, to remain in hiding and denial from the obvious maladies of society, then we also choose to remain as blindfolded passengers on a ship - that we *choose* to sail in - without caring in which direction we're being led by its captain, or the state of that captain's mind - we also refuse to acknowledge that there *is* a captain at all. Who is the captain? That's a good question!

Our characters have been formed to function in a low vibrational world; it's a world that shapes and conditions us according to its wishes and a world that insists not only on our compliance, but that we pass our conditioning, fears and compliance onto our offspring. We're taught that 'knowledge is power', but *what* knowledge and *whose* knowledge is not something we tend to think about or whether or not this knowledge is true - regardless, we accept it as truth. True power and knowledge is not something that we can learn from books or inherit from others - it can be found in the hearts of each and every one of us, because *that's* where it resides and where it has *always* resided. Realising and accepting this situation is the hardest part of knowing ourselves, because it's difficult to accept that the person we thought was 'uniquely' us, was moulded by the society we're living in and that in many respects, we really are just following a script. The first move to 'know thy *self*' is to question, question, and question again - everything that we've been taught without bias, without conditioning, without getting all hot and bothered and without lashing out at the system - after all, it was us who created it. We must wipe our slate clean and to begin with it's not an easy process, because we *have* to realise the futility of the way we've been living before we see anything new. Persevere, and our world changes into a far more beautiful and meaningful place to live in - this is *not* a hypothetical statement.

Chapter 48

Memory and Thought

There's no such thing as dirty water - despite contaminants, its essence remains pure.

You may be thinking about the above quote - trying to work out if it's true or not. Drawing on information stored in your memory you may come to an 'agree' or 'disagree' conclusion, or maybe you'll want to think about it some more. Every moment of our lives we're thinking about something; some of these thoughts bring pleasure and some can be so disturbing that it's hard to believe we're having them. From the moment we wake up to the moment we fall asleep, and on into the dream world, our brains are working away at something - the cogs keep turning. There are times we're so deep in thought that the world around us disappears as we go further into our minds, perhaps to wrestle with some problem, relive an occasion or to seek escape - whatever reason, it's our private space and we retreat to it often. There are other times when we can't escape our thoughts rambling on and on, accusing us, berating us, reminding us - over and over we replay them like a stuck record; if only we could silence the incessant chatter we'd get some peace of mind. Temporary escape may come by turning on our radio or television or by going out into the noise of the street, hoping that on our return we'll find welcome silence. Whatever we think about, we do by accessing memories - our past - and when we turn to distractions we *add* to and *edit* those memories, thus causing more noise rather than alleviating it. Every thought we think belongs to us *if* we adopt it; if we think negative thoughts and see negative images then *negativity* becomes the state of our mind. We can't exist without thinking; everything we do, say, see, smell or touch involves thought and once experienced, becomes a new memory - what we look back on and forward to. Our thoughts control our decisions, so it's important to watch them closely as they arise, question where they come from, and to follow that question through.

Reflecting on 'memory' and 'thought' is something that's occupied me for many years. At first, I was confounded as I became aware of my own thoughts and began to think about the thinking process. It seemed as though there was a disconnection from myself whenever I thought on the questions; who's doing the thinking, what *is* thinking, what *is* a thought and how is it that I'm able to *think* about thinking? The deeper I delved into these questions the more confused I became - not because it was complicated but because I'd never thought about it before. I also became increasingly aware that to go further along my 'path', I had to erase every trace of 'me'. 'Me' is what I've *become* and the 'construct' for 'me' contains all the information I've ever absorbed and held onto - information stuck like 'reminder notes' (memories) on my mind. In other words, 'me' is a conglomeration of *all* my personal experiences - all of my memories.

'Me' is an inner world that can't be known by looking outside - it's not physical. 'Me' has to be deconstructed and will strongly resist that process, which it does for several reasons - including that it wants to survive, making the task intensely arduous - requiring our full attention. Consequently, we cling to our images and do our best to become 'someone' that confirms our existence - to play our chosen roles in this world (doctor, housewife, politician, accountant, etc.) to the best of our ability. Here's an example of what I mean. I may ask myself 'Who am I?' and the automatic answer would be 'Renée' but I know that's not who I am, so I question how that automatic answer came about. I answer 'Renée' because that's what I've been called all my life - that's the name people use when they refer to me - it's the lie that I've made true. It's the name I turn around to when I hear it and say 'Yes?', it's the name on identity documents and countless other places, it's where 'me' can be 'found', but it's not *me*. It's just a name I learnt to respond and pin memories to; for example, Renée likes 'this', doesn't like 'that' and belongs to a particular group, nation or class system. Over the years, the name Renée has been kneaded repeatedly until it was exactly the right texture and consistency to become what I've come to know as 'me'. This is how our characters are gradually formed as we become deeply conditioned to believe in the images, words and judgements we associate with them. These 'descriptions' become our memories and we pay just as much attention to them as we do the images, words and judgements others have formed about us; we're totally engrossed in our egos and the feedback we receive about them - our egos have made our bodies their home. Some of these memories are lies, some are truths and some are lies that we've made true. Have you ever thought about what it is that makes you 'you'?

~~~

This is a hard-going chapter and I promise you I won't be offended if you skip ahead to the next one, or even put the book down. For me however, it's my passion/purpose and I must continue to write it - at times, it all makes my head spin, but it's a feeling that urges me on rather than pushes me back. No matter what we do to disguise the truth about ourselves or pretend that a truth doesn't exist, no matter how busy or distracted we keep ourselves so we don't have to think about these things, they'll *always* be there lurking and nagging in the background reminding us what frauds we are.

~~~

An actor can't *become* someone else, but he can play a role and this process requires a good memory. The actor has to learn to speak in the voice/accent of the character he wishes to portray, learning the character's mannerisms, thought processes, prejudices, body language and even what he likes to eat or drink. He must behave and look like the character - top hat, flat cap, weapons, costumes and other accessories - whatever he needs to be convincing. He has to absorb all this information and then the 'memories' can be accessed via thought - as soon as he needs them. To play a role well an actor must have the memories and thoughts of his character; he must *become* the character he wishes to play - effectively, becoming the character's ego. At the end of the play however, the actor drops the façade and returns to 'himself' once more. I'd suggest that the 'parts' of the actor and the character he plays could easily become intermingled as, when playing another role, it's inevitable that some memories must 'stick' - after all, these created our personalities to begin with.

An actor learns his part and replays it often during rehearsals and actual performances to such an extent that he may not even think about his lines or actions, as they become second nature - an alter-ego. These memories are always accessible for him to recall and should he falter slightly, there are directors and other stage staff to prompt him. There's often a transition where an actor comes off stage and is still 'in character' - he's not yet fully returned to his own, particularly if he's played his role well. It's a bit like coming off the motorway; it takes a while to get used to driving slower again and it's easy to pick up speed without realising that we're driving over the speed limit. We've become so fully engrossed in the roles we play that we're unaware we're playing them - we can't see that we're made up of memories; the memories of the people who gave them to us - the memories we've cached. We're ingenious actors so it's no wonder we don't want to let go of our roles - our multiple 'me's.

Needless-to-say, I now appreciate why people don't like to think about these things. Delving into the mysterious or unknown can be frightening - so much so that we prefer to immerse ourselves in the many familiar distractions that society has to offer; entertainment, information, exercise, travel, work, fantasy and consumption. In particular, we immerse ourselves in future projects such as preparing adequately for our old age, a wedding, a birth or next year's holiday - *anything* but face the possibility of quietly thinking. I've lost count of the number of people who have told me they 'don't like to think', but they do it all the time; what they really mean is that they don't like to think below the surface. For some however, like me, there's no choice but to 'delve' - nothing has changed my life so much for the better than self-reflection and a firm commitment to 'unlearn' the lot. As I wrote in my introduction, the restlessness I feel calls me with some urgency - I'm more than happy to answer that call, wherever it may lead.

~~~

Our minds are so full of contaminants that we can't see - or conceive of - that which is pure; we also don't accept - or know - that our minds are contaminated at all. For whatever reason, our innocence has been diluted by conditioning, prejudices, ownership, polluted dreams and identities that can never belong to us - identities made up of the ideas and images that our senses have been, and still are, bombarded with from the moment of our birth. Most importantly, we adapt these images according to our perception of the environment we live in - how we've been and continue to be conditioned. Thought creates our images; mother cooking in the kitchen, father supporting the family, pink for girls and blue for boys are just a few of the more traditional ones and we carry these images into our future, which is also the past. The future being the past takes a while to get to grips with, but let's keep it simple - what can you think about for the future that hasn't come from past conditioning and therefore experience? Thought creates and maintains our beliefs, fears and wishes; thought controls us and thought interrupts any attempt by us to be free from it. We can't imagine a perfect world because we don't *live* in one and have seen only the ideas and imagined worlds of the media. Take for example the images and ideas in the film *The Time Machine*, based on H. G. Wells' book. Utopia wasn't all it seemed to be; there was mischief going on behind the scenes - mischief that the passive population were oblivious to. Had the whole film been about happy people sitting by the river with everything they needed, we would've been bored stiff while watching it. Our interest however, is maintained and believability sustained when we add a little mystery regarding time, together with a few familiar character types and mischievous situations - we take a framework we like the sound of - like the *Garden of Eden* for example - and then fill in the blanks according to our conditioning.

Another reason we can't imagine a perfect world is because to do so means dismantling the one we're living in - letting go of what defines us - the idea of 'Me'. To dismantle what we 'know' to be true is tantamount to psychological suicide - no-one wants to live without their beloved identity and its various branches of inter-relationships; mother, brother, friend etc. To imagine a perfect world we must first face the horror and lies about the one we live in; we have to recognise the illusions and little-by-little, take them apart - it's necessary to erase *all* thoughts about who we think we are, before discovering that there's much more to us. We have to recognise that thought is memory - thought is the past and thoughts are what the world is made up of and influenced by - thought is confined and therefore *limited*. One difficulty in realising this is that we're left with no niche to belong to anymore; we're exposed, alone, naked in no-man's-land and way beyond our conditioned comfort zones - very few people are prepared to venture that far out of bounds. It's *not* an easy journey and we can't force ourselves to begin it; it begins when we want it to and not a moment before.

Another concept that's difficult to grasp is that we're 'One' - humanity. We can't be told that we're 'One' because we don't have the memories/thoughts that allow us to process the concept - it's alien to us. Our conditioned memories limit us to the barriers and borders that we've grown up with; nations, countries, tribes, colours and families - these all lend credence to separation rather than Oneness. We can only *realise* that we're 'One' for ourselves and the tendency is to ridicule anyone who tries to tell us otherwise, as they're 'threatening' our traditions. The problem however, isn't about 'threatening' traditions - it's about thinking on another frequency - it's about change and to change we have to be prepared to leave all the things we were doing before behind.

I digressed a little - thought is like that.

When we think, we tend to go by the marked footpath - the way we've always gone - our conditioned route. When we recognise and are willing to accept that our thoughts are *not* our own we then access something new - something eternal, sacred and immediate. To put thought into perspective we have to look closely, as best we can, at what it is. There are no thoughts - absolutely none - that haven't been given to us by society and that includes by our families. We've been taught by education and advertising to have thoughts about things; like 'happy families', relationships, 'success' and disaster; we've been shown so many models of these and through association with them, outline and fill in our lives, ambitions and dreams; these thoughts are from memory and formulaic - they're seriously flawed inasmuch as they can't deliver what they promise. A thought comes from a memory - it comes from our experiences. It would be very difficult, if not impossible, to locate our first thought - from our first experience - or to remember the discussions of our parents or nursing staff around us at the moment of our births:

- 'It's a boy.'
- 'He's perfect.'
- 'Let's call him Jack.'
- 'He weighs 7lbs.'

Without language how can a baby receive and process this information? I say without language, but I'd suggest it would be more accurate to say that he's unable to respond yet. We don't know if he's able to *understand* what we're saying - even if on some other level - but can't rule out the possibility and this would be a frustrating experience for the child if it were the case; we also can't rule out that thought may well begin in the womb. We can ask questions about our existence as we grow older, but the responses given to us can only come from the past. To elaborate a little more on this point, we get answers from reference books, from the media, from people we know or from our own memories - these answers are located in the past and there are a great many of them to amuse ourselves with. It's for this reason that searching for 'truth' on the outside is futile.

Quintessentially, there's something behind our memories and thoughts - something resistant to being conditioned yet at the same time, accepts this conditioning as the 'norm'. We can't see beyond this norm because we're conditioned not to; we must stay in line fearing consequences, should we choose to do otherwise. Yet there are times when we get to glimpse through the veil of conditioning - rather like getting a glimpse of the sun through heavy clouds; the same clouds that quickly cover it up again. Perhaps we convince ourselves that we never actually saw the sun - whereas we know we did, but choose to ignore any thoughts that tell us otherwise. We choose the thoughts and memories that bring us the most comfort and security. When I think of marmalade I think of 'marmalade on toast' and would venture that this is true for most people, but, for me to begin putting marmalade on jacket potatoes for example, could cause consternation for those familiar to me - raising not only eyebrows, but all sorts of questions regarding my 'sanity'. To act beyond our conditioning is *so* socially unacceptable that we bring pressure on those who do, to 'reform' themselves by stepping back into line - we prefer them to be like us because that doesn't threaten the *status quo*. New thoughts, that contradict the old, are unacceptable to the majority of us; we go to great lengths to upgrade everything in this world, except our minds - we resist this adaptation.

I'd suggest that we must have known - or had access to finding out - what we were doing here *before* we became so heavily indoctrinated, thus causing us to forget all about it - why else are we not encouraged to remember, discuss and study this topic; it's an important topic for every one of us, but instead of looking at it, we bury it beneath a great deal of unimportant diversionary nonsense. It's this nonsense that blocks all possible access points to that which is eternal. What's clear to me is that something existed *before* our characters were moulded - a predisposition. 'Me' is and continues to be a bundle of memories and thinking is the tool I use to access them. These memories are everything we're conscious of; for example, our names, addresses, professions, titles, opinions, fears, hates, histories, beliefs, rituals, sentiments and hopes. They're our stored experiences; they're the contents of our minds or if you will, the seeds from which our egos took root and flourished. We can only be free when we're free of thought and that's only possible in the Now as this is where we breach the limitations of thought itself and therefore, our fears - where there's no ego, space or time. If we try to stop thinking we can't; there are always thoughts keeping us busy and they come and go - at random - like confusing dreams, picked and collected from different periods of our lives that have nothing to do with where we are now. When we look closely at - or at least allocate a little of our precious time to the nature of *thought* then our lives can change significantly and in that process, the world becomes more magnificent and mysterious than we ever thought it could be. Memory then, is all we've absorbed - thought is playing back those memories. Thinking then, is a process by which we search through our databanks in search of those memories and assemble them according to our disposition. Where those memories lead us to and how much time we choose to linger with them is entirely up to us.

Chapter 49

Taking Stock - A Perspective

*The world doesn't care about us,
because we don't care about it.*

To see the world in a different 'light' it's necessary to realise that life isn't like a film, book or soap opera. There are no choreographed fight scenes down our streets where no-one gets injured, no-one who wakes up in the mornings with their makeup intact, no 'lady in the red dress', no perfect figure, no spotless complexion, no spaceship hovering a few hundred feet above us and no fire-breathing dragons - above all, no superhero that's going to save us from ourselves; life just isn't like that. The world seen through the filters of the media is entirely different to the one we recognise in our society, yet fantasy is very much a part of our 'reality' and we accept it as such. Images - such as the above - are promoted heavily and their effect distorts perception and perspective, leading to feelings of inadequacy, powerlessness and apathy. Such feelings leave us prey to whatever society provides us with, so that we may seek 'perfection' by comparing ourselves to those who have 'it' and those who haven't. These images are controls by which we're steered towards illusions - like games or trends - where we can dream and become whatever we want to be. But they're not *our* dreams - they're manufactured 'junk food' - they're spam for our brains! The spell of these dreams is easily broken when we catch a glimpse of ourselves in a mirror or wake up in the mornings either alone, or perhaps next to a frog who failed to turn into a prince - no wonder we return to our more comfortable and acceptable illusions. While there's nothing wrong with doing this, if it gets us through the day, what if we could set ourselves free by looking at what's really happening - at how the world is being manipulated and how the majority of people have been drawn into an intricate 'spider's web' of distractions and illusions. Because many can't see that they're living in a controlled environment, it's understandable that they've no wish to break free from it.

So what?

If we've been attracted into a 'web' then it follows that something did the attracting; *what* that is isn't important - only that we submit and agree to live under its cloak of deceit. This leaves us feeling powerless because our power is in someone *else's* hands, by our choice. Multiply that power by the world's population and it becomes apparent how the world has become so unbalanced - the few have a great deal. We've become so locked into the pull of desire, fear, success, failure, protection and separation that we actually believe one human being is more powerful than another - that they've an advantage over us, perhaps by having been born in the right place at the right time. This isn't the case; however, we believe it to be true and give other people the authority to control the lives of ourselves and our children. Perhaps you can't see this, but then I invite you to think about who decides when to invade another country, who pays for it and who's told that it's in the interest of *our* safety; isn't it more in the interests of those who want to continue being in control? Those same people make up our laws, educate our children, judge others, control our media, earn huge salaries and through 'VIP status' or 'diplomatic immunity' are given exemption from taking responsibility for their actions - they don't subject themselves to the laws they impose on us. Most importantly, think about who voted them into office on a wave of enthusiasm encouraged by the media and our 'fed-up-ness' with things the way they are - unhindered by the knowledge that *nothing* is going to change for the better. For every cause and effect there are consequences - there'll always be a price to pay for our apathy and reliance on our various elected 'authorities'.

Who are the authorities? We are. There's no real domination or submission, there's simply an imbalance, kept in place by our fears. Each one of us is different inasmuch as we were born into different cultural environments - environments that existed *before* our 'birth'. Environments created to maintain separation in such a way that the system we created grows stronger and more violent as that division continues; like us, it began with the first division of a 'cell' and has continued exponentially ever since. So why do we follow the laws of others? That's a *very* good question and needs meditating on, but mostly because there *are* laws and, even though some are illogical, we're conditioned to obey them - 'Simple Simon' says, and we do. The trouble with laws is that we become dependent on them to tell us what we can and can't do, and then complain when these laws are enforced - we've lost our ability to filter out the nonsense. We want other people to submit to these laws, even when we don't always obey them ourselves - we can be rather bossy and superior; the 'artful' bend these laws to suit their own agendas. Why do we have laws at all? That's a good question too. We have laws because we're irresponsible and selfish - it's that simple. For example, we need speed limits because we speed and put others at risk when we're doing it. A concept that's unfamiliar to many is that, in some cases, the laws really *are* for our protection - too often from ourselves. However, the laws are created - and enforced - by the same sickness of mind that made the need for them necessary, so what we get is more disorder and no justice. The more we behave 'badly', the more new laws will be created; for example, litter laws are necessary *only* because we throw our litter onto pavements and driving laws, because we drive recklessly and inconsiderately. We don't *need* the laws at all. What we need is to take responsibility - to allow ourselves to evolve in a way that widens our perspective, so we see that the way we behave has an effect on everything and everyone around us, and to *care* about that. If we're to evolve, psychologically, then we must become a law unto ourselves - for the *good* of mankind, not the detriment; if we choose not to - yes, it *is* a choice - then our prospects are rather bleak.

~~~

As individuals, can we do anything about what's happening all over the world? No! There's nothing we can do. That statement should have the effect of taking a heavy weight off our minds but it doesn't; it leaves us feeling apathetic and more powerless than ever. The world outside of our own perspective can't be changed by us personally. *Everyone* has to change - to stop doing whatever they're doing and take stock, rather than examine the world as 'armchair activists' focused on the large variety of world issues our minds are constantly directed towards. Bearing this in mind we know the world's population is not going to have that enviable 'light bulb' moment at the same time, so we do what we've always done - wait for someone or something to flick the switch for us - maybe by divine intervention or a superhero; who knows? The problem is that we don't see the whole picture, but only snippets. By way of illustration, the job of one person in this world may be to stamp out a metal shape and another's, somewhere else in the world, is to form that shape in to a part that gets sent on elsewhere to be attached to a frame of some sort. None of these workers know or care what's being constructed, how other members of the team are contributing towards it, or what its ultimate purpose is. We care only for the money we receive in our wage packets, so that we're able to pay our ever increasing bills, feed our families, accumulate 'more' and continue to heedlessly consume our world.

~~~

When the sky and outer space are beyond our reach and our ability to 'leave the planet' is limited to being up in one of our various flying machines - with the inevitable return to earth - everything can feel a little hopeless. We hear a great deal of bad news - every day - and sometimes even good news can feel 'bad', if it leaves us feeling frustrated or envious. Consequently, in 'powerless mode', we become engrossed in the various diversions provided for us - be it work or play - as they give the illusion of being in control while we're having a 'good time' or trying to 'make something of ourselves'. We temporarily forget about - or rather put to the back of our minds - all the things we're dissatisfied with - we don't like to think about them. We prefer the illusion of being in control, because we're uncomfortable with the noise of our thoughts when everything around us is silent - when we're alone. We're more comfortable living with the noise and chaos of society; when the world is screaming at us, *we* don't have to scream at it. Certainly the diversions we're surrounded by can leave us entertained and often amused, but they also leave us feeling undervalued, insignificant and ignored - we don't like to feel that way. These diversions also encourage us to 'join in' so we become actors, online chefs, exhibitionists and comedians for example - hoping for likes, followers and approval; we look for something or someone to acknowledge and take notice of our very existence, but it's all rather cliché and the vast majority of us remain invisible, despite our masks of anticipated/achieved popularity or fame. We take whatever we can get, but underneath there's a scream, a sorrow and a person who knows they're effectively banging their head against a brick wall - a person who's lost in this world, just like the rest of us.

It sounds hopeless doesn't it, but I invite you to think about whose voice is telling you that? Isn't it the voice of the ego that's 'quite comfortable as it is' and has no intention of exerting itself in order to change? We've been given the ability to find meaning in our lives - to work out what we're doing here and to have compassion for each other. We hear that distant voice - behind the ego - that we so often ignore in favour of our desires and comforts. We tune it out, rather like a television or radio station, to prevent the cross-talk interfering with our chosen frequency and so that we can't hear anything else, we turn up the volume. If we *really* want to change we need to tune in to the voice we ignore and see the ego for what it is - a creation of our mind. If we don't - if we remain between 'stations'

- then all we'll ever hear is white noise. Be aware that the mind is a clever trickster and offers us any number of 'good reasons' to remain as we are - it doesn't want us to change frequency by giving up its creation or allowing us a vision of a better world. The mind is our prison and its walls have been continuously reinforced for a long, long time. I'm not going to tell you that it's easy to free ourselves from within these walls, because that wouldn't be true. I can however, assure you that changing ourselves changes the way we see the world and though that can be a herculean task, it's worth the effort - *if* we don't give up. During the course of our lifetimes we've suffered many disappointments and setbacks; we've also been discouraged from doing 'our own thing' unless it suits the agenda of society. For these reasons we don't expect or believe that anything positive will or can take place in our lives - *that's* what I mean by giving up.

~~~

A play begins when the curtains open and ends when they close again; our lives begin when we're born, and end when our eyes close for the last time. We fear the end, but not what we put between it and the beginning; we don't give this much intelligent thought at all. Our lives are important enough for us to be here, so they should also be important enough for us to participate in the world in a meaningful and responsible way, as opposed to being an audience for those who wish to control us, as though we'd somehow drawn the 'short straw' on who takes charge. We feel obliged and accept unquestioningly living in *their* world, rather than creating our own. It doesn't matter what circumstances we're born into. What matters is how our *minds* develop and how we lift ourselves out of fear, dependence, helplessness, self-pity and despair.

Humanity needs a 'sea change', a change of mindset, and that mindset changes a little each time one of us puts our 'weapons' down; it isn't an *en masse* overnight process. By weapons, I don't just mean guns; I also mean gossip, jealousy, envy, hatred, spite, judgement, anger and snobbery - wielded by over-inflated egos. When we raise our consciousness and see the bigger picture, it isn't possible to behave in a destructive or inconsiderate manner. I'd suggest that we're not here to 'succeed' in this world; we're not here to win a war; we're here to evolve and to transform ourselves - psychologically. We're here to raise the level of our consciousness and right now - for the majority - it's being lowered by, amongst other things, our encouraged need to 'out-do' each other. Any form of competition is separation; if we meet, you may want to show me what you do and how you do it so much better than I can, and I may wish to show you the same thing from my perspective. This situation results in competitiveness and comparison - it may also get us the approval, admiration, recognition and acceptance that we all seek, but there are consequences. When we strive to become Number One, we're striving for someone else not to be good enough; when we strive to 'have' we strive for someone else to 'have not'.

No-one cares about us more than we do. We're more than a little interested in *ourselves* and for this reason we're not very good at seeing perspective, if it doesn't agree with our own. If we have a problem then that problem is as big - if not bigger - than the world and to all intents and purposes, we're alone with it. At our lowest point, like when we lose our job or a relationship ends, our lives feel like they've come to an end and nothing can ease our mind or make us feel better. As far as we're concerned, in situations such as these, the rest of the world doesn't exist as no-one understands the urgency of our situation with the same intensity that we do, neither will they give it priority. Sure, we can discuss our problems with friends or even acquaintances, but mostly - like us - they'll be more concerned with their own and more importantly, they really can't help us by bringing back what we've 'lost' - they can only console us and what practical use is that consolation. The world can support us when things get tough and it may genuinely try to help, but it can't solve our problems, live our lives for us or give them meaning. No matter how busy our social life is - real or virtual - we're each of us entirely alone with our thoughts and have an agenda seen *only* from our *own* perspective - our true intentions are rarely aired.

Between the covers of birth and death we write our unique stories - mostly tragic or full of missed opportunities and possibilities, rather than 'happy ever after' endings. Is it any wonder then, that our literature and other media are full of those same horrors, reflecting, reinforcing and magnifying them - after all, *we* are the writers of it. It's not that we're 'bad' inside, we just want someone else to show us the way, to solve our problems *for* us, so that we no longer have to be afraid and then we'll be happy - a 'when my boat comes in' mentality. As I mentioned earlier, life just isn't like that and we're lazy when it comes to doing things that are good for us; we also want someone to follow - someone to go first, for them to take the risks thereby clearing our path - a sort of guarantee that we won't stumble, fall or set off any 'explosions'. Ironically, we also want to be followed in some way - we're both sheep and shepherd. This is very much part of the nature of our world today, as is profoundly evident on our social media 'friends' and 'follow' lists. We can accept life as it is, as many prefer to do, or stop and take stock - to examine well our situation and overcome the belief that we can't change ourselves. We can start writing a new chapter any time we want to; all that's needed is a change of perspective - a change that happens by itself when we look at the whole picture.

Sometimes discerning what's happening is just a question of changing our perspective. If for example. there's a 1 in 100 chance of winning the lottery, we get more of an idea about what that means when we see that there's a 99 in 100 chance of losing. If the lottery were advertised this way we wouldn't buy tickets. When we turn things around they'll look very different. However, we're taught to think about the odds of *winning* and the word sticks. We're attached to 'hope' and getting 'lucky' - we choose these, even though we know it's futile. We can't see the truth about our world whilst arguing against it. For example, we choose to use the word 'winning' as opposed to 'losing', because no one wants to hear about losing, despite - in the case of the lottery - it being the more likely outcome.

~~~

Think about which characters would get the most exposure if you decided to put your story onto paper; in other words, who dominates your thoughts and by definition, your life. In my case it was my father, and an autobiography I drafted was nothing more than a sob story in which he played the 'starring role'. I came to realise that I was nothing more than an extra in my own life story with no lines of my own - therefore, I burnt it, because my father was starring in *my* life instead of me. Once I realised this, it became unacceptable to continue giving him so much space in *my* mind - it wasn't good for me. We have to realise that we're strange, very strange, and that we do the craziest things; for example, going on a diet and perhaps rewarding ourselves once a week for the effort we made, with something that *isn't* good for us - we call it a 'treat'. We rarely have our own best interests at heart. If we make little efforts to change the way we think and behave, then the world we see will begin to change for the better and we'll start to 'know ourselves' in a whole new and intelligent way - if we up the ante, it'll change much faster.

It's important not to see ourselves as victims of the authorities - like us, they're an audience. They watch us for change just as we watch them, and through statistics and observation they know how to keep us occupied and entertained. They give us what we want - someone else to take responsibility, and we give them what they want - 'power' and 'control'. Our feedback through various channels, informs the authorities about the mood of the general public and our own genius creates new fads and technological advances to placate us, but only with what we're able to absorb at the time. In other words, as long as we want to play games then games are what we'll create. Our games, phones and computers get frequent 'updates', but our minds don't; we can only upgrade that ourselves - yes, we can 'upgrade' it - and that can't happen as long as we allow our minds to continuously be infected by the various viral activities of society. There's a big difference between being controlled by society's wishes for us, and really being in control ourselves. It's that frequency thing again; when we're ready to change then it'll happen and not a moment before; until then we must continue to live under the parental arm and control of the society we created - it's there both for our protection and destruction and will be, for as long as we choose not to take responsibility for ourselves. It's a symbiotic relationship and it'll remain that way, until we take our power back. The authorities have no power without our compliance. It's our power that not only drives, but strengthens and advances the system - without that power we're greatly weakened. To vastly simplify this point; our compliance is the only power our elected authorities have - they'll hold on to it, until we're ready and responsible enough to handle it ourselves.

Chapter 50

Relationships

As we climb a mountain, the valley becomes clearer and clearer.

During the course of our lifetime, we encounter many different people - some from our own culture and others from significantly different ones. Some of these encounters may last for just a split second - as with passers-by - and sometimes we establish relationships for a lifetime. There are people who we meet at the moment of their birth and others at the moment of their death. Stranger, are the relationships that only take place in our imaginations, such as with a 'celebrity' or a character in a book or film. No matter what the type of meeting, we 'eye up' and categorise each other based on our conditioned images, prejudices and fears - always aware of any possible threat to our 'stability' and in particular to our 'safety' - we're *en garde*. We're humanity - the *human* family - but we've been divided into nations, colours, religions, age groups, classes, levels of education, the Smiths and the Jones's. It's these divisions that cause all of our problems as we strive to fulfil our own agendas - on our own 'side', behind our own 'flag' and these are our first priority; we tend to offer only 'spare change' for anything else. Regardless of the conditions under which we meet - because of the images that divide us - we can never fully know anyone, unless we're willing to drop all conditioned responses, to see our extended 'family' through unfettered eyes.

Relationships are complex and if we're honest, few of us welcome so-called 'outsiders' into our lives or speak to them on an equal footing - an outsider, being someone who doesn't fit into our accepted culturally-conditioned environment. Such outsiders have had different experiences to our own - some better, some worse, and it's through our biased experiences and adopted opinions that we judge them.

These judgements are often based on propaganda spread by the media, such as about immigrants waiting to enter 'our' country; we worry that they'll drain us of our resources when in truth it's more likely that we've drained them of theirs, which is why they seek our help now. Other outsiders are those we fleetingly pass by without any real contact; for example, once, whilst driving, I caught sight of a lorry coming my way and as we passed by each other I saw the driver's face.

I remember thinking that I'd never know who the man was; I'd never know how he's suffered, what he's going through now, where he's going, where he came from, or whether he has similar thoughts as he passes other people by. We generally encounter people every day of our lives and most of them we don't give a second thought to; however, our worlds *do* meet - albeit briefly. For example:

- Passively, as when standing in a queue.
- Actively, when greeting a colleague or client.
- Peacefully, at mutually agreeable venues
- Suspiciously, when meeting for the first time.
- Hopefully, when noticing a beneficial opportunity.
- Violently, to one degree or another, such as when or being 'pushed and shoved' through a crowd.

When meeting people for the first time we pigeon hole them into categories; such as, threat, naïve, 'keep at a distance', attractive, 'useful person to know' or 'avoid at all costs'; there are far too many to list and some of these are physical, some psychological, but *all* of our scrutinised categories and judgements are based on our past experiences. We euphemistically call this 'summing someone up', but when we do that we could miss a magic moment or a kindness that could result from such a chance encounter, simply because we look for confirmation of our judgement, which can obscure anything to the contrary. We brush shoulders in one way or another with other people during our daily lives, never noticing them, never knowing them and if we're honest, never really caring. We miss out on so many opportunities to make a difference when we fail to notice the world around us - when we're in 'I' 'Me' 'My' mode.

Circumstantial relationships are common and given little thought. We're quick to judge people if they're connected to someone we once knew; for example, the new girlfriend of an ex-boyfriend we feel resentment towards. No matter who our 'ex' dates, we'd likely hate them on first sight if we still have feelings for him; more likely we'd dislike them even before we met as jealousy and pride kick in. If however, we were to meet the same girl under different circumstances - like at a party - we'd probably get on rather well; after all, we must have something in common to have attracted the same man. So many of our mutually beneficial relationships are shallow, and reciprocal only if we're on the same 'team' such as in schools, sports, sects or competing businesses; should someone change allegiance, then our feelings towards them become more or less favourable than they were before - our friend then becomes our enemy or our enemy our friend - raising the question what exactly is it we require of someone in order to accept them as a friend. We've probably all been in relationships where we're expected to drop someone simply because our 'best friend' has fallen out with them - many comply with this demand; we miss out on so much when we allow ourselves to be divided by circumstance. There's also a dark side to circumstantial relationships where we're manipulated - or manipulate - as a means to an end and these are the most destructive of relationships as they invoke mistrust, betrayal and the like - they're far more common than most people would like to admit. Personal and business relationships are often based on an 'agreement' whereby as long as each person is doing what the other one wants things run smoothly; questioning in such a relationship can start sparks flying and bring the relationship to a swift end; for example, when a child disagrees with a parent, or an employee with his boss; when two sticks are rubbed together they'll produce a fire.

Families create the most complicated of relationships and based on current knowledge, we don't choose which family to become a part of. The word 'family' implies closeness, but we know that most families are anything but. If we look at humanity as a whole it's possible to see why that is - family members are just as divided as anyone else and only a surname (a tag or a label) connects them. Being a family is really just another form of separation - a further division - a division from everyone else. The ethnocentric nature of families demand that they stick together no matter what - because of this, the blood bond is difficult to break away from or to do without. It would cause us more loneliness than ever *not* to be a part of a family - we can't just leave one and join another; an adopted family member will always remain just that, no matter how much affection may be felt for them - often apparent in moments of high dudgeon. In reality, families are divided amongst themselves and each member has their own strong views. No matter how one particular view may be frowned upon or discouraged by other family members, it *can't* be changed or destroyed and will smoulder in our hearts until we're able, or decide to go our own way - perhaps as the 'black sheep', perhaps on a 'guilt trip' for standing up for ourselves instead of living with a loyalty that's one-sided. If we turn our backs on our own beliefs, we can end up remaining bitter for the rest of our lives - a bitterness that ferments and is detrimental only to ourselves. What can we do if we find ourselves in this position? I can only give you the benefit of my experience, which involved waiting until I was *legally* and *mentally* old enough to make my own decisions (wisely or not), yet all the while, observing the situation and learning from it; in particular, learning that I could only change myself, *never* others - despite the apparent 'unfairness' and 'injustice' of it all. This understanding was key to my letting go, though it took many years and much strife for me to come to terms with.

A married couple will often stay together, even if their relationship is destructive, for a variety of reasons including for the 'benefit' of the children, yet many choose to divorce; when this happens we tend to leave a trail of victims behind. Divorce is not just the separation of two people who no longer get along - any children are affected by the division and also the relatives and friends of the two families that were forged together when the marriage took place. On divorce, members of the family become polarised, based on who they 'supported' before the marriage - things that were once considered 'ours' now become 'yours' and 'mine', if they're not broken in the battle, and here I'm not only referring to material belongings. As with friendships, a relationship with a family can be dependent on whose side we're on and if that includes the separation of children from one of their parents or their grandparents, then that's what we'll work to bring about - allowing personal feelings, pride and judgment to take precedence over kindness or the welfare and consideration of others.

Somewhere along the line we've gone horribly wrong in our ideas about what it means to be a family. Consider this. We create new families, not just for biological reasons, but also and often foremost by reason of conditioned sentimentality - such as romance - and a need for security in a society that encourages us to be dependent on it. We search for our 'happy ever after' home because we feel lost, need somewhere to belong, somewhere we feel safe, and a 'family' relationship is one of the ways in which we feel this; a career away from a family environment is another, but *both* are illusions - both create continuity of what we're seeking security from. There's something status-hugging about getting married and starting a family; we construct life-size doll's houses and fill them with everything we can get into them including children, gadgets, furniture, toys etc. - some of us decide we'd be better off living alone. Having attained these 'ideals' we spend our lives striving to maintain the *status quo* often putting our children into some form of 'day care' - including schools - in order to do that. This is the situation and example that we pass on to our children, which can never change anything in the world for the better; it's frustrating and leads to further painful division - often a division between parents and their children causing bitterness and resentment. At some point, we're going to have to make sense of the increasing disruption going on in the world - we can do that by first seeing what's going on in our *own*.

When the whole of anything is divided it no longer *seems* to be complete; though that *is* stating the obvious, it's something that doesn't occur to many people. Humanity has been mischievously fractured by an unstable mind (*our* mind) and the cracks have been filled with conflict with all its attendant hatred, sorrow, violence and fear, forming a mosaic that has some semblance of One - but it's a rather ugly and heavily conditioned One - having the effect of further dividing people. Humanity is *still* complete - it can never be anything else - *but*, it's a 'complete mess'! We need to clean up our act by raking out that hard and inflexible filling and replacing it with love - a love that will draw the pieces together rather than keeping them apart. We also need to pay attention to our relationships and see them for what they are, then and only then can compassion and empathy flourish in our society. As long as we're slaves to a society that persists in driving us into situations that cause further instability in the world, we'll remain as we are, as we've been for a *very* long time - searching for a place where we can live in peace without fear of disruption - searching for our home, not in outer space, but in our hearts.

Too often missing from our relationships - I'd suggest *most* of the time - is selflessness. No matter how much we think we're considering the thoughts and feelings of another person, it's hard to remove the ego from our interactions. Being selfless doesn't come easy; there's always that internal accountant trying to balance the books - scrutinising any payment that doesn't promise some sort of return. In the end, we place relationships in the debtor's journal awaiting a repayment; for example, doing a favour for someone and thinking 'they owe me', even if we try to push that thought away. We need to make the accountant redundant and not refill the position - though our ego will put forward suitable replacements for consideration.

When we learn to 'give' with no thought of a return we develop the most complete and important relationship we can ever have. This is the relationship we must forge with ourselves, and *this* is the relationship we put up the most resistance to 'having'; this is the *only* relationship in which we can ever find peace - the relationship in which we're at ease and the relationship in which the ego can't dominate. From our births to our deaths we spend *every* second with ourselves - awake and asleep - on holiday or not - and *every* one of them is precious; we can never be away from ourselves - our true nature - no matter how high a wall we build to keep it hidden. Death can come to any one of us at any moment without prior warning and few are prepared for it - most are still grasping for the things we *can't* keep; only a few have gone into themselves with the dedication required to discover their 'root' - a root from which we can never be torn. Our journey and the state of mind we're in when we die *is* important - the state of our body is not. Although some people have buried this realisation deeper than others, no matter how much we deny it, no matter how many arguments we create to avoid seeing the truth, no matter how much we torture ourselves with inner debates on matters such as 'life after death' in whatever form we choose to imagine, we *know* our lives have purpose and meaning *now* - this knowledge is innate!

Chapter 51

The Control Conundrum

There's no control without consent and no consent without control.

When you're next out and about take a look at a newspaper stand - you'll find there's *nothing* on it that inspires or motivates, nothing life-changing and nothing that's not been seen before. The newspaper headlines grind at our emotions, fill us with anxiety, anger, envy, outrage, fear and guilt sending us further into our shells, yet we continue to buy them in order to 'keep up-to-date' with what's going on in the world - it's expected of us and we like doing it. The headlines, emblazoned on the front pages, are generally about attacks, robberies, murders, corruption, drugs, missing children, injustice and badly behaving 'celebrities' of one sort or another - different faces, ages or backgrounds, but essentially the same old fear-inducing stories - there's no balance. Someone, somewhere wants to keep us in a state of anxiety; why don't we question that? Whether we're aware of it or not we *are* influenced by these front pages as we scan over them - they leave us feeling deflated and powerless to change anything and to compound this, we feel compelled to wallow in the *full* story. Just who is in control of this situation?

The flood of negative information from newspaper headlines, advertisements and countless other media - impossible to entirely avoid - is unknowingly absorbed, too often leaving us with an inexplicable background feeling of impending doom. Avert our eyes from the headlines and we'll find 'feel good' diversions such as hobby, holiday, property, car, pet, fashion and glamour magazines, puzzle books, confectionery, fizzy drinks and sandwiches; these are some of the antidotes we happily turn to - putting us 'back in control', or so we believe, but they're there for the purpose of igniting our desires, consoling and distracting us; they temporarily make us feel better and like other 'pain killers' it's only a matter of time before we require another dose. It's in our nature to want to be in control of our lives, in any way that we can; however, we're being ingeniously directed - under assault - at *every* turn.

There's another pervasive diversion from reality and that's gaming. We're bombarded - on our various devices - with notifications of someone's high score, someone's latest post, invitations to play etc. - the temptation to 'play' can be irresistible. We lose ourselves in gaming worlds because we're unable to comprehend or face the horrors of our own. Whether or not we like them, whether or not we play them, gaming is now a huge part of our world. Games fully absorb us into them while we're playing; they give us a feeling of being in control, a feeling that evaporates when we're away from our screens or virtual reality headsets; because of this, these games *are* addictive - we're far too quick to deny this fact. When we shoot at or kill other players, rob banks, drop bombs or whatever we do in these games we can't be arrested, tried or convicted - we get away scot-free. We take risks while participating in the games, knowing that we can't be harmed in any way - risks we wouldn't take in 'real life - there are no injuries, no deaths and no responsibilities. Shooting at someone in a game in today's world is equivalent to knocking over a tin soldier, or playing 'cowboys and Indians' in 'times gone by'. We can choose to behave violently, destroy the world and set ourselves up as heroes or villains without any apparent consequences. Consequences or not, violence is the act we're committing whether in real life or the gaming world; the majority of these games *are* violent in one way or another - increasingly gratuitous - as, inevitably, are our thoughts when we play them.

In a world we appear to have no control over it's no wonder we immerse ourselves in these fantasies - fantasies that give us, albeit an illusion, the feeling of being in control. We become so immersed in these games that we forget what time it is, whether or not we're hungry, all about the environment our body exists in and the people we share that environment with; gaming is an *out-of-body* experience - it's escapism. When our concentration is interrupted we get irritated - sometimes angry - out of all proportion, even if the call is to come down for a meal. When away from our screens for longer periods of time all we can think of is getting back to the game. We don't want to be pulled out of our fantasies back into the 'reality' that we're rejecting. I've seen extreme examples of this where nothing matters except 'The Game', not even food, hygiene or sleep; the games further divide those who are playing them from those who don't - often destroying personal or business relationships. It becomes apparent, when you take a step back and really look at the world, that it's awash with games of one sort or another; sporting, digital, shows, lotteries and countless other forms of games, including the mind games we play with ourselves and each other. There are consequences to this state of affairs. While we're busy in the playground our world, is being destroyed all around us and people everywhere are suffering. Instead of being in control of our world, we're controlled by the world of games. We're advancing technologically, but not physically (so many are sick in our world) or spiritually (so many have no hope left) or psychologically (we can no longer think for ourselves) and therefore, have no control over our lives. While we're influenced and controlled by these reality-altering games, instead of considering our existence and helping mankind out of its decline, our lives have no worthwhile meaning or value. Our life-clock however, is still ticking away as a reminder that our time here is passing.

~~~

Recognising what we can and can't change in society is an important part of changing ourselves and consequently, our world. Changing ourselves is a choice - do it or don't. If we decide to change then with that decision comes freedom from the diversions of those who wish to maintain the *status quo*, by appealing to and controlling our desire for consolation and distraction from our pains; consolation and distractions that generally aren't good for our physical *or* mental health - which is just one reason why we lead such unhealthy and stressful lives - leaving ourselves little time or inclination to make any kind of life-changing decisions. Imagine a film scene where someone has suffered a shock of some kind; in most cases are they not offered a sedative, cigarette or alcoholic drink to calm themselves? We're influenced by this suggestion and reach for drugs, alcohol, cigarettes or food when we need support, but they never support us; they provide an unhealthy distraction as we temporarily put our woes to one side - our sorrows can be suppressed, but they can't be drowned. When we reach for these distractions it's *us* who are in control of our actions, *us* who decide to bury our problems by not thinking about and elevating ourselves above entrapment; this is submitting ourselves to the control of others in a society that prefers us not to think at all; we willingly put our lives, and responsibility for them, in the hands of others. Paradoxically, the person who is being controlled is the one in control - being controlled is a choice. We're not naturally 'controllees', but take on the 'role' when we're afraid of possible repercussions and also when it's beneficial to us. Control - or rather authority over our actions - *has* never and *can* never been removed from us.

So much of the world, as portrayed, is out of our control and the most stable position for an individual to be in, is that of 'observer' - otherwise all we do is 'chase our tails'; the world is so out of control that no-one can possibly keep up with it. One piece of information conflicts with another and one of the greatest indicators of this is in our software 'updates'. When programs on my computer upgrade, others have to keep up with them or they don't function correctly anymore; for example, when our computer operating systems are updated - other programs may have to change with it or they become out-of-date and consequently, incompatible. My computer is always whirling away in the background updating something or another and this updating significantly slows down whatever I'm doing at the time - sometimes bringing it to a grinding halt, unless I make a decision to disconnect from the Internet and then my time is under my control. The same applies to our mobile phones. When I switch mine on in the mornings, more often than not it wants to update several applications to 'improve' my 'user experience' - this morning there were ten, but I experienced no improvement whatsoever. If we *don't* click in a box 'agreeing' to the update, then we may not be able to use the application and as many applications are interconnected this can cause operating problems - we've no control over this situation except to make a choice 'to agree' or 'not agree' in which case the application - and possibly others -

won't function? No wonder it's so difficult to get off the 'wheel' of upgrades, upgrades and yet *more* upgrades - for everything but our minds. Like the programs that won't work without changes, neither will we; we have to get off the wheel. In the world we're creating, the need for money and possessions now far outweigh the need for intelligence, compassion or love for each other.

If we choose to abstain from keeping 'up-to-date', by distancing ourselves from 'current affairs' and spending our time away from the chaos, then we're largely seen as not caring about what's going on in the world, which in most cases couldn't be further from the truth. Choosing not to swim in dirty water doesn't mean we don't care that it's dirty - it means that we prefer it to be clean. This action is not a slant against those who choose to remain as they are; it's a decision to remove ourselves from an unhealthy environment and take back control of our own lives, as far as is possible, without outside influence; it's a personal decision not to live in fear anymore - no matter what. It's also a firm decision to do anything we can to 'enquire' into the questions 'Who am I?' and 'What am I doing here?' even if the answers can't be fully understood during our lifetime. If our decision is in earnest, then the urge to change is so powerful that *nothing* can divert us.

~~~

Beneath the surface we're in full control of our own lives making choices every day; such as, what channel to watch, turn left or right, go to work or choose whether or not to finish reading a book; we make hundreds - if not thousands - of decisions every day without being aware that we're making them. Each choice we make produces a different effect on our lives; for example, the moment we choose to step into a road can result in us safely crossing it, serious injury, or even our death. We 'conduct' our lives *day-to-day* regardless of our circumstances or physical bodies; even from a hospital bed we can still smile - it's our energy that counts. We're *alive*. As long as we're alive, like 'a live wire', we're not disconnected from the energy that runs through us, but we *can* choose in which direction that energy flows and whether or not to suppress it. We can disconnect from our sorrows and pains and re-connect to what we've ignored for so long; what lies beneath our various masks - our fundamental nature, which is good. We can *choose* to be directed and follow the crowd, or to direct ourselves - following our own path. Our lives are full of contradiction and when it comes to talking about control there's more contradiction than ever. 'The control conundrum' is, who, if anybody, is in control of our lives? Ironically, there *is* no actual control - only the effects of the choices we make based on the influences we're surrounded by.

Chapter 52

Endurance

Endurance is the strength to cope with a hardship in whatever form it presents itself.

Whatever age you are, whatever your character, skin colour, no matter what the condition of your health and regardless of whether you smoke, drink alcohol, eat junk food or not; regardless of whether you have tattoos, qualifications or have lost one or even all of your limbs - here you are reading this sentence; you've made it through *all* your problems and every one of those moments you believed you *couldn't* go on any longer - those moments when you wanted the ground beneath your feet to split open and swallow you up, burying you forever as your world came to a heart-breaking end. Every one of us has survived what we thought we couldn't, and that says a lot about the resolve of the human race to endure whatever's put in front of it, and about our resilience and ability to come back stronger than ever. Brilliant, aren't we? However, like all thoughts that I allow to seed there's more to endurance than that.

The 1980's Japanese show 'Endurance' holds the title in *The Guinness Book of Records* as the 'Most Extreme Game Show'. I don't need to go into examples of the rounds, but to win this show contestants push themselves to their limits by *volunteering* to suffer exquisite pain, degradation and humiliation, and, from the expressions on their faces - they love every minute of it; however, it's not just the contestants who love these shows but the audience too - without a show there's nothing for an audience to see and without an audience, there's not much point in putting on a show. As an audience, our minds put us in more or less the same mental state as the contestants whilst in reality, we're sitting on the edge of our seats peeping through our fingers or curling our toes, as we pick up on the energy and revel in the 'courage' of the contestants to endure what we (as virtual contestants) quite possibly couldn't. If we choose to sit on a throne of momentary 'stardom', which is what we get from participating in a television game show, a throne of self-delusion or any other throne then that's what we'll do - no matter what hardships we may have to endure whilst sitting on it. We have a tendency to want to prove ourselves *to ourselves* by pushing our limits of tolerance and that manifests itself in various forms of suffering; we'll put ourselves through a lot in order to fit into society. We endure - we always have!

Our lives have much in common with this Japanese game show, in that we volunteer to endure suffering - to one degree or another - in exchange for 'prizes' in much the same way; these prizes are not necessarily tangible and could be anything from a medal to approbation. We go to great pains keeping up appearances for our neighbours, colleagues, acquaintances, family or friends - necessary when we live in a way that requires us to have so many complicated inter-relationships. In most cases, we can't reveal our nature to everyone we know, as we behave in a different way with each of them. To an employer we behave in a way that's acceptable to him in order to take home a salary - our 'prize'; it's the *price* we're willing to endure in order to have a nice home with all the related 'trimmings'. In most cases, we wouldn't want to keep our jobs if it weren't for the fact that we need a salary to pay our bills; generally, we don't work for the love of the job but out of necessity - it's an investment. We can do the same thing with relationships; I know people who have remained in very stressful situations simply because they don't want to divide their home or give up the income and comfort that they've built up over the years - so they endure the misery in order to hold onto their possessions and comforts - very few are able to break away from a situation like this.

One of the problems with endurance is that once we pass our chosen targets, we set ourselves further ones; humans like to push far and beyond the limits they have surpassed. Imagine if you will, someone who goes to the gym for the purpose of building muscles; the extreme of them will never have enough 'bulk' for their liking, and so end up looking 'deformed' in the most horrible way - it's self-inflicted. We talk about space, reaching for the moon, perhaps Mars, setting ourselves targets and then we'll want to go further - no distance will ever be far enough to satisfy us. The issue here is desire - a desire to surpass and as always with humans that results in competition, as the only thing we can really try to surpass is each other; the muscles are needed to be stronger than someone else, the space travel because we want to 'get there' before anyone else, and of course money - we'll never have enough of that. At this point I'm reminded of the old adage 'give them an inch and they'll take a mile'. We will endure - and cause others to endure - a great deal to achieve our goals.

We treat our bodies as though they were crash test dummies - testing them quite often to destruction. We starve them, overfeed them, poison them with alcohol and tobacco, eat over-processed modified 'food', pollute our vital air and water, and take drugs for entertainment; we're making ourselves *and* our planet ill and refuse to see that it's all self-induced; we've emotionally disconnected from what we're doing and the consequences of it. But, unlike crash test dummies our bodies aren't replaceable and we have to endure the results of our 'dare devil' activities. How much will we agree to endure before we tap into our intelligence and say 'enough is *enough*' instead of 'bring it on'? If it's still going on and getting worse, which it is, then we're pretty much okay with what's happening and don't want it to stop - at the very least, we don't want to do anything that will cause it to stop. We tend to go through life as willing packhorses ladened down with unnecessary loads. We *could* shed our load and walk away from it, but with that shedding comes the loss of a certain perverse status that we're unwilling (*not* unable) to give up - so we 'dutifully' endure whatever's put on us to keep that status going.

By now I expect some people are thinking about the endurance of an illness we can do nothing about, the pain of a cancer sufferer, the suffering of an abused child or a person who's lost someone dear to them. So, for example, what about the death of a loved one you may ask? That depends on your view of death - of what death is. To many people it's something to be feared, to others it means we go to a 'better' place. There are conditioned responses to death depending on our culture, and beliefs - how we endure the pain of the death of someone close to us depends upon that conditioning. Life however, will always go on and for me, as long as we're alive it's our responsibility to make the best of what's in front of us, even if that's pain - and yes, I've endured a lot of it. We never lose anyone at all, we do however, wish we could've held onto a relationship we've lost and *this* wish is for our own benefit, not the benefit of the person who 'died'. I could give endless examples like this, but these pains - that humanity must currently endure - are caused by the division of humanity from itself; they're the symptoms of a greater illness - the illness of the divided collective mind, currently in destructive 'I' 'Me' 'My' mode. If we were psychologically mature we'd realise that there's much more to us than our bodies and therefore, though we'd feel sorrow if someone close to us died, we'd be far better equipped to cope with it - and to put it into perspective, by knowing that the death of our body is as natural as the birth of it.

~~~

It's often said that we have to do the right things for the right reasons and I'd posture that the same applies to endurance. What do I mean by this? An extreme example might be holding onto a hot iron bar and enduring the pain for no reason other than pride (a challenge perhaps) as opposed to holding onto an iron bar - that has become hot - to keep a door open so that people can escape from a burning building. One of these actions is foolish and the other an unselfish act performed in order to save lives. It's not that we've *endured* that's important, but the dignity with which we did it and the strength gained from our experience. The 'condition' of the trail of memories and choices that we leave behind us matters; for example, we can remember a tough childhood as an experience that made us who we are today and in that way positively benefit from it, or we can remember our suffering in a way that perpetuates and accentuates it, preventing us from moving on as we continue to endure the same suffering, re-living it again and again in our minds - I did this for a great many years. There's enough pain and suffering in this world, without us volunteering to unnecessarily endure more. Through dispassionate self-observation we can learn much from the experiences that brought us to where we are at this very moment, and we can share that learning with others, as I'm doing with you. How we approach suffering and how we choose to endure it from this moment on is entirely up to us.

Chapter 53

Plan B

*When we realise the futility of living the way we do,
the process of change has begun.*

If we're honest, the majority of us tend to think of ourselves as inadequate in some way, mostly because we're conditioned to live up to the unattainable standards pushed onto us by society and in particular, by the media. It's inevitable that we'll 'fail' to live up to these standards no matter how hard we try to meet them, because the frontiers keep moving; there's a line that's near on impossible to cross; the competition is fierce and most of us are too tired to fight our way through it. Too many 'hopefuls' are grappling for the same targets; such as, security, romance, beauty, fame, approval or just an ounce of recognition, but the majority of us soon discover that we're 'excess to requirements'; yet *still* we come in droves - ever hopeful and ill-prepared for what lies ahead. We live in a dysfunctional society - one that still has wars, poverty, mass chaos and a burgeoning population - a world full of lies, corruption, external dreams and internal illusions; the world's committing suicide and doesn't give two hoots as long as it's 'business as usual' today - Now Syndrome*. As individuals we're encouraged to do the best we can with our lives - to succeed - but society, as a whole, is more than a little bent on 'failing' - it doesn't do or want what's good for it, but craves what's expedient. 'Plan A' isn't in our best interest and, as avoidable disaster looms, too few people are prepared to give any attention to the possibility of a 'Plan B' - if only we'd give this a little thought.

We divert ourselves from the agonies and frustrations society puts upon us - putting them to the back of our minds; by for example, flexing our muscles at the gym, taking up hobbies, socialising or seeking a good education, but what's the point of any of these; what use are they with regard to the psychological advancement of humanity and what do they really do for us as individuals? These activities do no more than make us look like a better product than we actually are - great packaging on not-so-desirable contents; however, this packaging was designed by those who profit from keeping us in a state of struggle and an illusion that we can be anything other than who we are. We need to be willing to stretch our minds rather than our muscles. The more we try 'to be' something or someone else, the more we thicken our masks and disguises and the less able we are to silence the noise in our minds; we can't see the beauty or simplicity of what lies beneath these masks and therefore, can never reach our full potential. Without peace of mind - whatever we do and wherever we go - we'll face the same problems because that's the world we've elected to live in - a refusal to change what we're doing, is an endorsement to keep things the way they are.

We live by Plan A - what we're doing right now and have been doing all of our lives with no positive change in sight - on the contrary, things in the world are becoming more and more insane and recent elections show that clearly. What I see is choice without choice; a choice between candidates who - according to propaganda - are no better than each other or anyone else for that matter. Despite being fully aware of the hullabaloo, we go along with the drama and *still* choose one of the candidates, whilst complaining about the stupidity of it all, as though we were unable to do anything about the situation. Society expects everyone to vote - to do their 'duty' - so we tend to vote for a candidate who purports to suit our agenda, even though we *know* it's all a contrivance. There's *always* a Plan B - a plan we must elect to implement ourselves and each one of us has the power to choose it, but first we must stop pleading helplessness. Say for example, you're given the choice between eating a rich chocolate fudge cake or an equally rich heavily-iced fruit cake - the debate begins, but as we consider the merits of each offering, we rarely consider the third choice of not eating either one of them, because conditioning demands a choice be made. The choice of not eating isn't *actually* a choice, but rather it's a developed freedom of the mind that doesn't consider either cake - there's no attraction to them. When there's *no* attraction there *is* no decision or consideration necessary; it's something we *feel* rather than have to think about and this feeling puts distance between ourselves and the question - we become mere observers of it.

Most of us have tried to avoid the call of the confectionery aisle in supermarkets at some point in our lives, but then leave the store with a bar of chocolate or packet of something that in some way we regret buying, particularly after we've eaten it. We didn't implement or think about Plan B; however, when we do implement Plan B and manage to leave a supermarket without those 'goodies' we feel pretty good, albeit temporarily as because of our success, we usually reward ourselves on our next scheduled visit, if not sooner. The feel good factor that we experience, in our current state of mind, is so unfamiliar that it gets rejected out of hand because we feel 'unworthy' of sustaining it, causing us to give up almost immediately as our targets are so far away in the future - a future that we may never reach and are willing to trade in for our more immediate desires (Plan A). Have you ever felt on a 'high' after reading a self-help book, going to an aerobics class or perhaps watching an uplifting film? I have. After reading a book many years ago I felt as though I were walking on air. This feeling lasted for about a week, but what I felt was the energy of the book, rather than any of my own, which is why this feeling didn't last any longer. The vast majority of us have experienced this feeling in one form or another *and* the fall that ensues once we settle back into our more familiar mind dramas, problems and routines - our new-found resolve falling by the wayside.

The continuity of the 'lift' we feel living by Plan B happens because we've decided to give our lives a meaning - a meaning that doesn't depend on remuneration or approval and a meaning that enables us to stop doing the things that bring stress, worry and fear into our lives. Take for example, when we look to get fit or to lose a few pounds, deep down we're looking for the approval of others, but mostly for our own; our heart isn't really into the weight loss, but more the image we'll have of ourselves should we succeed. Because we're trying to change our shape we begin with a negative image of ourselves and struggle with various diets, classes and exercise regimes - with varying levels of success. Because we're 'on a diet' we look to when we can come 'off' it, at which point the reverse begins to happen and the process restarts with all the stress and hassle that goes with it. What we really need is a sea change of the way we live and then we'll become healthier and happier with ourselves. More beneficial however, is the sea change for our mind - to filter out the excess daily nonsense that's being fed into it, to remove ourselves from negative situations and to clear out the historical ghosts that haunt us day and night. If we really want our lives to change - we have to *make* those changes, and make them permanent. Plan B requires mental housekeeping and the development of our observational skills - a mastery over ourselves and all that occurs in our lives; it takes time to develop these skills. Though I know this without a shadow of a doubt, I'm still having to work at it.

~~~

Imagine a world where we work and live for the good of each other; a world where humanity gives back as much as it takes and doesn't live in fear of governments or next door neighbours; a world where we care for each other without hatred or hierarchy, without poverty or greed, without fears or locks and without hunger or excess. It's rather hard to do because we're so set in our ways that such a Utopia is nothing more than a distant fantasy, like any other, that can't be fully imagined or realised with our minds in their current state of consciousness - unable to conceive of anything outside it - just as when our curtains are closed we can't see what's on the other side of them. When we begin to see the futility of Plan A, it's like seeing light coming through the cracks of the curtains, which we then draw back enabling ourselves to see the limitless possibilities that lie before us - possibilities that exist beyond the realms of understanding by our Plan A conditioned minds. Plan B!

Plan A is that which is offered to us by society - a plan we delight in complaining about, yet happily follow as it demands nothing of us other than our compliance. Plan B, on the other hand, is facing up to the reality and the futility of Plan A, putting aside our fears of being unable to survive without it. Living by Plan B is not a choice *per se*, but more of a realisation that living by Plan A creates havoc in the world. The corollary is that though we no longer need to fully participate in Plan A, we still have to live in the world; therefore, we can't reject the ground we walk on, but rather must strive to leave less of an imprint on it, and for it not to leave its imprint on us. Of course, there's always the danger of trying to fix Plan A with parts of Plan B - to have the best of both worlds - but this won't work because the mindset of Plan B is totally different to that of Plan A; it would be like adding fresh apples to a bowl of rotting ones in the hope of stopping the rot. When we switch to Plan B we arrive at an indefinable space where we're no longer following *any* plan - we instinctively know what we now need to do for the good of humanity *and do it*, even if that contribution might only be a small one, it *is* better than nothing at all. But why are so few people interested in Plan B? Could it be that Plan B demands something of us - a shift from our familiar existence and to do something different? Though many people love to hear or talk about Plan B it's nothing more to them than a flight of fantasy or a 'What if?', never realising that they have the power to make the change today, preferring to dismiss it as a 'not in my life time' phenomenon. Plan B has to be realised for oneself and when it is, what happens next is entirely up to you.

* *A term I used in my chapter 'Sensation, Desire and Relevant Reflections'*

Chapter 54

A Little More Taking Stock

To climb out of the deep dark hole we dug for ourselves is the hardest thing to do - the key to achieving it is wanting to do it badly enough.

We were born into a living nightmare - no sane person can deny that. As children we struggled to fathom what we saw, looking at it with bewilderment rather than wonder. Even as adults, we've all stood back and looked at the world, knowing that it's crazy as it seamlessly relates to us one frightening story after another - many happening simultaneously; physically, we can't go anywhere else so we do our best to slot in wherever we can - we have to like it or lump it - it's all we've got. An adage I heard a lot in my youth was 'if you can't beat them, join them' - with society the way it is, this isn't exactly good advice'; however, after years of struggling to make sense of a world that *can't* be made sense of, as adults, this is what we tend to do. Such capitulation locks us into a madness that we're both surrounded by and at the mercy of - we become participants at a grotesque masked ball, either dancing or 'sitting one out'. Like guests at the ball, we think we won't be recognised; the majority of us however, can see clearly what lies beneath the masks of others - as clearly as they can see behind ours; they've learnt to fit in just as we have. This knowledge is treated as 'taboo' - a tacit agreement to keep each other's secret while we play out our roles. Without this agreement we'd be stripped of our faux identities and such exposure could cause chaos and confusion; initially, it can be a shock to suddenly be in a position where we judge ourselves, as we've previously judged others.

So we adapt and learn to lie - to fit in with the *status quo*. These lies protect us from ourselves *and* others; we need them in order to hide our underlying vulnerability and because we tell so many of them, they eventually become our truth - the mind supplying the evidence and encouragement we need to convince ourselves of their veracity. I was witness to a good example of this at the time of the 9/11 incident; what happened regarding the actual event is not of concern here, as the mass of information spawning from the incident is so overwhelming that no-one will ever discover what really happened - some know, some think they do and many neither know nor care. Anyway, I mentioned to a friend that I'd seen a video apparently showing a *live* news broadcast from the scene reporting on a building that had collapsed, while it was shown as *still* erect in the background behind the reporter.

Whether or not this film had been manipulated is of no concern to me, but my friend's reaction to this information was that the film studios were *very* busy and probably got their films mixed up - the validity of the information and the integrity of the television company were in her view incontrovertible - she believed that which made her the most comfortable and the idea that the building was simultaneously erect *and* down was 'explained' away, rather than questioned. There's a strange paradox at work in the world whereby 'tongue-in-cheek' we say it must be true as it was 'in the papers' or 'on the television'; however, at the same time, we receive it as a truth; our minds pass it through the filters that present us with a story we can more readily accept - making incidental the parts that don't fit our truth. Perhaps this is why we can so easily watch horror on our screens or read it in our books and newspapers and not cry out loud - we're de-sensitised to it and a horror story on the news has no more inner effect on us than a horror film we watch for pleasure; we don't shed the tears we ought to be drowning in, and would be if we were willing to change our perspective.

It's in our nature to filter out what we don't want to see or hear and turn it into a truth that suits us better. We're unreliable narrators, which is why two people can witness the same incident and - at a later date - give an account of two very different stories about what happened. In much the same way, two people can read the same book or watch the same film and take away different meanings from them; for example, a philosopher and a scientist will dissect the bible in different ways - each finding what they want to find. We might get confused about dates, names, places or faces, but when we tell our stories - particularly if we repeat them often enough - we'll believe them to be true; we all know that this situation causes conflict, particularly in personal relationships. This knowledge opens up all sorts of queries when it comes to thinking about juries or witness statements, and is just one reason why more than one account or opinion is required - even then they can't be relied on. We'll never be capable of judging each other in a way free from all bias, until we've judged ourselves. The mind of humanity is sick, it's confused and doesn't know truth from lies; it doesn't know because it's so caught up in 'I' 'Me' 'My' mode that it can't stand back and observe the bigger picture - also because we have too much irrelevant information in our minds and no room for anything new. If we stood back and took a good look at ourselves - first as individuals and then as a whole - we *would* drown in our own tears. It's then, when we observe ourselves, that the extent of our sickness is revealed. Few of us are prepared to admit to the folly of our own ways - we're not very good at admitting when we're wrong or that we've been foolish; vulnerability in society is strongly discouraged.

To remain in the madness of the world, taking whatever happens to be on offer - whether appealing or not - simply because it's 'sold' to us as a necessity, keeps us coming back for more as we increasingly need to alleviate the mental and physical pains of living, which paradoxically, are caused by the very quest to alleviate them - making it all hurt so much more. We make the most of what's available, enjoying the entertainment, material things and other distractions while we have the opportunity to do so, but this is a grab-it-while-you-can attitude towards life that throws caution to the wind, regardless of the consequences for ourselves or future generations - it's been done this way for a long time. We don't consider what we're *actually* doing, why we're living in a nightmare we can't seem to wake from, or why we're unable to live freely without the need for outside authority. We allow our minds to be manipulated and they've become twisted and dulled beyond recognition. We gave up asking the innocent questions of our childhood because they were frowned upon and considered to be 'childish'; as a result, we slowly developed a thoughtless and carefree attitude towards life, desiring only the pleasures we could find in it - our hearts hardened.

~~~

It occurred to me while writing this chapter that I've never really thought about what an adult is. I know that it's a 'big person' and that it somewhat eagerly, assumes control of its life when it 'comes of age'. I know also that adults pay more for tickets and can get into places and do things that are for 'adults only', but what actually *is* an adult? Our influences and beliefs change gradually over the course of our lifetimes - so gradually that we don't notice them - but after a while the metamorphosis from innocent child into adult is blatant. There are many ways to describe what an adult is, but mostly it's an innocent child who as a result of successful indoctrination and growing 'bigger' can now do the things that were on their banned list when they were small, without the risk of censure or having to provide identification to prove that they're of 'legal age'; for example, to buy alcohol, tobacco or x-rated materials. In other words, 'adult' is a license to do all the things forbidden to the innocent - most often carried out behind closed doors. An adult has learnt to abide by the rules of an unwell society and to enforce those same rules upon 'newcomers' to the human race - towering over them as indoctrinators and thus carrying on the cycle. Adults are under the illusion that they're in control of their world, whereas they're actually *out* of control. Amongst other things, being an adult is also a licence to behave badly - very badly if we choose to do so. I suppose in some ways, you could compare the psychological process of becoming an adult to an expanding balloon (creating our egos); society blows information into the balloon and as it does the balloon inflates; the process of unlearning can be likened to deflating the balloon - returning to a state of innocence - which is *not* the same as being 'childish' or 'naïve'.

When we were young and innocent we believed everything we were told, not because we were naïve or stupid, but rather because we loved and trusted the people we were surrounded and directed by - our care was entirely in their hands. We loved the stories they told and were protected from the 'news' and other adult occupations as we were generally - in my day at least - tucked up in bed at these times. Slowly, as we grew older, the levels of corruption and frustration of our world dawned on us; such as, the world is a tough place to live in, it's not fair, Father Christmas isn't all he seems to be and neither are our myths or legends - we felt let down, ill-prepared for life and very much alone. For all the knowledge we've been given we still have no idea what we're doing or who we are. In many ways we're worse off than the innocent children we once were - at least then we had something or someone we could put our trust in - something to believe in, or hope for. But not all is lost. By returning to our innocence we combine the best of being a child with that of an adult and come to realise that the only person we can really put our trust in is ourselves - our lives are now in our own hands, with all that implies. Reflecting on this helps us develop an understanding of our circumstances, but not the knowledge of how we found ourselves so vulnerable in them - what lies before and beyond our lives must, it seems, remain a mystery for now. When we answer our 'call', our attention turns away from the horror and sorrow of this world - which we can't change - back to a state of wonderment at our surroundings, but this time in awe of them rather than bewilderment.

Chapter 55

Stepping out of Time

When we step out of time we also step out of space and can find ourselves somewhat out of tune.

We can march in time, keep in step with this world and all it has to offer, good or bad, accepting the *status quo* and our eventual demise, or we can dare to step out of time, aspire to greater heights and march to our own rhythm.

As far as we can tell - due to our limited perspective - the reality in which we live is finite; there's a beginning and an end - the part in the middle is what we call life. Like it or not, we're governed by laws we didn't vote for - the laws of the physical universe, from whichever scientific discipline, that control every aspect of our lives. We take many of them for granted; when we lay a table for a meal we expect the plates and cutlery to stay where we put them - not to float off somewhere less convenient; those same laws cause our vases to break if we drop them. Scientists have tried to understand these physical laws and use them to our advantage - or disadvantage - by combining them *or* using one against the other; for example, getting a plane to lift off the ground or finding new ways to devastate entire cities. With such focus on the physical side of our world it's hardly surprising there's no place for the extraordinary - thinking is 'well-grounded' and 'conclusive'; there's nothing that can't be explained away by good scientific reasoning. Should anything extraordinary raise its head, there are any number of well-meaning (or not as the case may be) learned journals, professors, teachers or rationalists down the pub to explain the phenomenon away to their own satisfaction, based on their biases and experiences. There's no room for miracles in this physical materialistic world and the entertaining of such is considered the forte of religious crack-pots or those needing to see a psychiatrist, so that they can be re-integrated into the 'real world'. There's a reluctance to consider stepping out of this physical existence, to contemplate the metaphysical or to go beyond what we *think* we know - it's out of our comfort zone. We brush aside our non-physical nature - which is as much a part of us as our hands and feet are - preferring, it seems, the mind-numbing 'around the clock' familiarity of the existence that keeps us firmly entrenched in the physical mind-set, until our inevitable demise.

~~~

I made it down a long flight of stairs by taking just two steps; I've done the same thing before without taking any steps at all and sometimes I don't make it to the bottom of the stairs as they morph into a path through a forest, or I find myself walking along a beautiful sandy seashore ... I'm driving a car but the road ahead of me disappears and then I'm surrounded by walls that are shrinking the space around me, but I don't crash into them and they soon morph into something else and in a flash I'm walking our dog in the countryside or sitting at my desk, which may or may not be in my home - where it should be. I cross a road in a single step and as I put my foot down the path I thought I'd stepped onto dissolves into a giant puddle and I watch, fascinated, as the ripples spread out. I walk on water and walk through walls; sometimes I even fly and once I had a houseful of friends all speaking in what I thought was Chinese - I understood them - though I can't speak a word of it.

No, I haven't lost the plot; I'm talking about dreams. Dreams are strange because they don't make sense and defy what we think of as the laws of physics - the laws that trap us in what we know as 'reality'. Strangely, in our dreams, nothing seems to be out-of-place or give rise to concern - it all seems perfectly 'normal'. When we wake from these dreams, we can no longer do the impossible and find ourselves once again limited by the restrictions of time and space. There are enough books and opinions on what dreams, out-of-body experiences and illusions are and, as always, science is doing its best to explain these things to us - saving us the trouble of thinking for ourselves. However, I like to explore my world for myself and observe what I see, which if you think about it is what the authors of books, purveyors of opinions and scientists do as well - so I'm going to talk about how these things occur in *my* world, because this *is* my world and *everything* in it is coming from my mind - how can it possibly come from anywhere else.

On the point of defying the 'laws of physics' in our dreams; so what? Dreams are as much a part of our lives as our day-to-day activities are when we're awake. The laws of physics are concerned with matter and energy, yet so much about us is non-physical; for example, our minds, dreams and imaginations; why do we need sleep, or why do we dream. Much of our life is spent asleep and somehow we don't consider the relevance of this. We see sleeping as essential rest from the day's activities that exhaust us - sometimes collapsing into a heap on our beds, until the following morning when we start those activities all over again, perhaps beginning our first conversation of the day with 'I had this really weird dream last night' and after recounting it, never giving it another thought. There's more to our sleep than that. We drift into unconsciousness, as day drifts into night; there's no proof whatsoever that we're anywhere at all when we're asleep, even if there's a witness who states that they saw us lying in our bed. Does the world exist at all when we're not 'here'? This question is increasingly interesting for me.

As a child and well into my adulthood I experienced repeating dreams; I woke up at the same point each time - other dreams had recurring themes running through them in a variety of different situations. One of these themes is 'voicelessness'. I've often been calling out to someone I wanted to help in some way, or warn against an impending danger, but no sound comes out of my mouth - as though I were mute - and I feel unable to move closer to them. Sometimes there are other people around and I call out for assistance, but still I've no voice. Usually this voicelessness dream occurs when someone is drowning in the sea or sinking into the land or quicksand; I hold my hand out, stretching it as far as I can, but can't reach the hand they're holding out to me. I used to find this dream disconcerting and frustrating. I'd watch until the person disappeared completely and then wake up in a sweat. So what could these dreams be about? In my younger years I'd often see simple solutions to other people's problems, but was rarely asked for my opinion and to have given it when it wasn't asked for - which I did on numerous occasions - was akin to pulling a dog's tail; I learnt this lesson the hard way. Perhaps the hand in the dream was not really reaching out to me, but to someone else that I couldn't see - or perhaps the person holding out their hand wanted to drag me down with them. No doubt there are many possible interpretations, but the way I see it, we re-write our waking reality in our dreams, removing time and space, making them surreal and adding extra drama. Just as in my dreams, I couldn't help anyone in 'real life' and had no voice - no-one listened. What I've learnt from realising this is that we can't help people who don't want to be helped, even if they appear to be reaching out to us.

It has been said that if we die in a dream we die in 'real life', but I don't see how anyone could possibly prove it. I seemingly died many times in dreams from being shot, falling or being hit by a car. I can't say for sure that I wouldn't have survived these experiences as I subsequently woke up, with the odd feeling that I'd somehow dropped back into my body. I'd suggest that perhaps it's the same with 'near death experiences' for no-one can see beyond death; no-one can see beyond the mystery of life - we can only speculate and speculation comes from conditioned memories. I'd suggest that our dreams are a form of housekeeping - where we can work on unresolved issues and fears - and just as with the clutter in a house that hasn't been touched for years, the contents of our minds are in a state of disarray. We each have one home (our mind) and in it are stored all the moments of our lives - every touch, taste, wish, hope, joy, ache, pain and heartbreak. There's much mind-management to be done before we can see our world more clearly and only we can do that work - no-one else can do it for us. When we make a start on our 'housekeeping' there can be a lot of dust and clutter to work through, but gradually we come to know and realise many things; such as, our five senses lock us into believing this physical world is real and 'all there is' - they confirm its existence and apparent solidity and deny any other explanation or exploration - all of our physical experiences have come through our senses.

When we're prepared to step out of time, our spiritual sense opens up a whole new world of possibilities, but like the sailors of old, who were frightened to sail too close to the horizon in case they fell off the edge of the world, we can experience similar fears of the unknown - we've become so locked into the physical world that we're afraid to step out of it. Magic and spirituality have become 'spooky' themes that are explained away as 'fantasy' by the realm of entertainment and in so doing, come to have no more meaning than amusing hocus pocus - or not so amusing horror (though entertaining for some of us). If we choose to *stay* in time then we'll continue to be haunted by the memories and events of our pasts, and those of others too - such as the victims of war. Our past is *full* of horrors and our future is going to be bleak, if we continue to do what we're doing - causing and perpetuating mischief in our world.

By 'stepping out of time' we connect to something different - something indefinable and unfamiliar - but to connect to this we need to disconnect - mentally - from the way we're living now. We can do this by realising not only the illusory nature of the world we live in but the negligent way in which we live in it - a negligence that's causing our world to go downhill fast - filling it with sorrow, unnecessary illness and destruction along the way. When we open our eyes - perhaps peeping through our fingers - to some painful truths, we gradually become aware of our surroundings in a new way; our world becomes surreal and less scary and the monsters we once closed our eyes to aren't there anymore. However, we have to *stay* connected to this mindset otherwise we'll revert to our old habits, hear the same old song we've always heard, and the monsters will reappear. The very act of stepping out of one situation places us into another, just as though we were walking from one room to the next.

The quality of our experience in this world depends on the choices we make; for example, what film to watch, what career to pursue or which train to take. The memories from whichever film we choose to watch get etched onto our minds and inevitably weave themselves into our dreams; the career we choose will shape many parts of our lives and the next train we board could turn out to be a life or death situation. We hold onto bitterness, anger, vengeance, spite and other unhealthy feelings that come from our past, without realising that they not only destroy our future, but turn our dreams into nightmares - they're internalised and control our lives, harming only ourselves rather than our chosen 'targets'. Our lives are fragile yet we live them carelessly and thoughtlessly assuming that tomorrow will always arrive because it's noted - in so many different ways - on our calendars. We're here to write our own lyrics, play our own music and dance our own dance, but the problem is we're doing it under the clockwork direction of external influence and conditioning; we should be playing in our own 'one man band' - considerately - for the benefit of ourselves and others, but somewhere along the line our lives were hijacked and we're now dancing to someone else's tune.

Time; we live by it, eat by it, work by it, play by it and at an *unknown* time we're going to have to 'die' by it. I mentioned earlier that many seem to prefer the mind-numbing 'around the clock' familiarity of our physical mind-set, but there's so much more to us if we dare to contemplate the metaphysical, and go beyond what we *think* we know. *Now* is the time, our chance, our opportunity to do just that, while the clock is still ticking.

Chapter 56

A Touch of Feeling

When we feel love for ourselves, we'll feel love for all others.

Life is something we have to fully experience to the end; we can't run away from caring about the outside world, and expect to feel happy on the inside.

We *all* have feelings but do we ever intelligently think about what they are? As with all my questions, the more I think about them the more obscure they become, yet all my life I've spoken about my feelings and the feelings of people I've come into contact with. We 'feel' every moment of our lives, even in our dreams, and we'd not get far without doing so - feelings are an essential part of us. As with all subjects that I begin to focus on, the experience is like opening a trunk; the contents of which unpack themselves as we rummage through it. We begin to see things we already know very well and have no need for external references to back up what we find; having said that, discussing the subject with like-minded people can be fun and reveal even more, provided the parties concerned are listening to each other. As I'm making notes, it becomes clear that this is an *enormous* subject that can't be contained in one chapter, let alone a book, so I'm going to skim over what opening up the trunk has revealed to me so far.

What is a feeling? Essentially, it's a sense - our feelings allow us to be sensitive to all that we're surrounded by. We have five senses that confirm our physical world, but we also have senses that relate to the 'metaphysical' and we refer to them frequently without realising it; examples are:

- I feel you're upset about something.
- The experience left a bad taste in my mouth.
- I see what you mean.
- I smell a rat.
- I heard a voice inside my head.

- I feel like I'm being watched.
- I sense danger.
- I was touched by their generosity.

A feeling is a body, egoic or other metaphysical reaction relating to an event - external or internal; such as another person, a passion, a suspicion or for that matter, anything we come into contact with or have experienced - it begins with thought. By bodily reaction I mean, for example, when we come out in goose-bumps or break out in a cold sweat - by egoic reaction, when we take offense or have our pride hurt. Like the physical five senses, our feelings and emotions make us aware of the external world. Through these feelings we experience fear, sadness, happiness, danger and many other reactions that we express as emotions - we couldn't exist without them. Whereas our metaphysical senses allow us to be *aware* of our world, our five physical senses confirm its *existence* and help us to navigate our way through it. Without these senses we can't experience the world, though we *can* manage with the loss of some of them as is the case with those of us who are unable to hear, speak or see. The majority of us - including me - can't imagine what it would be like to live in a world where we can't see, touch, taste, hear or smell. We need at *least* one of our physical senses to confirm that we're living in a world *at all* and therein lies a good philosophical argument for existence itself - an argument that can't be tested because it can never be completely experienced.

Let's expand on an item from the above list - 'I *feel* like I'm being watched'. Remember, that this is *only* a feeling with no physical evidence to back it up - we've no idea where it came from or why we're feeling it, but it can have a great effect on us. Our minds '*real*-ise' the experience and won't leave it alone - *physicalising* and emotionalising it. The feeling of being watched leaves us with uncomfortable emotions of uncertainty, insecurity or vulnerability as our personal space appears to have been invaded from afar. These emotions can pass through us in a flash or linger and compound, depending on the attention we're prepared to give them - possibly leading to further upset, tears or even blind panic, depending on the situation. If we're outdoors at the time of this feeling we usually look around to ensure our security and, if we're indoors and discover - or believe - that we really *are* being watched we may decide to close the curtains and check that our doors and windows are locked. In both cases, our reaction - physical and emotional - tends to come from a place of fear rather than certainty. Our reaction to the feeling of 'being watched' (true or imagined) is based on what our minds have absorbed - much of it horror and other negativity - and our imagination, feeding on these memories, creates a fearful experience.

To digress a little, I'd suggest that the root of the 'feeling of being watched' began when we were babies; we've *always* been watched and continue to be watched - also criticised or compared - in one way or another by our parents, siblings, teachers, friends, employers and surveillance equipment. We've become so accustomed to being watched that we not only *feel* it, but now also watch ourselves *and* each other - walking along the street, in mirrors, through windows or keyholes, at work, at play and on social media etc. The result of continuous observation and comparison - leading to our inevitable self-micro-management - is what causes us to become self-conscious; we've been moulded, criticised, cajoled or even abused into a 'shape' that a fractured and disgruntled society finds acceptable. This distorted image of ourselves becomes, not what we *are* but what we've come to *believe* we are - an image we go all out to protect in order to *remain* acceptable - so that we still exist - and this is what makes us emotionally fragile - we become defensive. Our intense conditioning prevents us from thinking about ourselves as we *truly* are, because we've become so attached to the images of 'I' 'Me' and 'My'. We don't have the ability to fully conceive the truth about ourselves and no-one can convince us otherwise until we want to see it - we wouldn't believe them. However, we *do* have 'feelings' that tell us quite clearly that there's more to us than our wardrobes, tax numbers or social media profiles; we're frauds - we know it - we *feel* it.

~~~

Feelings we can't contain, or control, plague our minds day and night - they cause us to lose sleep and wake the following morning often more tired than when we went to bed. Sometimes this is in excited anticipation of an event such as Christmas day, starting a new job, going on holiday, our last day at school or perhaps our birthday, but at other times the 'plague' follows an event, like being left standing at the aisle, the death of a family member or a heated argument we got into; in these situations our feelings are so intense that we can't be cheered up or reasoned with. I'm sure many of us have tossed and turned all night - over a situation we could've handled differently - re-playing the scene as it actually happened including feeling all the emotions we felt at the time *and* - with the benefit of hindsight - re-writing our various preferred versions of it. In the case of a death in the family, or a friend for that matter, the emotions of 'regret' and 'remorse' torture us about things we failed to do; such as, 'I could've been kinder', 'I shouldn't have said this or that', 'I never said *I love you*', 'I shouldn't have wished you harm' or 'I put off saying sorry for too long' - all of which are now too late to remedy; we tend to take time for granted - thinking we've plenty of it - and then beat ourselves up when it runs out.

Our mind dramas come from events in our pasts or anticipated futures, but the emotions we feel are always in the Now. If we focus on this fact as and when the dramas take place we gain a greater awareness of how our minds work; watching our thoughts and reactions to whatever life puts in front of us, as and when it happens - life becomes a 'Live' event rather than a review of the past. With this realisation comes the ability to free ourselves from the restraints of our pasts - regardless of whether events took place fifteen years or fifteen minutes ago - nothing good can come from dwelling on them. It can take a while to adapt our way of thinking, but I promise that if you persevere and repeat the exercise it'll become clear. Old habits can take a long time to free ourselves from; they're past events we *prefer* to repeat and hold onto rather than evict - they literally 'in-habit' us. We'll still feel sorrow and pain when things go wrong in our lives or don't go the way we want them to - it's a part of our human condition, but we'll be better equipped to heal ourselves and put things into perspective, instead of allowing our feelings to get in the way of intelligent judgement and action - it takes practise.

Life isn't fair - it never has been. I was placed into an orphanage at the age of nine months and had to live with all the dramas that go with such a predicament. At the time I was too young to control events in my life, or society's will to crush me - a task I later took over responsibility for. To my knowledge, we've no control on where, when or to whom we're born; however, as we grow older we have the power to make choices that shape our world and the most major of those choices is to take back control of our lives, by not allowing the past or society to intimidate or guide us - we can't change them when we're children, but we *can* remove their strong and erroneous influence once we reach adulthood. If we choose *not* to then the past and present situation in society will continue to control how we think, feel and behave for the best part of our lives - feeling all the unwanted emotions that go with that decision.

~~~

There are times when our emotions are remembered - like a gun that fires a bullet when the trigger is pulled or a light that comes on when the switch is flicked; we carry these dormant emotions around with us for our whole lives and they can be highly destructive. Remembered emotions lie dormant until an external action is applied, like a wrong word someone says to us, a large utility bill that arrives in the post or the sight of a long forgotten enemy - perhaps from our school days. In the case of the first example we may associate the word with an unpleasant past event and it can feel like re-living an experience we've no wish to re-live - in the second case we may feel the emotion of frustration at once again being short of funds. The third example is more complicated as an enemy from our school days would probably invoke *many* nasty emotions that we've no wish to return to feeling and, believed we'd left behind us. Another example of a remembered emotion is that which we long to feel again, because to be without the feeling is too painful; for example, when we 'fall in love' because we *need* to be in love or when we're on the rebound - neither of which are in our best interest.

We need to learn how to re-act to situations that recur in our lives by recognising that we lash out to protect ourselves from re-experiencing things that disturbed us in the past. If we don't learn this, then we'll spend the rest of our lives feeling angry, defensive, snappy, sulky, uncertain of ourselves or seeking to re-experience happy 'times gone by' - taking us away from the life that's happening *now* - *not* in the past. We don't necessarily know that we're remembering an emotion when we react to triggers; too often these emotions are buried deep within us and because they're unresolved, exert a force that manifests itself as over-sensitivity - an adult can display out of proportion reactions to even the smallest slight if he was subjected to hyper-criticism as a child.

~~~

Up until now I've discussed our *own* feelings, but it's important to widen our perspective and examine how we actually feel about others when, for example, we pass a crash scene - most of us would be horrified to realise how limited our feelings are for the people involved. Almost everyone in the world is in pain and has suffered as much, perhaps more, than we have. We like our social media pages to be filled with 'inspirational' material, but we blend this inspiration with horror on our next post - not unlike 'have longer eye lashes' advertisements between earthquake or other disaster news flashes. How can we change this situation? One of the best ways to do this is to recognise that our emotions are erratic and irrational - we change from one moment to the next, forgetting - or not recognising - what matters most. We like to think that we're caring, loving and warm people; that may be the case amongst our close-knit family and friends but how many of us extend that warmth to those who don't live in our relatively small social circles - those we tend to pass by or comfort with charitable pennies or empty words - some of us don't even spare those. Think about beggars, an elderly person we brush past, a passed-out drunkard or the homeless in the street for example; we can be unkind in our judgements of these people - judgements we've been conditioned to feel; these people are not only symptoms of the dysfunctional and selfish environment that we've created, they serve as unwelcome reminders of it.

When we meet another person we don't tend to see their pain as we're more focused on what they look like, what they do for a living, how scruffily they're dressed, who does their hair or perhaps what they can do for us - socialising etc. But inside each beggar, elderly person, passed-out drunkard or homeless person whose path we cross is a sad story that has left them in their unfortunate circumstances; their world is very lonely and generally, we feel no real compassion or pity for them - we don't even acknowledge them.

When did we stop caring outside of our personal circle? To share in the sadness of another person is a difficult thing, especially when we're generally unable to help them out of their situation other than to offer a few words of comfort or hold their hand. Our ability to sympathise is largely limited to feeling apologetic for someone's situation - and to commiserate with them, but we can't really help them beyond that; their pain persists until they reach a point where they're able to lessen it or let it go - which is sometimes never. We see worldwide pain and suffering every day of our lives through our various media outlets - some of it horrifying and all of it unacceptable. We *have* to look away and forget about it, as most of the stories are so far away from where we live and work that we're unable to offer help - other than financial - which history proves is never a solution to the problem - or we can expose the news, by forwarding the stories to others in the hope that *they'll* be able to do something about it. We have our own problems to think about that are closer to home; we've the dog to walk, bills to pay, plumbing to fix, shopping, work to do, kids to feed and we're always on the 'Go' 'Go' 'Go' for one reason or another - such are the lifestyles we've unwisely created - *we're* in pain too.

Back to the question from another perspective 'When did we stop caring … ?' I don't believe we ever did - we maxed-out on empathy. We've empathised with so many situations that we're now exhausted, with nothing left to give to the sick, poor, tragic or hopeless - there are too many of them. The suffering of others has become the 'norm' and we no longer *see* the beggars in the street *or* realise that we walk around them as though they were a fixture, like a bollard. Whatever we *personally* do, it'll never be enough to stop the flow of suffering - we can't see the end of it. Stories in the news have become no more than our daily 'infotainment' - topics of 'cultured' or 'educated' discussion to spread, 'like' or 'thumbs up' on our media pages - they're no longer remarkable. So we shop, work, stop at coffee shops, entertain, amuse and occupy ourselves so that we don't have to think about or feel the outside world, but however much we do those things it still exists. The outside world is as much a part of us as our inside world but we feel powerless to change the first and unable to change the second; we *can* make choices in our personal 'circles' that make a difference to our lives (to have a baby or not, for example) - regardless of whether it's a positive or negative difference; the point is, it's something we have control over and we *like* to feel that we're in control.

Due to our conditioning, whether we like to believe we're conditioned or not, we don't fully understand our feelings or emotions - we don't talk easily about them. In many cases, feelings and emotions are things we've learnt to hide because it's 'sissy' or 'weak-minded' to show them; we're taught that we should be strong and able to take the blows of life without complaining about them. We're 'case-hardened' - or think we are - and expect others to be too. Because of this we're not always in control of our feelings as much as we'd like to be; for example, giving full rein to emotions like anger, rage, aggression, jealousy, extended sorrow or sadness.

These emotions - uncontrolled - are damaging not only to ourselves, but also to those on the receiving end of them. That we have these emotions is part of our human experience, but learning to keep them under control is an art we're far from mastering. We've all felt anger welling up inside us and to a large extent it's because we allowed its seed to sprout and our egos to water it, until it could no longer be contained. By observing how we react to various situations that we regularly and *repeatedly* encounter, we get to know that our emotions are out of control. When we *do* take an honest look at ourselves, and especially at how we react to others - watching the 'Live Event' - we begin to understand our feelings and emotions - we become emotionally mature. Such maturity makes us better equipped to deal with situations that arise - we begin to sympathise and empathise with others, rather than criticising or lashing out at them.

It's said that empathy is 'head' and sympathy 'heart'. Where that originates I've no idea and in my opinion it's irrelevant as are the origins of pity or compassion. We spend too much time analysing, labelling and mapping these things and not enough time *intelligently* feeling them. I say what does it matter where they come from as long as we're able to feel for and help other people - as long as we can say 'No, it's not okay that our world is like this' and *mean* it. Yes, empathy and sympathy are different, but they don't come from different places; I'd suggest that they come from our minds (which can't be located) - from the thoughts that are our experiences and in particular from our conditioned thoughts and responses. Feeling empathy and sympathy represent 'kindness' and *this* is what the world needs to focus on - not single trendy 'acts' of kindness; such as 'Free Hugs Here', but *ongoing* kindness towards everyone - a kindness mindset. When we turn our attention away from ourselves, it automatically turns towards the rest of the world; then - and only then - can we feel the pain, hear the voice and look into the eyes of others - only then can we empathise with the rest of humanity and be able to see the beggar, instead of the bollard.

Chapter 57

Gratitude

Gratitude is the appreciation of things not deserved, earned or demanded.

When we look inside *ourselves* we find a different world - a world much larger than the one we're familiar with and a world that's so full of revelations, that had someone recounted this knowledge to us, we wouldn't have believed them. For example, we discover how focused we are in 'I' 'Me' 'My' mode and don't give much thought to the rest of the world, as long as we're okay - our new world reveals much that we don't tend to like admitting about ourselves. Paradoxically, this process changes all we see on the outside too - it *must*, in the same way as changing our appearance changes what we see in a mirror. The world becomes a mystery again - a mystery that's been waiting for us to delve into it. We can unravel this mystery as far as it'll allow us to and in doing so, it reveals those beautiful things we've taken for granted for so long.

Again, paradoxically, the more we unravel the mystery the more of a mystery it becomes; however, something's different, *something* we're unable to put into words, *something* that changes our outlook on life bringing with it an energy that inspires and motivates us to explore further, and *something* that we can't show or adequately explain to another person.

On our journey, what we need to discover more than anything else are our *own* eyes, and we find them when we begin to piece together the puzzle of life - a puzzle that can't be explained until we come upon it for ourselves. Up until now we've tended to look at the world in a way that's expected of us; for example, being grateful that things aren't much worse than they are, being grateful that we *have* a job, being grateful that there's no war in *our* country and being grateful for our possessions. These are the things we're told we should be grateful for - we're 'guilted' into feeling bad about having something that's an inalienable right, by images and stories of people who have less than we do. As a child, when I didn't like something on my dinner plate, I was told I should be grateful for it and continually reminded about how many children around the world weren't as fortunate as I was - we grow up with a sense of guilt. Every one of us has a right to live in peace and to have enough food, water and shelter. Our encouragement to be grateful for these 'essential for living' things is a diversion - it keeps us from seeing the things we really *should* feel gratitude for; it also encourages us to be grateful for things that are 'sold' back to us - like water - but they're already ours. We *share* this planet and no one person has more right to the water on it than another. This sort of encouraged gratitude is not gratitude at all, but rather it instils the fear that we may one day not have water, food or shelter - a fear not lost on a society that encourages dependence on it to provide for our needs. Consequently, we comply with a system that demands we adequately prepare for our old age - which we may never reach - instead of living now, and also that we live in fear of going hungry, thirsty or living on the streets. One side effect of this fear is that we become self-protective thus, as the years pass, we care first and foremost for ourselves; another effect is that we're far too busy with our day-to-day activities to think about the core of our existence.

~~~

Gratitude isn't a reply to a fulfilled desire or something that's happened to us by chance. I remember once coming home and as I reached the gate having tears running down my face; I wore a huge smile at the same time and had no idea why, but did feel grateful 'to be' in this state of what I can only describe as joy. Gratitude is a thankfulness that passes through us; it's there one minute and gone the next, but it leaves a lasting memory of that moment that we don't forget, though we've no idea why this feeling of gratitude arose in us in the first place. A few years back these happy teary moments occurred to me all the time; I'd come back from shopping and enter the house in tears - prompting questions asking me what was wrong, but these moments were beyond explanation - they were to be experienced, not analysed. After a while, my 'moments' were just smiled at and accepted as something that was happening to me - a change taking place. Eventually, the tears and smiles gave way to what I can only describe as a profound understanding - I'd changed. Gratitude is a state of mind that can't be expressed by words or actions - such as 'thank you' or exchanging gifts; as our awareness grows, it develops into a 'state' of appreciation that alters the way we approach life.

I find myself trying to remember when these feelings began and I can't be sure, but I do know that it was at a time when I was prepared to take back 'control' of my life. That is to say, I was no longer living in expectation that good things would come knocking at my door or looking to find any happiness outside of myself, or in anybody else for that matter - I'd stopped feeling hard-done-by and began taking responsibility for my life. I put myself in the driving seat and had no idea where my journey would end; I *still* don't, but I *do* know that my life now has purpose and that I alone am responsible for the choices I make *and* the consequences of those choices. Being in the driving seat means I can observe and react to - or not as the case may be - my actions and thoughts as and when they occur. Through such inner observation - if we're prepared to reflect on what we find - we come to realise that we're judgemental, hypocritical, envious, jealous, critical and spiritually aimless. Probably the most insightful revelations are that we're not the perfect beings we once thought ourselves to be, that we knew this all along and that life isn't a battle between us and the rest of the world, but rather a battle to overcome ourselves - our inimitable egos - and in doing so, we develop a new and wider-angled understanding of the outside world.

The more we know and accept about ourselves, the more we're able to discern - without prejudice - what we see on the outside. Acknowledging our own behaviour and reactions to events that occur in our lives causes a change in us - we 'grow *up*' in our awareness, raising our vibration and reconnecting to a higher knowledge; it's to this phenomenon that I attribute the joyful teary moments I mentioned earlier. However, if we continue to live our lives focusing our attention on the outside without growing 'up', then we'll always be in a state of looking for that *something* 'missing' in our lives, but never finding it. We don't know what that something is, but we'll never feel complete without it and have nothing to feel truly grateful for. Realising this not only 'lightens our load', but brings clarity to our lives in a way that inspires gratitude, enabling us to live serenely, instead of trying to cram everything we can into our lives before our inevitable 'demise' - the pressure is off. The clock still ticks, the world still spins, everyone gets on with their business and it's all happening very nicely without our full attention, as it always did; what changes is our attachment to it - our fears subside, we're less self-engrossed and no longer need approval or approbation. The world reacts to us according to how *we* react to it; everything outside is what we perceive and how we choose to interact with that perception.

The seed of gratitude is planted when our perception of the world changes - when we learn to see it more fully. As long as we see the world as something we have to function in - effectively 'clocking in' when we wake up to become part of the machine and 'clocking out' again when we fall asleep - we'll be unable to see the beauty and mystery of it - a mystery we're not here to solve, but to discover, learn and grow 'up' from during the course of our lives, however long - or short - they may turn out to be. When gratitude grows in us it alters our attitude towards the outside world - our focus of attention changes and with it our priorities; we're no longer attached to the material things that once attracted us, because we see the temporary nature of things - they no longer hold us captive.

We're all challenged in one way or another and those challenges are irrelevant when talking about gratitude. What matters is *how* we live our lives and that we learn to live virtuously at every moment, rather than living in a past that we *allow* to define and therefore limit us. No matter what our circumstances we can all appreciate the beauty of life, the mysteries within it and live with every part of our being - physical and metaphysical - so that we become whole. Our world becomes a larger place (in our mind) in a smaller space, with no need to explore outside for what we'll never find - that innate 'Who am I?' knowledge that we seek. I walk down the street, but no longer feel intrinsically part of it; I'm watching the world from a different space and I'm grateful for that - grateful to *know* that I'm on a journey - with a purpose - when before I was so lost, needy, insecure, going from one birthday to another, one home to another, one marriage to another, one fashion to another and above all, one mistake to another. I'm done searching for my place in this world because I've found it, inside, and my wish is to help others to find theirs.

Chapter 58

If I Told You

Disappointment is anticipation turned to ashes.

When we've had enough. When life feels meaningless. When we can't see where we're going and wonder what we're doing here at all, we've two choices. We can bob up and down in the river of our thoughts (content or otherwise) - which I did for a long time - or we can strike out for the bank and hope there'll be something there when we climb out. Knowledge that there's *something* beyond this existence comes from a continuous investigation of ourselves, a willingness to turn over every stone and most importantly, not to give up when things get tough. Things *do* get tough and we can often wonder what point there is in continuing, but it's only a wave and when we're vigilant, it doesn't take long before we recognise the pattern of those waves coming and going, or to know that we can be carried closer to the bank with each wave we encounter - if we choose not to drown beneath it.

If I told you
That our pains are not worth keeping
That our worries aren't worth weeping
Would you let it all go,
If I told you
That our fears are all unfounded
That our tears are all unsounded
Could you let it all go, if I told you …

Or would you hold on tightly to it
Let it rule and break your spirit
Build a wall and not smash through it,
If I told you
And if I showed you all your might
Would you stand right up and fight
Or meekly crumble to the floor
Forever suffer more and more.

If I told you
What we seek is all inside
That we've never really tried
Would you let it all go,
If I told you
That your feet have not been grounded
That we leave this life astounded
Would you let it all go, if I told you …

Or would you show your frozen heart
Shout and scream and fall apart
Pin a point upon your chart,
If I told you

And if I showed you all your power
Would you climb up to that tower
Or continue on your path
Always cry and never laugh

If I show you
That it's pointless to delay
That the beast is ours to slay
That it's love that we deny
How the mind is cruel and sly
That the pains of yesterday
Are now very far away
That there's no point laying low
That it's life we must outgrow
When we walk around that bend
It's ourselves we must befriend
That our tears need not be cried
Only you and I decide

Would you let it all go, if I told you ...

Chapter 59

Wrapping Up

Tears that fall on barren land produce nothing - they're cried in vain.

Our lives are short; at one extreme, they're so short that we don't even get the chance to blink and at the other they seem to drag on for so long that we want 'out' - particularly if we're frail and in bad health. Few of us take the time to ponder the meaning of our lives and though we're unable to fully determine where we come from, who we are or where we're going, we *are* able to feel an innate 'sense' that there's more to us than this life; for me, this couldn't be more clear, but I've had to start from scratch by questioning *everything* I've ever been taught, without taking in more rogue information. In the past we were educated to search for information in museums, libraries, books or to listen to our teachers; nowadays, we turn to the internet as the font of all wisdom, but it's only humanity's 'recycle bin'. This is fine if we want to know how to bake a cake or determine the molecular weight of lead, but not much use in our search to find out who we are. The internet is far from being wise, but it *is* bursting with everything we've explored, hidden and revealed or don't want to know about; none of the information can be relied on when asking the question 'Who am I?' All we can expect to come across on the internet are the 'opinions' of others and those who agree or disagree with them - more conflict, leaving us none the wiser.

We all have innate intelligence, but our authorities aren't leading with it - just look at what's happening to our world and how, by proxy, we're allowing them to do it. Our own intelligence grows when we choose to stop conforming to conventional standards; standards that history informs us are low indeed, and by recognising that we've created an ugly mess of the world - not by chance, not by accident, but willingly with full knowledge of the possible consequences. It's this mess that keeps us living in fear because we *know* where it eventually leads and we've been - and are still being - conditioned to feel powerless to do anything about it. Despite the horrible consequences of our apathy we wait, comply and support our tainted society, convinced that we're helpless or perhaps in need of some sort of salvation, that's always arriving ... soon.

When we pick up a book to read, and aren't enjoying it - perhaps because we find it offensive, too violent or just plain boring, we put it down again or throw it into the bin; when we watch a film and dislike it for the same reasons we turn it off. However, when we see and think about all the 'bad' we've created in the world we do *nothing* against it, because we fear saying 'No' to our various authorities and losing what we've got - we can't see the bin or the off switch. We can say 'No' to a regime just as we do the book or film, or anything else for that matter - we *always* have a choice. It's only our 'what's the point' attitude and fear that pin us to our seats - fear of the imaginary consequences that have been instilled into us. Even if we're not spiritually minded it's clear that things aren't getting any better in the world and that our lives are going to come to an end at some point; it's a pretty good call to think about 'what happens next', rather than doing nothing or hedging our bets. Every one of us has the opportunity to change while we're still alive - to raise our vibration - and based on my personal experience

I'd suggest that it's a good idea not to put that change off; we *must* keep moving by mental exercise - only then can we grow stronger, psychologically. Every moment is important because our heart beats for a limited time, and we don't know in advance when it's going to stop - the clock is ticking.

We spend our time here learning how things are from our parents and society; how we can best prepare ourselves to survive in this 'dog-eat-dog' world. Our education encourages us to compete with each other for the best paid jobs, in order to find security and purchase our own homes; it teaches us about the horrors of the past and how science will create a better future for us all. But science attempts to identify what can't be identified and to control what can't be controlled; it's limited and will *always* be limited because it relies on thought, which is limited; it's also under the control of an increasingly insane world that's going from strength to strength - nothing good can come from it until we grow 'up'. All the while, towns become more crowded, more and more people are without employment, corporations get richer and there's more and more disruption, confusion, corruption, perversion and separation going on in the world - online and off - *everybody* knows this. This is an over simplification of what's happening to our world right now, but as you're reading this book I prefer to credit you with enough intelligence to be aware of the rest, and to know that things aren't improving for ourselves or future generations. If we ignore a problem, it doesn't mean that it doesn't exist - it'll grow larger, fester and throb away in the back of our minds; it will ache in our hearts until *we* resolve it. Despite certain appearances and claims by our authorities, *no-one* is actually fighting for us, no-one ever has, no-one is indispensable in what they're doing; the battle we must *all* one day face is to overcome our apathy and *only* then can we come to know ourselves (as best we can) and until we do, the battle will continue to be played out and torment us. We must walk alone, but fight together - for One cause, instead of against each other.

~~~

Human beings have an innate need for companionship of some sort; if we're feeling lonely we turn on the television, message an internet 'friend' or play with apps on our mobile phones - as long as there's someone, or something, we can interact with; it doesn't necessarily have to be personal contact - what we need is to feel 'connected' in some way. Though we don't want to hear the negative and senseless chatter in our minds, there are times when we need to be alone and gather our thoughts for a while, which we don't mind doing as long as we know there's someone to talk to, should at any time we feel the need for it. In today's world being 'alone' for a while can be problematic, even when we're sleeping; it's difficult to be quiet when we're surrounded by noises and lights that are distracting - the hum of a refrigerator, the glow of an alarm clock, an incoming message, a neighbour returning home late or a car driving past can interfere with our peace - disturbance of some kind is very much a part of our world. We don't know *how* to be quiet, as noise has become so familiar to us that total silence can feel disorientating and frightening - a somewhat claustrophobic, alien and lonely experience, until we learn to enjoy being in our own company. We hear the noise of our minds more clearly when our surroundings are silent - we're then able to observe ourselves and see how uncomfortable we feel in our own company; this is the true meaning of loneliness. No-one feels lonely when at peace with themselves, but when we're not we can become desperate for a voice on the end of the phone, someone to socialise with, an outside activity, or a partner to keep us company - we always want a distraction of some kind.

On this journey we must be prepared, if necessary, to give up a lot - friends included. As we raise our consciousness level, the psychological distance between us and the people we know increases - we no longer speak the same language or have much in common; we're literally on a different wave length. At get-togethers for example, we may see a hand waving in this 'distance' and not know whether it's waving 'hello' or saying 'goodbye', but as our vibration rises we become more and more comfortable quietly observing our outside world (in all its madness) and with being alone - more and more comfortable with the silence that we find inside. The world no longer feels frightening or lonely and we no longer depend on outside activity for comfort or company - we see the hand waving and, in that moment, it matters not whether it's saying hello or goodbye.

The 'divine' and 'holy' are concepts that we dismiss with comments such as 'there's no old man with a beard sitting on a cloud looking down on us' - silly, because there isn't a person in the world who actually believes that there is. These comments and symbols are the tools we use to dismiss subjects we've made 'taboo' or 'weird'. They tend to be subjects that challenge the lifestyles we wish to pursue - the things we want to do without anyone tapping us on the shoulder. Though there's much to complain about in the world, we've no real wish to change - our fear of change is stronger than our curiosity or need to explore the contents of our minds. We're One; One world, One love, One consciousness, One family - One humanity trying hard to make sense of itself, and until we do we have One problem - love is missing from our lives. We must find this love again if we're ever going to live in peace, *first* for ourselves and only then for all others, but we can't find it if we continue to hold onto judgement, hatred, bitterness, jealousies, pain or other suffering - there's no place for these emotions when we live 'in Love'. None of us have any idea how long we'll remain in this particular 'existence', so we shouldn't miss the opportunity to let go of fear and its hand maidens, and surrender to Love, while we still can - our time is too short to be wasted.

'The greatest thing you'll ever learn
is just to love and be loved in return.'

Nature Boy
Eben Ahbez

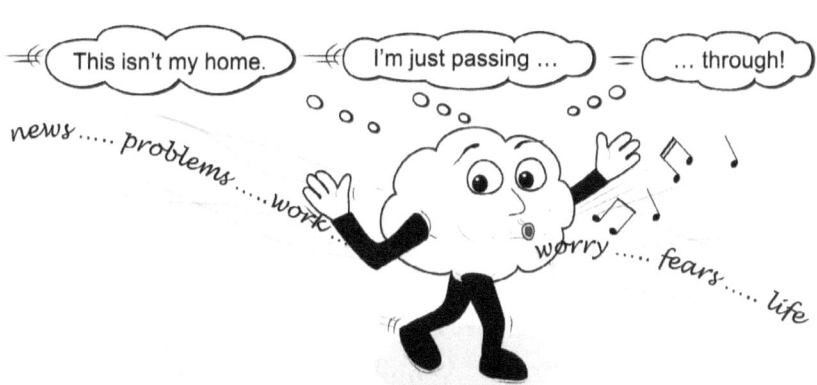

Bibliography

[1]   Davies, W. H. *Leisure*. (http://www.greenfolder.co.nz/WHD/poetry/Leisure.html [28th July 2013])

[2]   Google. (https://www.google.co.uk/#q=self+help [2 September 2013])

[3]   Confucius, *The Great Learning* (translated by James Legge). (Internet Classics Archive of MIT - http://classics.mit.edu/Confucius/learning.html [15th July 2013])

[4]   ushistory.org. Ancient Civilizations Online Textbook, *Gladiators, Chariots, and the Roman Games* (2013) (http://www.ushistory.org/civ/6e.asp [31st July 2013])

[5]   Sagan, Carl. Druyan, Ann. Soter, Steven (writers) *Cosmos: A Personal Voyage*, (Episode 9) *The Lives of the Stars*. (1980)

[6]   Gandhi, Mahatma. Gandhi International Institute for Peace, *Essential Quotes of Mahatma Gandhi* (http://www.gandhianpeace.com/quotes.html [28 August 2013])

[7]   Chesterton, G. K. *The Scandal of Father Brown*, (Chapter 'The Point of a Pin') (http://gutenberg.net.au/ebooks02/0201031.txt [11 Oct 2013])

[8]   Arunachala Ashrama. *The Teachings of Sri Ramana Maharshi*, (http://www.arunachala.org/ramana/teachings/ [17 July 2013])

[9]   Dictionary.com, (http://dictionary.reference.com/browse/philosophy [21 August 2013])

[10] Interview with Ian McNay on Conscious television. (http://www.youtube.com/watch?v=VYYXq1Ox4sk [8 August 2013])

[11] Biology Online, (http://www.biology-online.org/dictionary/Placebo_effect [10 Sept 2013])

[12] Francois Duc De La Rochefoucauld. *Reflections or Sentences and Moral Maxims* No. 119. (http://www.gutenberg.org/files/9105/9105-h/9105-h.htm [11 July 2013])

[13] Interview with Ian McNay on Conscious Television. (http://www.youtube.com/watch?v=-6kDMl6N3C4 [25 September 2013])

[14] *The Matrix* movie 1999 (Motion Picture, US: Warner Bros)

[15] Krishnamurti, Jiddu. - Krishnamurti Teachings in Krishnamurti's Journal (para. 169) (http://www.jkrishnamurti.org/krishnamurti-teachings/view-context.p?tid=42&chid=318&w=%22All+those+years+passed+without+leaving+scars&s=Context [18 September 2013])

NOTES

NOTES

NOTES

NOTES

NOTES

About the Author

Renée Paule was born in London and was brought up in an orphanage, despite having two living parents. Subjected to mental and physical cruelty, the trauma she suffered left her with twelve years of almost total amnesia. Six marriages later (four official), she chose to 'take stock' and began a process of questioning everything in her world.

Her take on life changed dramatically following a profound experience revealing the connection between herself and the Universe - there's no separation. With this realisation, she no longer accepted the 'face-value' world she'd once thought of as the norm.

Renée Paule wishes to share this knowledge and show how a change of perspective can provide an alternative to the topsy-turvy world that Humanity, on the whole, accepts as an inevitable way of life.

She now lives in Ireland.

www.reneepaule.com

www.ingramcontent.com/pod-product-compliance
Lightning Source LLC
Chambersburg PA
CBHW032013230426
43671CB00005B/66